MASASHI KISHIMOTO

Something I've been worrying about lately is whether or not to download digital copies of movies I've already bought on DVD or Blu-ray... There are also subscription services. Too many options!

AKIRA OKUBO

I've been living at a pretty relaxed pace, so the weekly schedule has been a shock to my system, but it's thanks to all of you that we've gotten this far. I hope you take your time and enjoy the story.

SAMURAI 8
THE TALE OF HACHIMARU
04

SHONEN JUMP Manga Edition

Story **MASASHI KISHIMOTO**
Art **AKIRA OKUBO**

Translation/STEPHEN PAUL
Touch-Up Art & Lettering/SNIR AHARON
Design/JULIAN [JR] ROBINSON
Editor/ALEXIS KIRSCH

SAMURAI8 HACHIMARUDEN © 2019 by Masashi Kishimoto, Akira Okubo
All rights reserved.
First published in Japan in 2019 by SHUEISHA Inc., Tokyo.
English translation rights arranged by SHUEISHA Inc.

The stories, characters and incidents mentioned in this publication are
entirely fictional.

Printed in the U.S.A.

Published by VIZ Media, LLC
P.O. Box 77010
San Francisco, CA 94107

10 9 8 7 6 5 4 3 2 1
First printing, November 2020

viz.com

shonenjump.com

PARENTAL ADVISORY
SAMURAI 8 is rated T for Teen and is
recommended for ages 13 and up. This
volume contains fantasy violence.

SAMURAI 8

THE TALE OF HACHIMARU

04

PARTNER

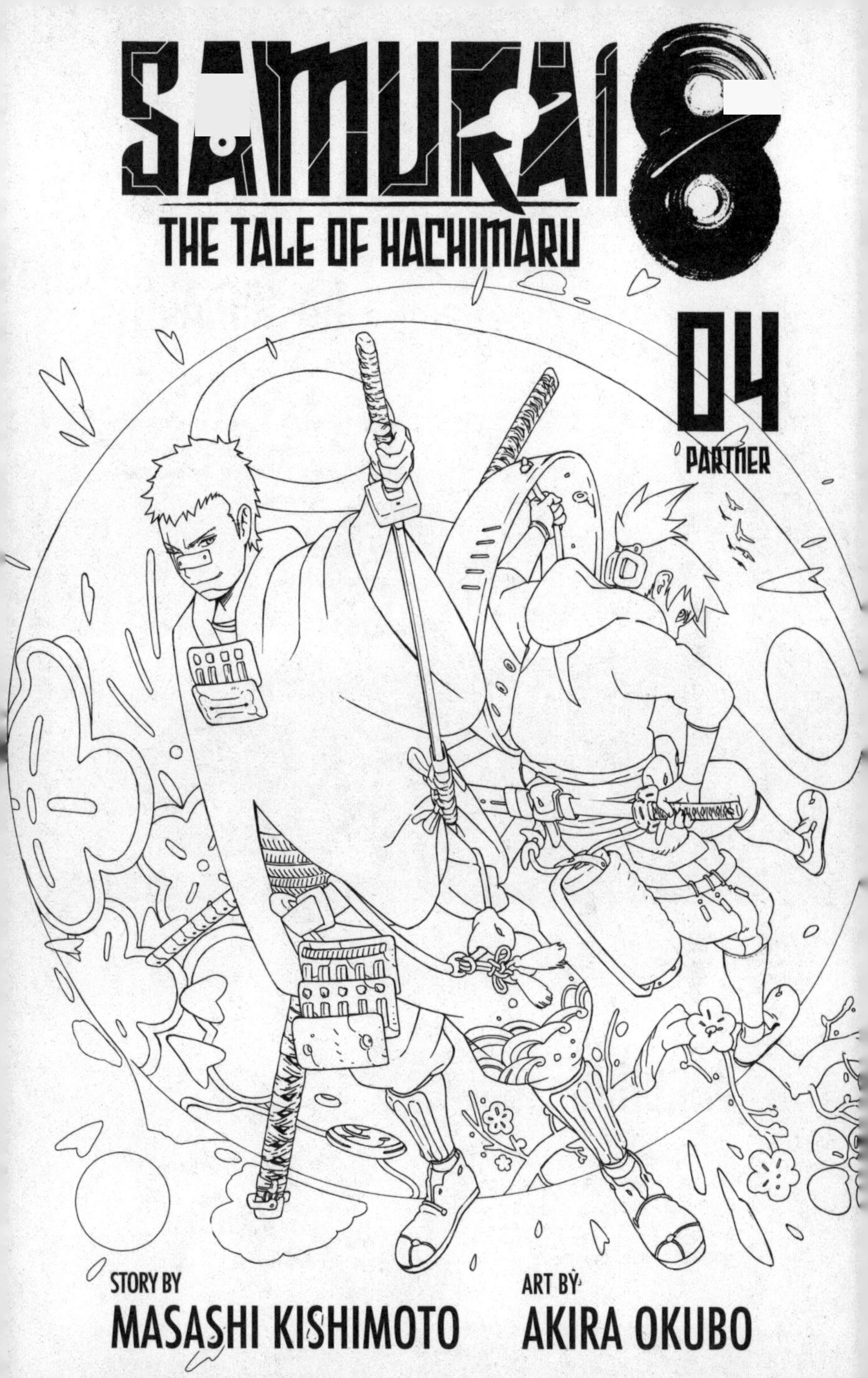

STORY BY
MASASHI KISHIMOTO

ART BY
AKIRA OKUBO

THE TALE OF HACHIMARU

CHARACTERS

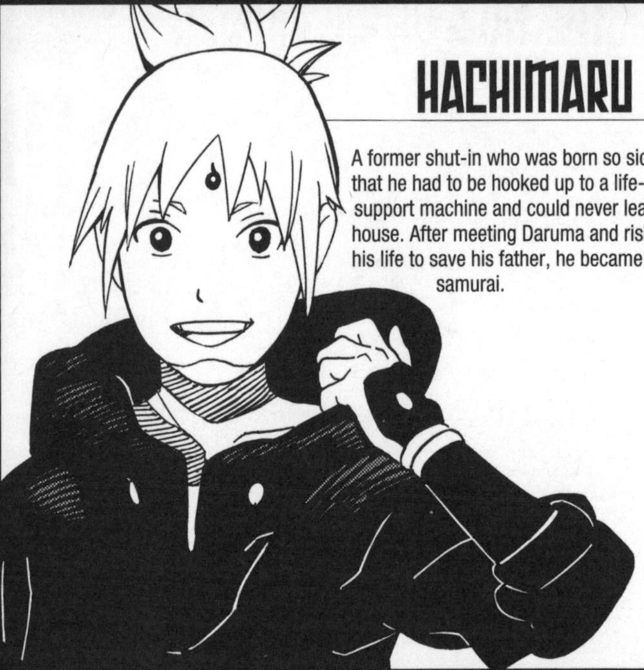

HACHIMARU

A former shut-in who was born so sickly that he had to be hooked up to a life-support machine and could never leave the house. After meeting Daruma and risking his life to save his father, he became a samurai.

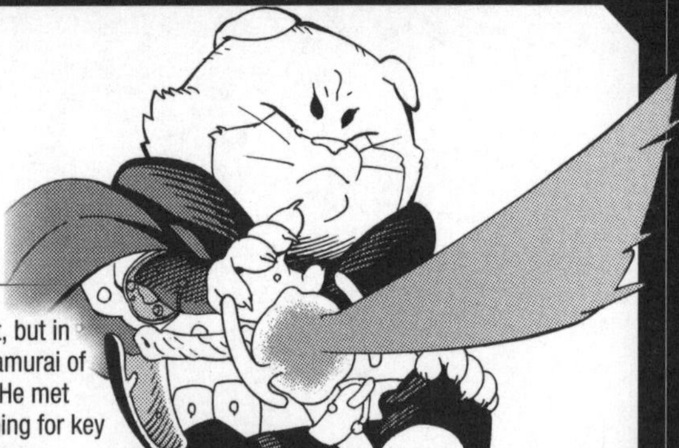

DARUMA

He looks like a lucky cat, but in fact he is a legendary samurai of the Kongo-Yasha Style. He met Hachimaru while searching for key samurai to save the galaxy.

SAMURAI 8

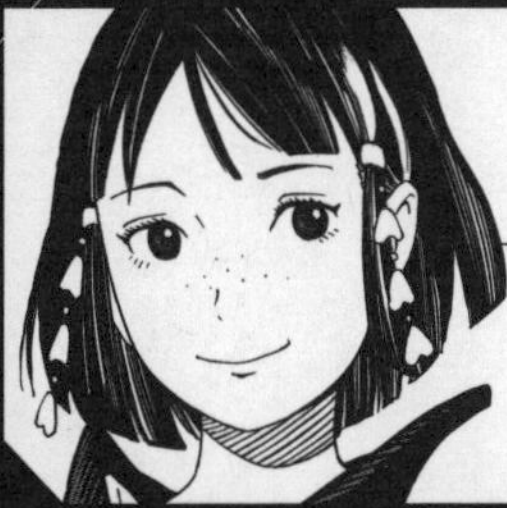

ANN

A young princess in training. She lost her Locker Ball, which is necessary to complete the samurai ritual.

HAYATARO

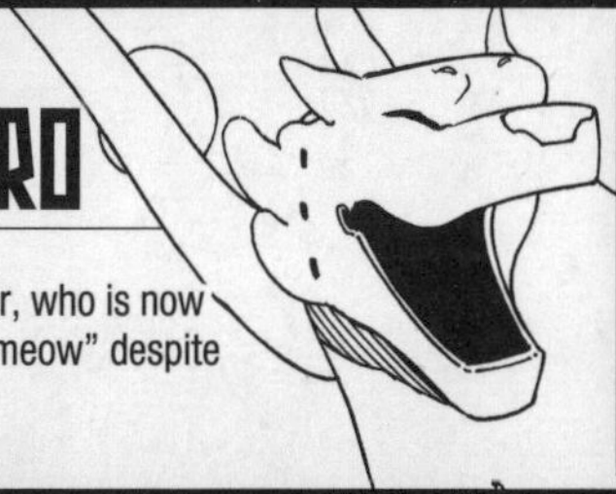

Hachimaru's Pet Holder, who is now his Key Holder. Says "meow" despite being a dog type.

WHAT IS A HOLDER?
A lifeform(?) that inhabits this galaxy. Their name changes based on their role: Pet Holder, Guard Holder, etc. Ones who serve a samurai master are called special Key Holders.

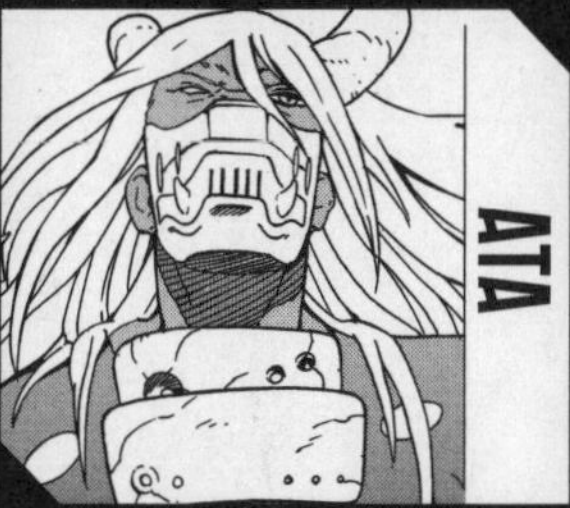
ATA

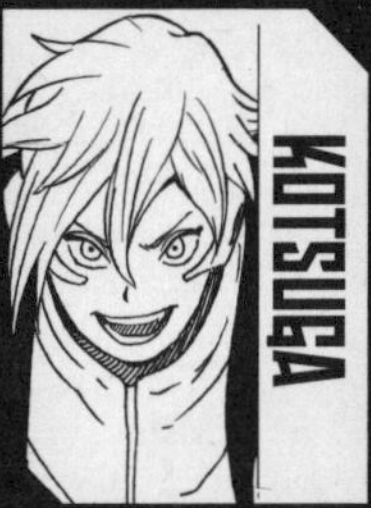
KOTSUGA

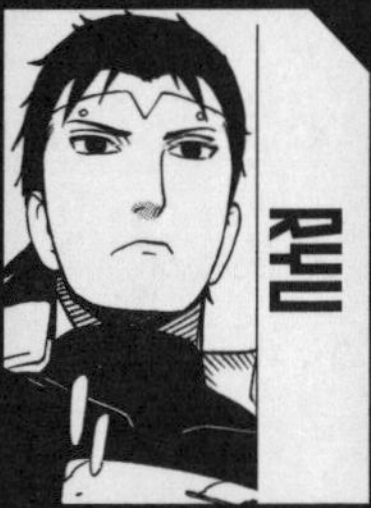
RYU

STORY

Hachimaru is a boy with a weak body. He can't survive without being hooked up to a life-support device, and he believes his dream of becoming a samurai will never to come true. But one day, he meets Daruma, a samurai in the form of a large, round cat. With the approval of the warrior god Fudo Myo-o, Hachimaru gains the life of a samurai!! While training under Daruma, Hachimaru gets attacked by the menacing Ata. Hachimaru's father sacrifices his own life to drive him off, but the effect is only temporary. Hachimaru decides to make his samurai calling to fulfill his promise to his father and protect the planet! The group heads out to space to look for companions, where they meet an eccentric pair named Kotsuga and Ryu, who invite them to take part in a battle royale. When Hachimaru is the last man standing, the tournament's organizer appears, but he's got other ideas in mind!!

SAMURAI 8
THE TALE OF HACHIMARU

04

PARTNERS

CONTENTS

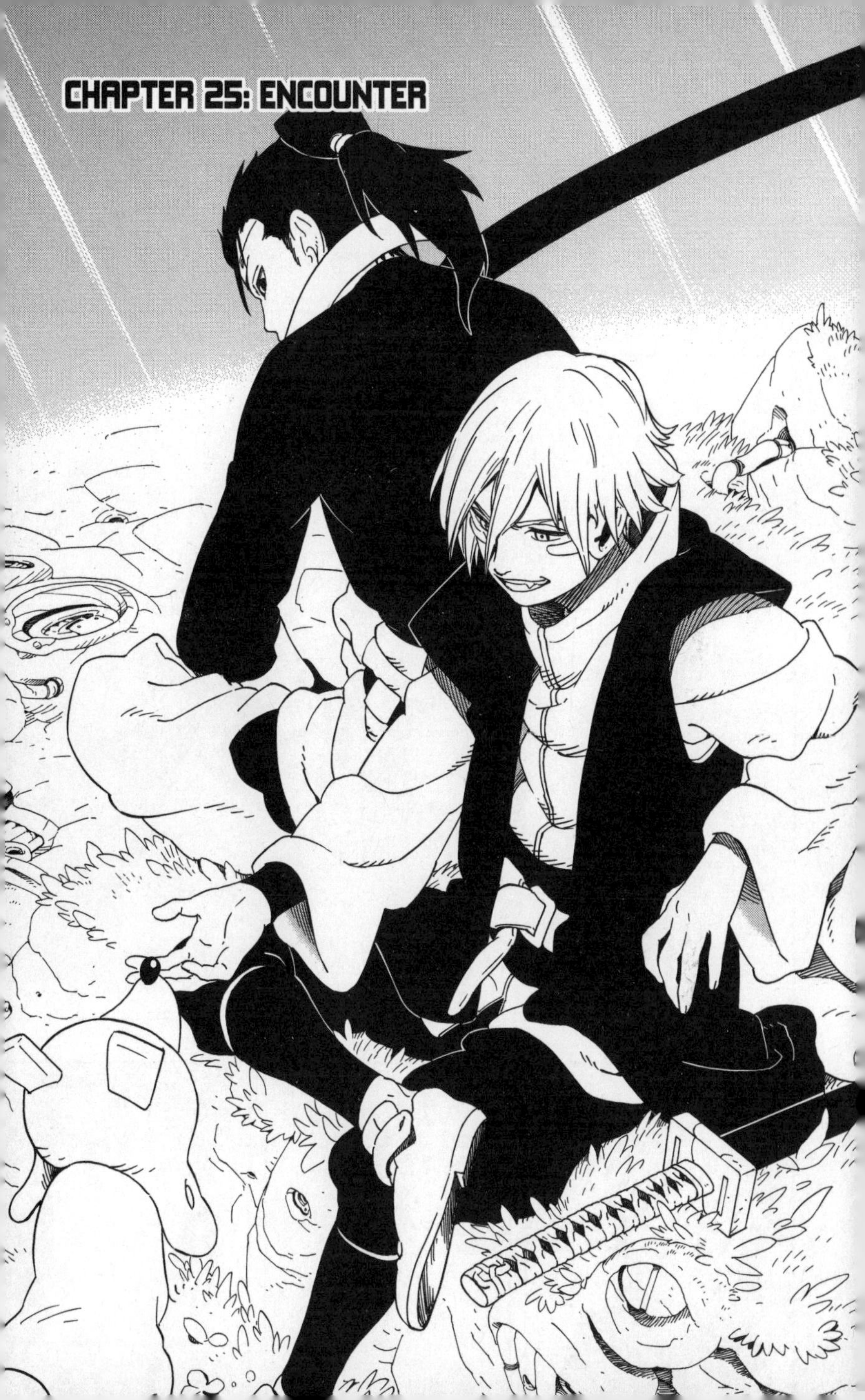
CHAPTER 25: ENCOUNTER

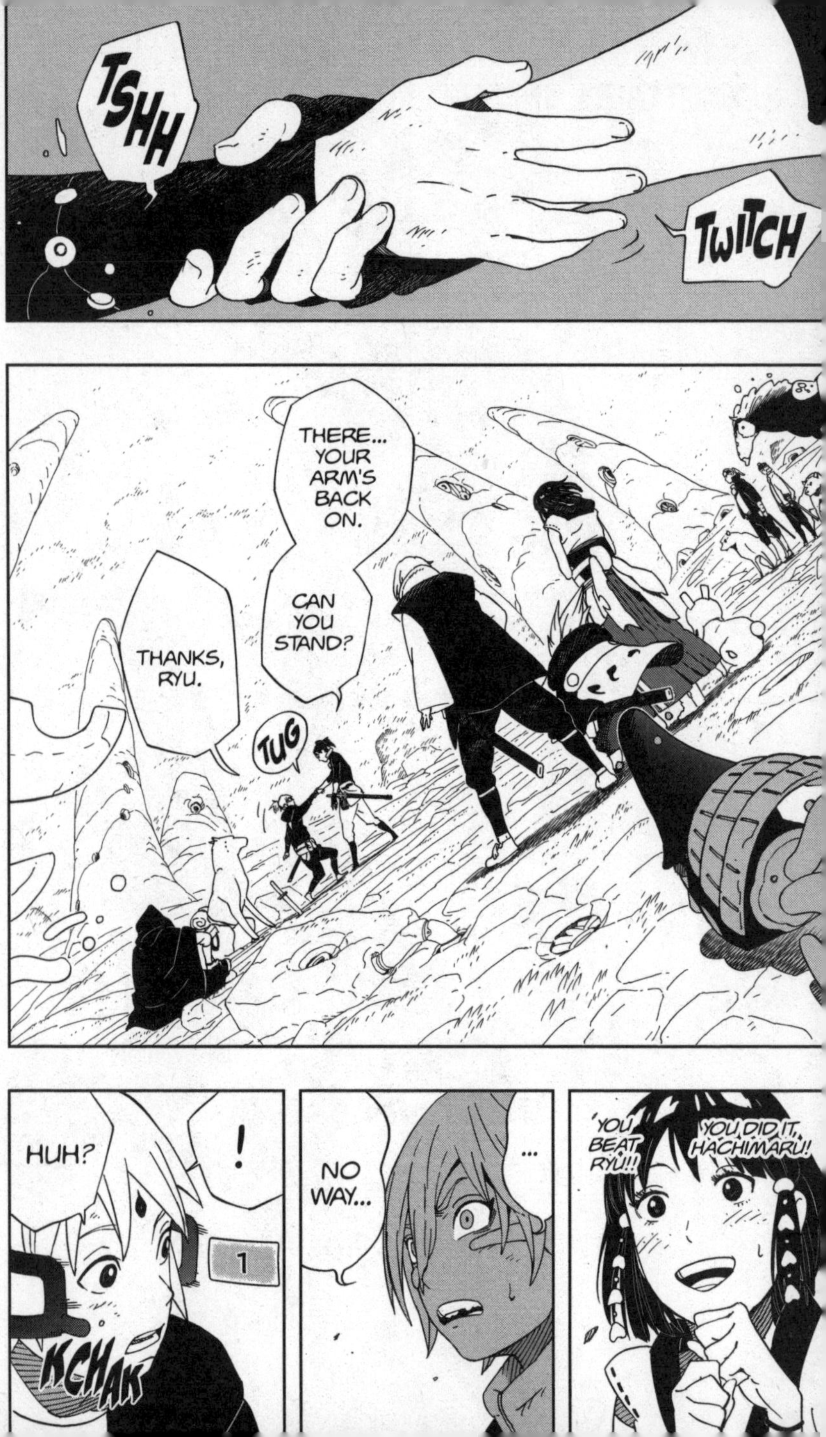
TWITCH
TSHH
THERE... YOUR ARM'S BACK ON.
CAN YOU STAND?
THANKS, RYU.
TUG
YOU DID IT, HACHIMARU!
YOU BEAT RYU!!
...
NO WAY...
!
HUH?
1
KCHAK

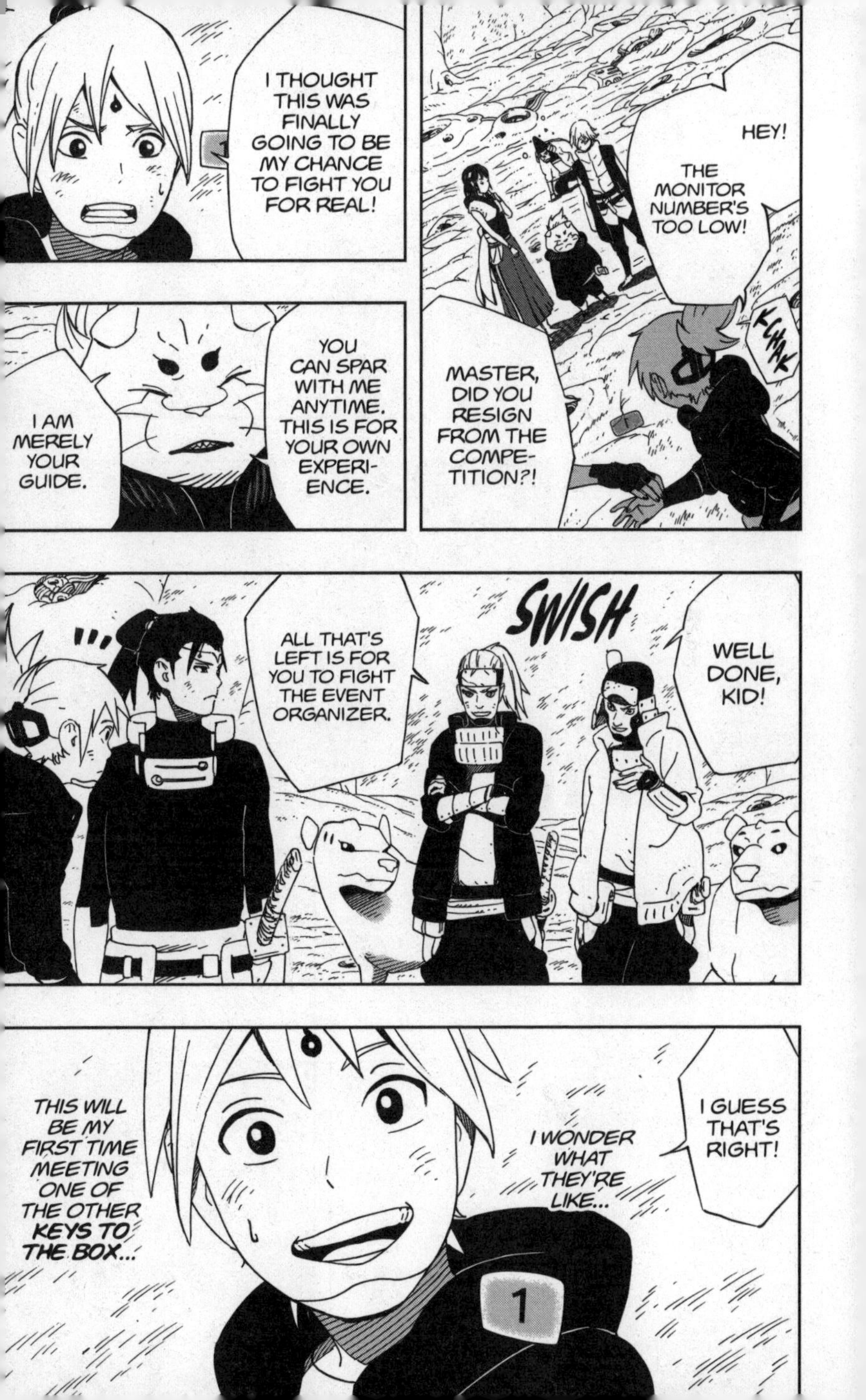
HEY!
THE MONITOR NUMBER'S TOO LOW!
K'CHAK
MASTER, DID YOU RESIGN FROM THE COMPE-TITION?!
I THOUGHT THIS WAS FINALLY GOING TO BE MY CHANCE TO FIGHT YOU FOR REAL!
YOU CAN SPAR WITH ME ANYTIME. THIS IS FOR YOUR OWN EXPERI-ENCE.
I AM MERELY YOUR GUIDE.
WELL DONE, KID!
SWISH
ALL THAT'S LEFT IS FOR YOU TO FIGHT THE EVENT ORGANIZER.
I GUESS THAT'S RIGHT!
I WONDER WHAT THEY'RE LIKE...
THIS WILL BE MY FIRST TIME MEETING ONE OF THE OTHER KEYS TO THE BOX...

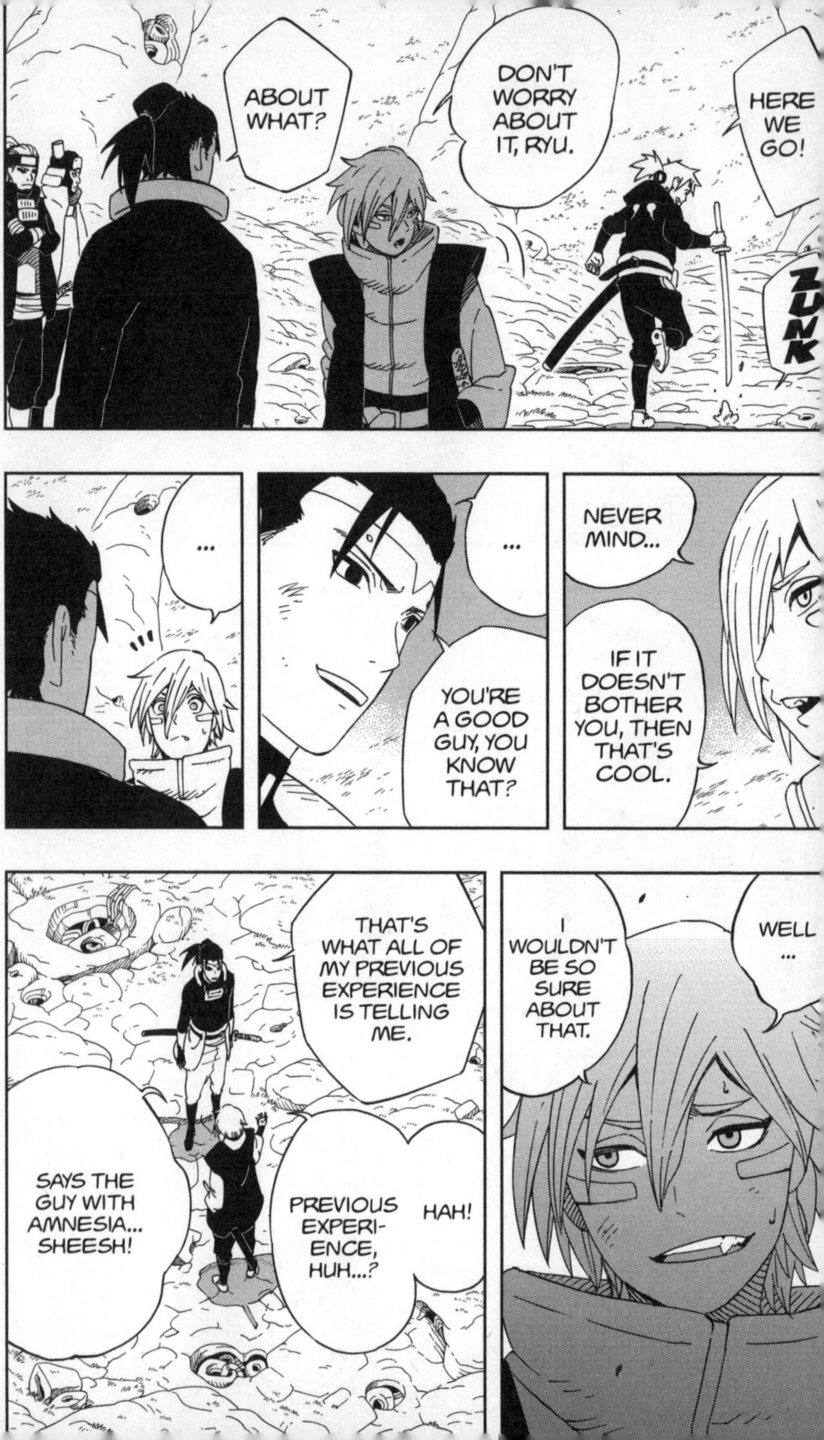
HERE WE GO!
ZUNK
DON'T WORRY ABOUT IT, RYU.
ABOUT WHAT?
NEVER MIND...
IF IT DOESN'T BOTHER YOU, THEN THAT'S COOL.
...
YOU'RE A GOOD GUY, YOU KNOW THAT?
...
WELL...
I WOULDN'T BE SO SURE ABOUT THAT.
THAT'S WHAT ALL OF MY PREVIOUS EXPERIENCE IS TELLING ME.
HAH!
PREVIOUS EXPERI-ENCE, HUH...?
SAYS THE GUY WITH AMNESIA... SHEESH!

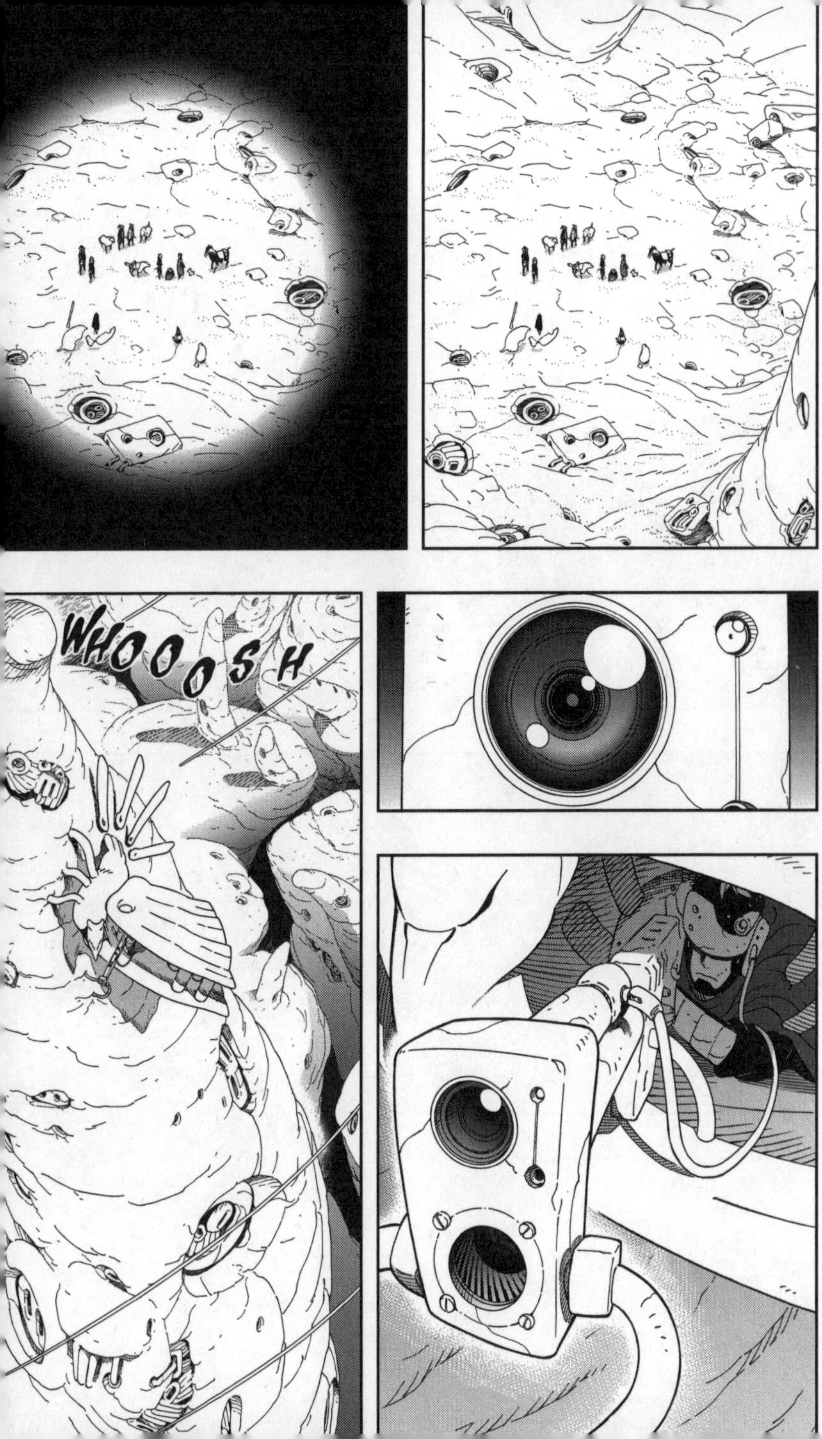
WHOOOSH

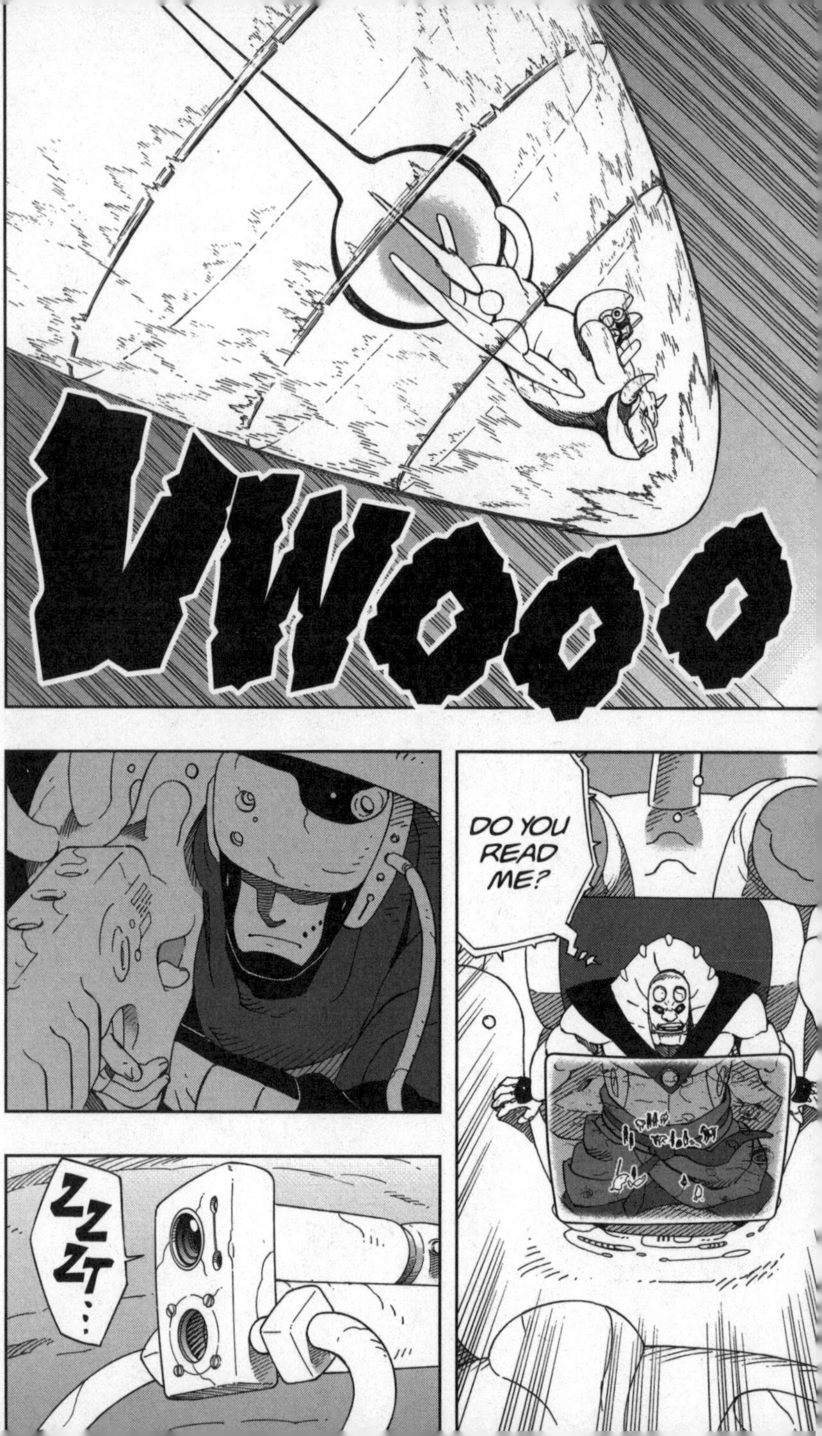
VWOOO
DO YOU READ ME?
ZZZT...

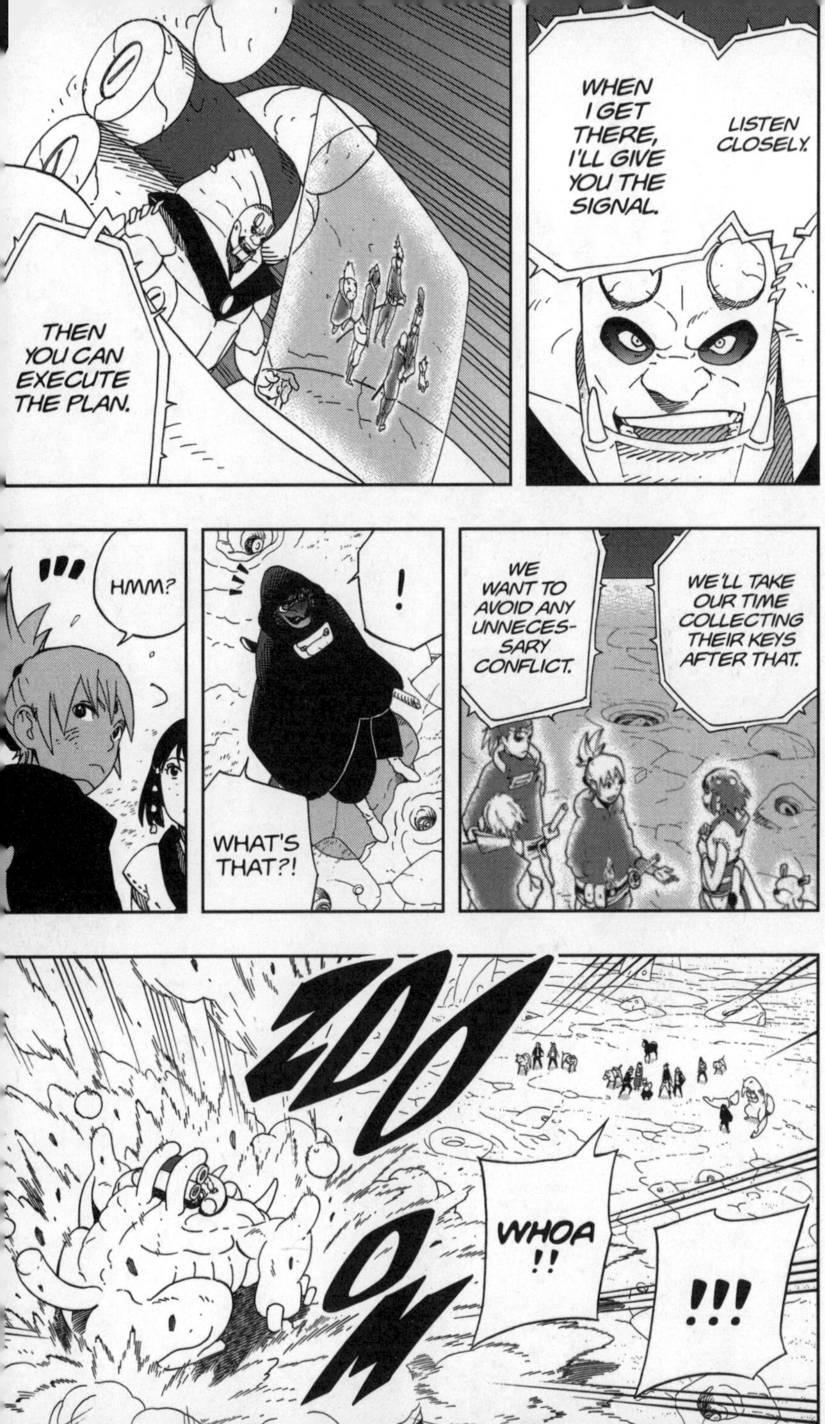
LISTEN CLOSELY.
WHEN I GET THERE, I'LL GIVE YOU THE SIGNAL.
THEN YOU CAN EXECUTE THE PLAN.
WE'LL TAKE OUR TIME COLLECTING THEIR KEYS AFTER THAT.
WE WANT TO AVOID ANY UNNECES-SARY CONFLICT.
!
WHAT'S THAT?!
HMM?
!!!
WHOA!!
ZDOOM

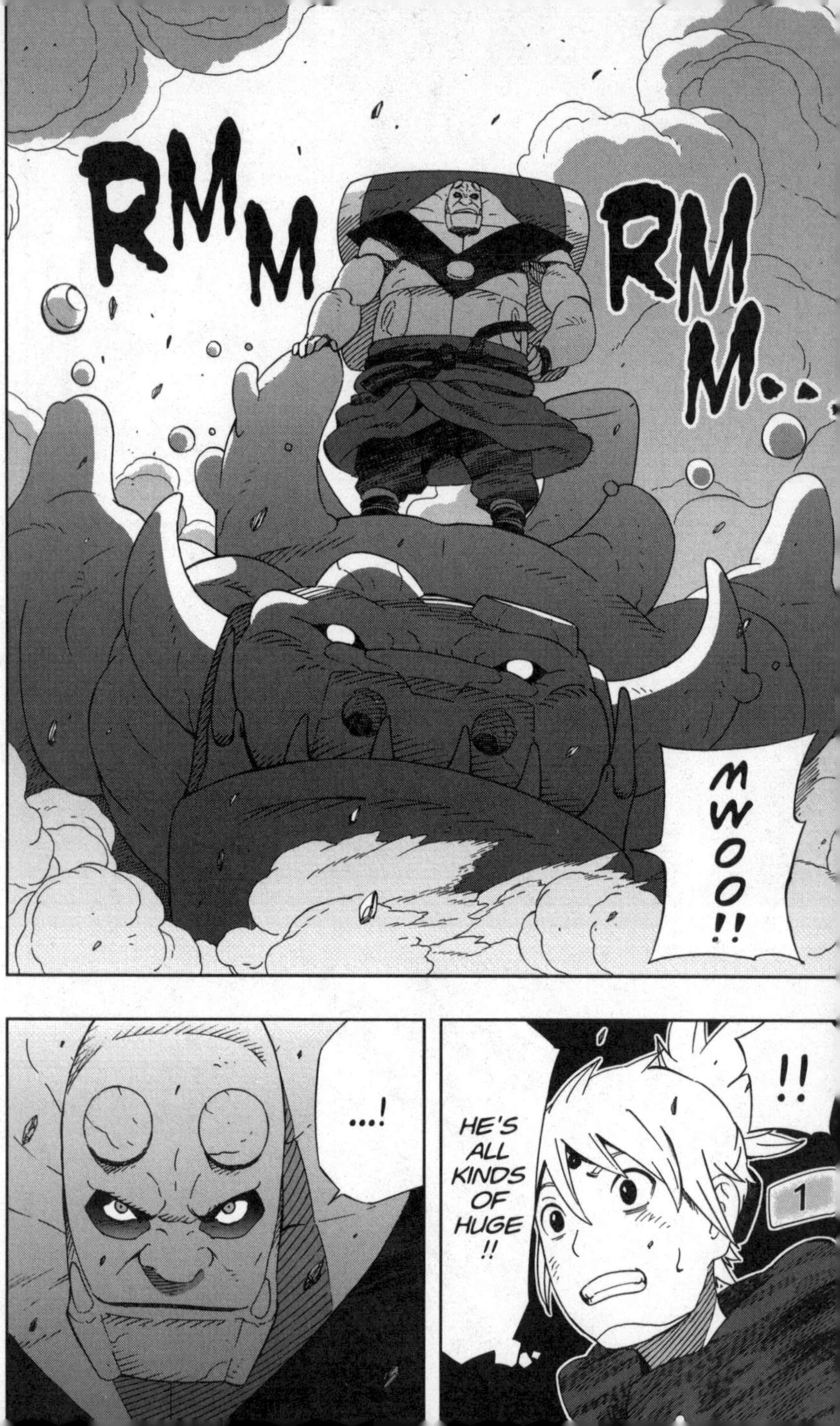
RMM M...
RMM
MWOO!!
!!
HE'S ALL KINDS OF HUGE!!
...!

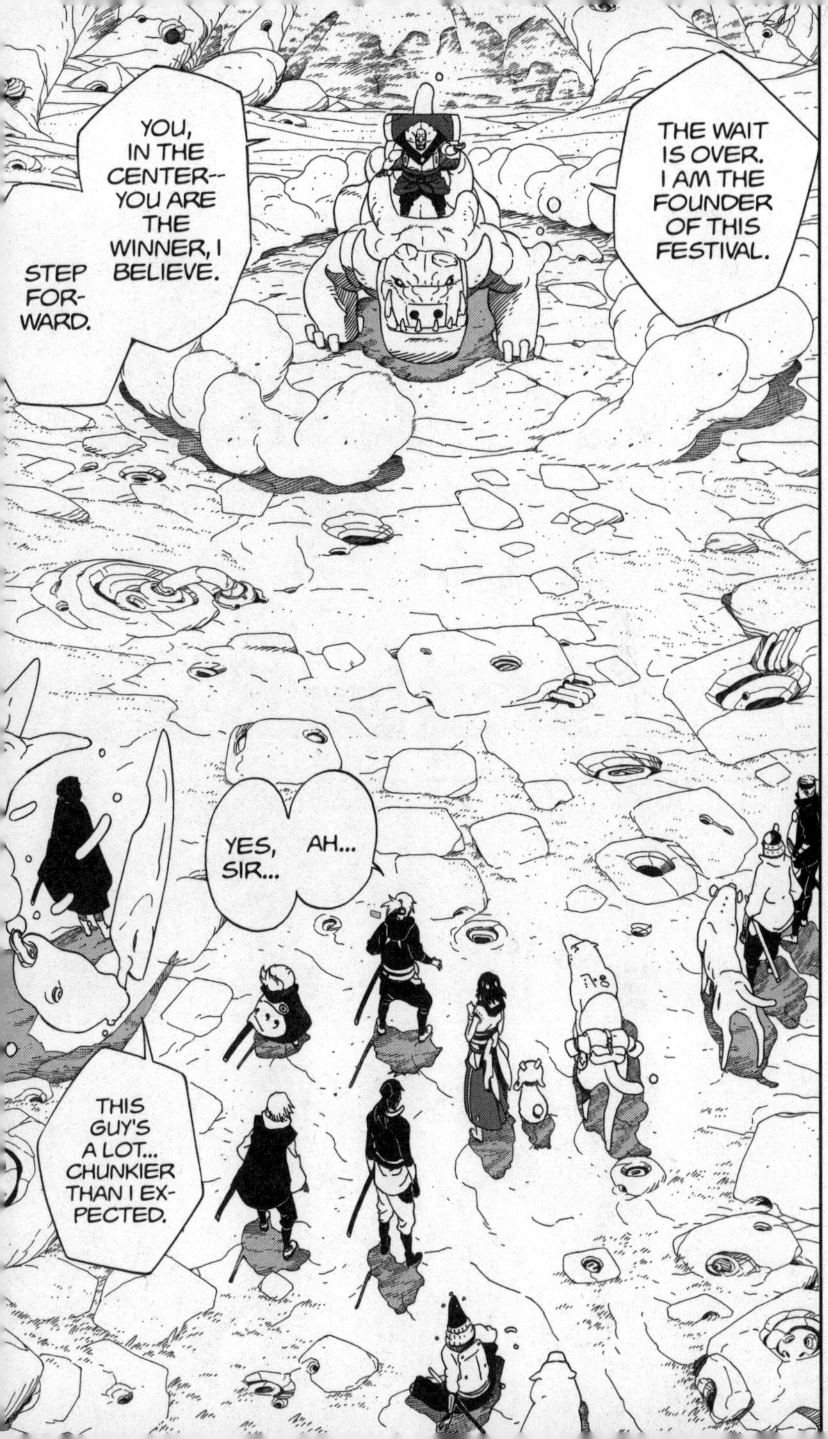
THE WAIT IS OVER. I AM THE FOUNDER OF THIS FESTIVAL.
YOU, IN THE CENTER-- YOU ARE THE WINNER, I BELIEVE.
STEP FOR-WARD.
AH...
YES, SIR...
THIS GUY'S A LOT... CHUNKIER THAN I EX-PECTED.

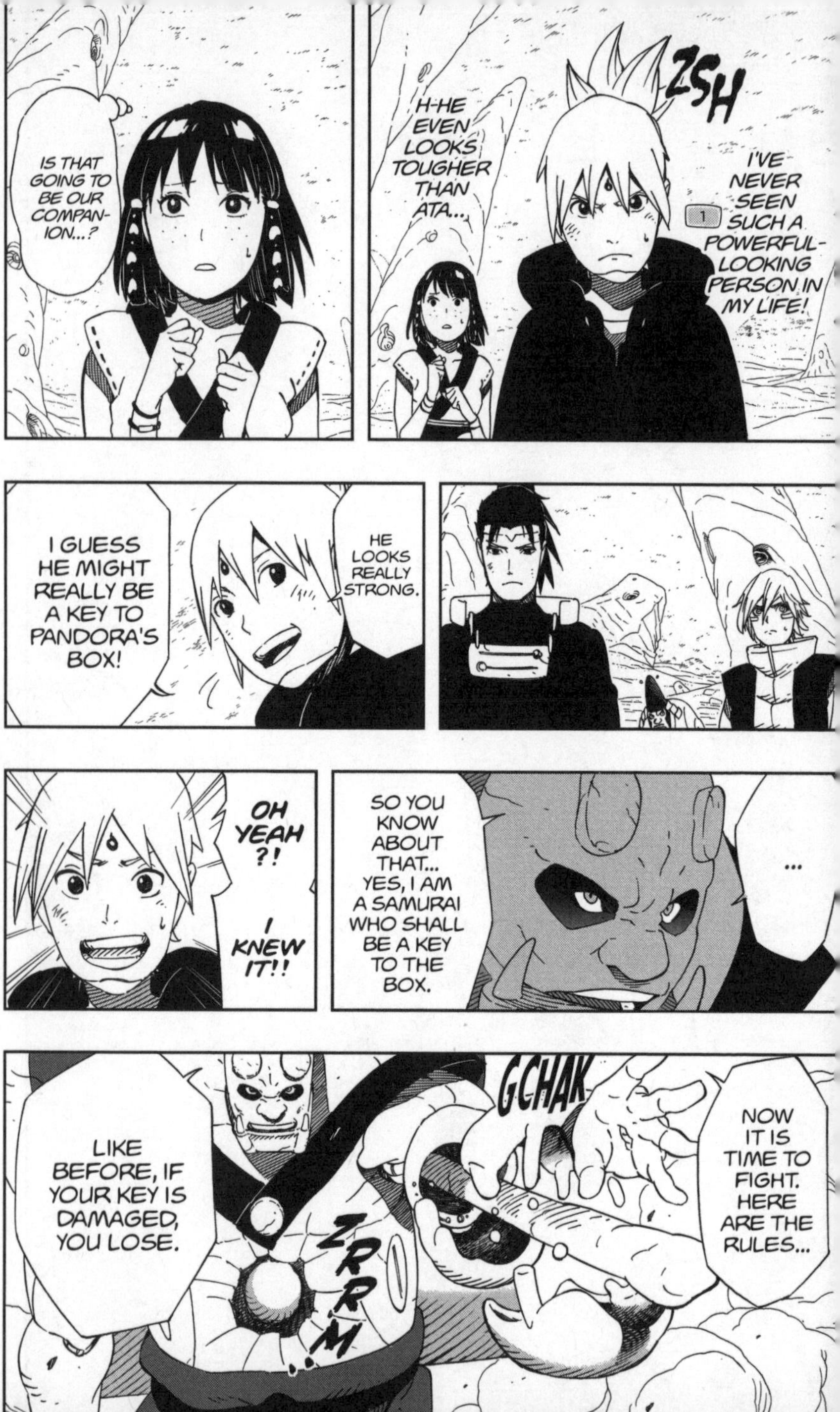
ZSH
I'VE NEVER SEEN SUCH A POWERFUL-LOOKING PERSON IN MY LIFE!
H-HE EVEN LOOKS TOUGHER THAN ATA...
IS THAT GOING TO BE OUR COMPANION...?
HE LOOKS REALLY STRONG.
I GUESS HE MIGHT REALLY BE A KEY TO PANDORA'S BOX!
...
SO YOU KNOW ABOUT THAT... YES, I AM A SAMURAI WHO SHALL BE A KEY TO THE BOX.
OH YEAH?!
I KNEW IT!!
NOW IT IS TIME TO FIGHT. HERE ARE THE RULES...
GCHAK
ZRRM
LIKE BEFORE, IF YOUR KEY IS DAMAGED, YOU LOSE.

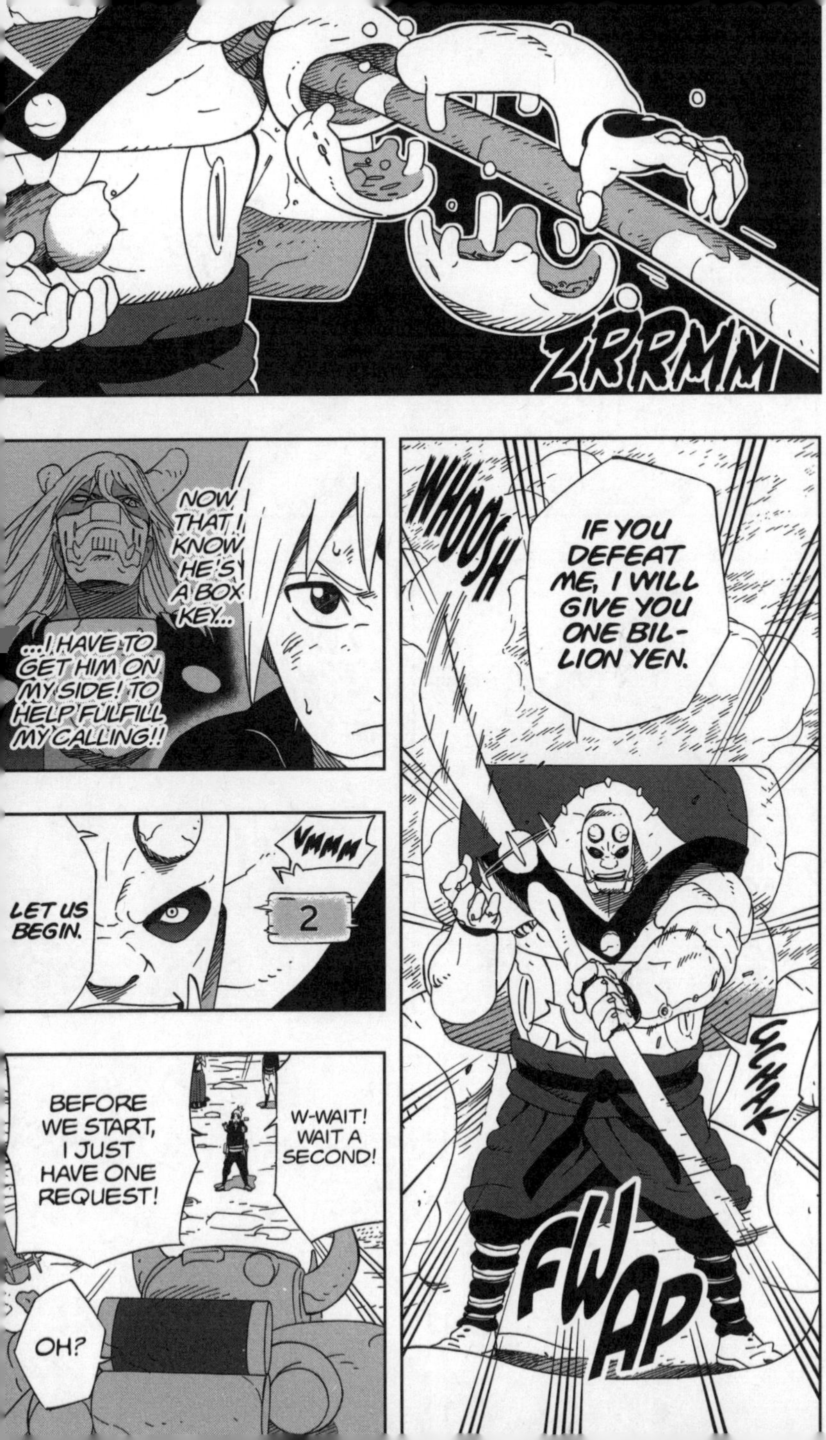
ZRRMM
NOW THAT I KNOW HE'S A BOX KEY...
...I HAVE TO GET HIM ON MY SIDE! TO HELP FULFILL MY CALLING!!
VMMM
2
LET US BEGIN.
W-WAIT! WAIT A SECOND!
BEFORE WE START, I JUST HAVE ONE REQUEST!
OH?
IF YOU DEFEAT ME, I WILL GIVE YOU ONE BIL-LION YEN.
WHOOSH
UCHAK
FWAP

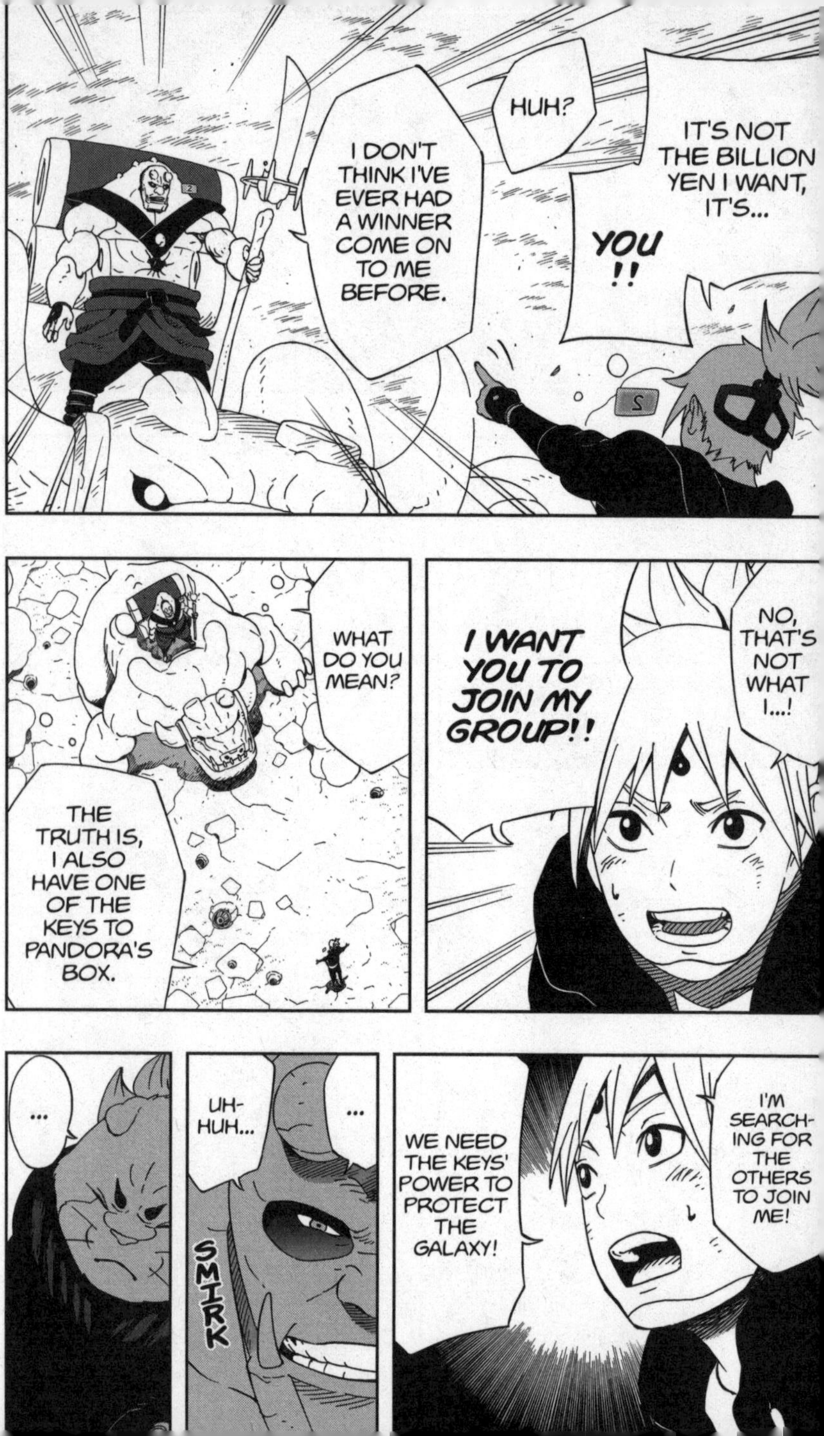
IT'S NOT THE BILLION YEN I WANT, IT'S...
YOU!!
HUH?
I DON'T THINK I'VE EVER HAD A WINNER COME ON TO ME BEFORE.
NO, THAT'S NOT WHAT I...!
I WANT YOU TO JOIN MY GROUP!!
WHAT DO YOU MEAN?
THE TRUTH IS, I ALSO HAVE ONE OF THE KEYS TO PANDORA'S BOX.
I'M SEARCHING FOR THE OTHERS TO JOIN ME!
WE NEED THE KEYS' POWER TO PROTECT THE GALAXY!
...
UH-HUH...
SMIRK
...

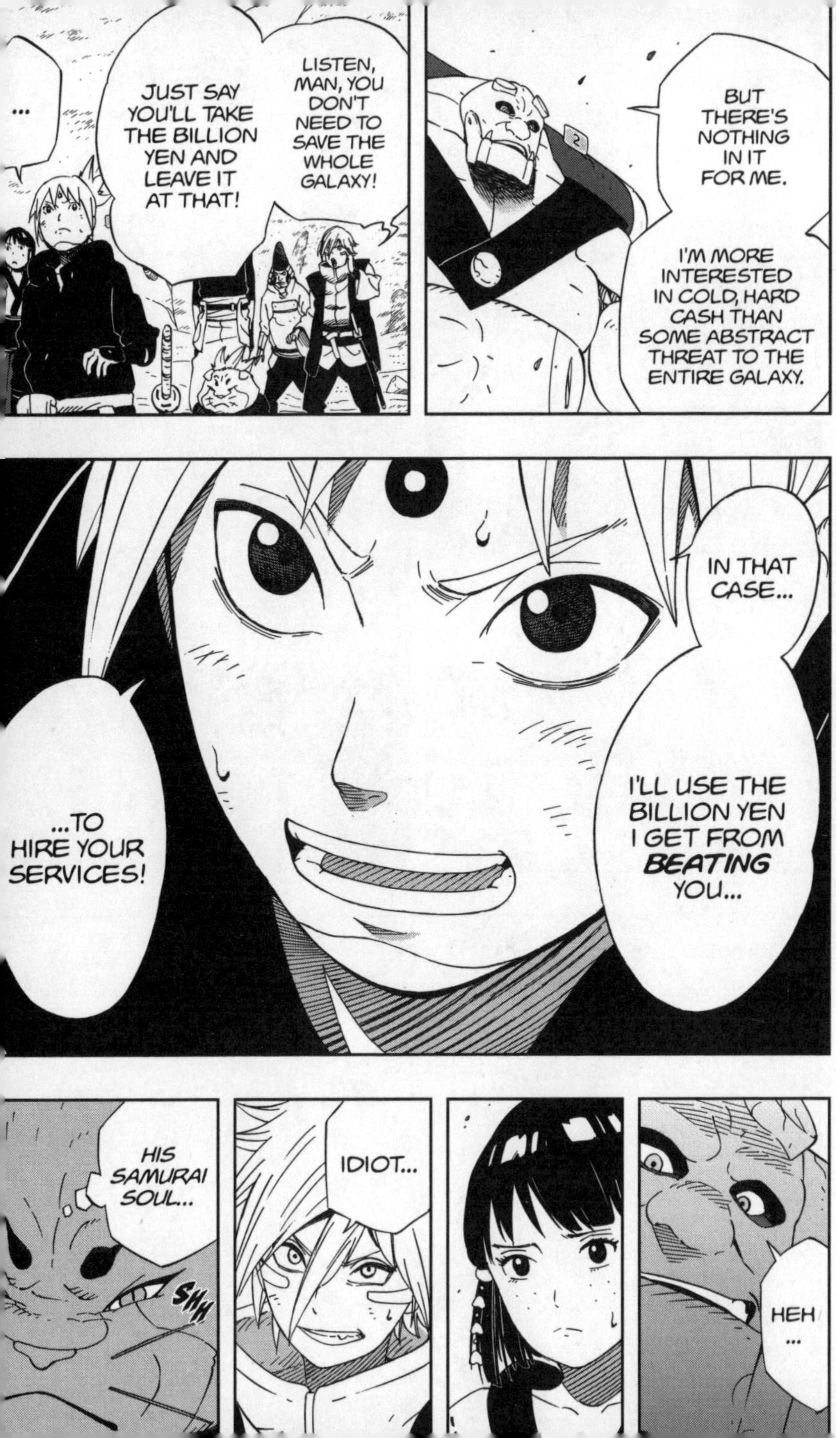
BUT THERE'S NOTHING IN IT FOR ME.
I'M MORE INTERESTED IN COLD, HARD CASH THAN SOME ABSTRACT THREAT TO THE ENTIRE GALAXY.
LISTEN, MAN, YOU DON'T NEED TO SAVE THE WHOLE GALAXY!
JUST SAY YOU'LL TAKE THE BILLION YEN AND LEAVE IT AT THAT!
...
IN THAT CASE...
I'LL USE THE BILLION YEN I GET FROM BEATING YOU...
...TO HIRE YOUR SERVICES!
HEH ...
IDIOT...
HIS SAMURAI SOUL...
SHH

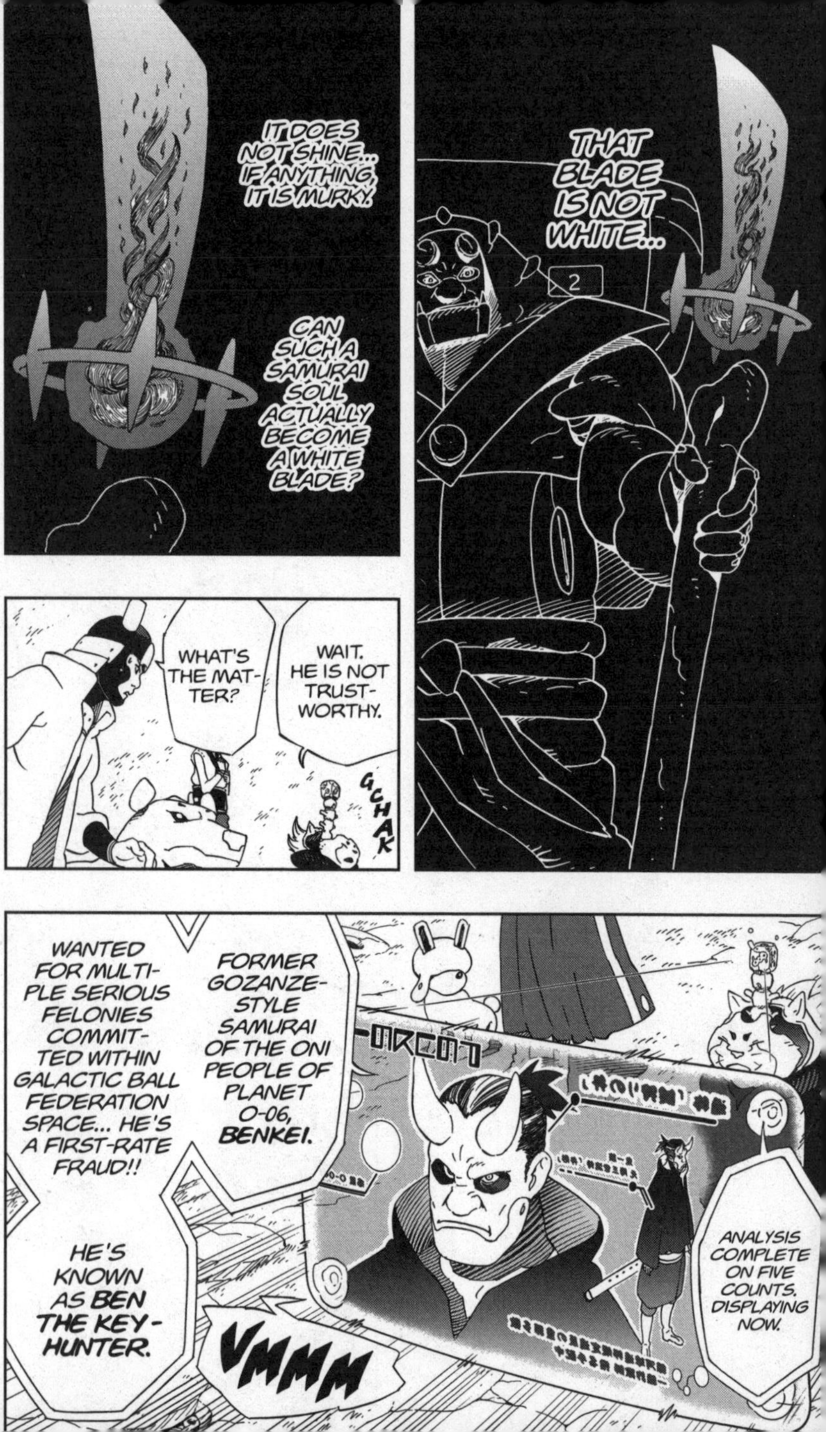
THAT BLADE IS NOT WHITE...
IT DOES NOT SHINE... IF ANYTHING, IT IS MURKY.
CAN SUCH A SAMURAI SOUL ACTUALLY BECOME A WHITE BLADE?
WAIT. HE IS NOT TRUST-WORTHY.
WHAT'S THE MAT-TER?
GCHAK
ANALYSIS COMPLETE ON FIVE COUNTS. DISPLAYING NOW.
FORMER GOZANZE-STYLE SAMURAI OF THE ONI PEOPLE OF PLANET O-06, BENKEI.
WANTED FOR MULTI-PLE SERIOUS FELONIES COMMIT-TED WITHIN GALACTIC BALL FEDERATION SPACE... HE'S A FIRST-RATE FRAUD!!
HE'S KNOWN AS BEN THE KEY-HUNTER.
VMMM

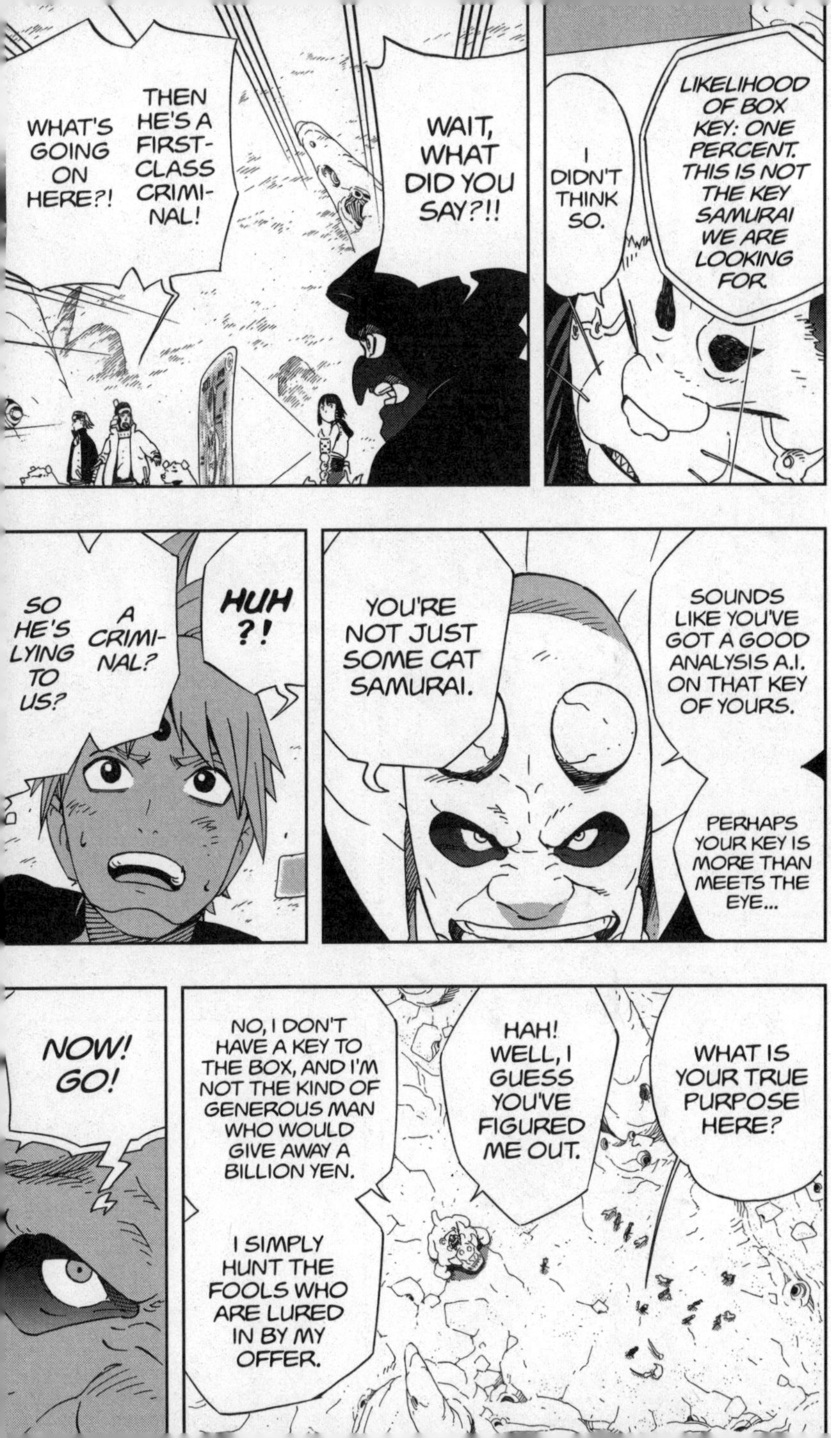
LIKELIHOOD OF BOX KEY: ONE PERCENT. THIS IS NOT THE KEY SAMURAI WE ARE LOOKING FOR.
I DIDN'T THINK SO.
WAIT, WHAT DID YOU SAY?!!
THEN HE'S A FIRST-CLASS CRIMINAL!
WHAT'S GOING ON HERE?!
SOUNDS LIKE YOU'VE GOT A GOOD ANALYSIS A.I. ON THAT KEY OF YOURS.
YOU'RE NOT JUST SOME CAT SAMURAI.
PERHAPS YOUR KEY IS MORE THAN MEETS THE EYE...
HUH?!
A CRIMINAL?
SO HE'S LYING TO US?
WHAT IS YOUR TRUE PURPOSE HERE?
HAH! WELL, I GUESS YOU'VE FIGURED ME OUT.
NO, I DON'T HAVE A KEY TO THE BOX, AND I'M NOT THE KIND OF GENEROUS MAN WHO WOULD GIVE AWAY A BILLION YEN.
I SIMPLY HUNT THE FOOLS WHO ARE LURED IN BY MY OFFER.
NOW! GO!

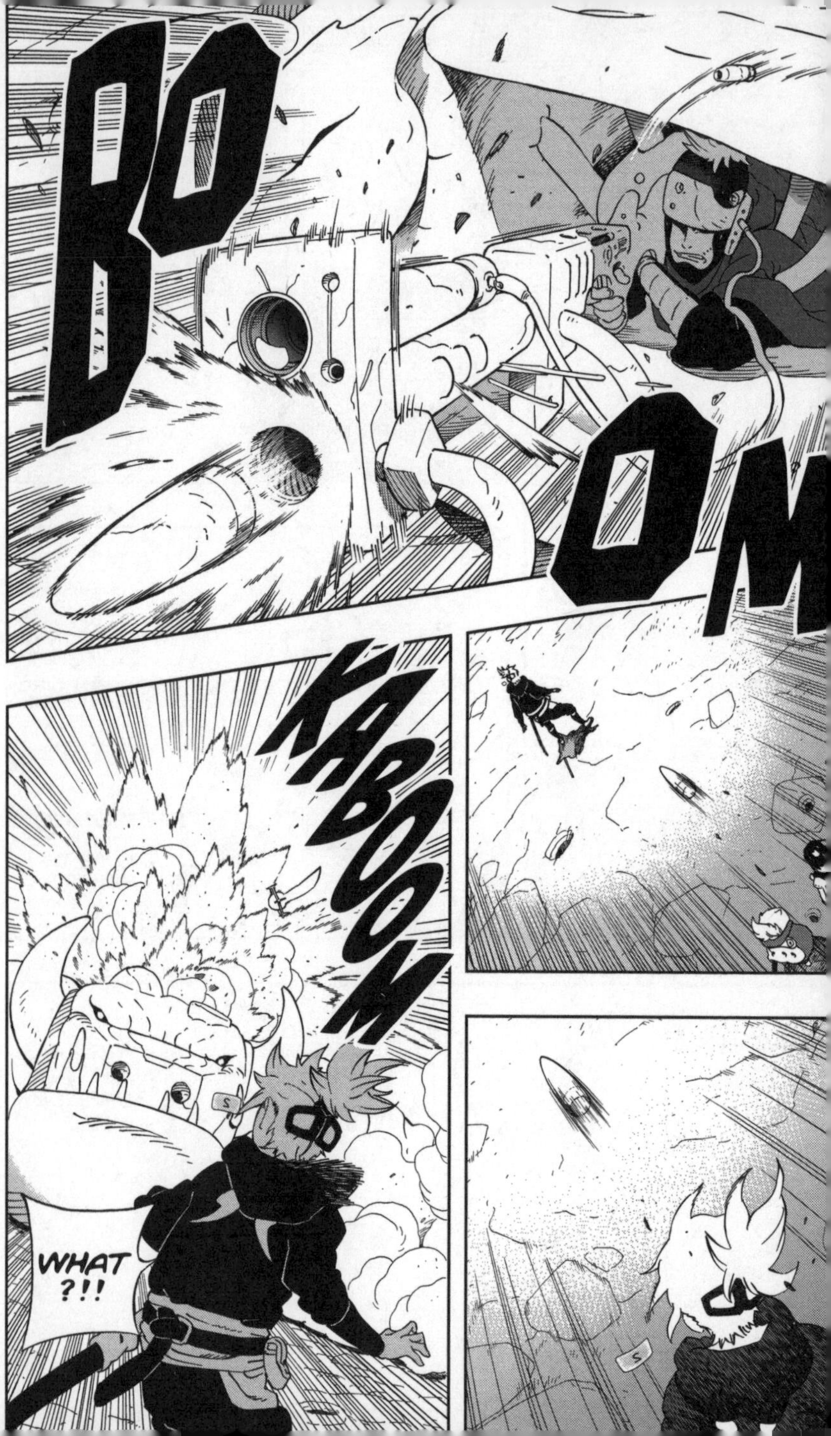
BOOM
KABOOM
WHAT?!!

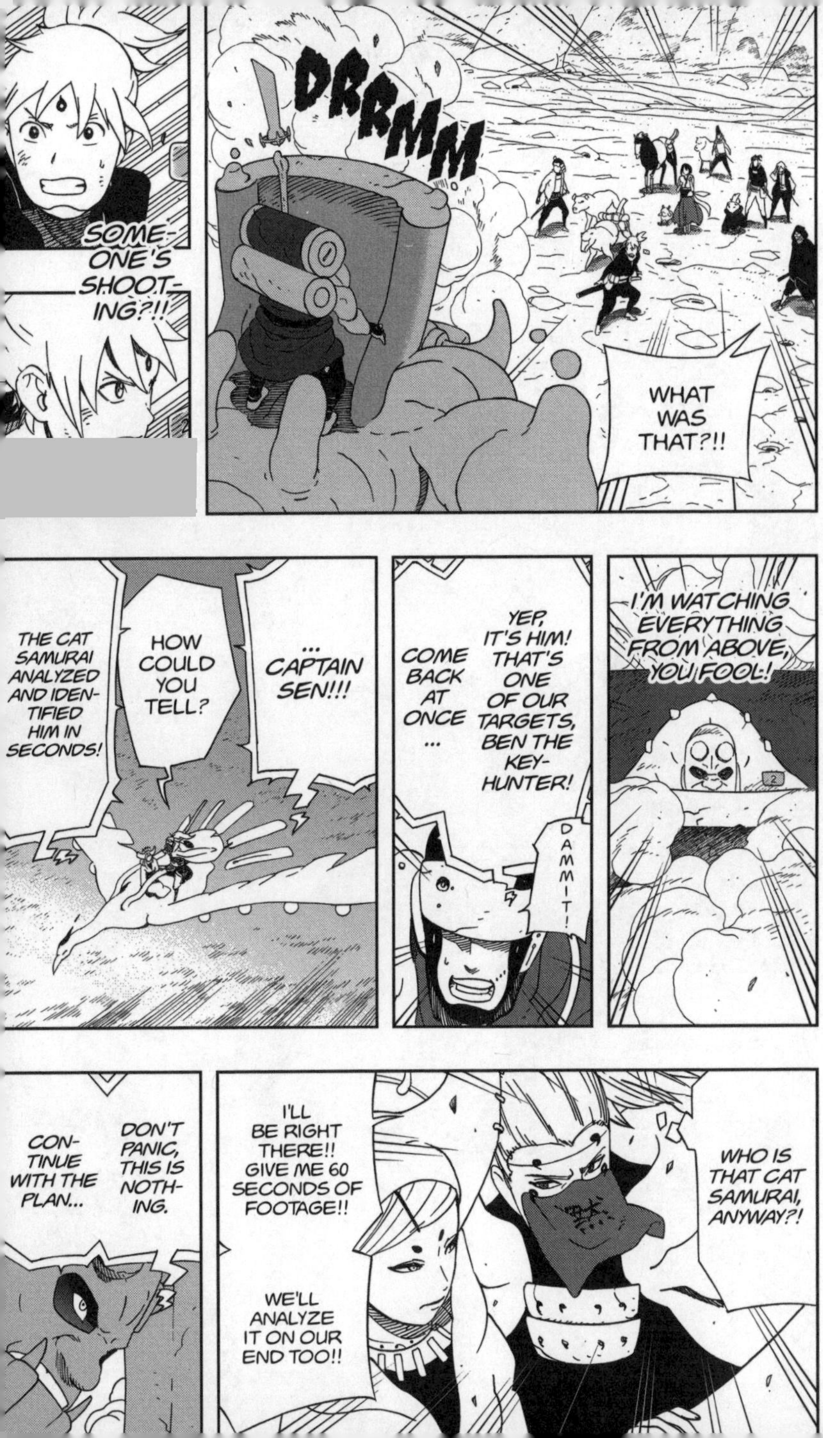
DRRMM
WHAT WAS THAT?!!
SOME-ONE'S SHOOT-ING?!!
I'M WATCHING EVERYTHING FROM ABOVE, YOU FOOL!
YEP, IT'S HIM! THAT'S ONE OF OUR TARGETS, BEN THE KEY-HUNTER!
COME BACK AT ONCE ...
DAMMIT!
... CAPTAIN SEN!!!
HOW COULD YOU TELL?
THE CAT SAMURAI ANALYZED AND IDEN-TIFIED HIM IN SECONDS!
WHO IS THAT CAT SAMURAI, ANYWAY?!
I'LL BE RIGHT THERE!! GIVE ME 60 SECONDS OF FOOTAGE!!
WE'LL ANALYZE IT ON OUR END TOO!!
DON'T PANIC, THIS IS NOTH-ING.
CON-TINUE WITH THE PLAN...

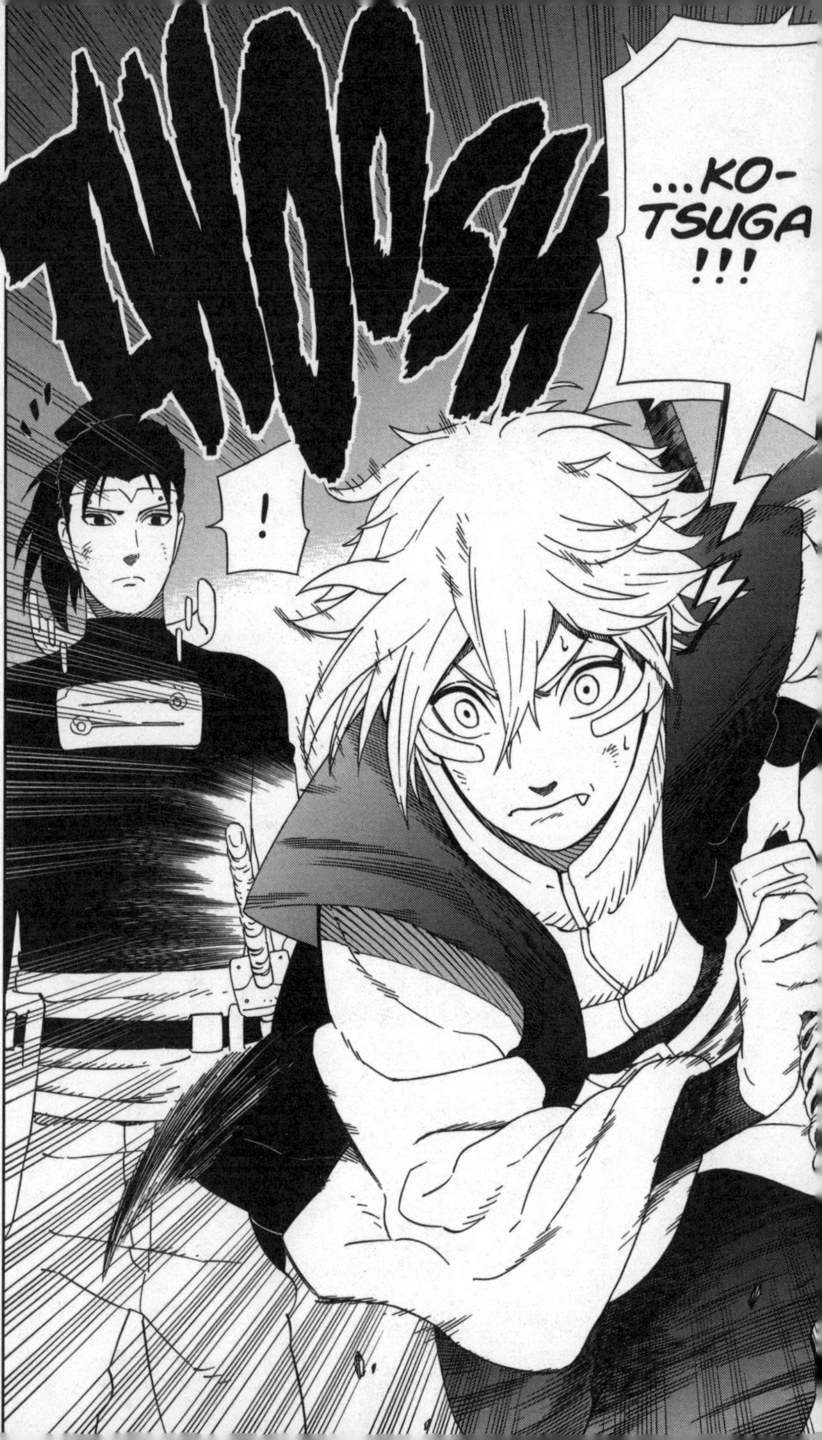
...KO-TSUGA!!!
!

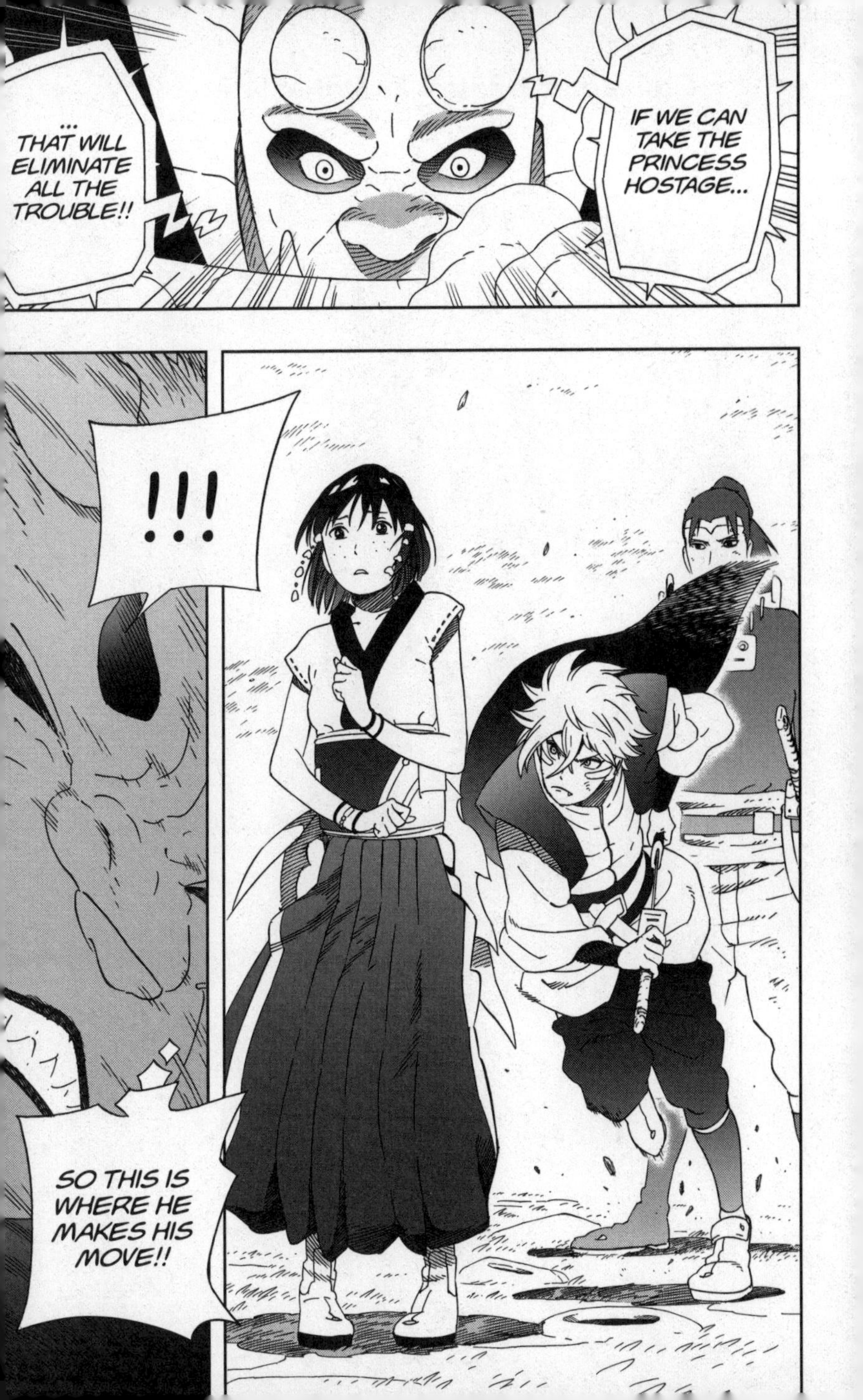
IF WE CAN TAKE THE PRINCESS HOSTAGE...
... THAT WILL ELIMINATE ALL THE TROUBLE!!
!!!
SO THIS IS WHERE HE MAKES HIS MOVE!!

Character Design Sketches: Benkei

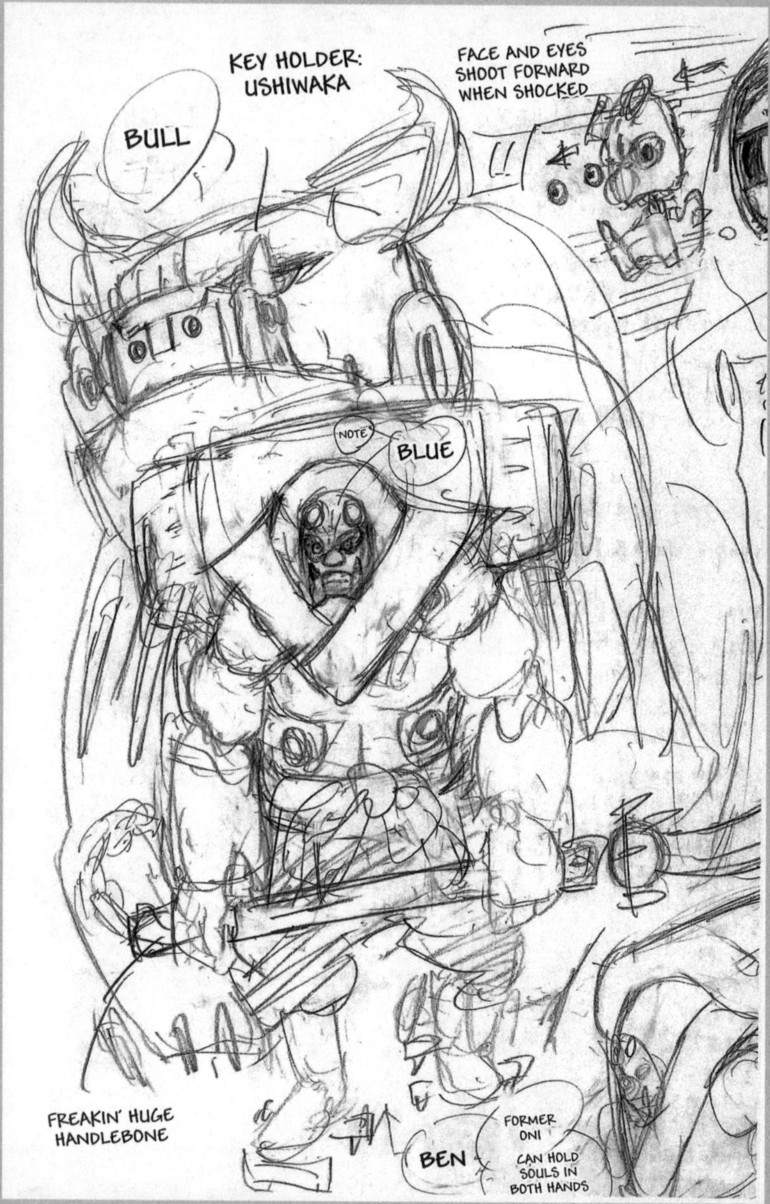
KEY HOLDER: USHIWAKA
FACE AND EYES SHOOT FORWARD WHEN SHOCKED
BULL
NOTE
BLUE
FREAKIN' HUGE HANDLEBONE
BEN
FORMER ONI
CAN HOLD SOULS IN BOTH HANDS

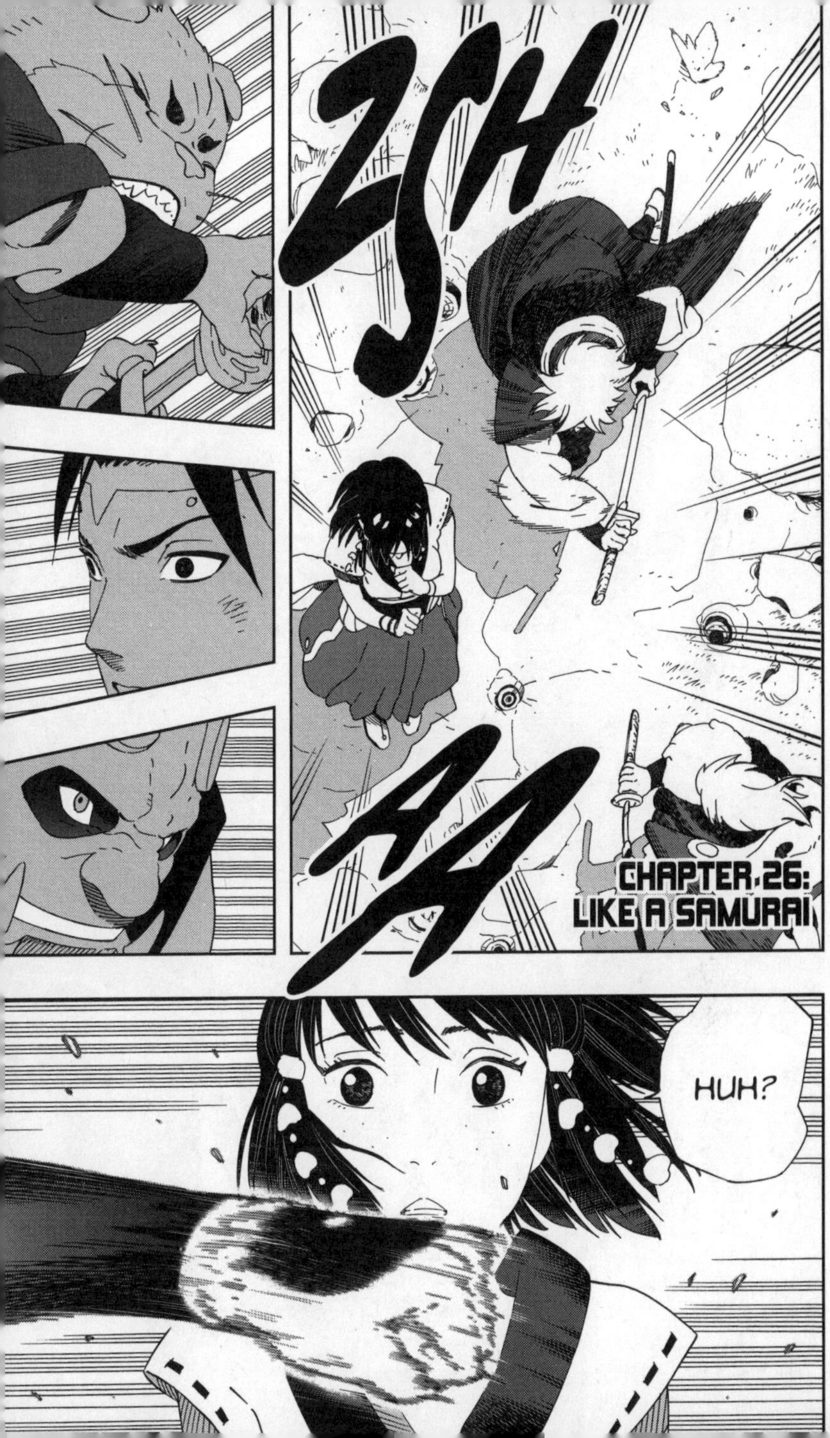
ZSH
AA
CHAPTER 26:
LIKE A SAMURAI
HUH?

CHAPTER 26: LIKE A SAMURAI

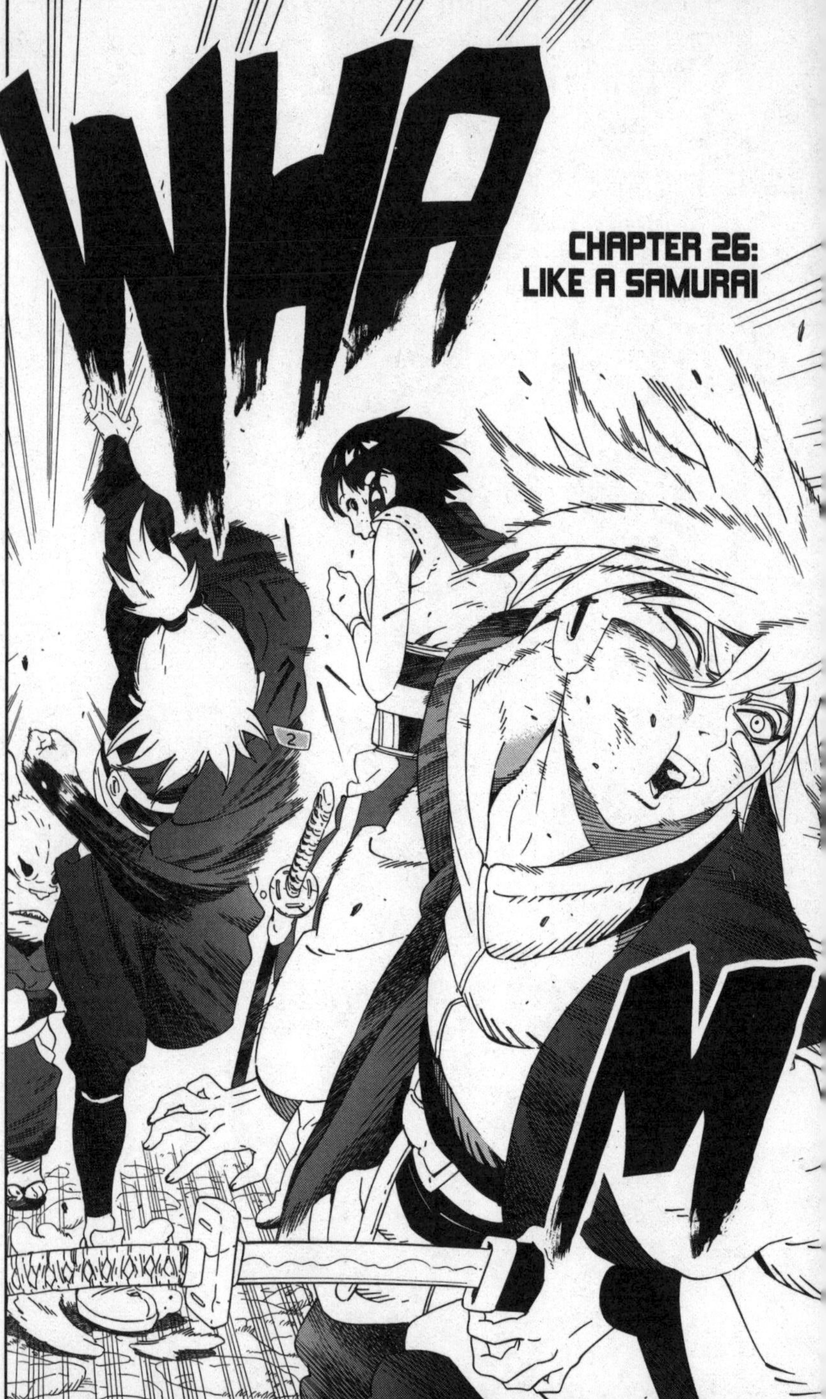
WHA
M

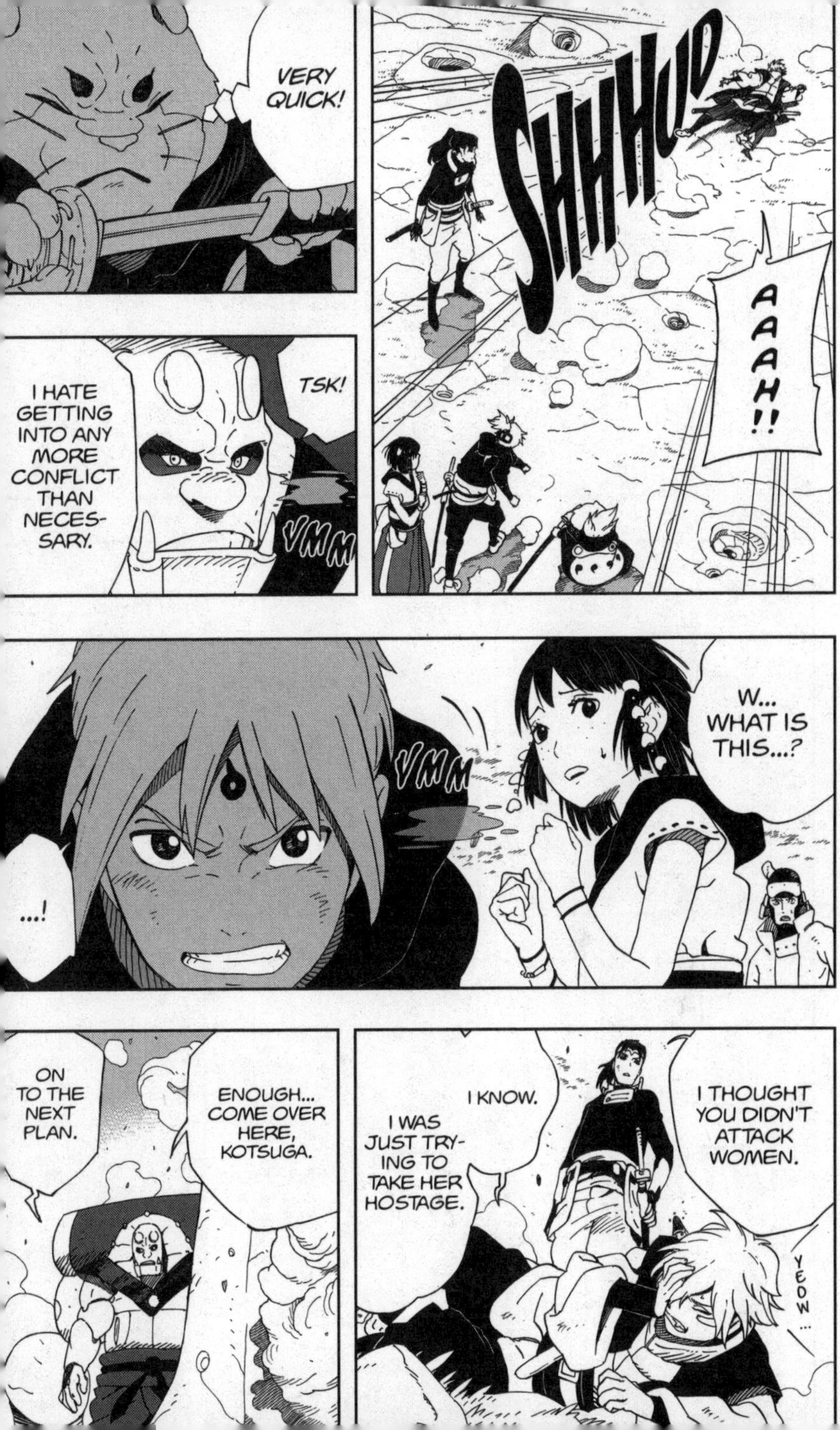
SHHHUD
AAAAH!!
VERY QUICK!
TSK!
I HATE GETTING INTO ANY MORE CONFLICT THAN NECES-SARY.
VMM
W... WHAT IS THIS...?
VMM
...!
I THOUGHT YOU DIDN'T ATTACK WOMEN.
I KNOW.
I WAS JUST TRY-ING TO TAKE HER HOSTAGE.
YEOW...
ENOUGH... COME OVER HERE, KOTSUGA.
ON TO THE NEXT PLAN.

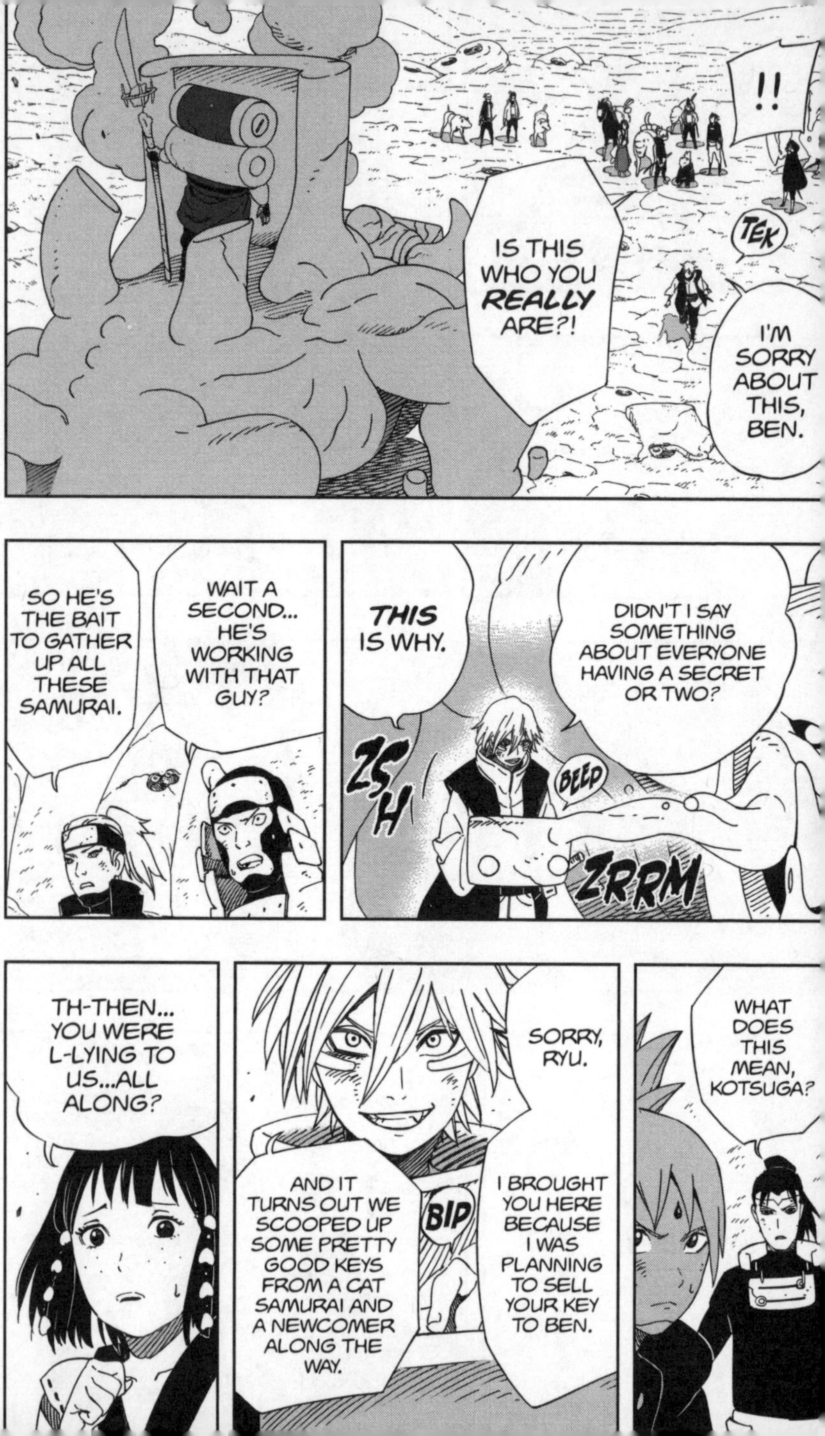
!!
TEK
IS THIS WHO YOU REALLY ARE?!
I'M SORRY ABOUT THIS, BEN.
DIDN'T I SAY SOMETHING ABOUT EVERYONE HAVING A SECRET OR TWO?
THIS IS WHY.
ZSH
BEEP
ZRRM
WAIT A SECOND... HE'S WORKING WITH THAT GUY?
SO HE'S THE BAIT TO GATHER UP ALL THESE SAMURAI.
WHAT DOES THIS MEAN, KOTSUGA?
SORRY, RYU.
I BROUGHT YOU HERE BECAUSE I WAS PLANNING TO SELL YOUR KEY TO BEN.
BIP
AND IT TURNS OUT WE SCOOPED UP SOME PRETTY GOOD KEYS FROM A CAT SAMURAI AND A NEWCOMER ALONG THE WAY.
TH-THEN... YOU WERE L-LYING TO US...ALL ALONG?

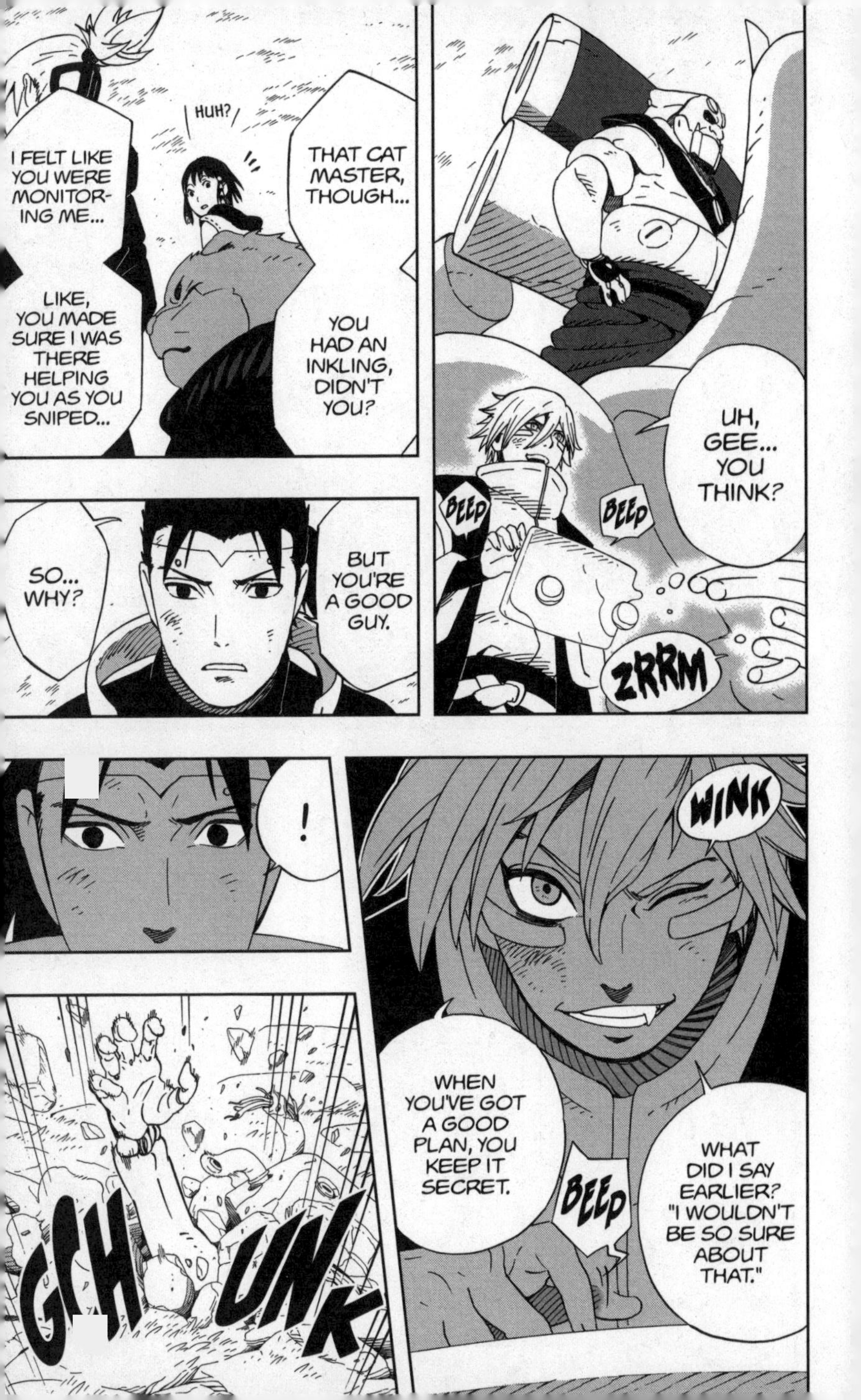
UH, GEE... YOU THINK?
BEEP
BEEP
ZRRM
THAT CAT MASTER, THOUGH...
HUH?
I FELT LIKE YOU WERE MONITORING ME...
YOU HAD AN INKLING, DIDN'T YOU?
LIKE, YOU MADE SURE I WAS THERE HELPING YOU AS YOU SNIPED...
BUT YOU'RE A GOOD GUY.
SO... WHY?
WINK
WHAT DID I SAY EARLIER? "I WOULDN'T BE SO SURE ABOUT THAT."
WHEN YOU'VE GOT A GOOD PLAN, YOU KEEP IT SECRET.
BEEP
!
GCHUNK

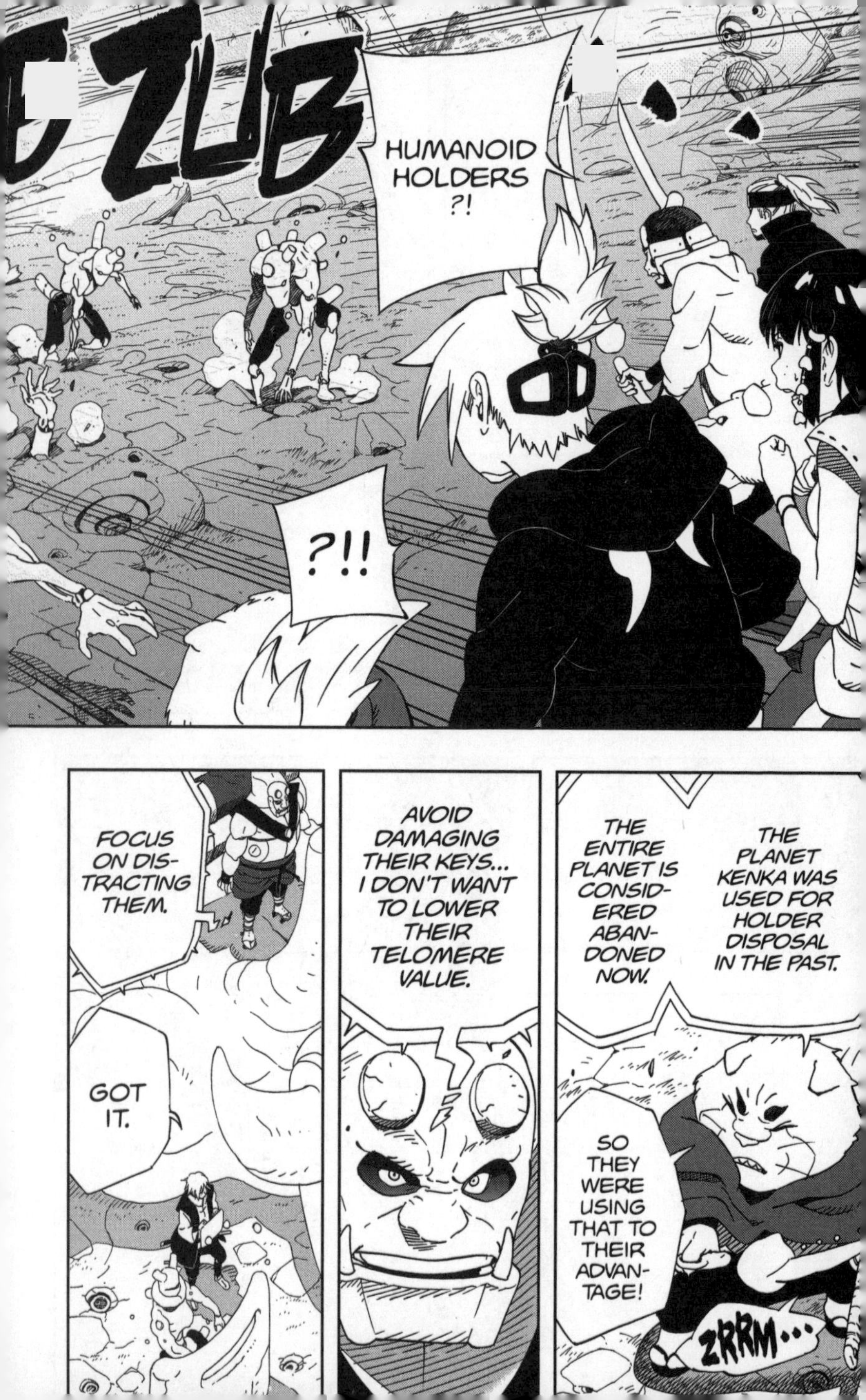
ZUB
HUMANOID HOLDERS ?!
?!!
THE PLANET KENKA WAS USED FOR HOLDER DISPOSAL IN THE PAST.
THE ENTIRE PLANET IS CONSIDERED ABANDONED NOW.
SO THEY WERE USING THAT TO THEIR ADVANTAGE!
ZRRM...
AVOID DAMAGING THEIR KEYS... I DON'T WANT TO LOWER THEIR TELOMERE VALUE.
FOCUS ON DISTRACTING THEM.
GOT IT.

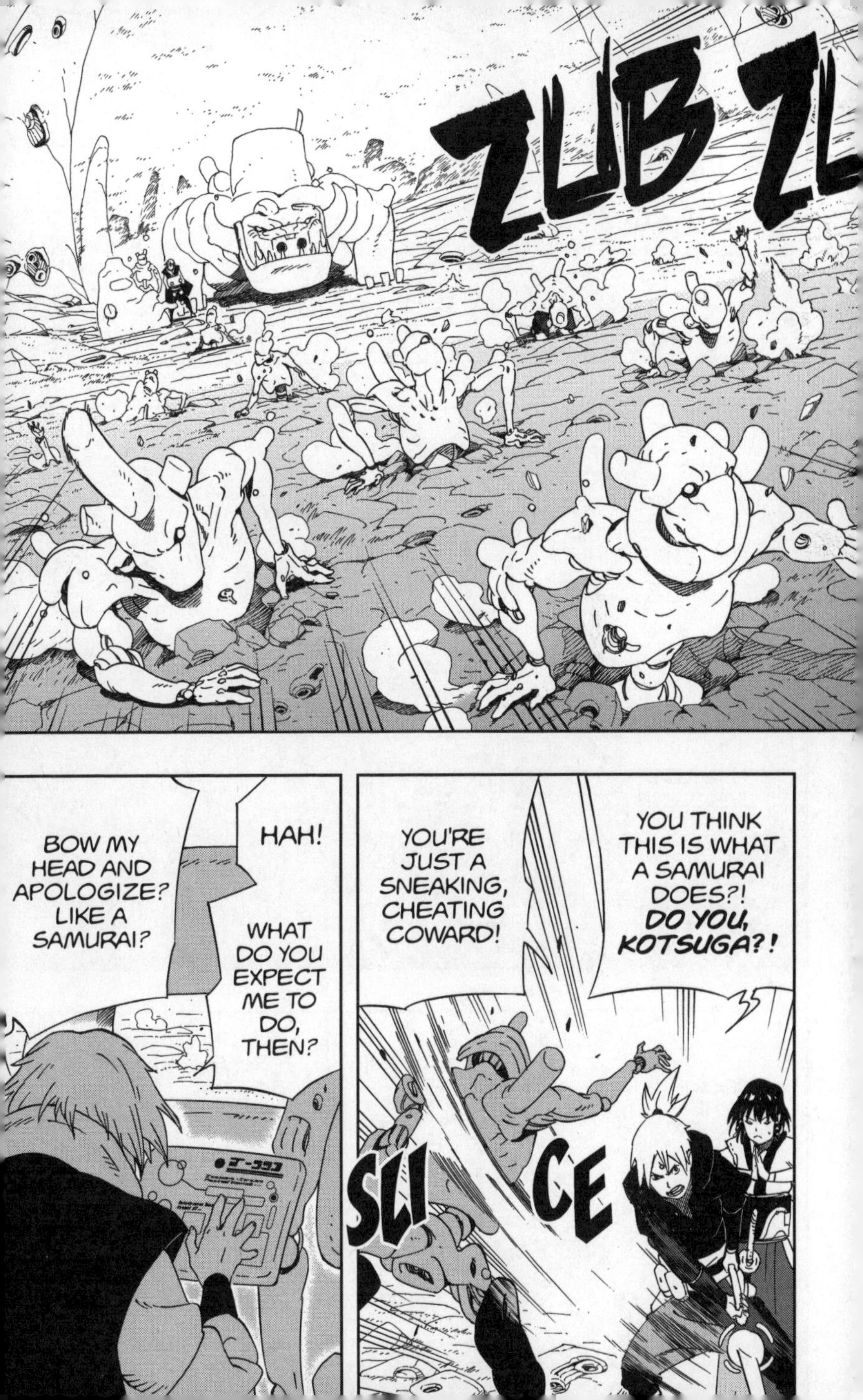
ZUB ZL
YOU THINK THIS IS WHAT A SAMURAI DOES?! DO YOU, KOTSUGA?!
YOU'RE JUST A SNEAKING, CHEATING COWARD!
SLICE
HAH!
WHAT DO YOU EXPECT ME TO DO, THEN?
BOW MY HEAD AND APOLOGIZE? LIKE A SAMURAI?

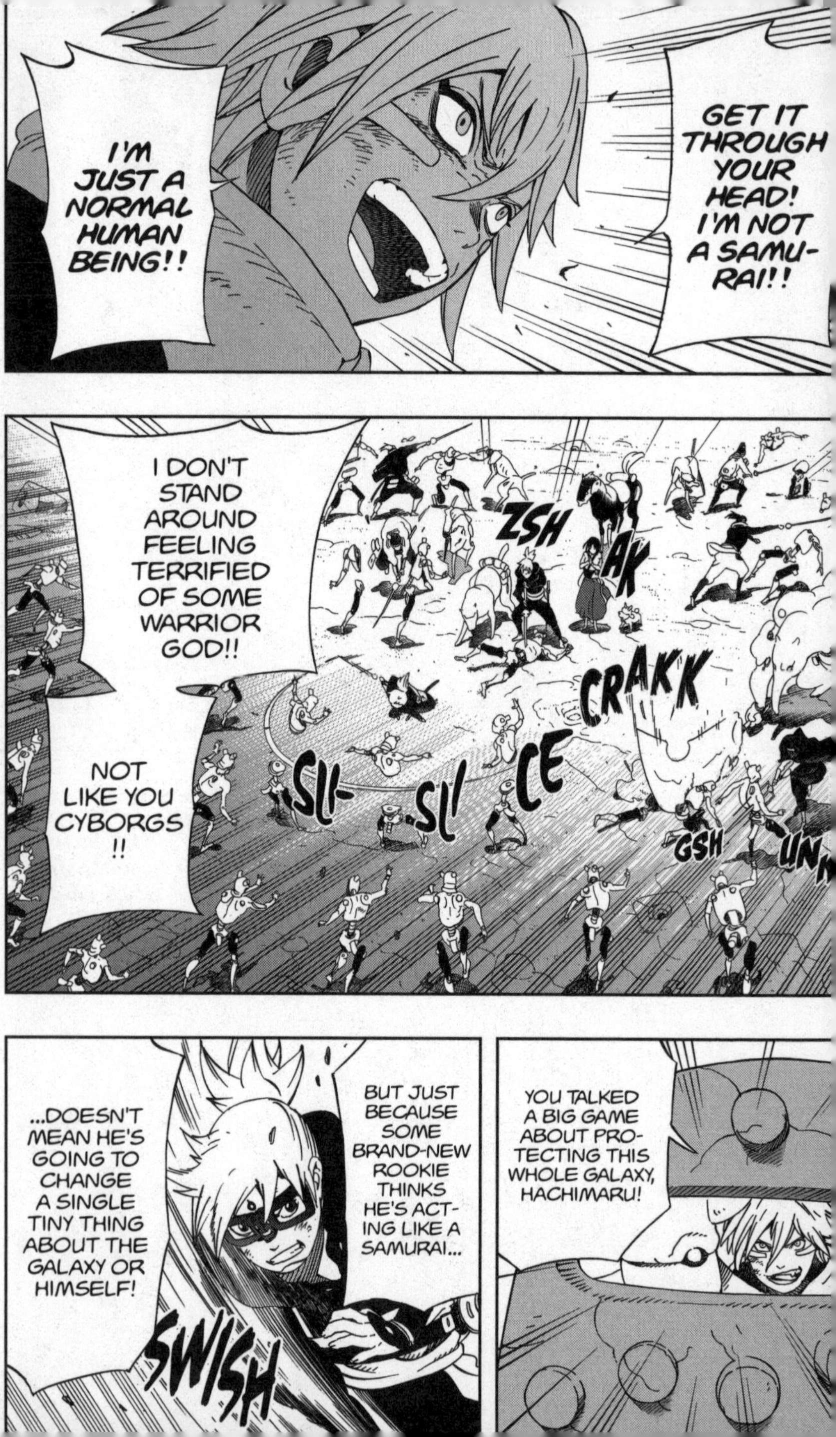
GET IT THROUGH YOUR HEAD! I'M NOT A SAMURAI!!
I'M JUST A NORMAL HUMAN BEING!!
ZSH
AK
I DON'T STAND AROUND FEELING TERRIFIED OF SOME WARRIOR GOD!!
CRAKK
NOT LIKE YOU CYBORGS!!
SLI- SLI CE
UNK
GSH
YOU TALKED A BIG GAME ABOUT PROTECTING THIS WHOLE GALAXY, HACHIMARU!
BUT JUST BECAUSE SOME BRAND-NEW ROOKIE THINKS HE'S ACTING LIKE A SAMURAI...
...DOESN'T MEAN HE'S GOING TO CHANGE A SINGLE TINY THING ABOUT THE GALAXY OR HIMSELF!
SWISH

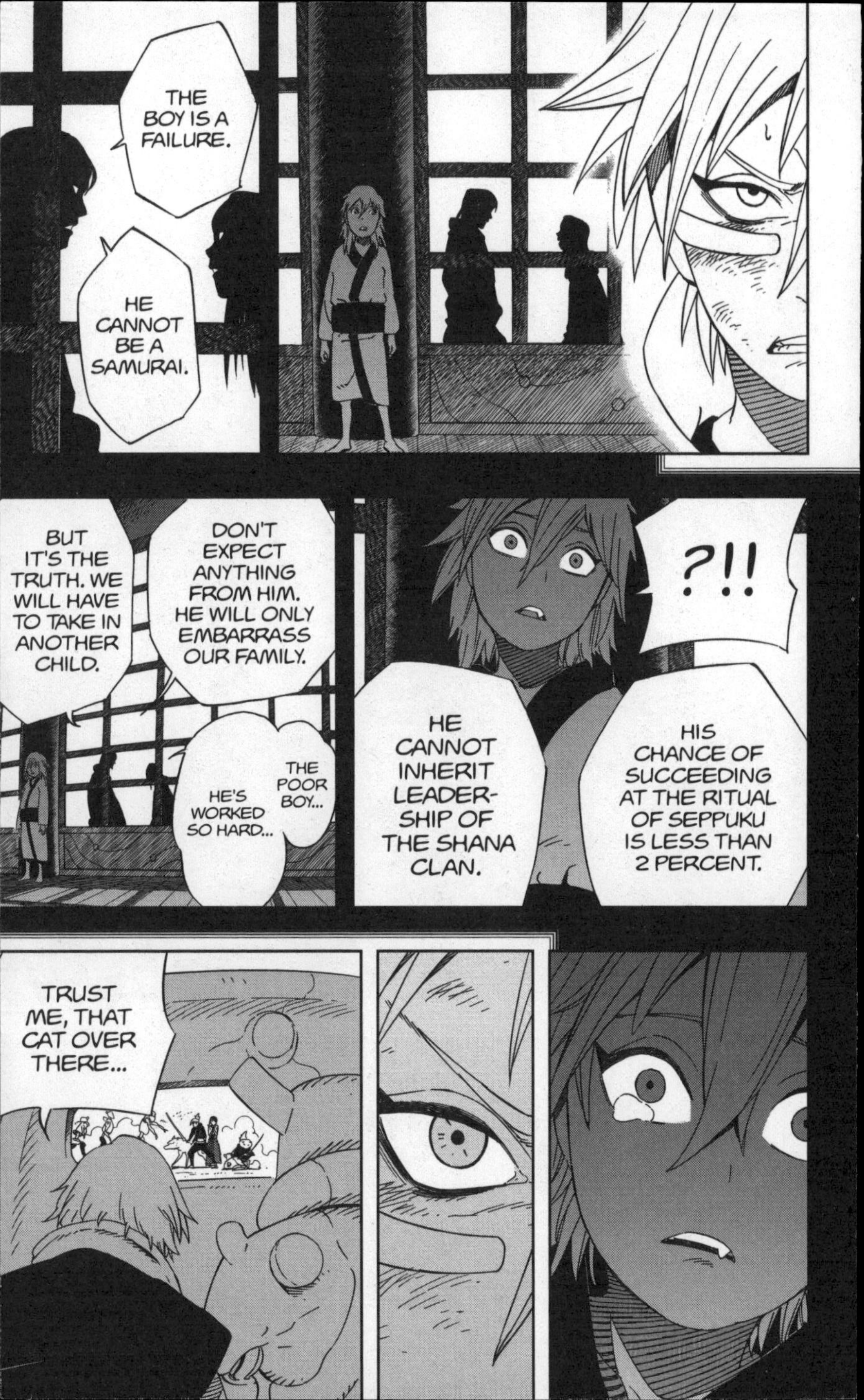
THE BOY IS A FAILURE.
HE CANNOT BE A SAMURAI.
?!!
HIS CHANCE OF SUCCEEDING AT THE RITUAL OF SEPPUKU IS LESS THAN 2 PERCENT.
HE CANNOT INHERIT LEADER-SHIP OF THE SHANA CLAN.
DON'T EXPECT ANYTHING FROM HIM. HE WILL ONLY EMBARRASS OUR FAMILY.
BUT IT'S THE TRUTH. WE WILL HAVE TO TAKE IN ANOTHER CHILD.
THE POOR BOY...
HE'S WORKED SO HARD...
TRUST ME, THAT CAT OVER THERE...

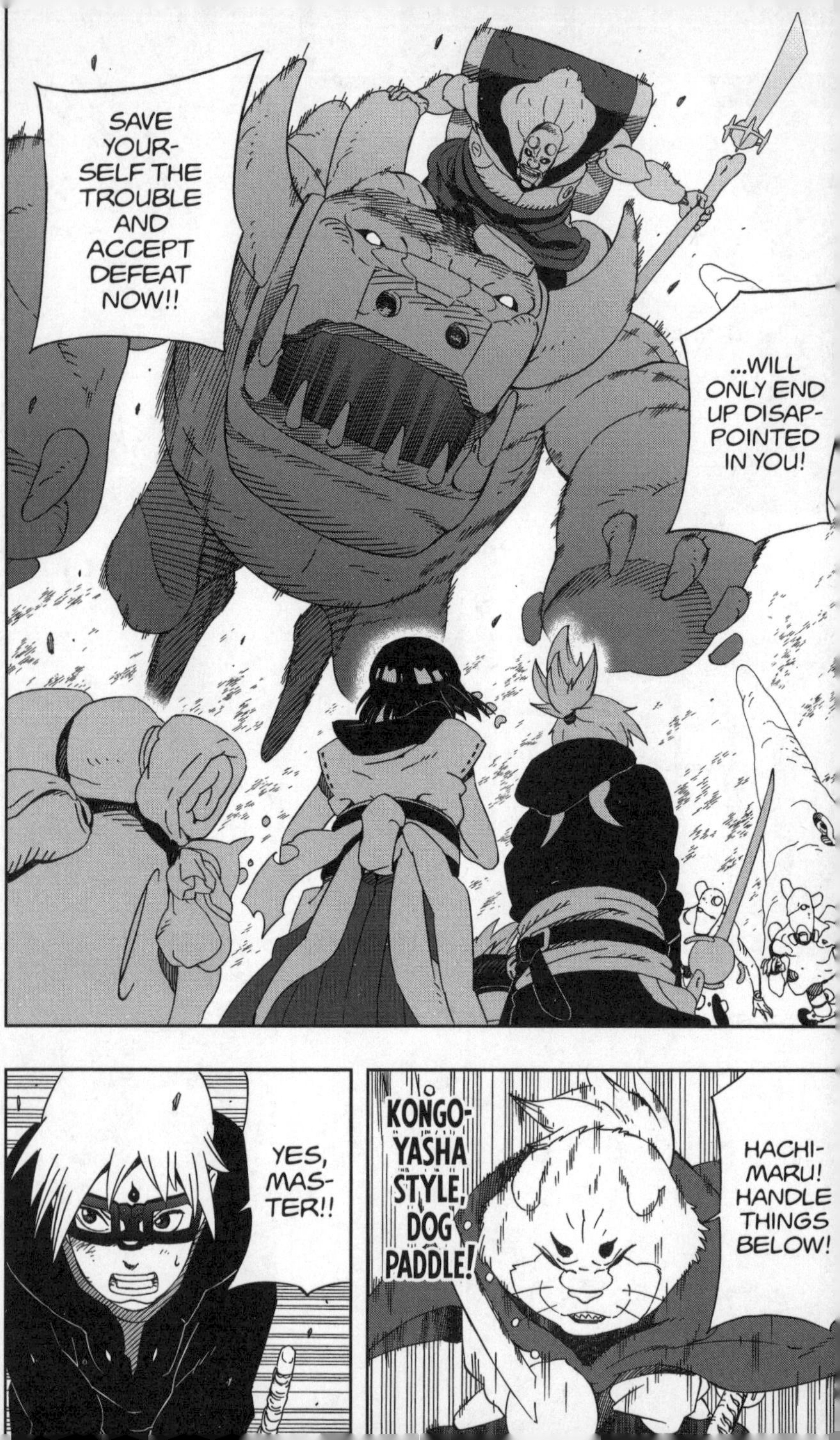
...WILL ONLY END UP DISAPPOINTED IN YOU!
SAVE YOURSELF THE TROUBLE AND ACCEPT DEFEAT NOW!!
HACHIMARU! HANDLE THINGS BELOW!
KONGO-YASHA STYLE, DOG PADDLE!
YES, MASTER!!

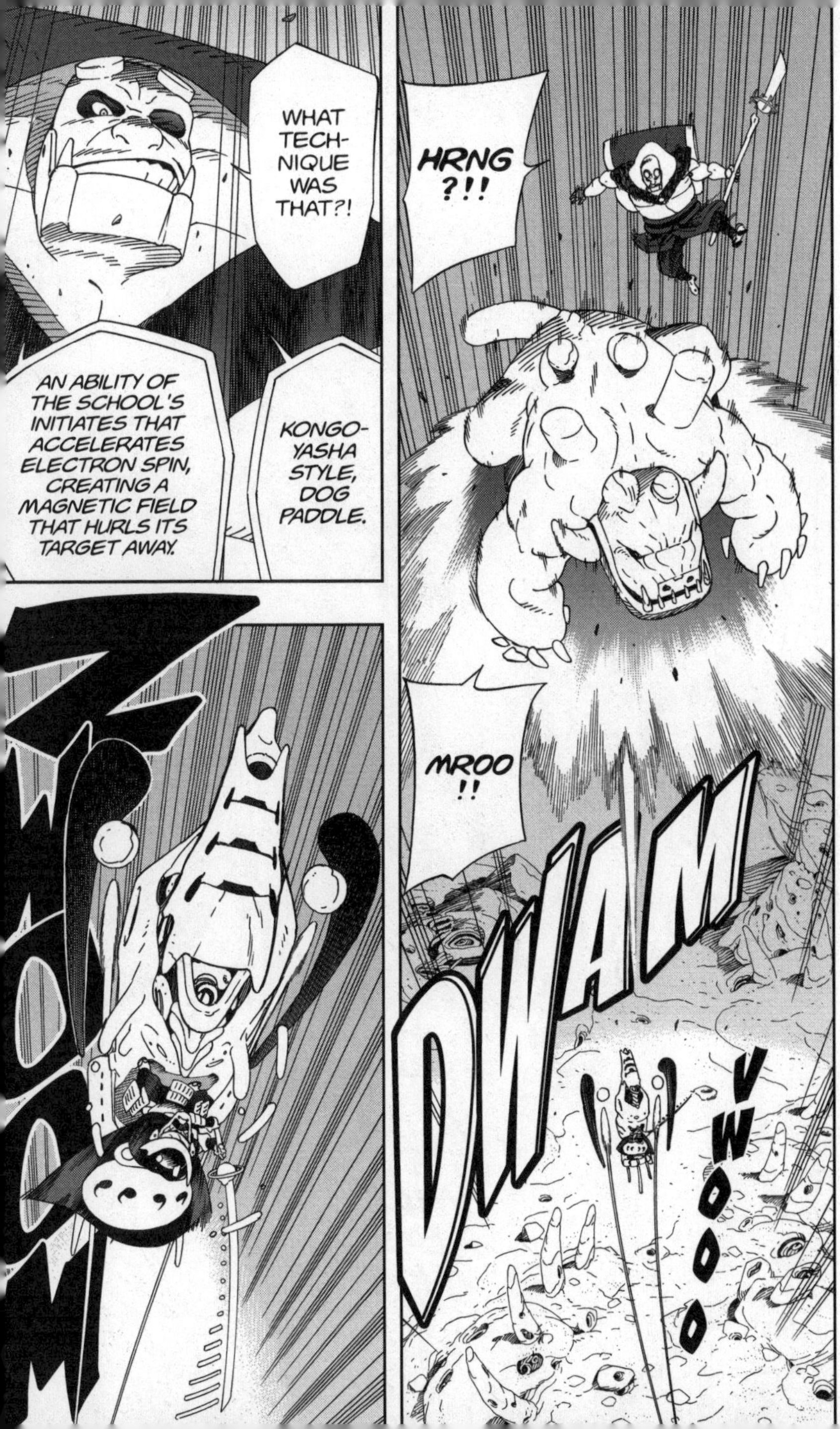
HRNG ?!!
MROO !!
DWAM
VWOOO
WHAT TECH-NIQUE WAS THAT?!
KONGO-YASHA STYLE, DOG PADDLE.
AN ABILITY OF THE SCHOOL'S INITIATES THAT ACCELERATES ELECTRON SPIN, CREATING A MAGNETIC FIELD THAT HURLS ITS TARGET AWAY.

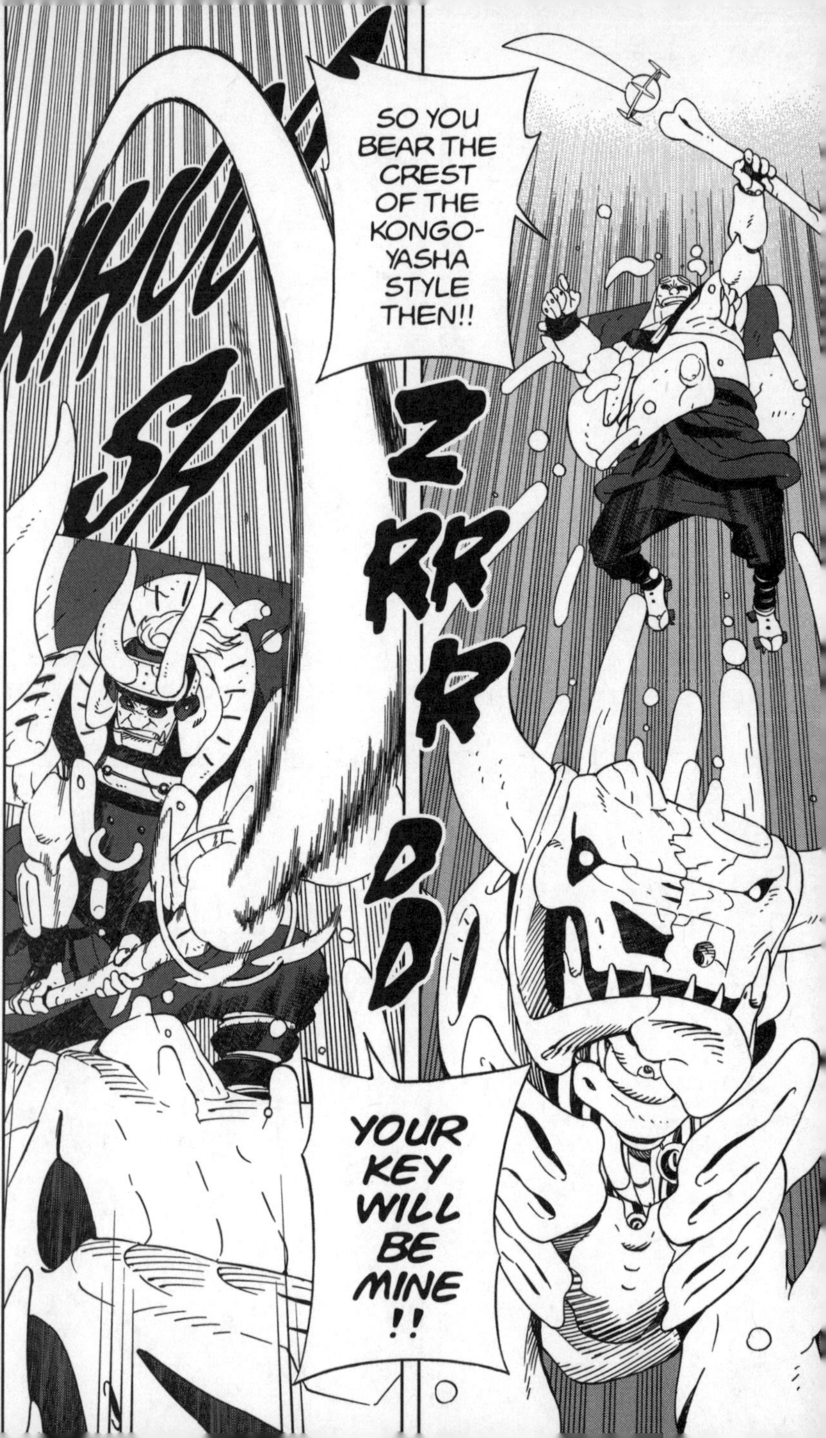

SO YOU BEAR THE CREST OF THE KONGO-YASHA STYLE THEN!!
ZRRRDD
YOUR KEY WILL BE MINE!!
WHOOSH

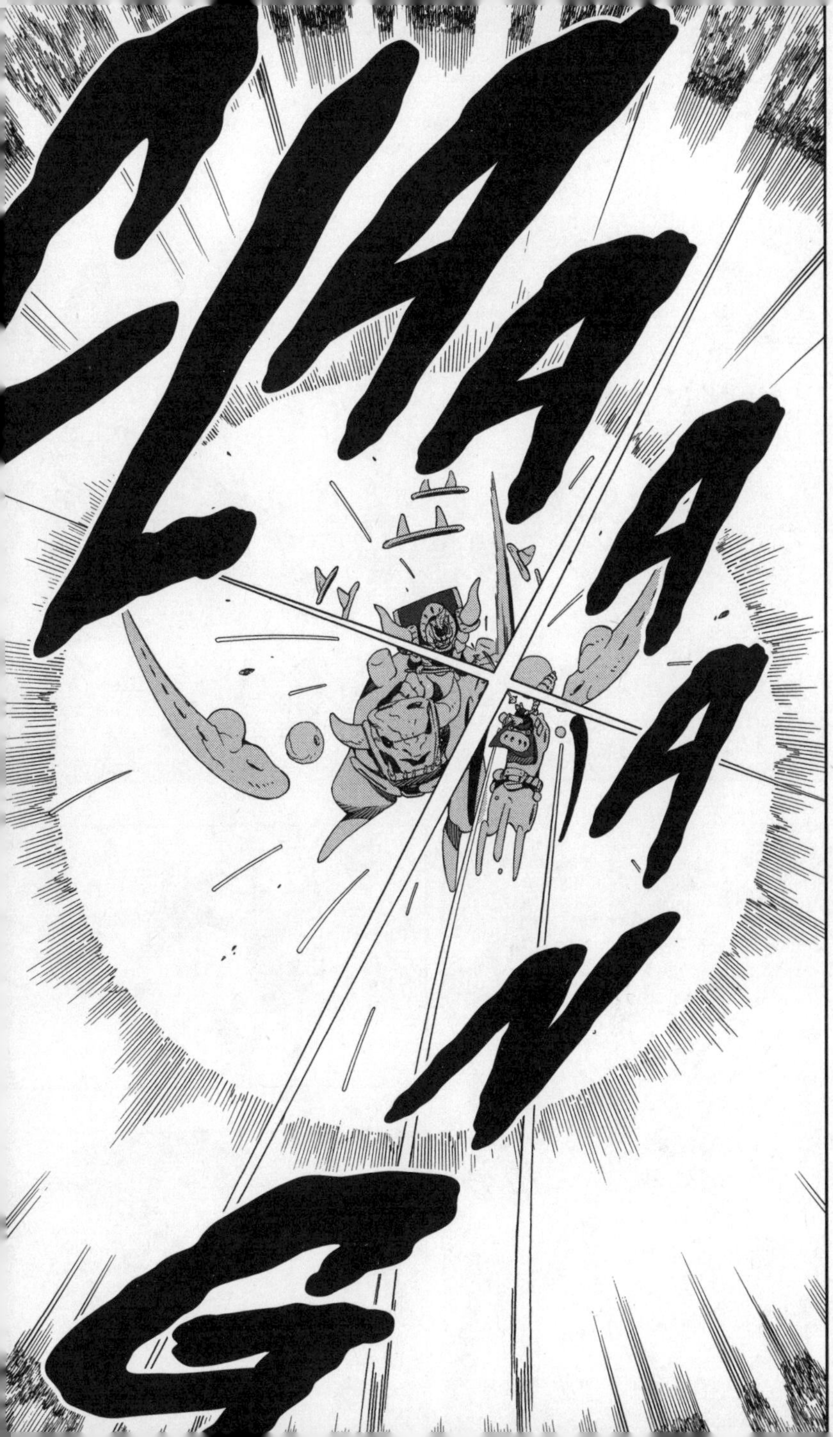
ZHAAANG

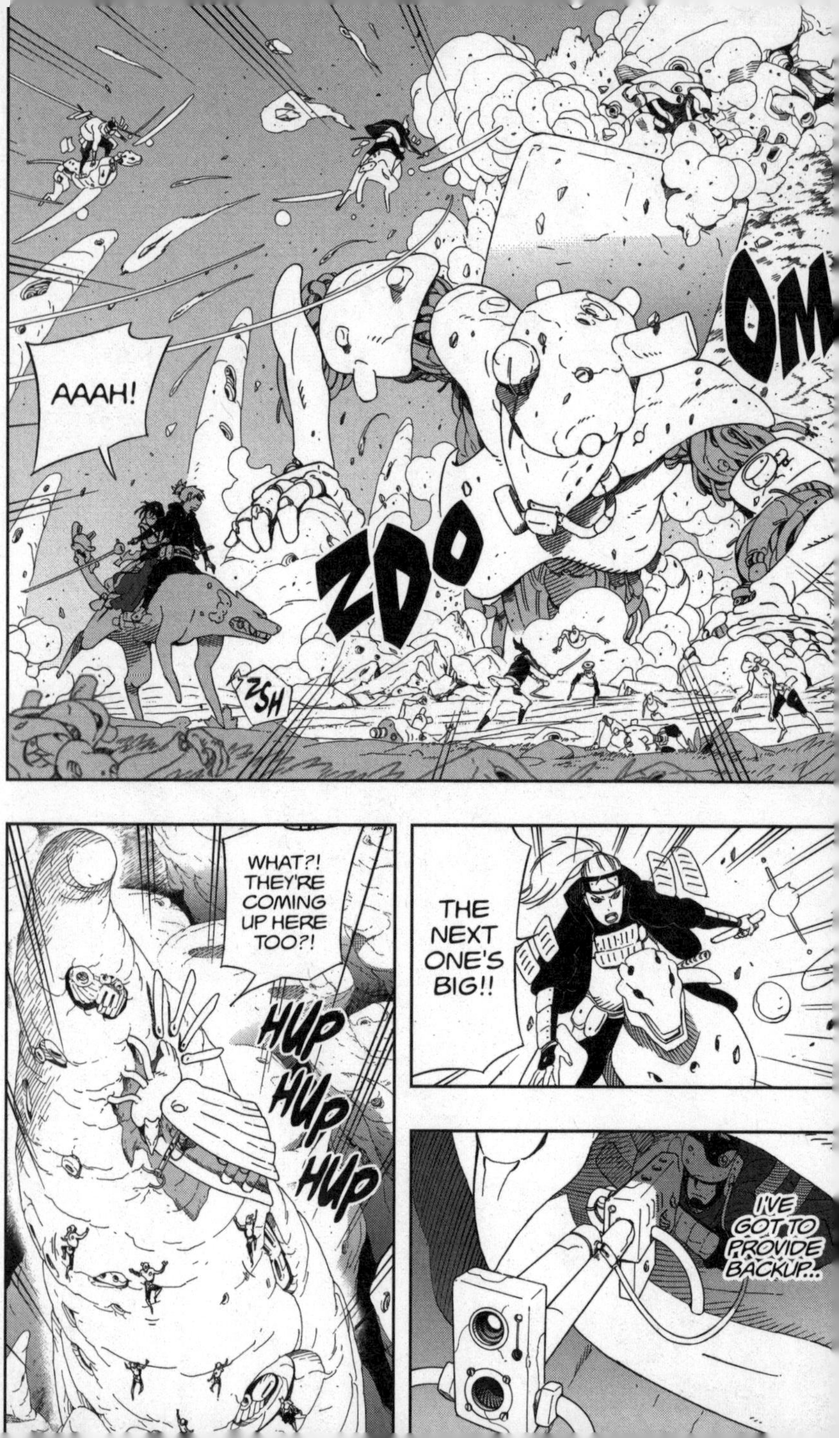
OM
AAAH!
ZDO
ZSH
THE NEXT ONE'S BIG!!
I'VE GOT TO PROVIDE BACKUP...
WHAT?! THEY'RE COMING UP HERE TOO?!
HUP HUP HUP

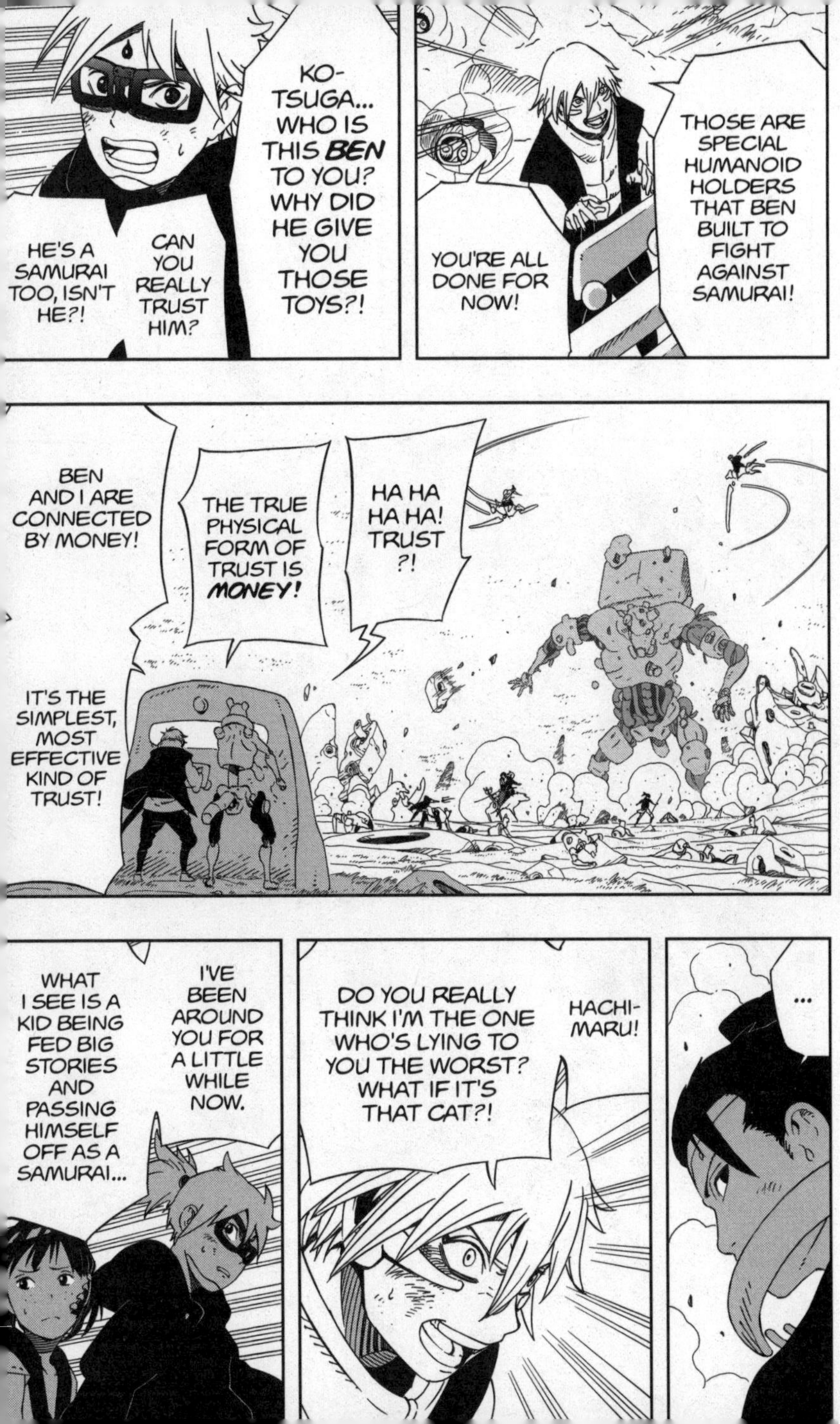
THOSE ARE SPECIAL HUMANOID HOLDERS THAT BEN BUILT TO FIGHT AGAINST SAMURAI!
YOU'RE ALL DONE FOR NOW!
KO-TSUGA... WHO IS THIS **BEN** TO YOU? WHY DID HE GIVE YOU THOSE TOYS?!
CAN YOU REALLY TRUST HIM?
HE'S A SAMURAI TOO, ISN'T HE?!
HA HA HA HA! TRUST?!
THE TRUE PHYSICAL FORM OF TRUST IS **MONEY!**
BEN AND I ARE CONNECTED BY MONEY!
IT'S THE SIMPLEST, MOST EFFECTIVE KIND OF TRUST!
...
HACHI-MARU!
DO YOU REALLY THINK I'M THE ONE WHO'S LYING TO YOU THE WORST? WHAT IF IT'S THAT CAT?!
I'VE BEEN AROUND YOU FOR A LITTLE WHILE NOW.
WHAT I SEE IS A KID BEING FED BIG STORIES AND PASSING HIMSELF OFF AS A SAMURAI...

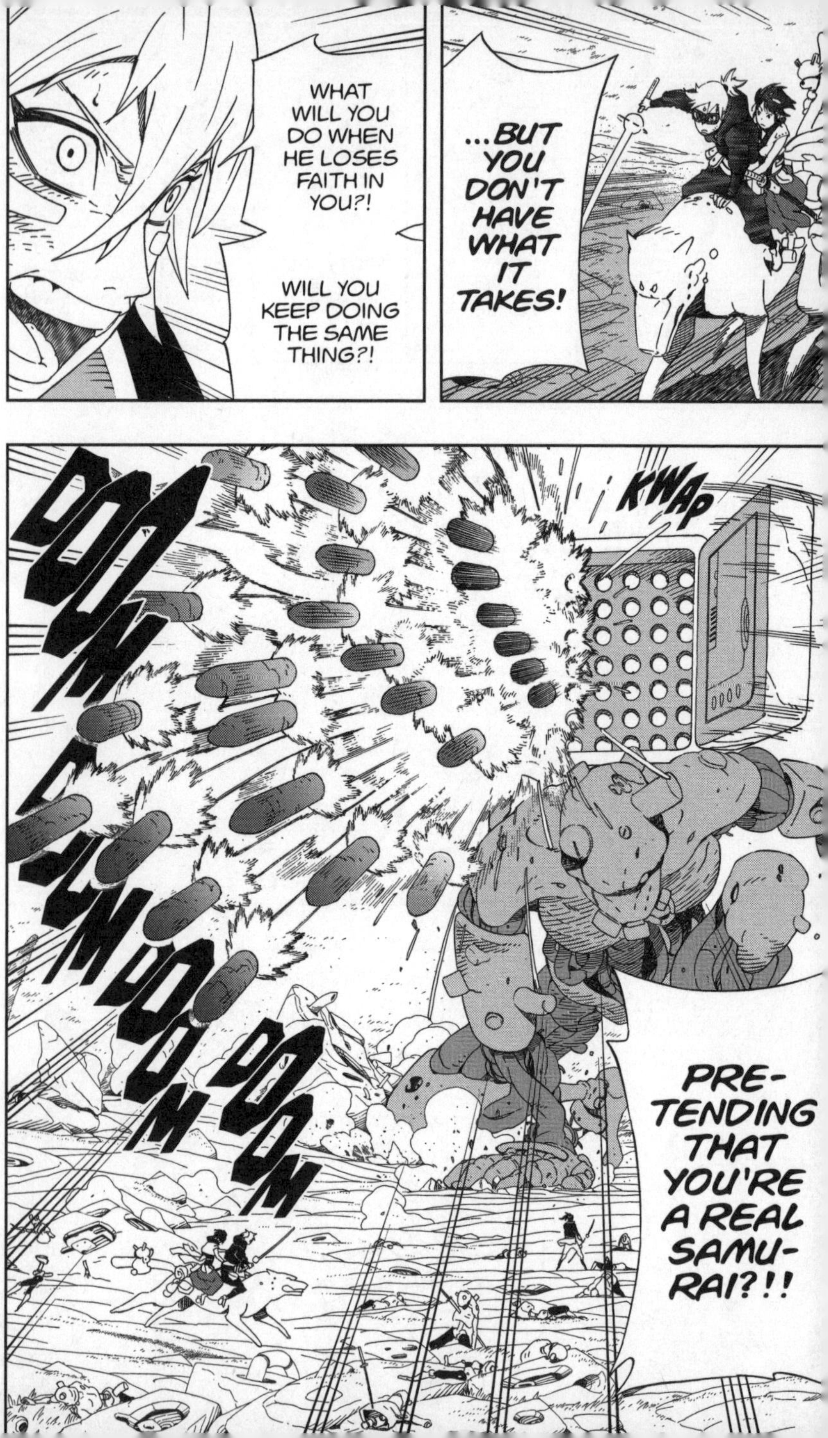
...BUT YOU DON'T HAVE WHAT IT TAKES!
WHAT WILL YOU DO WHEN HE LOSES FAITH IN YOU?!
WILL YOU KEEP DOING THE SAME THING?!
KWAP
PRE-TENDING THAT YOU'RE A REAL SAMU-RAI?!!
DOOM DOOM DOOM DOOM
DOOM

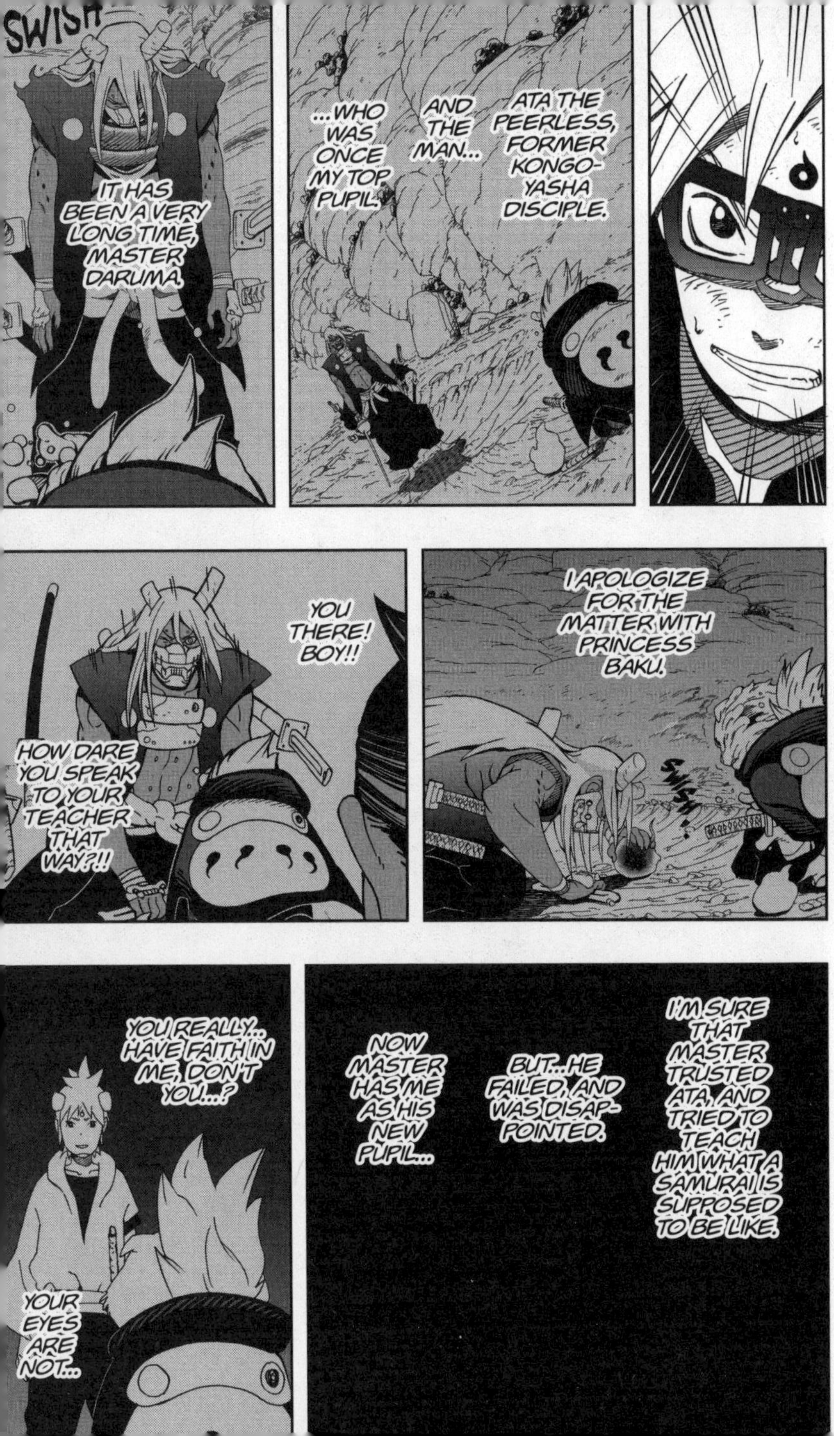
ATA THE PEERLESS, FORMER KONGO-YASHA DISCIPLE.
AND THE MAN...
...WHO WAS ONCE MY TOP PUPIL.
SWISH
IT HAS BEEN A VERY LONG TIME, MASTER DARUMA.
I APOLOGIZE FOR THE MATTER WITH PRINCESS BAKU.
SWISH
YOU THERE! BOY!!
HOW DARE YOU SPEAK TO YOUR TEACHER THAT WAY?!!
I'M SURE THAT MASTER TRUSTED ATA, AND TRIED TO TEACH HIM WHAT A SAMURAI IS SUPPOSED TO BE LIKE.
BUT... HE FAILED, AND WAS DISAP-POINTED.
NOW MASTER HAS ME AS HIS NEW PUPIL...
YOU REALLY... HAVE FAITH IN ME, DON'T YOU...?
YOUR EYES ARE NOT...

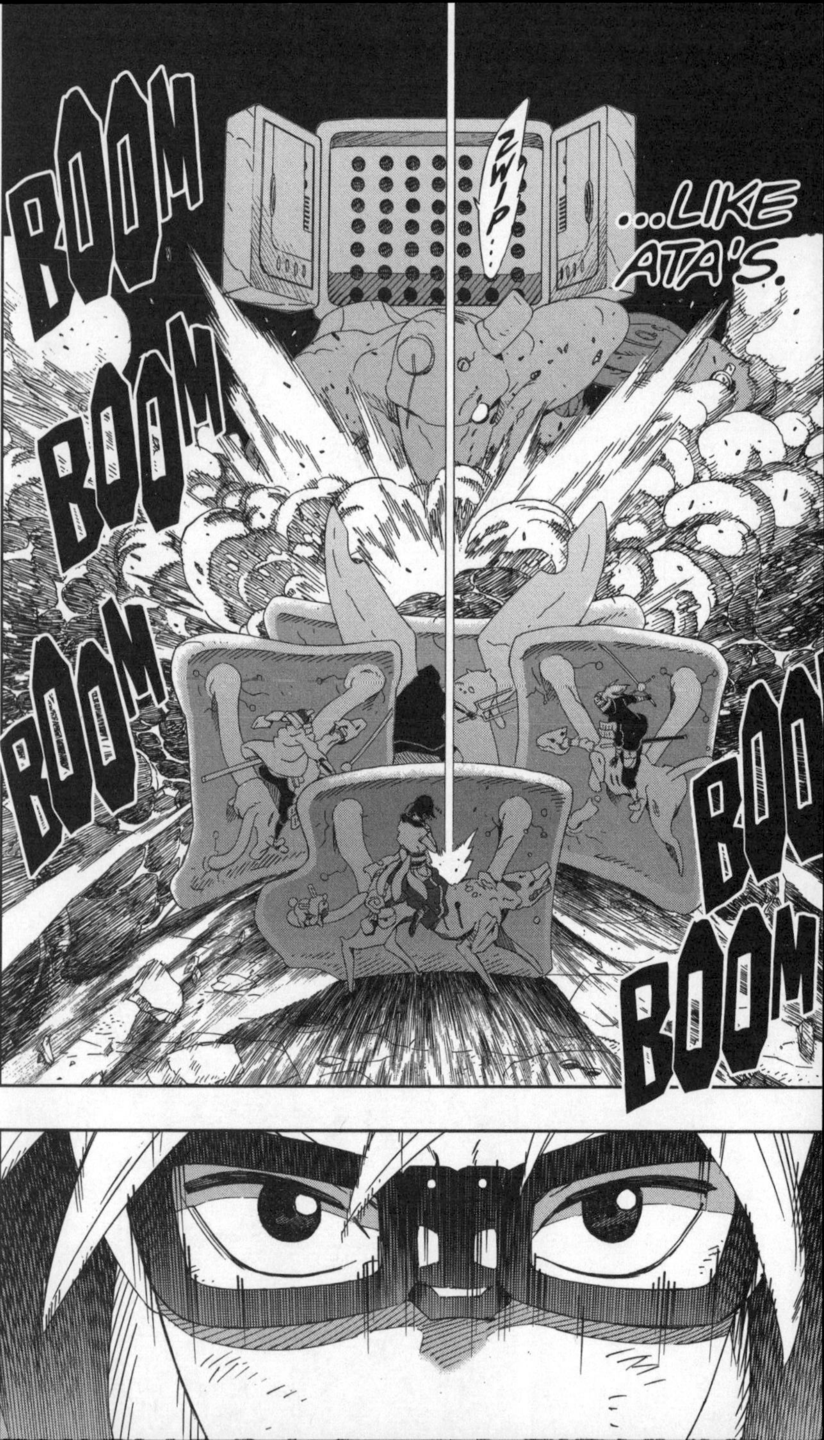
ZWIP...
...LIKE ATA'S.
BOOM
BOOM
BOOM
BOO
BOOM

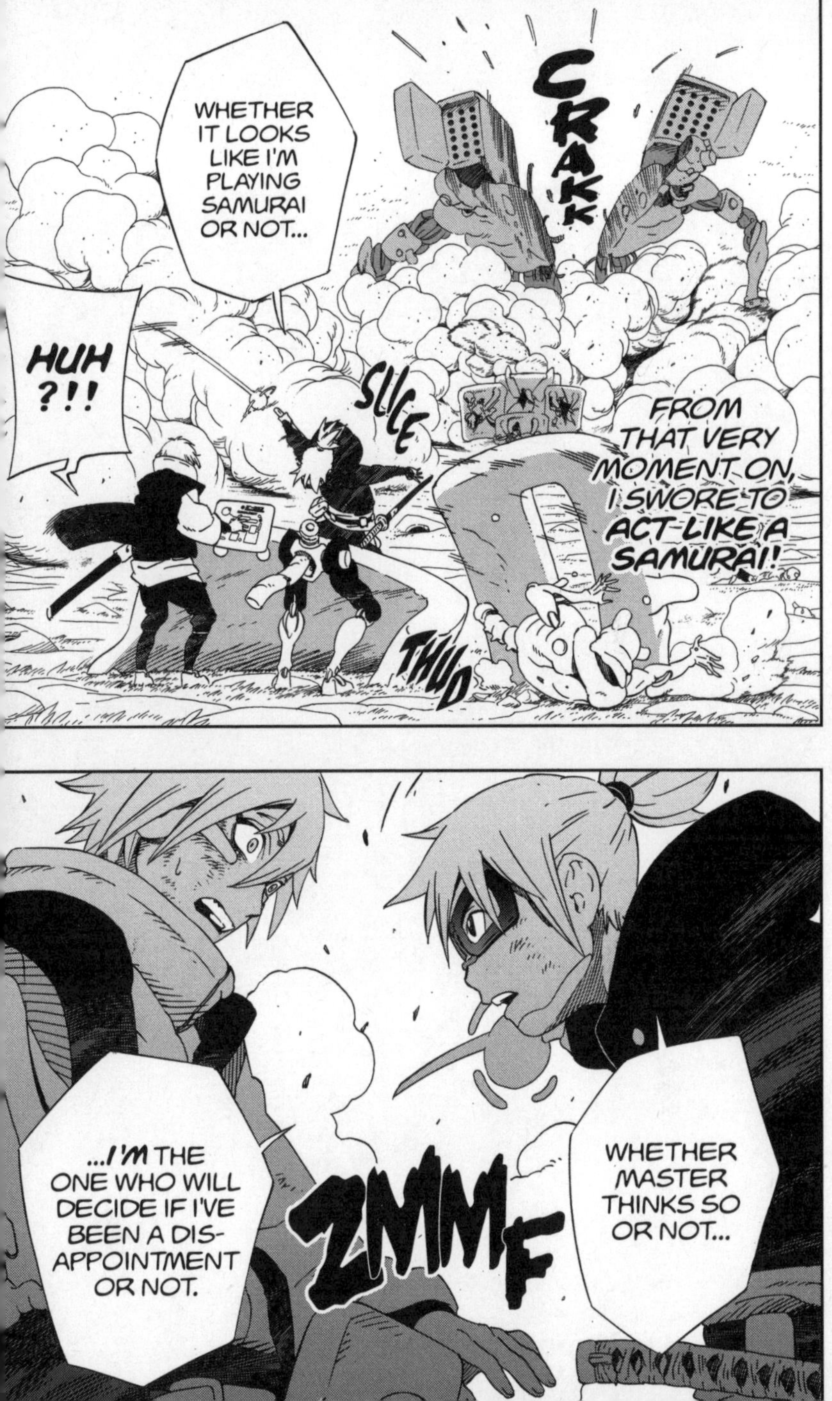
CRAKK
WHETHER IT LOOKS LIKE I'M PLAYING SAMURAI OR NOT...
FROM THAT VERY MOMENT ON, I SWORE TO ACT LIKE A SAMURAI!
SLICE
HUH ?!!
THUD
WHETHER MASTER THINKS SO OR NOT...
ZMMF
...I'M THE ONE WHO WILL DECIDE IF I'VE BEEN A DIS-APPOINTMENT OR NOT.

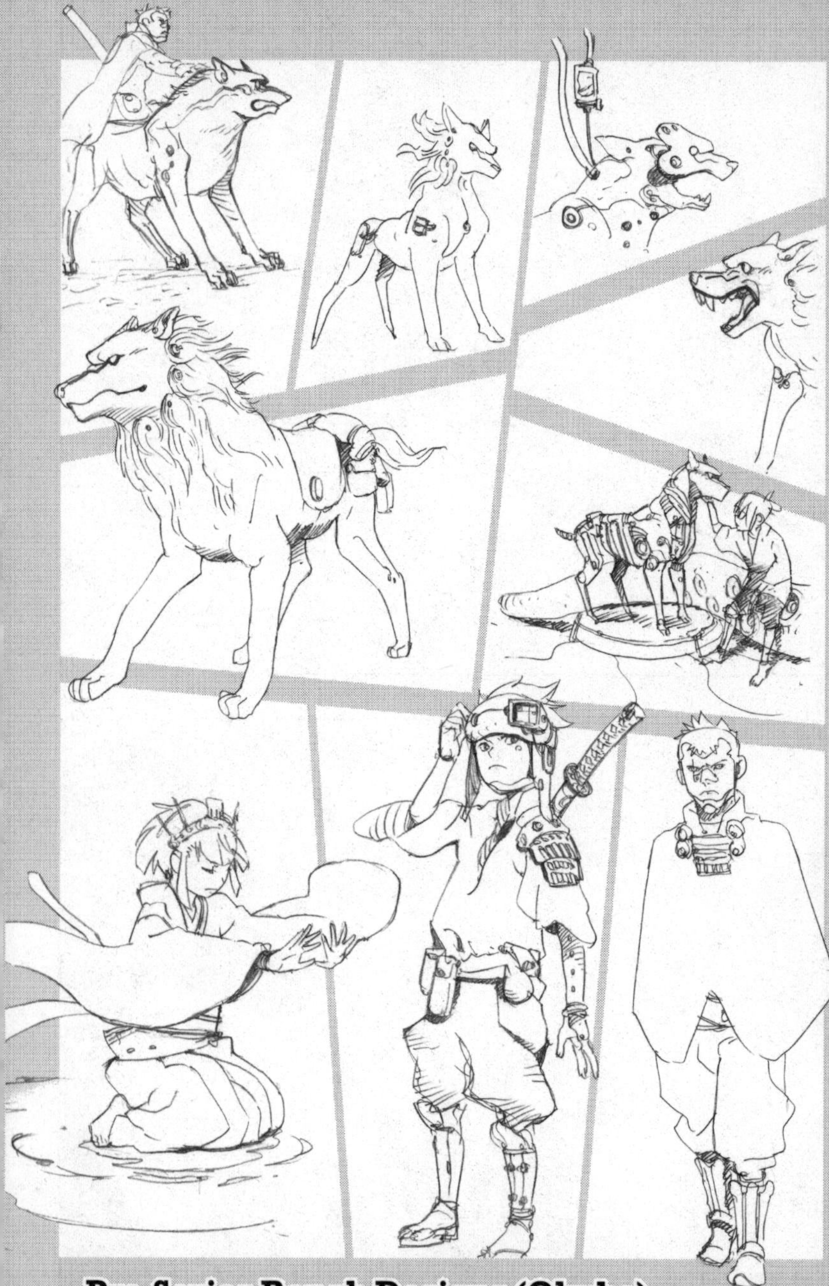

Pre-Series Rough Designs (Okubo)

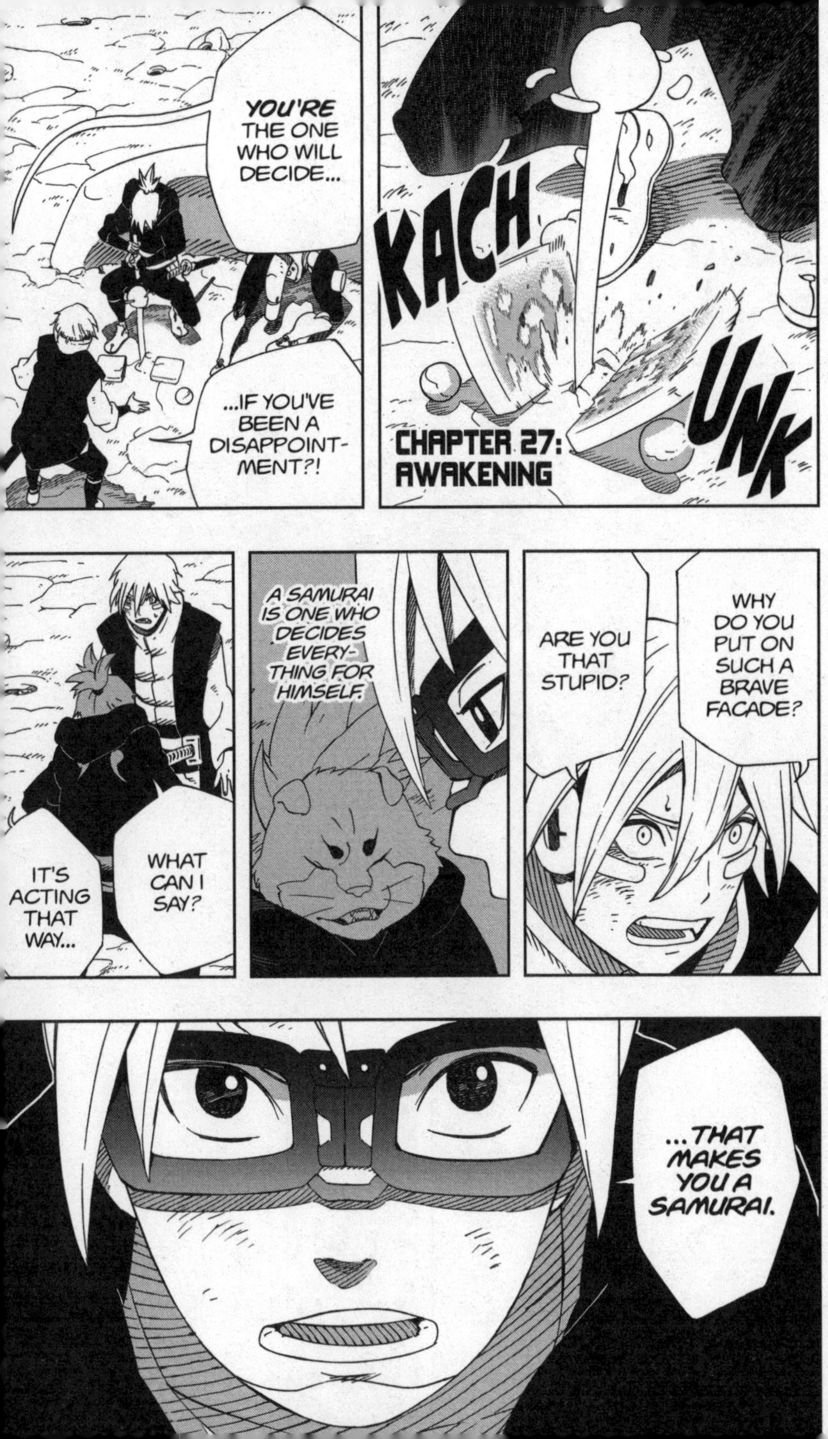
KACH
UNK
CHAPTER 27: AWAKENING
YOU'RE THE ONE WHO WILL DECIDE...
...IF YOU'VE BEEN A DISAPPOINT-MENT?!
WHY DO YOU PUT ON SUCH A BRAVE FACADE?
ARE YOU THAT STUPID?
A SAMURAI IS ONE WHO DECIDES EVERY-THING FOR HIMSELF.
WHAT CAN I SAY?
IT'S ACTING THAT WAY...
...THAT MAKES YOU A SAMURAI.

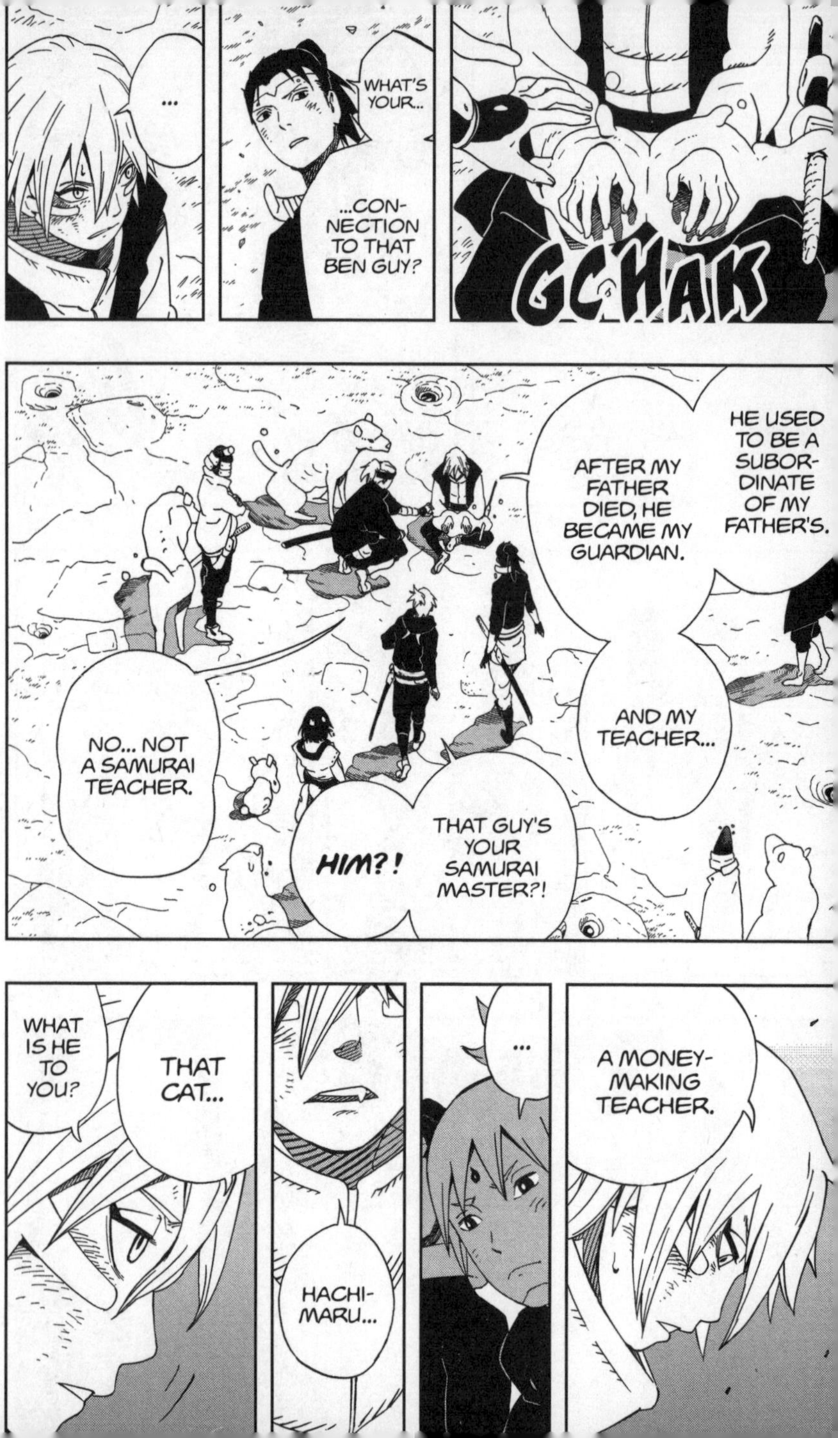
GCHAK
WHAT'S YOUR...
...CON-NECTION TO THAT BEN GUY?
...
HE USED TO BE A SUBOR-DINATE OF MY FATHER'S.
AFTER MY FATHER DIED, HE BECAME MY GUARDIAN.
AND MY TEACHER...
THAT GUY'S YOUR SAMURAI MASTER?!
HIM?!
NO... NOT A SAMURAI TEACHER.
A MONEY-MAKING TEACHER.
...
HACHI-MARU...
THAT CAT...
WHAT IS HE TO YOU?

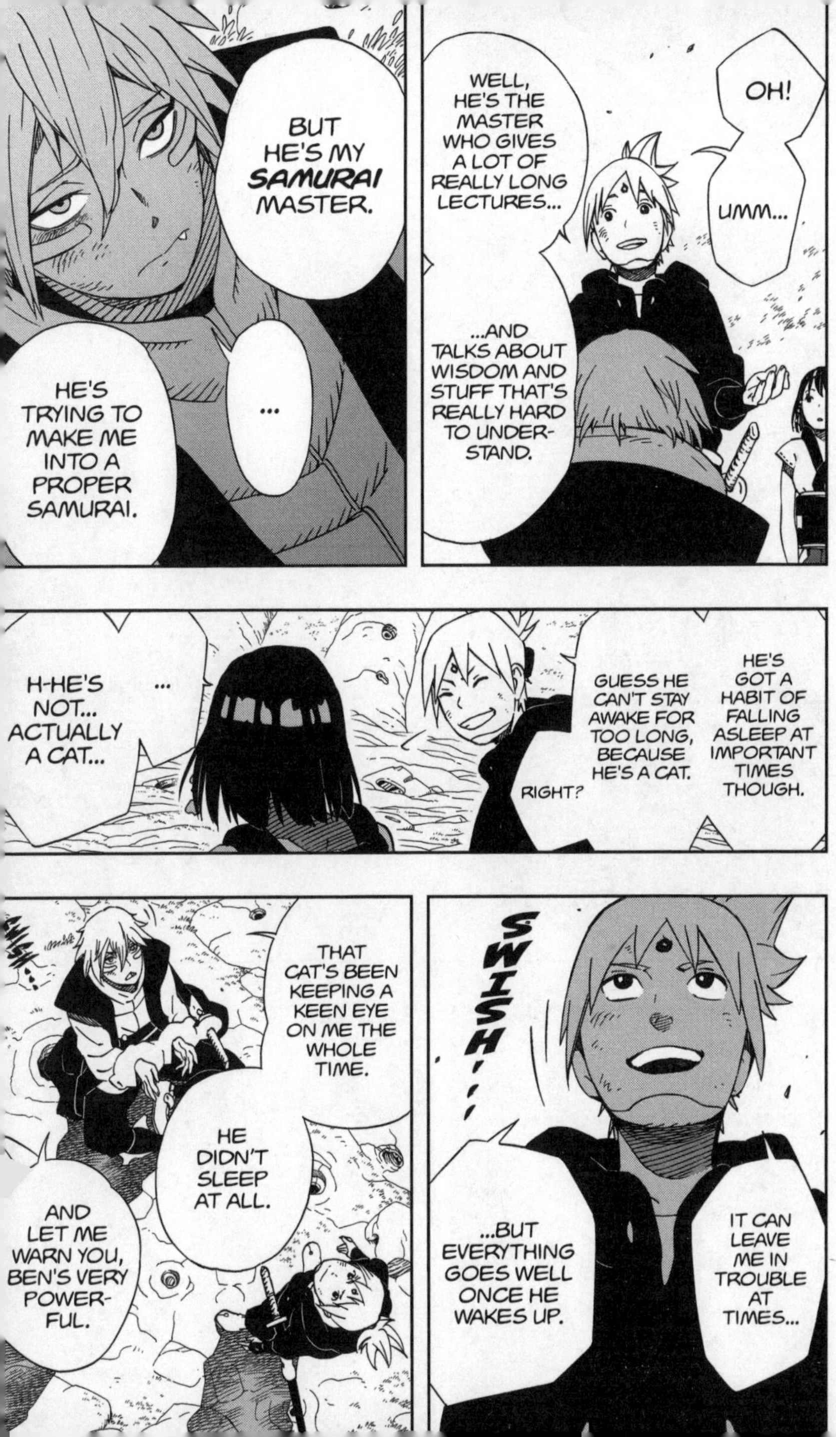
OH!
UMM...
WELL, HE'S THE MASTER WHO GIVES A LOT OF REALLY LONG LECTURES...
...AND TALKS ABOUT WISDOM AND STUFF THAT'S REALLY HARD TO UNDERSTAND.
BUT HE'S MY *SAMURAI* MASTER.
...
HE'S TRYING TO MAKE ME INTO A PROPER SAMURAI.
HE'S GOT A HABIT OF FALLING ASLEEP AT IMPORTANT TIMES THOUGH.
GUESS HE CAN'T STAY AWAKE FOR TOO LONG, BECAUSE HE'S A CAT.
RIGHT?
...
H-HE'S NOT... ACTUALLY A CAT...
SWISH!!!
IT CAN LEAVE ME IN TROUBLE AT TIMES...
...BUT EVERYTHING GOES WELL ONCE HE WAKES UP.
SWISH
THAT CAT'S BEEN KEEPING A KEEN EYE ON ME THE WHOLE TIME.
HE DIDN'T SLEEP AT ALL.
AND LET ME WARN YOU, BEN'S VERY POWERFUL.

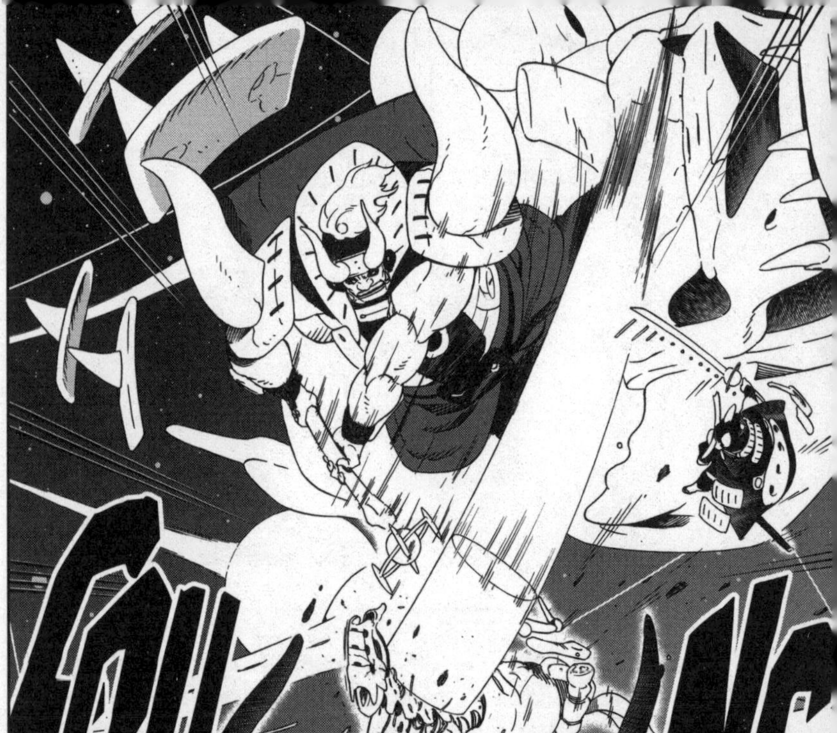

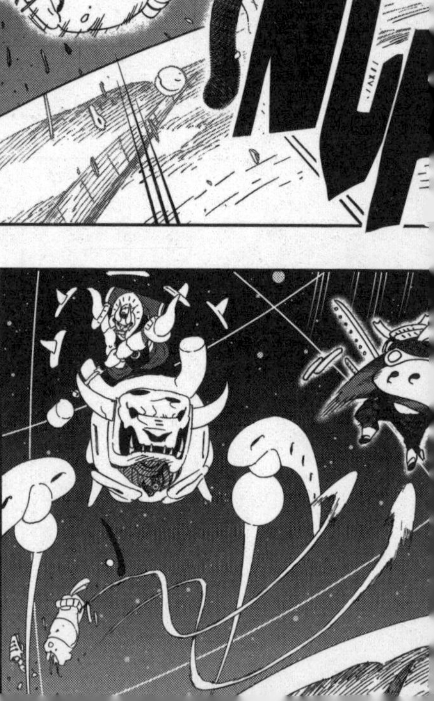

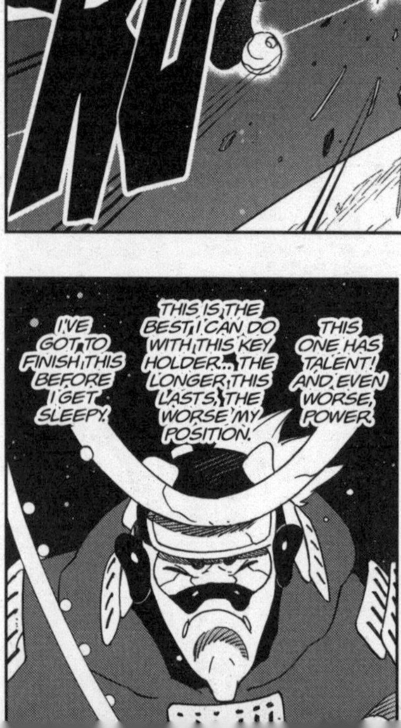
THIS ONE HAS TALENT! AND EVEN WORSE, POWER.
THIS IS THE BEST I CAN DO WITH THIS KEY HOLDER... THE LONGER THIS LASTS, THE WORSE MY POSITION.
I'VE GOT TO FINISH THIS BEFORE I GET SLEEPY.

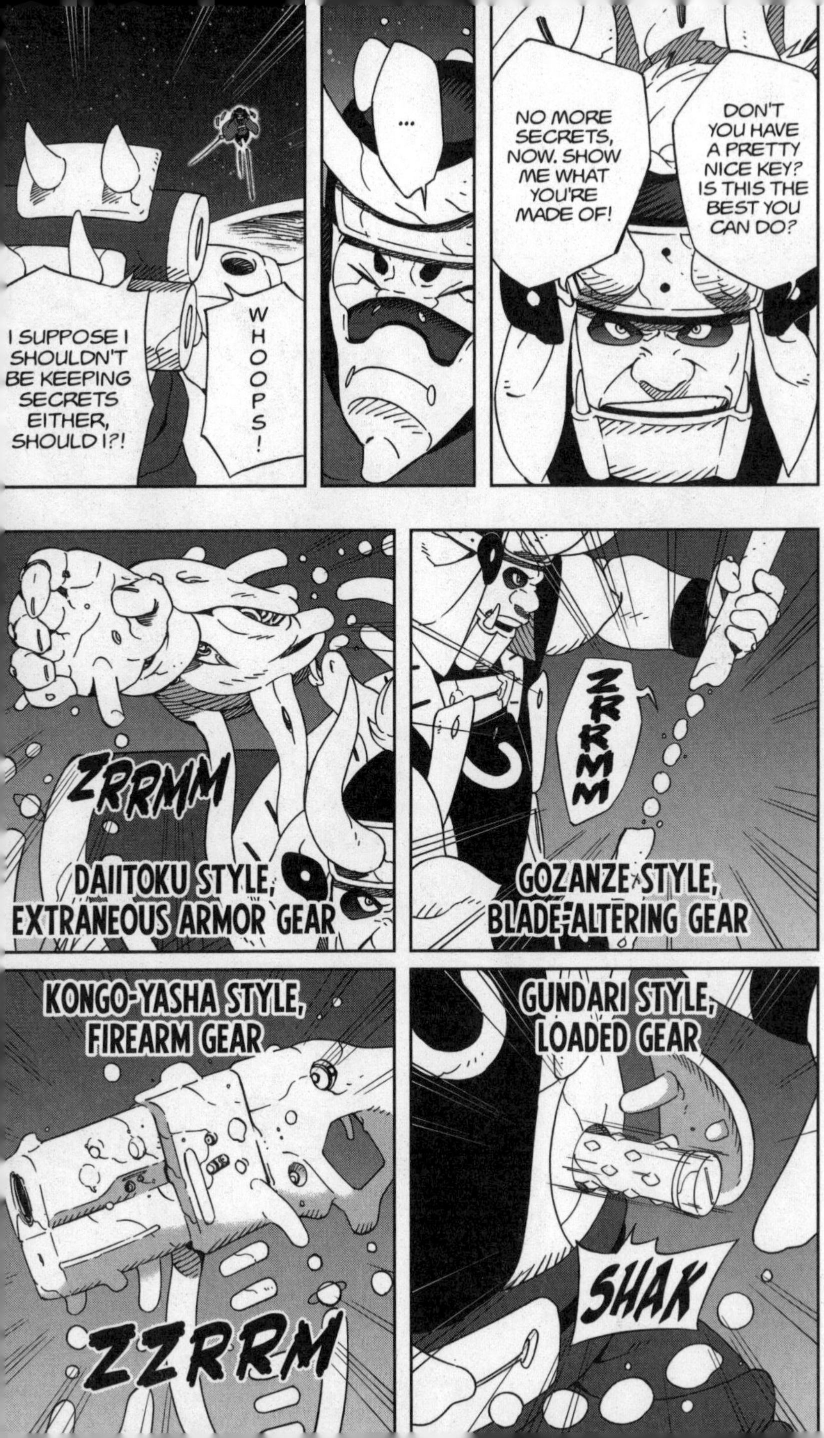

DON'T YOU HAVE A PRETTY NICE KEY? IS THIS THE BEST YOU CAN DO?
NO MORE SECRETS, NOW. SHOW ME WHAT YOU'RE MADE OF!
...
WHOOPS!
I SUPPOSE I SHOULDN'T BE KEEPING SECRETS EITHER, SHOULD I?!
ZRRMM
GOZANZE STYLE, BLADE-ALTERING GEAR
ZRRMM
DAIITOKU STYLE, EXTRANEOUS ARMOR GEAR
GUNDARI STYLE, LOADED GEAR
SHAK
KONGO-YASHA STYLE, FIREARM GEAR
ZZRRM

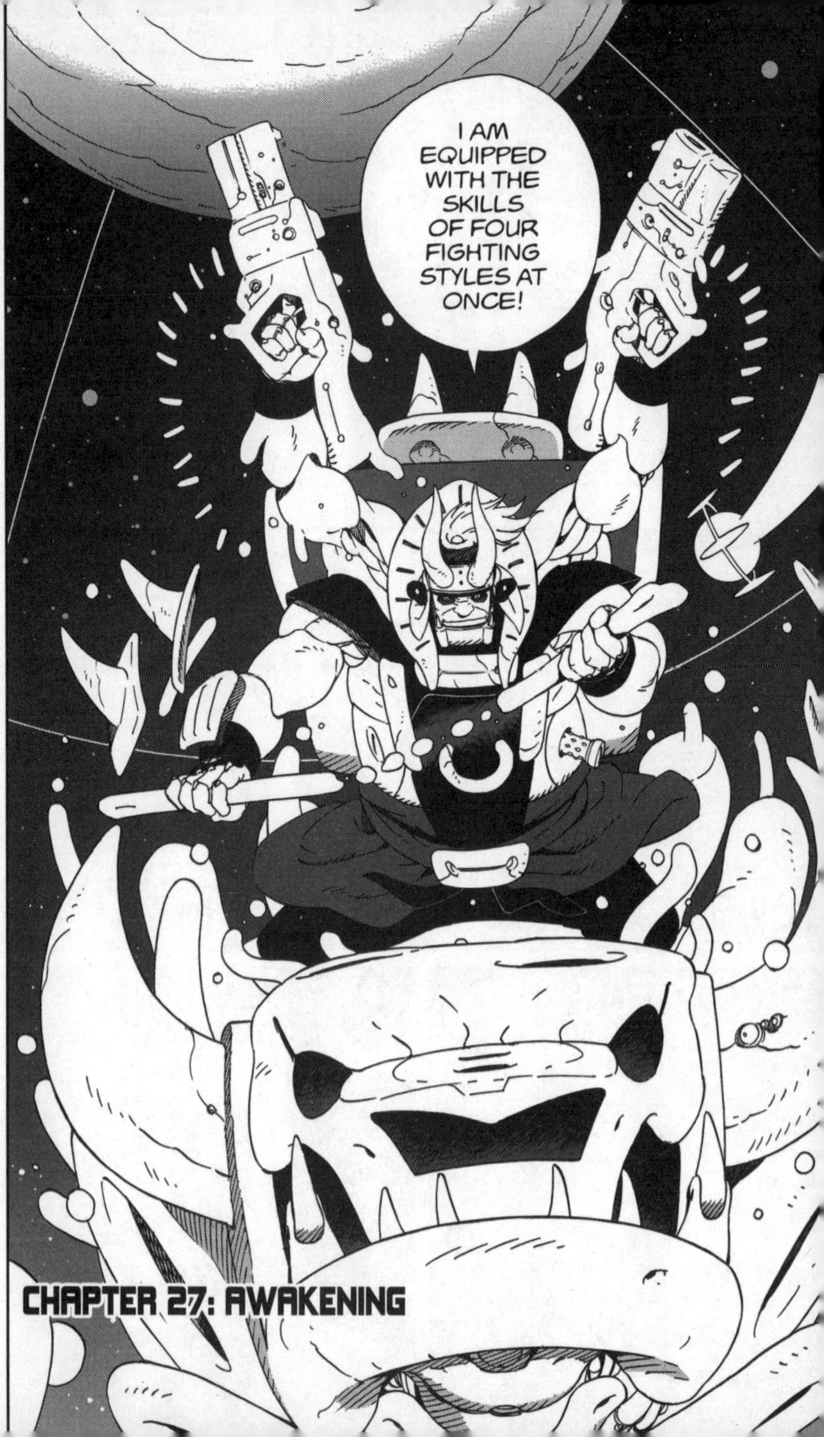
I AM EQUIPPED WITH THE SKILLS OF FOUR FIGHTING STYLES AT ONCE!
CHAPTER 27: AWAKENING

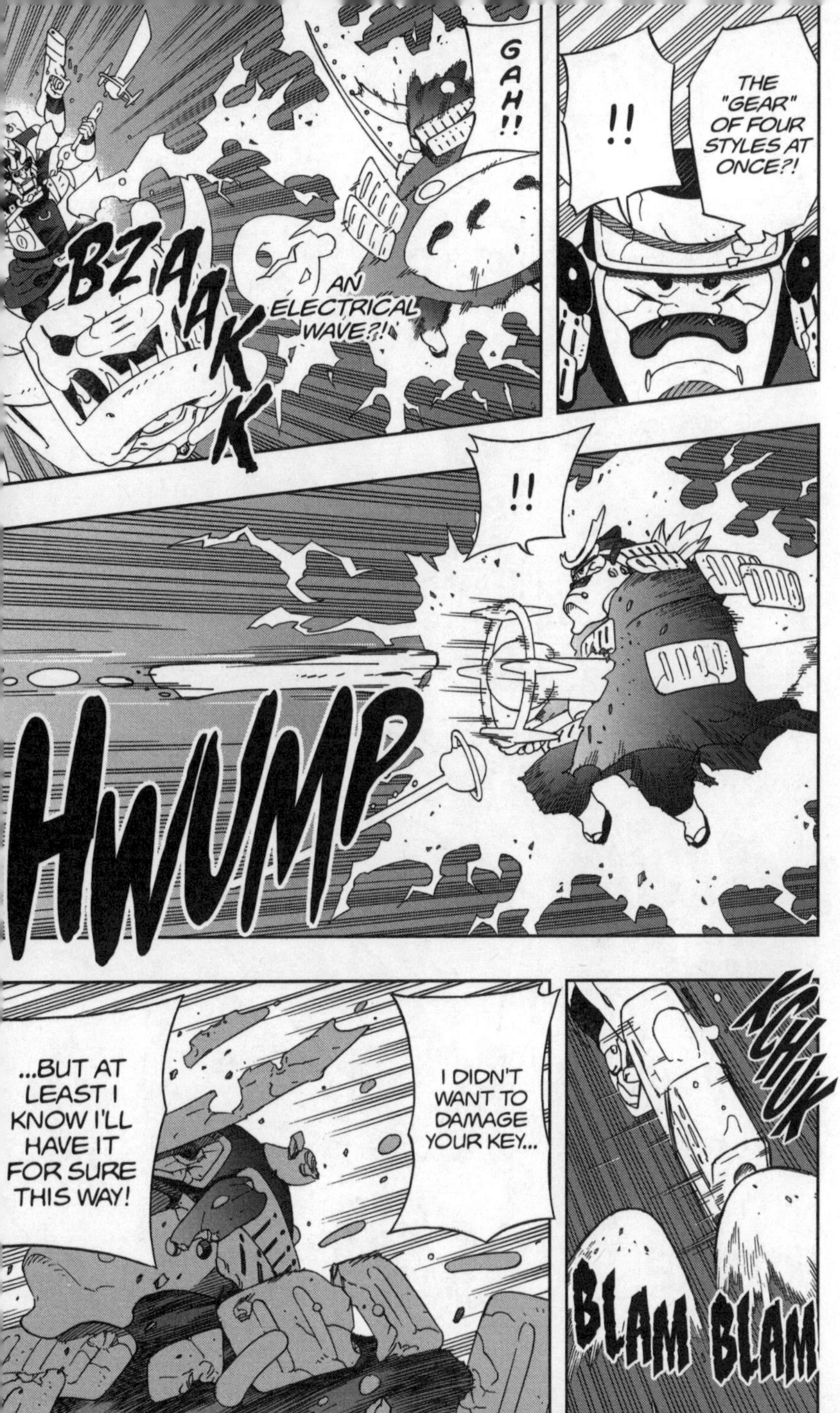
THE "GEAR" OF FOUR STYLES AT ONCE?!
!!
GAH!!
BZAAKK
AN ELECTRICAL WAVE?!
!!
HWUMP
KCHUK
BLAM BLAM
I DIDN'T WANT TO DAMAGE YOUR KEY...
...BUT AT LEAST I KNOW I'LL HAVE IT FOR SURE THIS WAY!

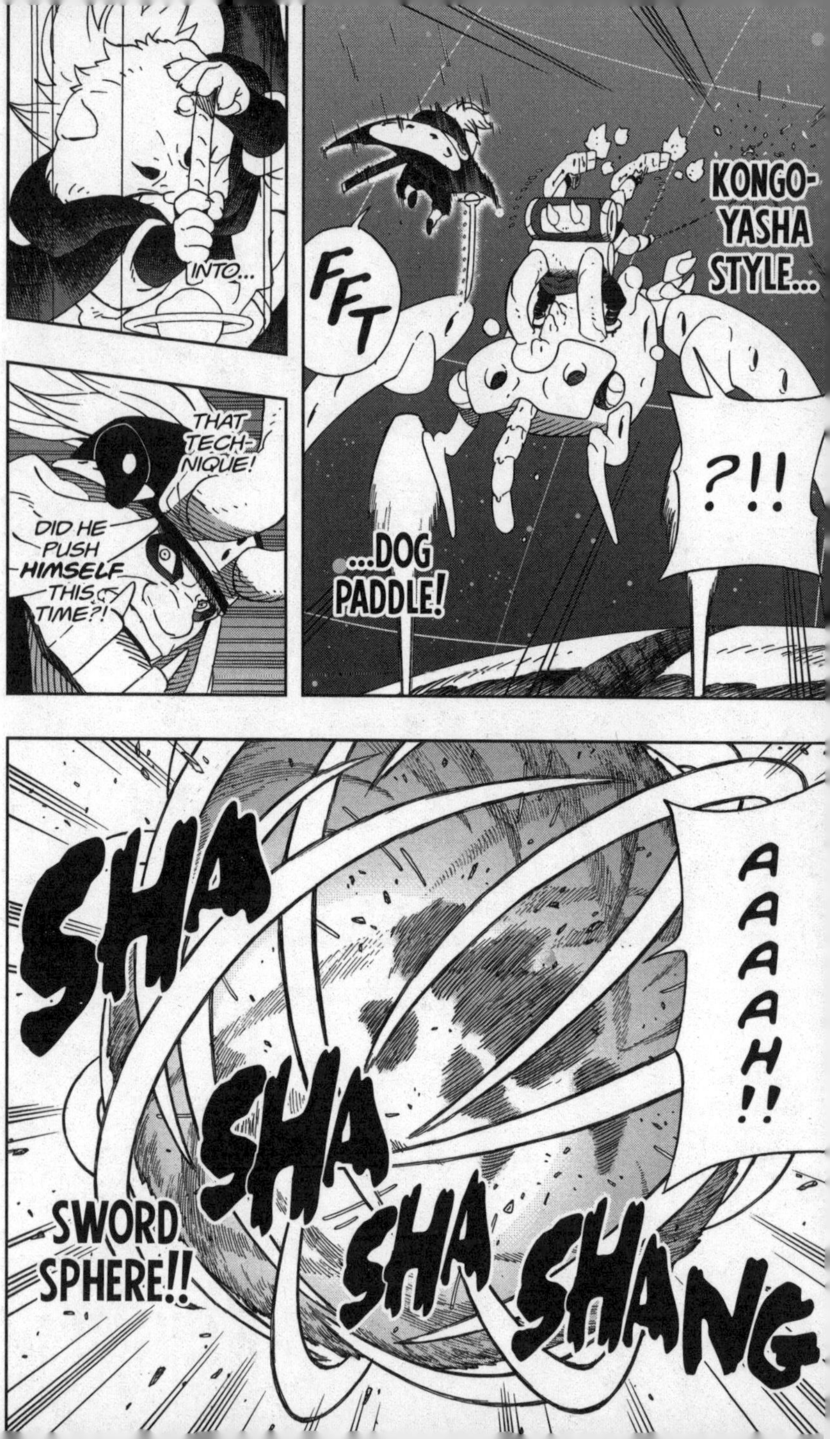
KONGO-YASHA STYLE...
FFT
?!!
...DOG PADDLE!
INTO...
THAT TECHNIQUE!
DID HE PUSH HIMSELF THIS TIME?!
AAAAAH!!
SHA
SHA
SHA
SHANG
SWORD SPHERE!!

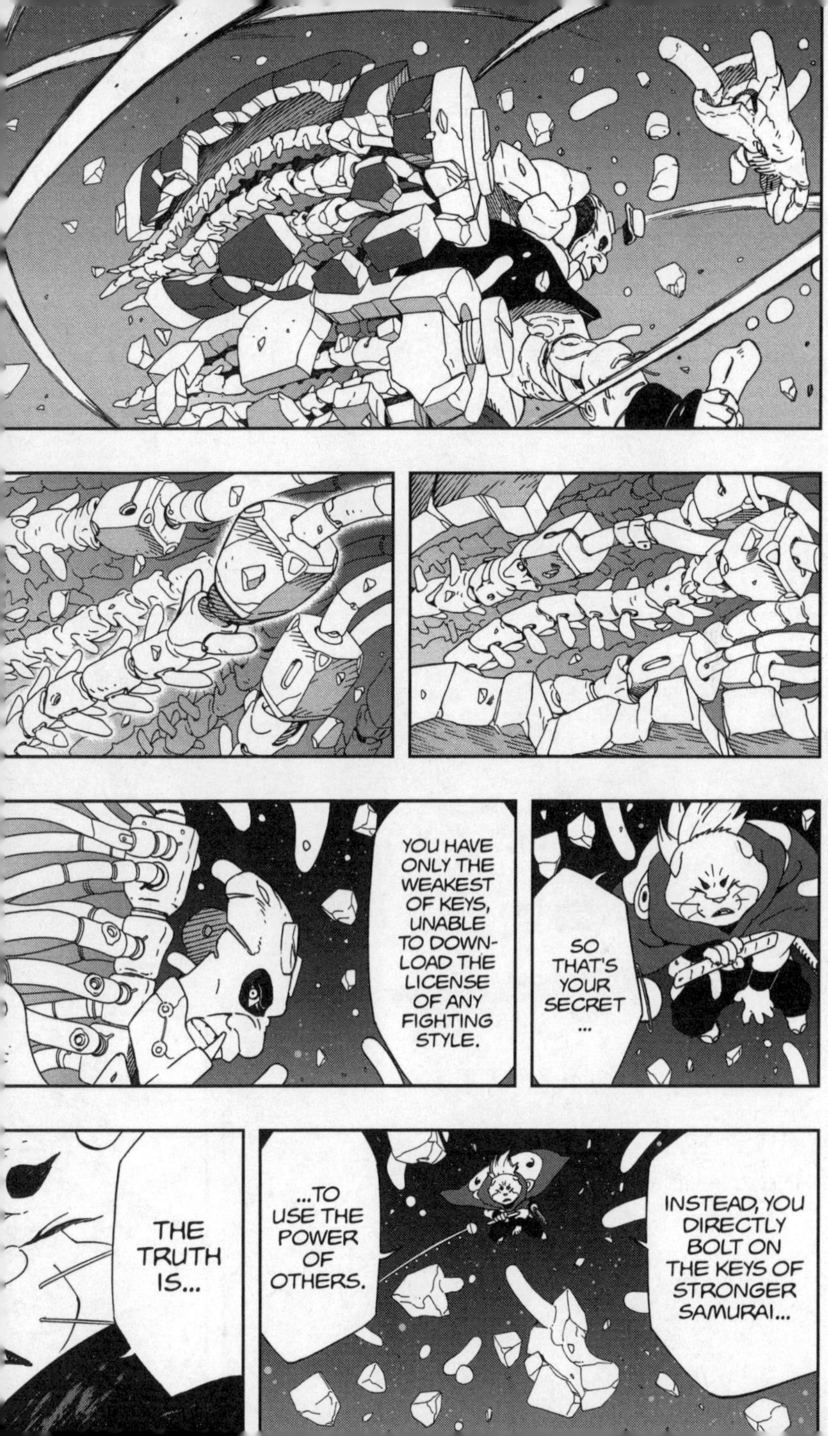
SO THAT'S YOUR SECRET...
YOU HAVE ONLY THE WEAKEST OF KEYS, UNABLE TO DOWN-LOAD THE LICENSE OF ANY FIGHTING STYLE.
INSTEAD, YOU DIRECTLY BOLT ON THE KEYS OF STRONGER SAMURAI...
...TO USE THE POWER OF OTHERS.
THE TRUTH IS...

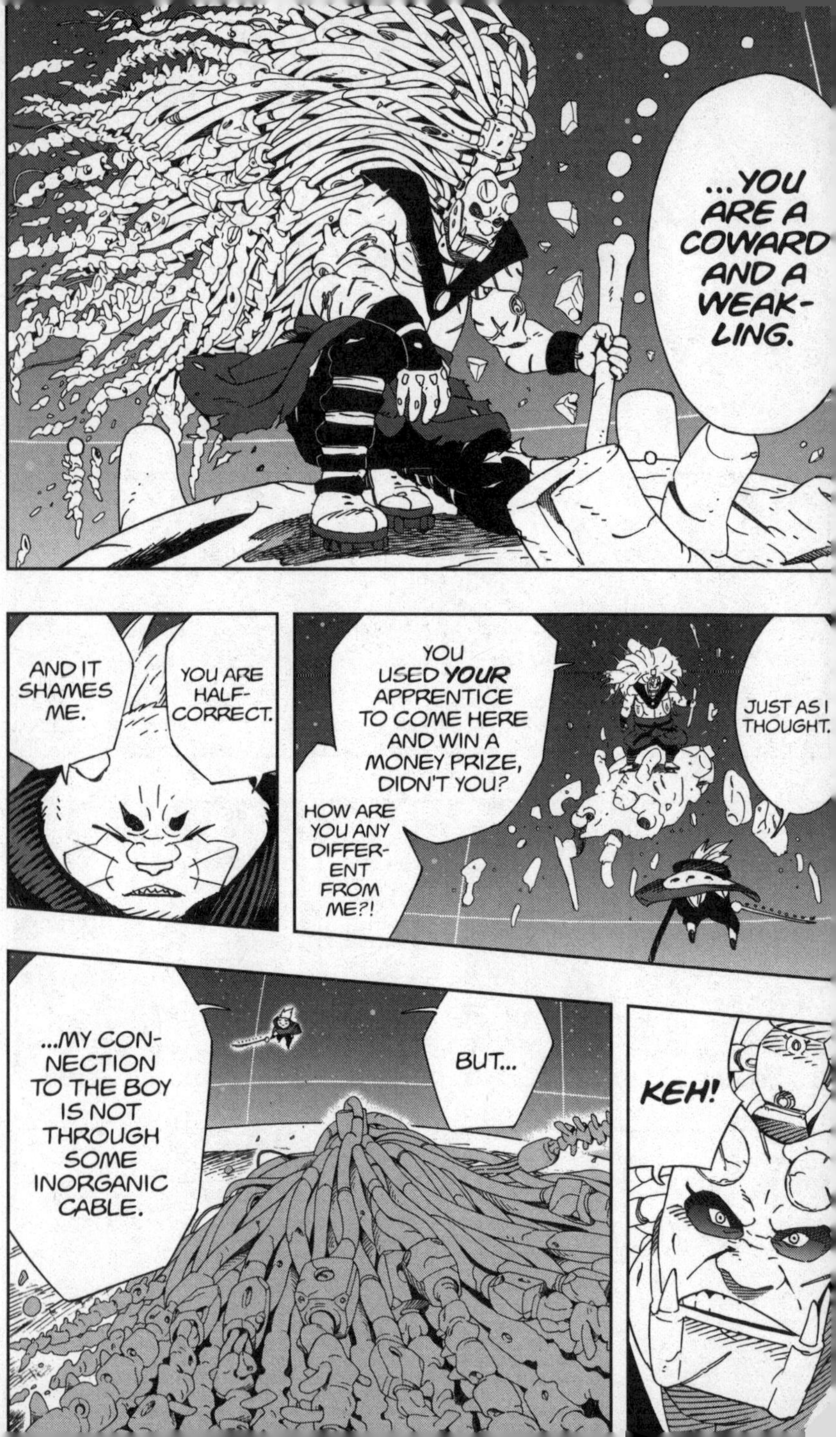
...YOU ARE A COWARD AND A WEAK-LING.
JUST AS I THOUGHT.
YOU USED **YOUR** APPRENTICE TO COME HERE AND WIN A MONEY PRIZE, DIDN'T YOU?
HOW ARE YOU ANY DIFFER-ENT FROM ME?!
YOU ARE HALF-CORRECT.
AND IT SHAMES ME.
KEH!
BUT...
...MY CON-NECTION TO THE BOY IS NOT THROUGH SOME INORGANIC CABLE.

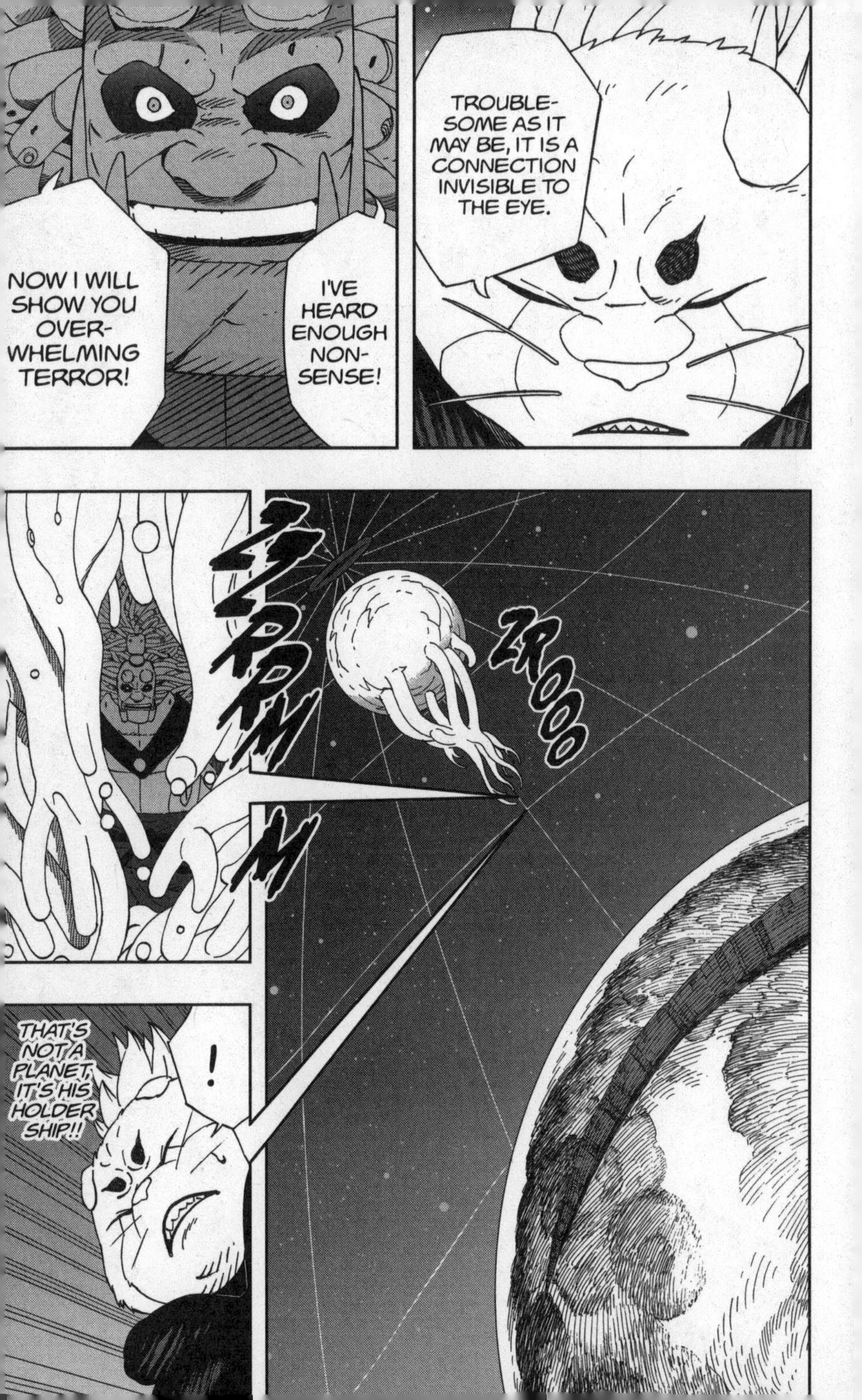
TROUBLE-SOME AS IT MAY BE, IT IS A CONNECTION INVISIBLE TO THE EYE.
I'VE HEARD ENOUGH NON-SENSE!
NOW I WILL SHOW YOU OVER-WHELMING TERROR!
ZROOO
ZZRRMM
M
!
THAT'S NOT A PLANET, IT'S HIS HOLDER SHIP!!

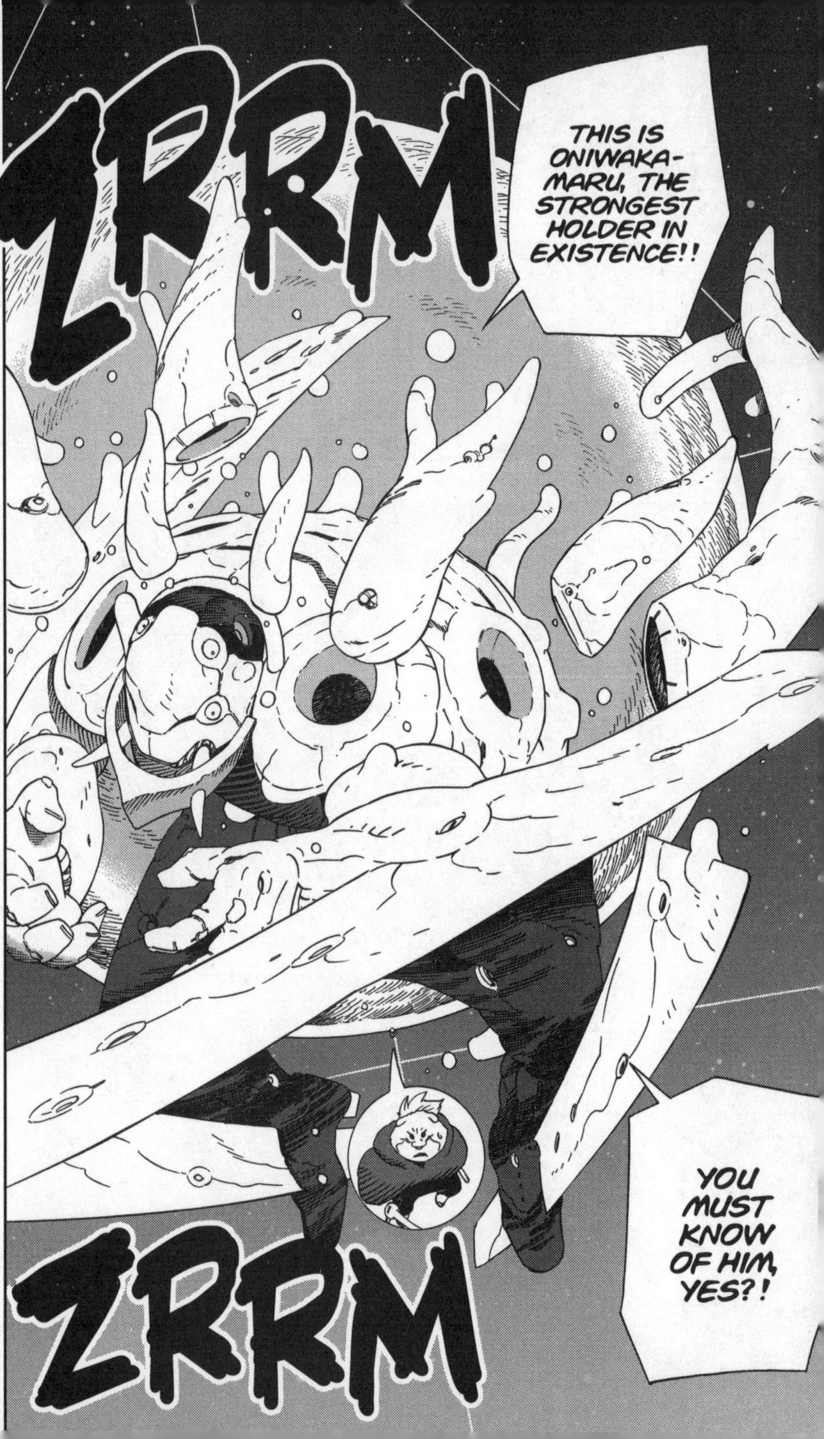
ZRRM
THIS IS ONIWAKA-MARU, THE STRONGEST HOLDER IN EXISTENCE!!
YOU MUST KNOW OF HIM, YES?!
ZRRM

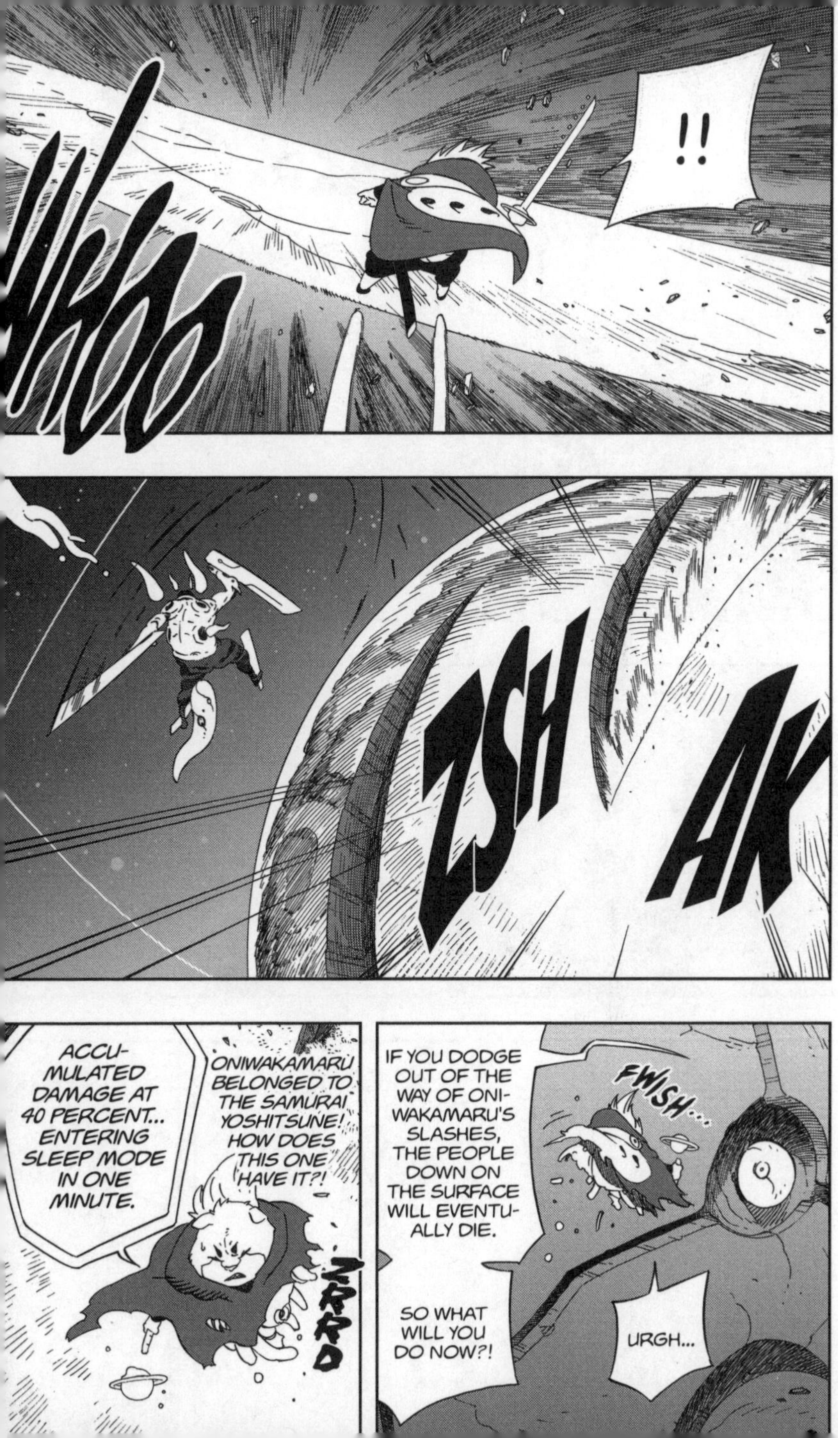
!!
WHOOO
ZSHAK
IF YOU DODGE OUT OF THE WAY OF ONI-WAKAMARU'S SLASHES, THE PEOPLE DOWN ON THE SURFACE WILL EVENTU-ALLY DIE.
FWISH...
SO WHAT WILL YOU DO NOW?!
URGH...
ONIWAKAMARU BELONGED TO THE SAMURAI YOSHITSUNE! HOW DOES THIS ONE HAVE IT?!
ACCU-MULATED DAMAGE AT 40 PERCENT... ENTERING SLEEP MODE IN ONE MINUTE.
ZRRRD

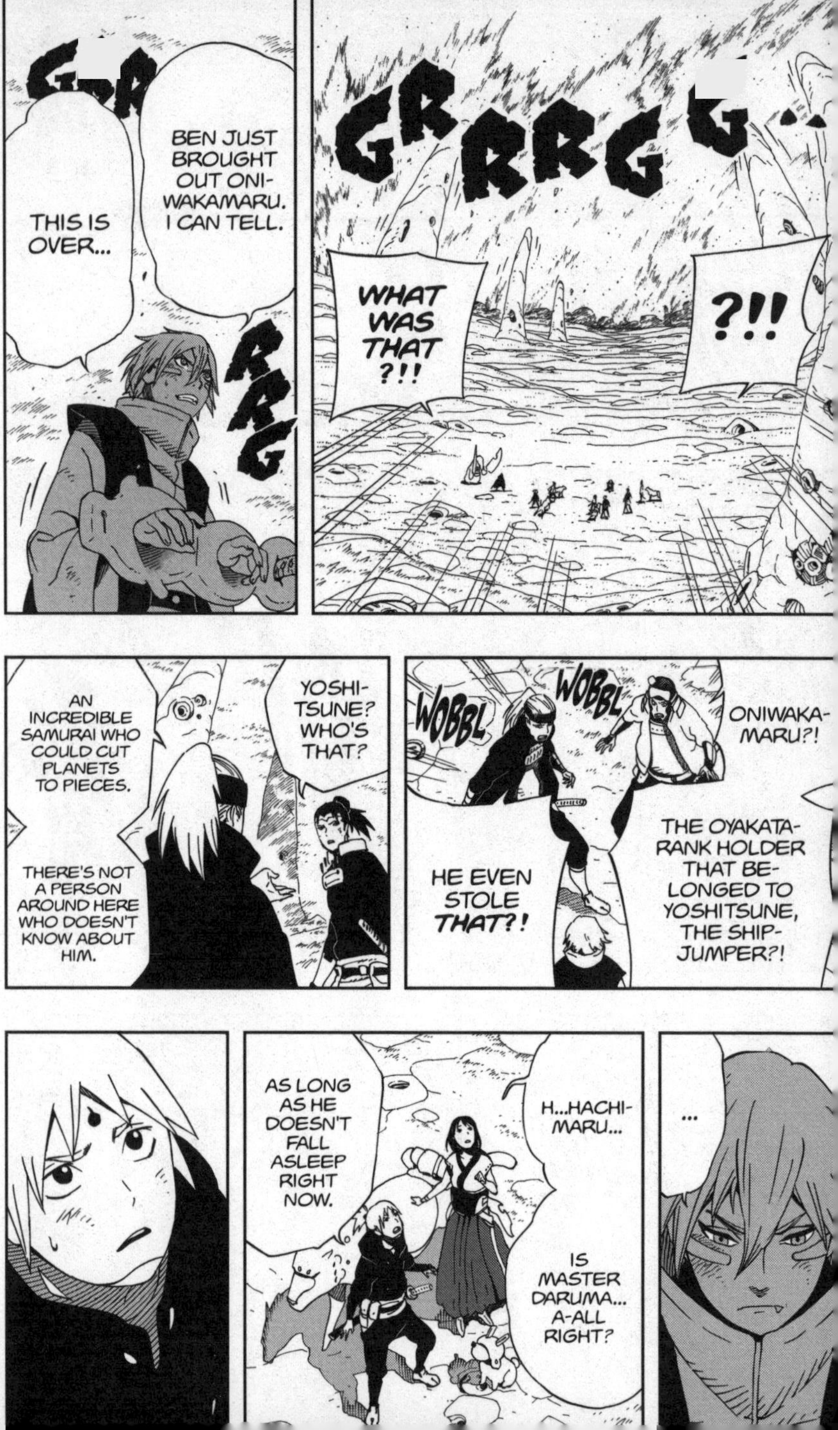
GRRRG...
?!!
WHAT WAS THAT?!!
BEN JUST BROUGHT OUT ONI-WAKAMARU. I CAN TELL.
THIS IS OVER...
RRG
ONIWAKA-MARU?!
WOBBL
WOBBL
THE OYAKATA-RANK HOLDER THAT BE-LONGED TO YOSHITSUNE, THE SHIP-JUMPER?!
HE EVEN STOLE THAT?!
YOSHI-TSUNE? WHO'S THAT?
AN INCREDIBLE SAMURAI WHO COULD CUT PLANETS TO PIECES.
THERE'S NOT A PERSON AROUND HERE WHO DOESN'T KNOW ABOUT HIM.
...
H...HACHI-MARU...
IS MASTER DARUMA... A-ALL RIGHT?
AS LONG AS HE DOESN'T FALL ASLEEP RIGHT NOW.

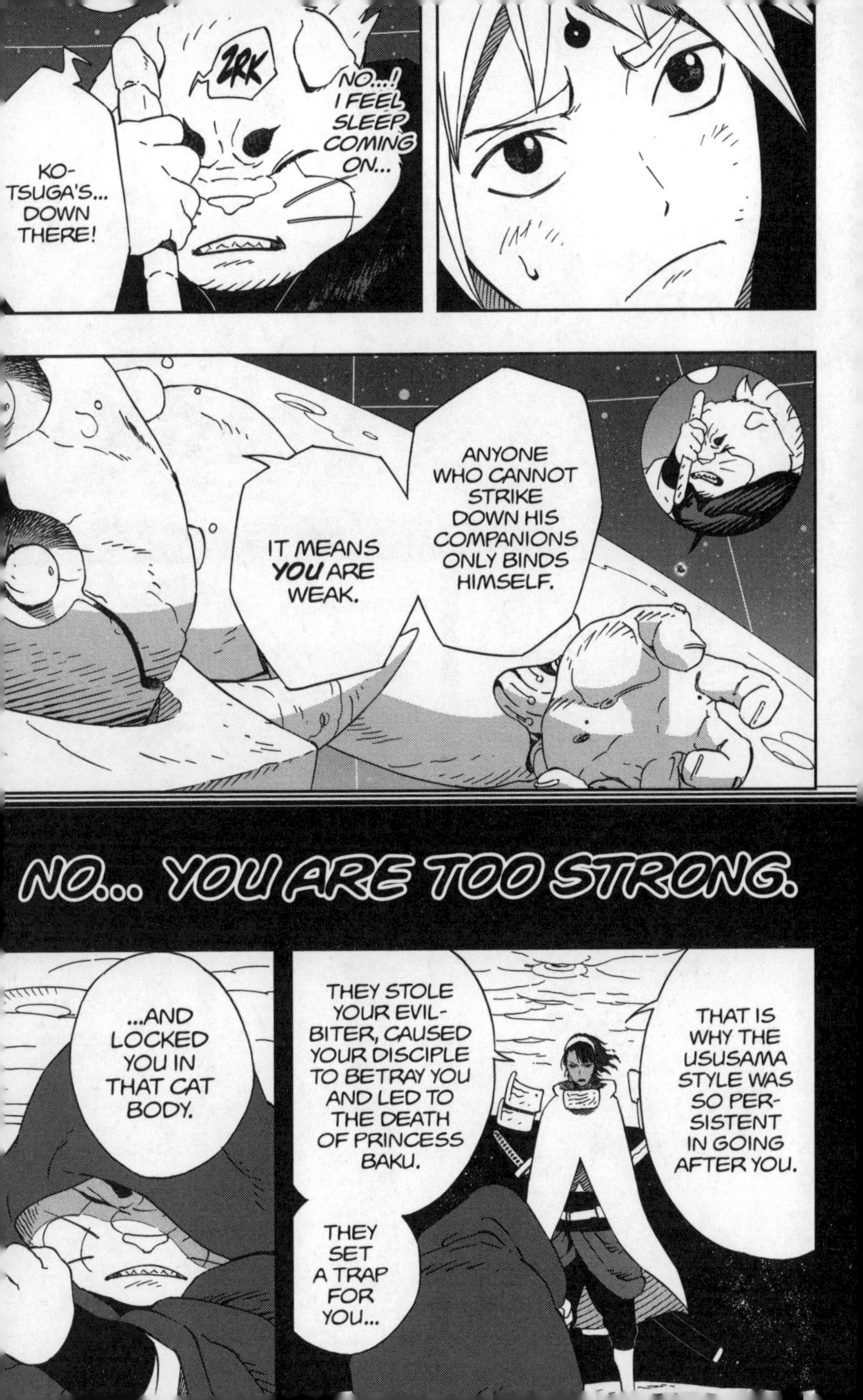
NO...! I FEEL SLEEP COMING ON...
ZRK
KO-TSUGA'S... DOWN THERE!
ANYONE WHO CANNOT STRIKE DOWN HIS COMPANIONS ONLY BINDS HIMSELF.
IT MEANS YOU ARE WEAK.
NO... YOU ARE TOO STRONG.
THAT IS WHY THE USUSAMA STYLE WAS SO PERSISTENT IN GOING AFTER YOU.
THEY STOLE YOUR EVIL-BITER, CAUSED YOUR DISCIPLE TO BETRAY YOU AND LED TO THE DEATH OF PRINCESS BAKU.
THEY SET A TRAP FOR YOU...
...AND LOCKED YOU IN THAT CAT BODY.

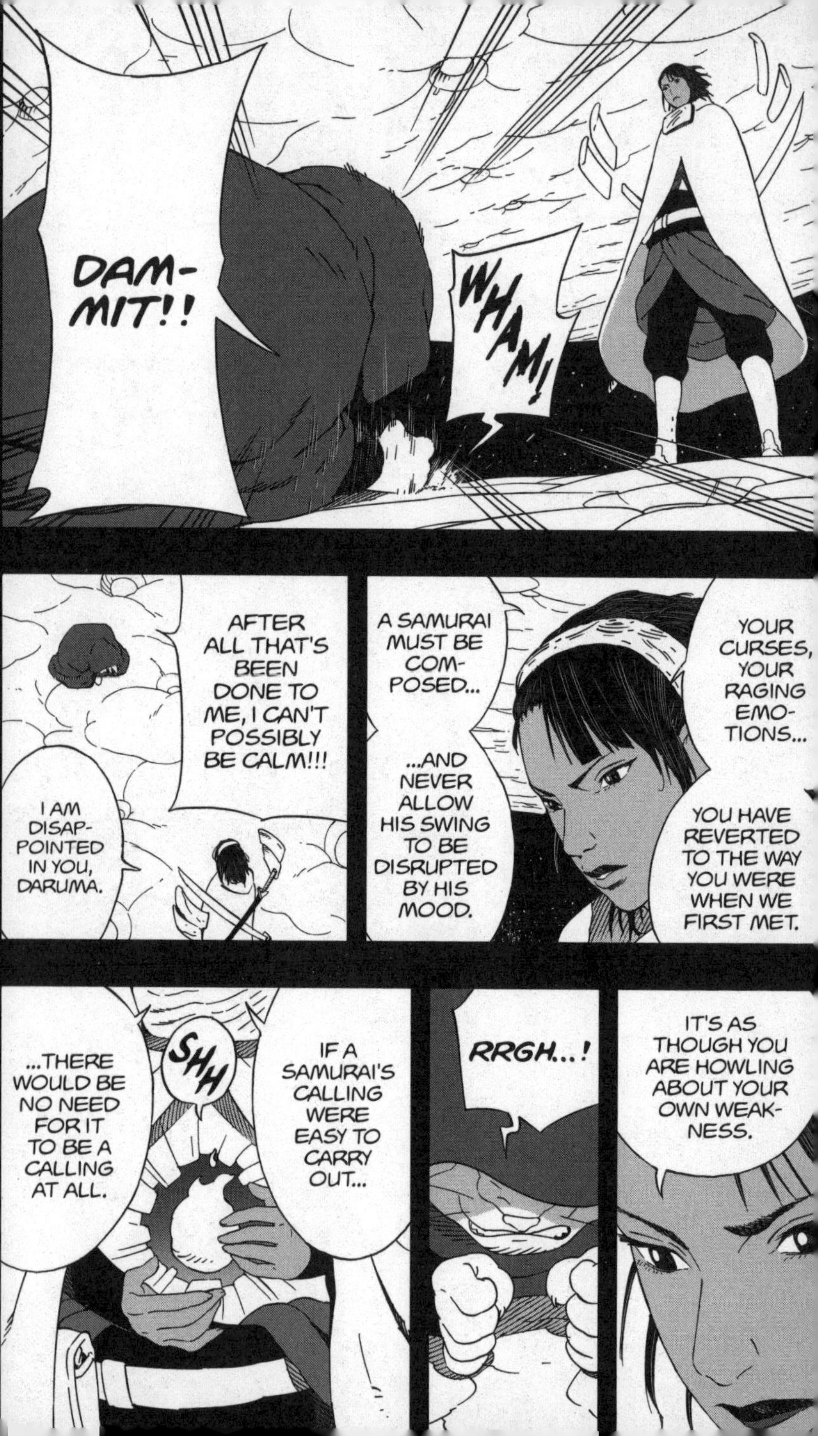
WHAM!
DAM-MIT!!
YOUR CURSES, YOUR RAGING EMO-TIONS...
YOU HAVE REVERTED TO THE WAY YOU WERE WHEN WE FIRST MET.
A SAMURAI MUST BE COM-POSED...
...AND NEVER ALLOW HIS SWING TO BE DISRUPTED BY HIS MOOD.
AFTER ALL THAT'S BEEN DONE TO ME, I CAN'T POSSIBLY BE CALM!!!
I AM DISAP-POINTED IN YOU, DARUMA.
IT'S AS THOUGH YOU ARE HOWLING ABOUT YOUR OWN WEAK-NESS.
RRGH...!
IF A SAMURAI'S CALLING WERE EASY TO CARRY OUT...
SHH
...THERE WOULD BE NO NEED FOR IT TO BE A CALLING AT ALL.

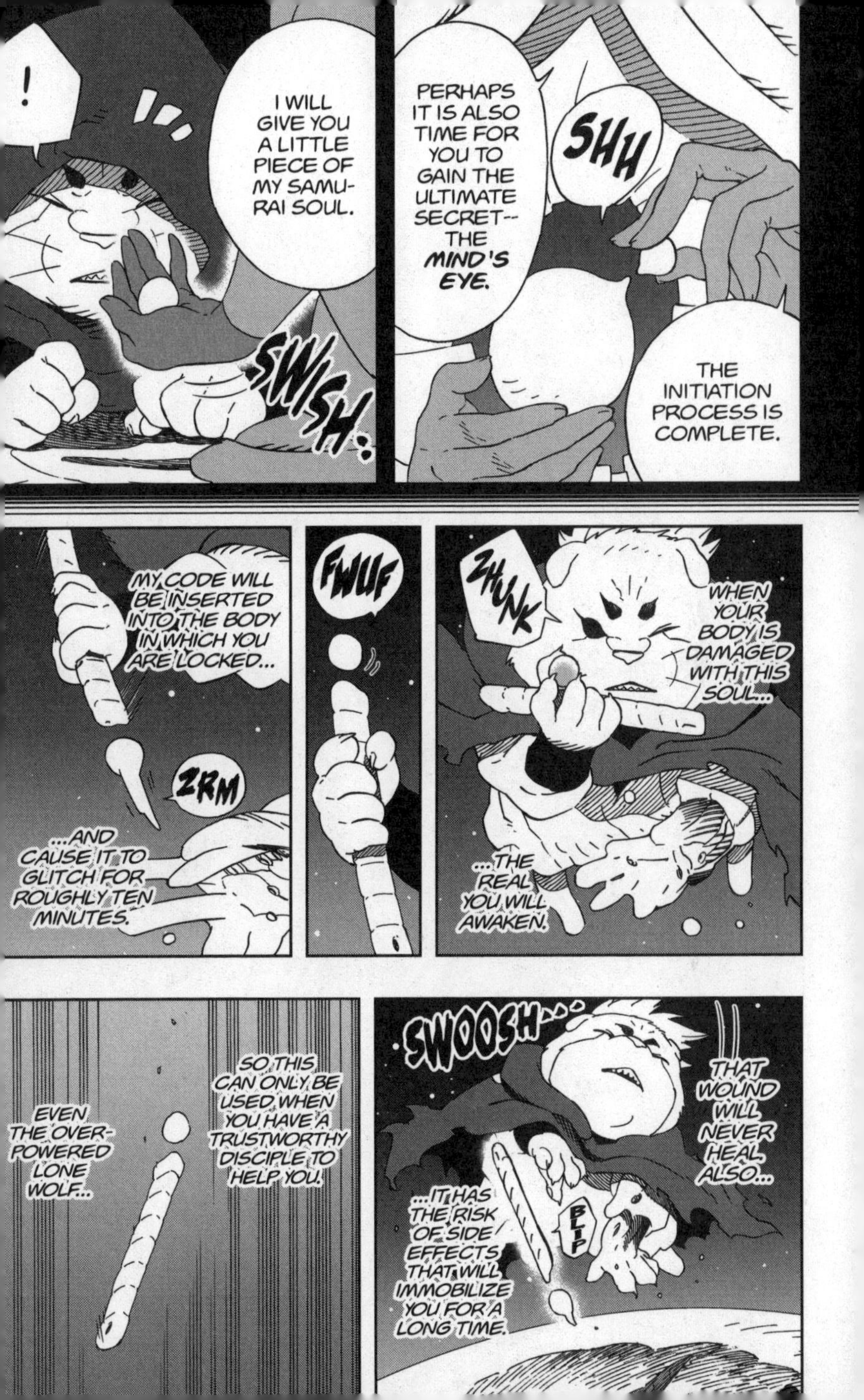
SHH
PERHAPS IT IS ALSO TIME FOR YOU TO GAIN THE ULTIMATE SECRET-- THE MIND'S EYE.
THE INITIATION PROCESS IS COMPLETE.
!
I WILL GIVE YOU A LITTLE PIECE OF MY SAMU-RAI SOUL.
SWISH
ZHUNK
WHEN YOUR BODY IS DAMAGED WITH THIS SOUL...
...THE REAL YOU WILL AWAKEN.
FWUF
MY CODE WILL BE INSERTED INTO THE BODY IN WHICH YOU ARE LOCKED...
ZRM
...AND CAUSE IT TO GLITCH FOR ROUGHLY TEN MINUTES.
SWOOSH
THAT WOUND WILL NEVER HEAL. ALSO...
BLIP
...IT HAS THE RISK OF SIDE EFFECTS THAT WILL IMMOBILIZE YOU FOR A LONG TIME.
SO THIS CAN ONLY BE USED WHEN YOU HAVE A TRUSTWORTHY DISCIPLE TO HELP YOU.
EVEN THE OVER-POWERED LONE WOLF...

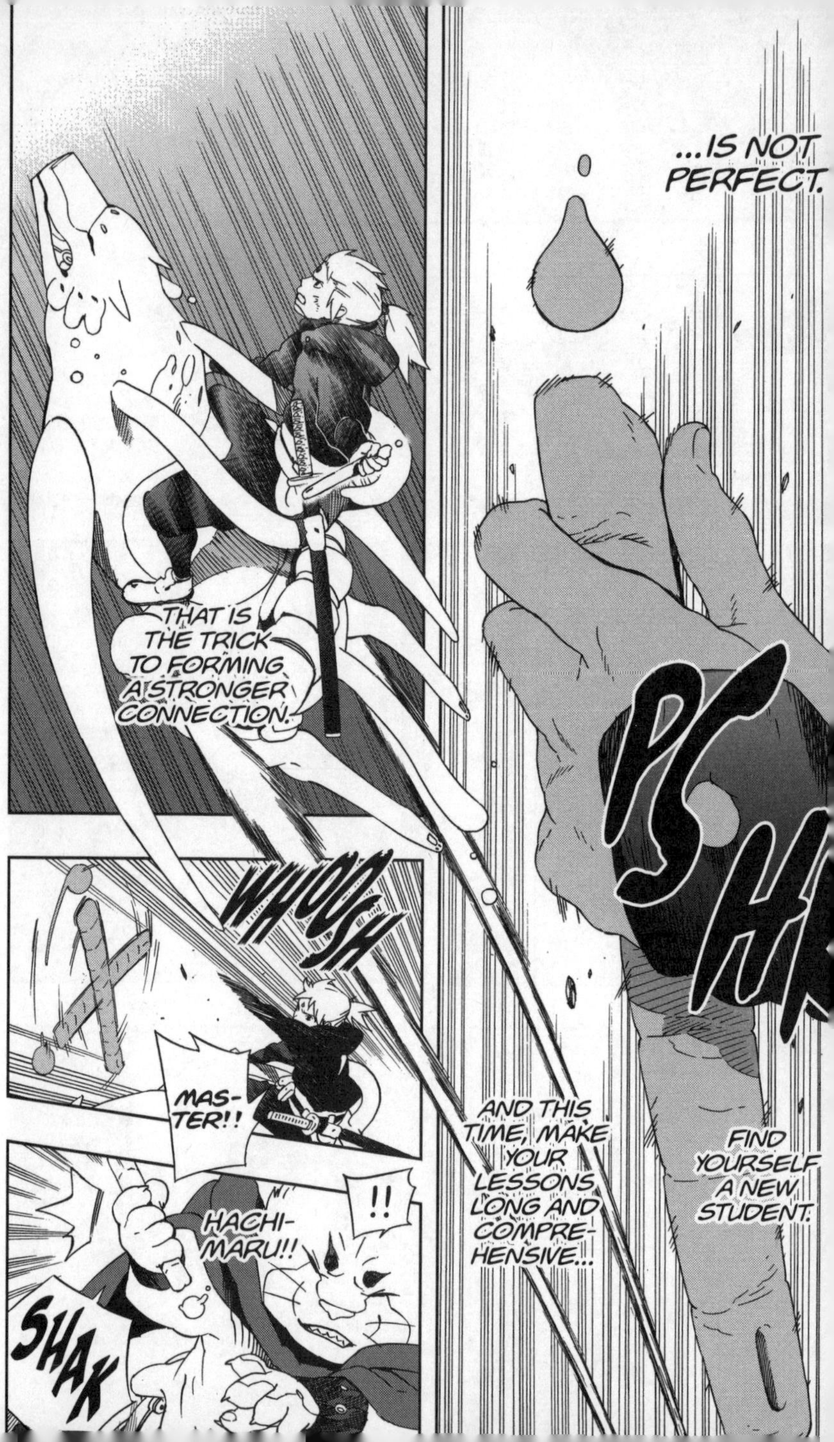
...IS NOT PERFECT.
FIND YOURSELF A NEW STUDENT.
AND THIS TIME, MAKE YOUR LESSONS LONG AND COMPRE-HENSIVE...
THAT IS THE TRICK TO FORMING A STRONGER CONNECTION.
WHOOSH
MAS-TER!!
!!
HACHI-MARU!!
SHAK

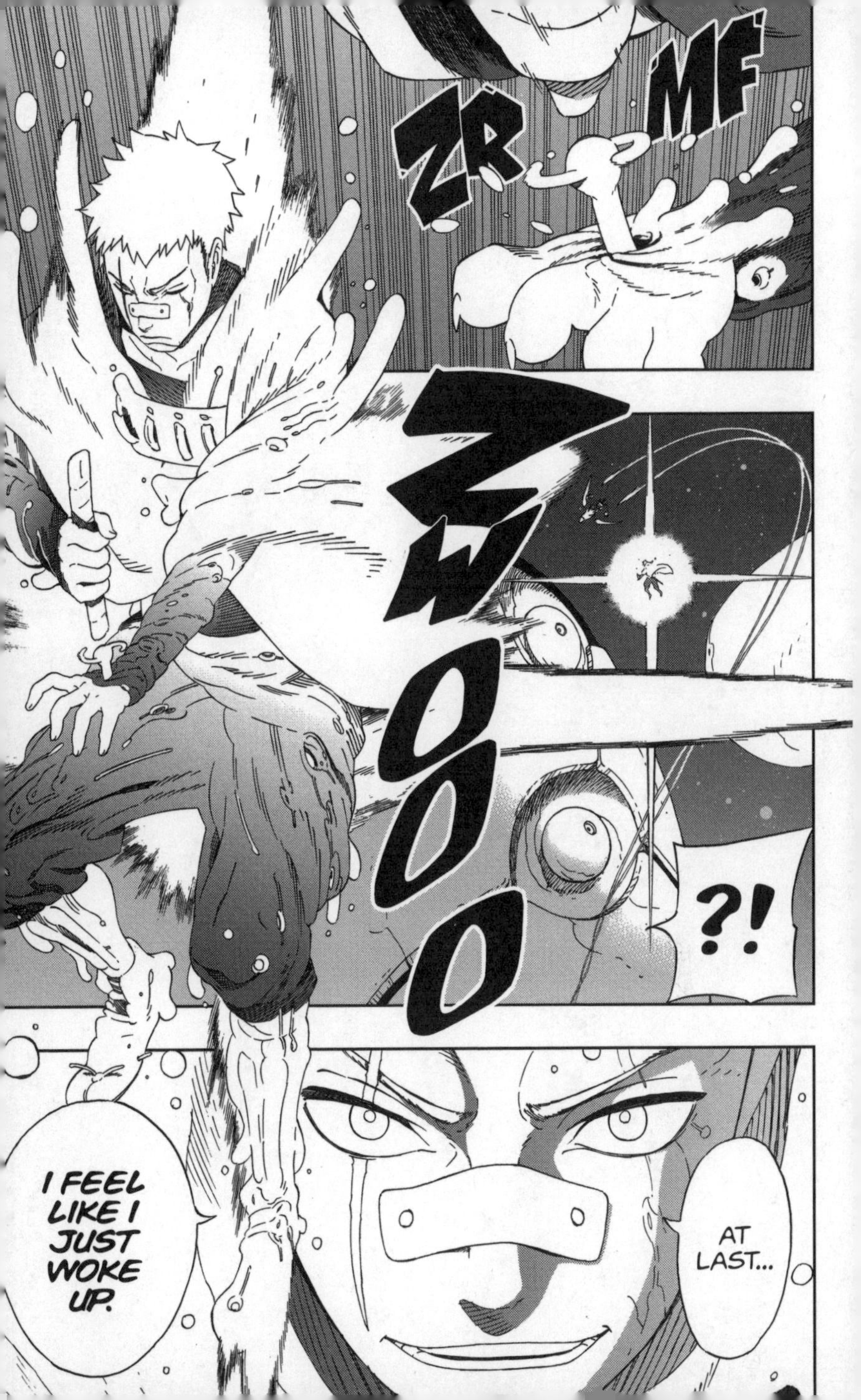
ZR
MF
ZWOOO
?!
AT LAST...
I FEEL LIKE I JUST WOKE UP.

Character Design Sketches: Oniwakamaru

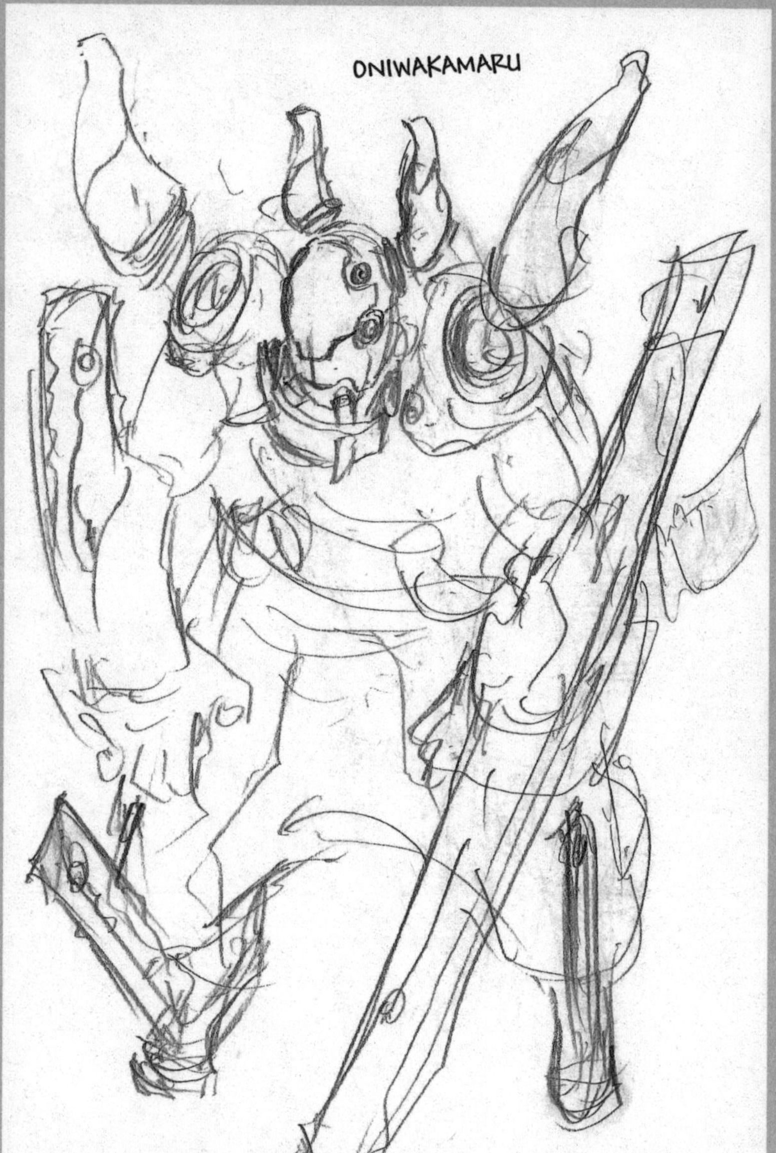
ONIWAKAMARU

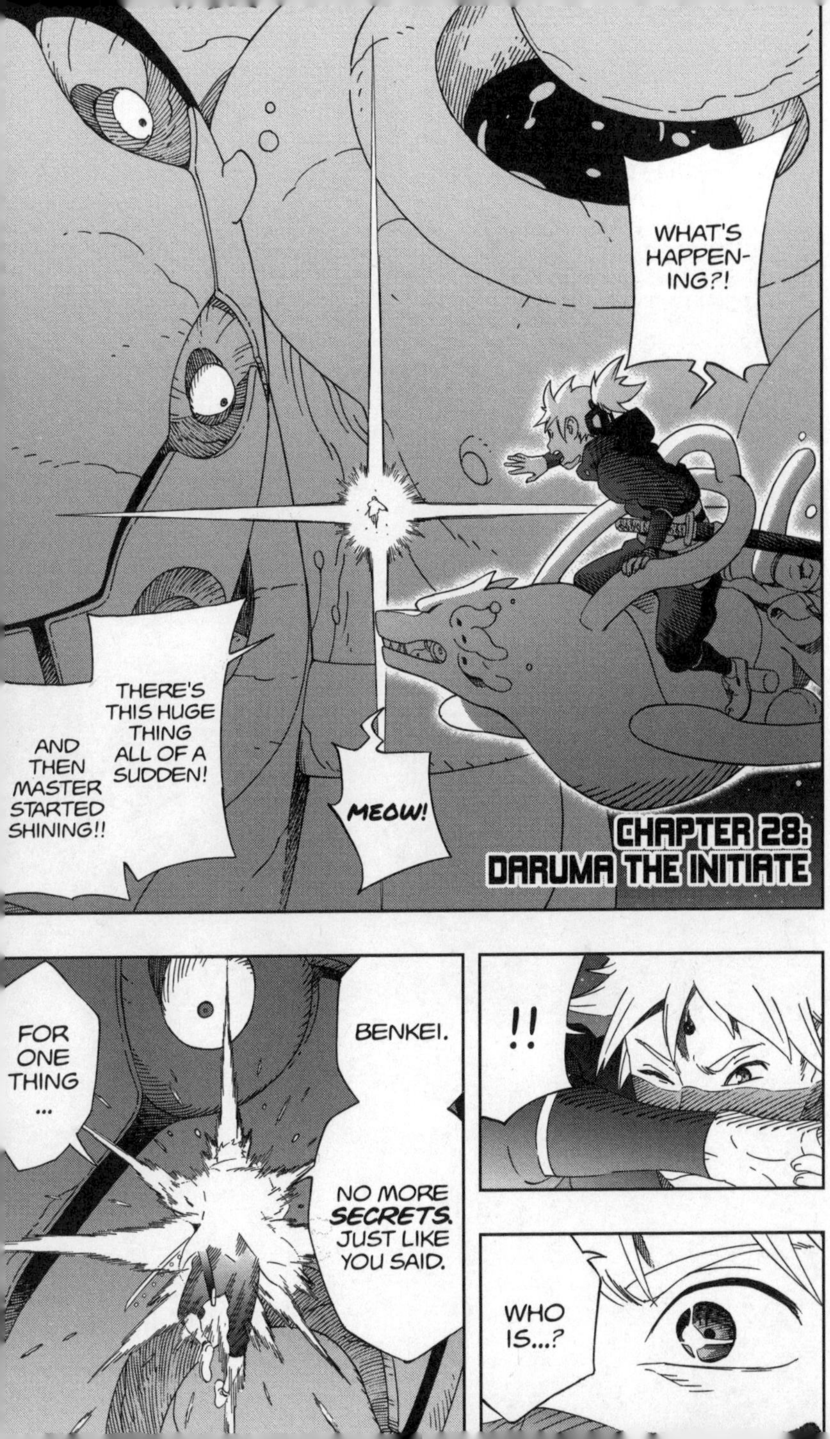

WHAT'S HAPPENING?!
THERE'S THIS HUGE THING ALL OF A SUDDEN!
AND THEN MASTER STARTED SHINING!!
MEOW!
CHAPTER 28: DARUMA THE INITIATE
!!
WHO IS...?
BENKEI.
FOR ONE THING ...
NO MORE SECRETS. JUST LIKE YOU SAID.

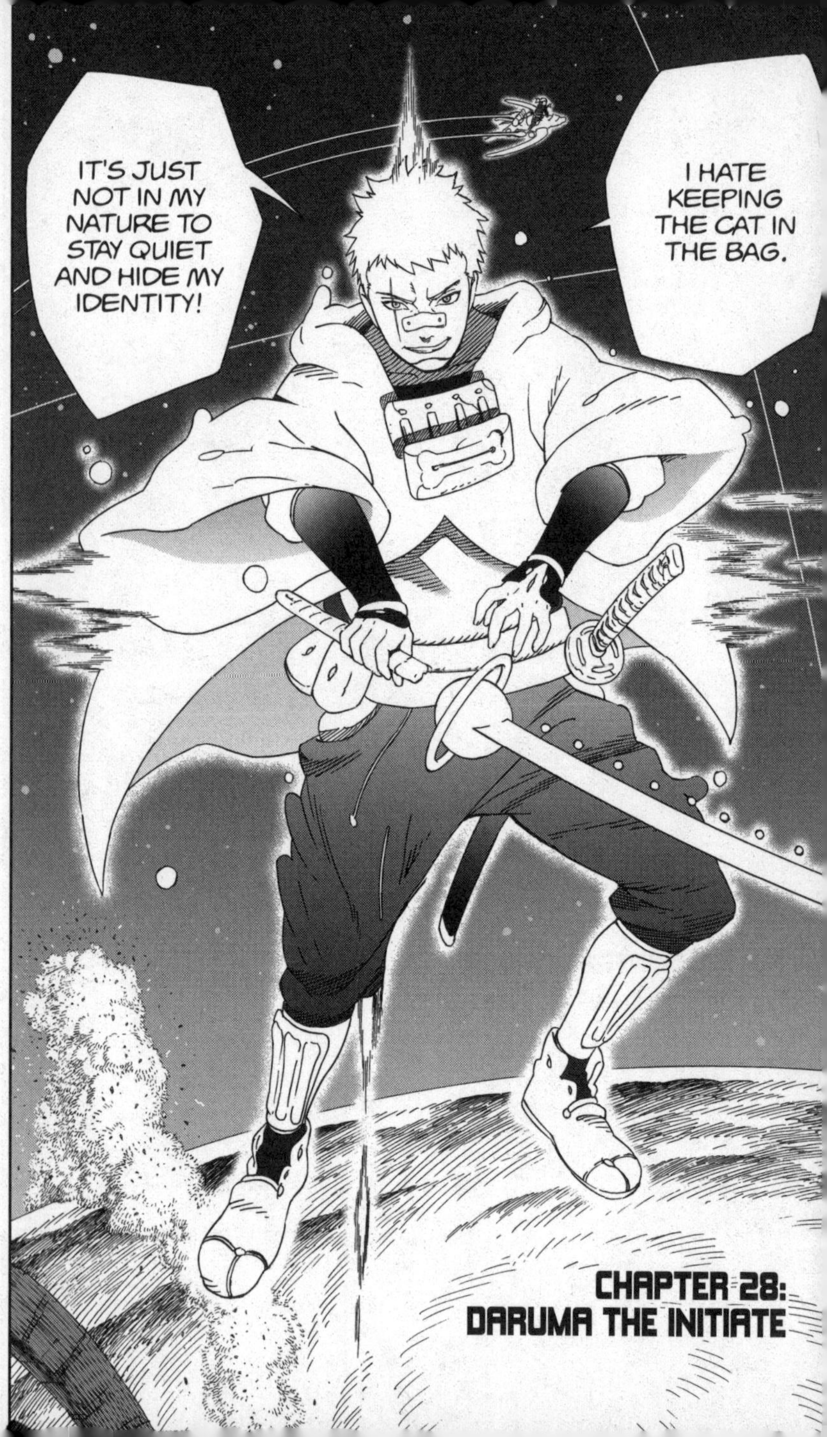
I HATE KEEPING THE CAT IN THE BAG.
IT'S JUST NOT IN MY NATURE TO STAY QUIET AND HIDE MY IDENTITY!
CHAPTER 28: DARUMA THE INITIATE

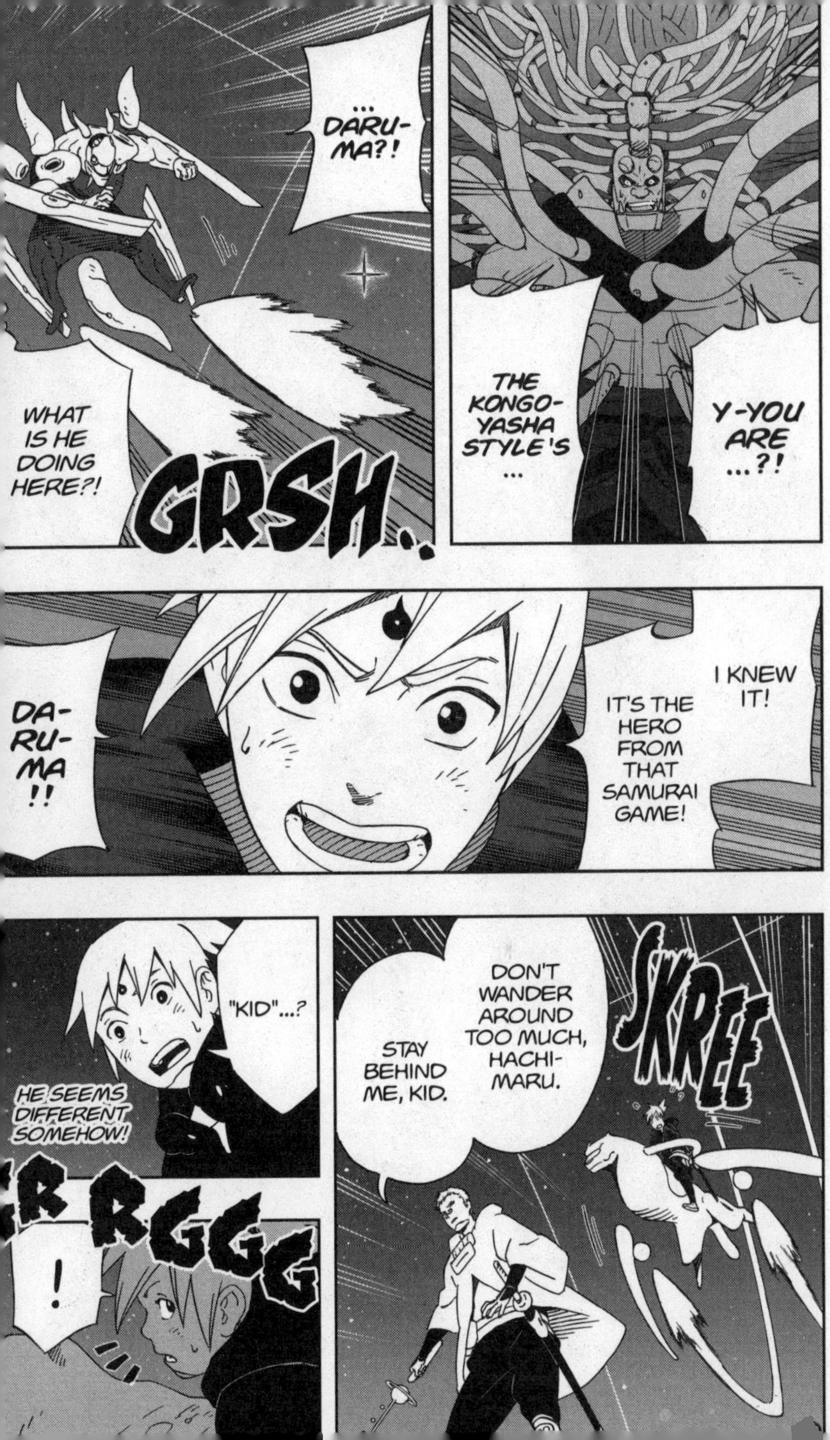

Y-YOU ARE ...?!
THE KONGO-YASHA STYLE'S ...
... DARU-MA?!
GRSH..
WHAT IS HE DOING HERE?!
I KNEW IT!
IT'S THE HERO FROM THAT SAMURAI GAME!
DA-RU-MA!!
SKREE
DON'T WANDER AROUND TOO MUCH, HACHI-MARU.
STAY BEHIND ME, KID.
"KID"...?
HE SEEMS DIFFERENT SOMEHOW!
RRGGG
!

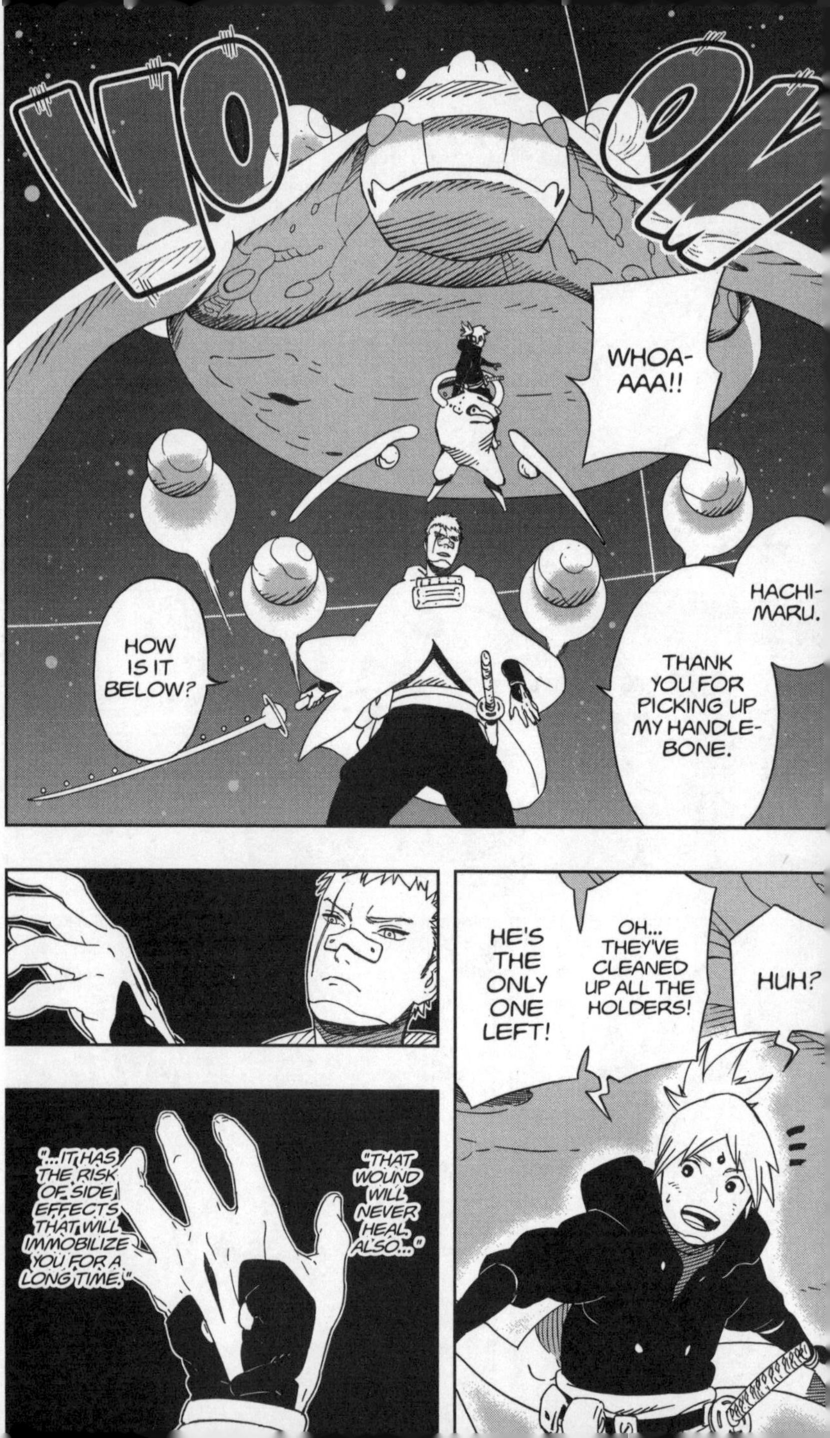
VOOM
WHOA-AAA!!
HACHI-MARU.
THANK YOU FOR PICKING UP MY HANDLE-BONE.
HOW IS IT BELOW?
HUH?
OH... THEY'VE CLEANED UP ALL THE HOLDERS!
HE'S THE ONLY ONE LEFT!
"THAT WOUND WILL NEVER HEAL. ALSO..."
"...IT HAS THE RISK OF SIDE EFFECTS THAT WILL IMMOBILIZE YOU FOR A LONG TIME."

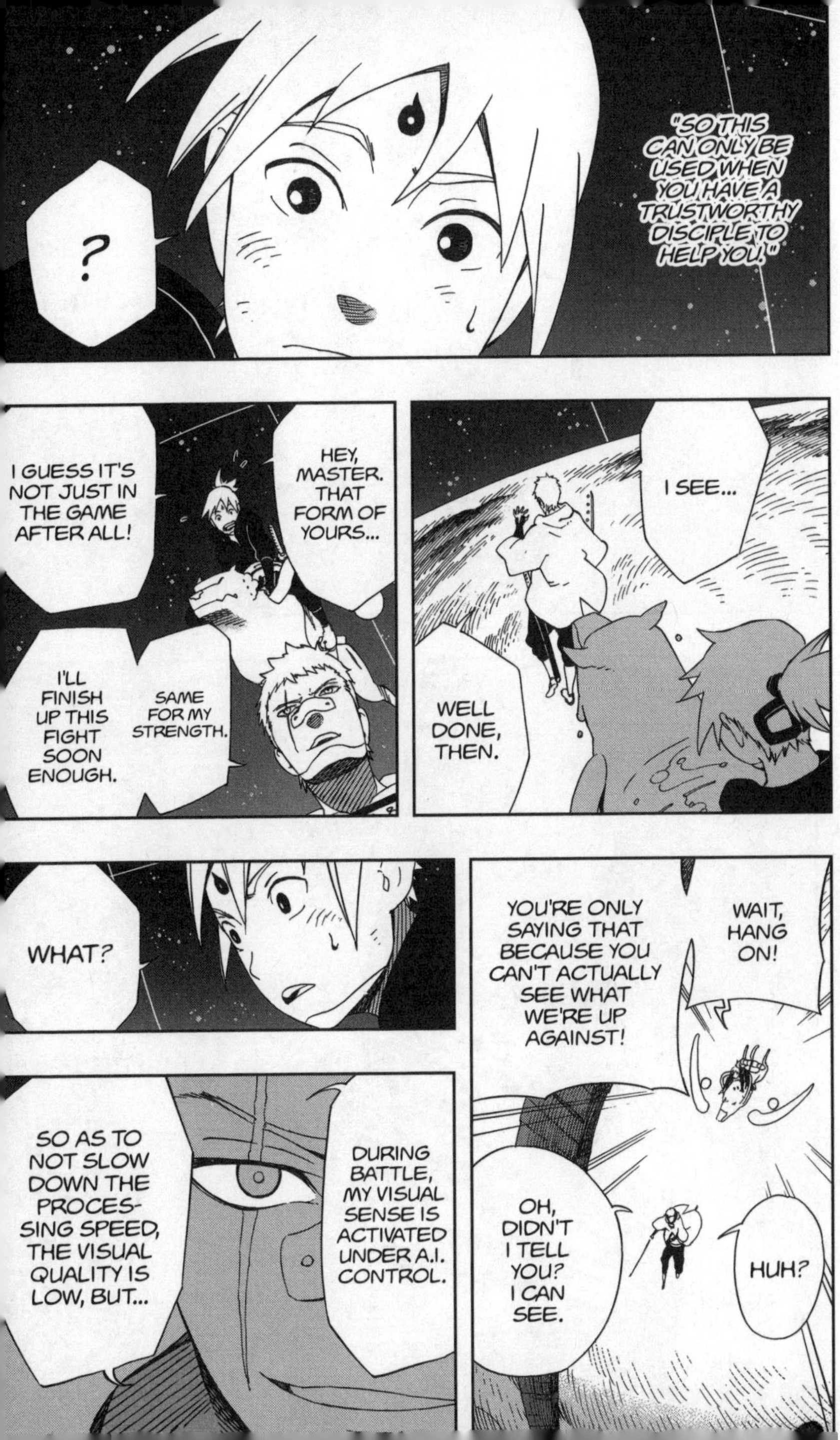
"SO THIS CAN ONLY BE USED WHEN YOU HAVE A TRUSTWORTHY DISCIPLE TO HELP YOU."
?
I SEE...
WELL DONE, THEN.
HEY, MASTER. THAT FORM OF YOURS...
I GUESS IT'S NOT JUST IN THE GAME AFTER ALL!
SAME FOR MY STRENGTH.
I'LL FINISH UP THIS FIGHT SOON ENOUGH.
WAIT, HANG ON!
YOU'RE ONLY SAYING THAT BECAUSE YOU CAN'T ACTUALLY SEE WHAT WE'RE UP AGAINST!
HUH?
OH, DIDN'T I TELL YOU? I CAN SEE.
WHAT?
DURING BATTLE, MY VISUAL SENSE IS ACTIVATED UNDER A.I. CONTROL.
SO AS TO NOT SLOW DOWN THE PROCES-SING SPEED, THE VISUAL QUALITY IS LOW, BUT...

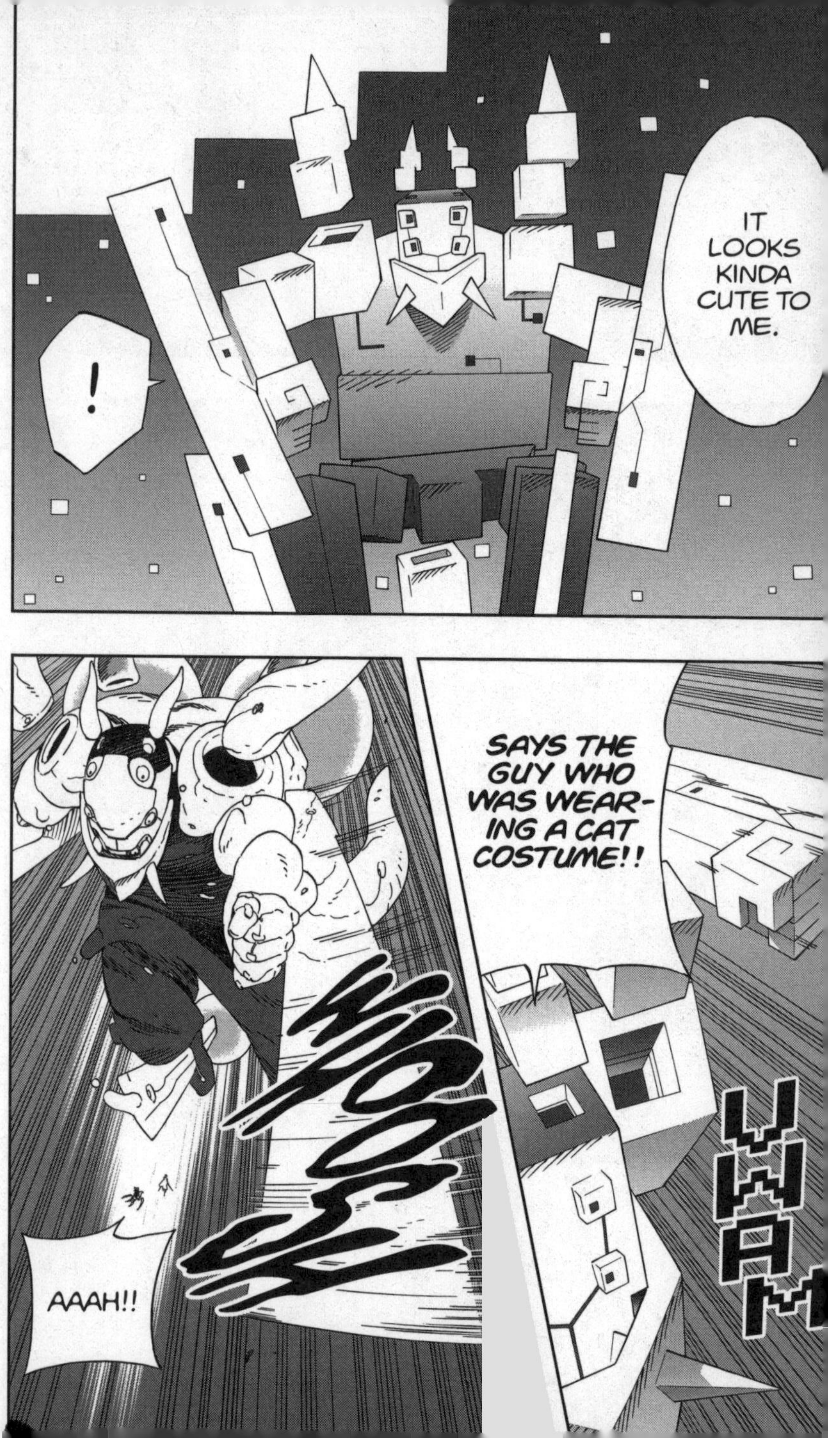
IT LOOKS KINDA CUTE TO ME.
!
SAYS THE GUY WHO WAS WEARING A CAT COSTUME!!
WWAM
WHOOSH
AAAH!!

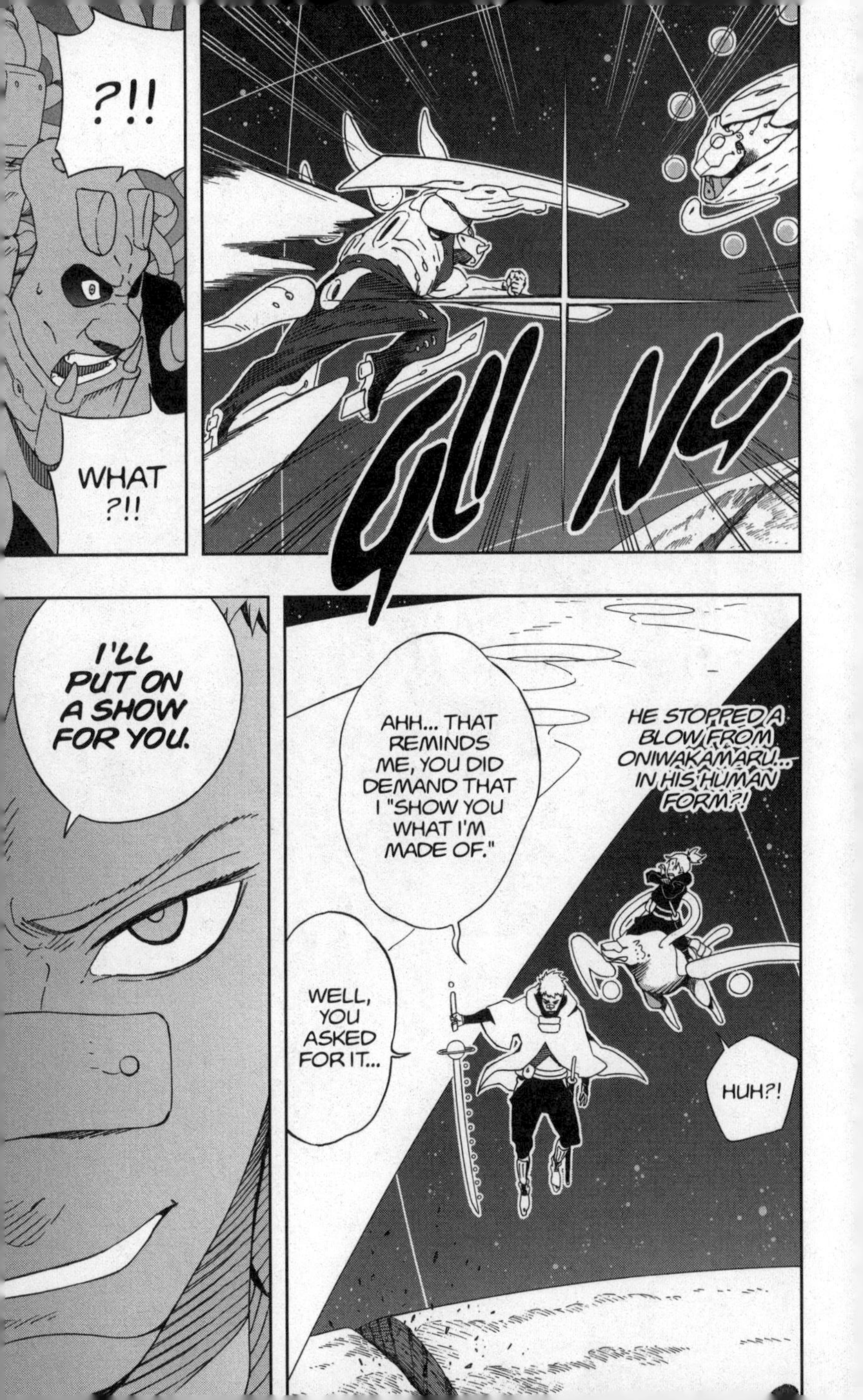
GIING
?!!
WHAT ?!!
HE STOPPED A BLOW FROM ONIWAKAMARU... IN HIS HUMAN FORM?!
AHH... THAT REMINDS ME, YOU DID DEMAND THAT I "SHOW YOU WHAT I'M MADE OF."
WELL, YOU ASKED FOR IT...
HUH?!
I'LL PUT ON A SHOW FOR YOU.

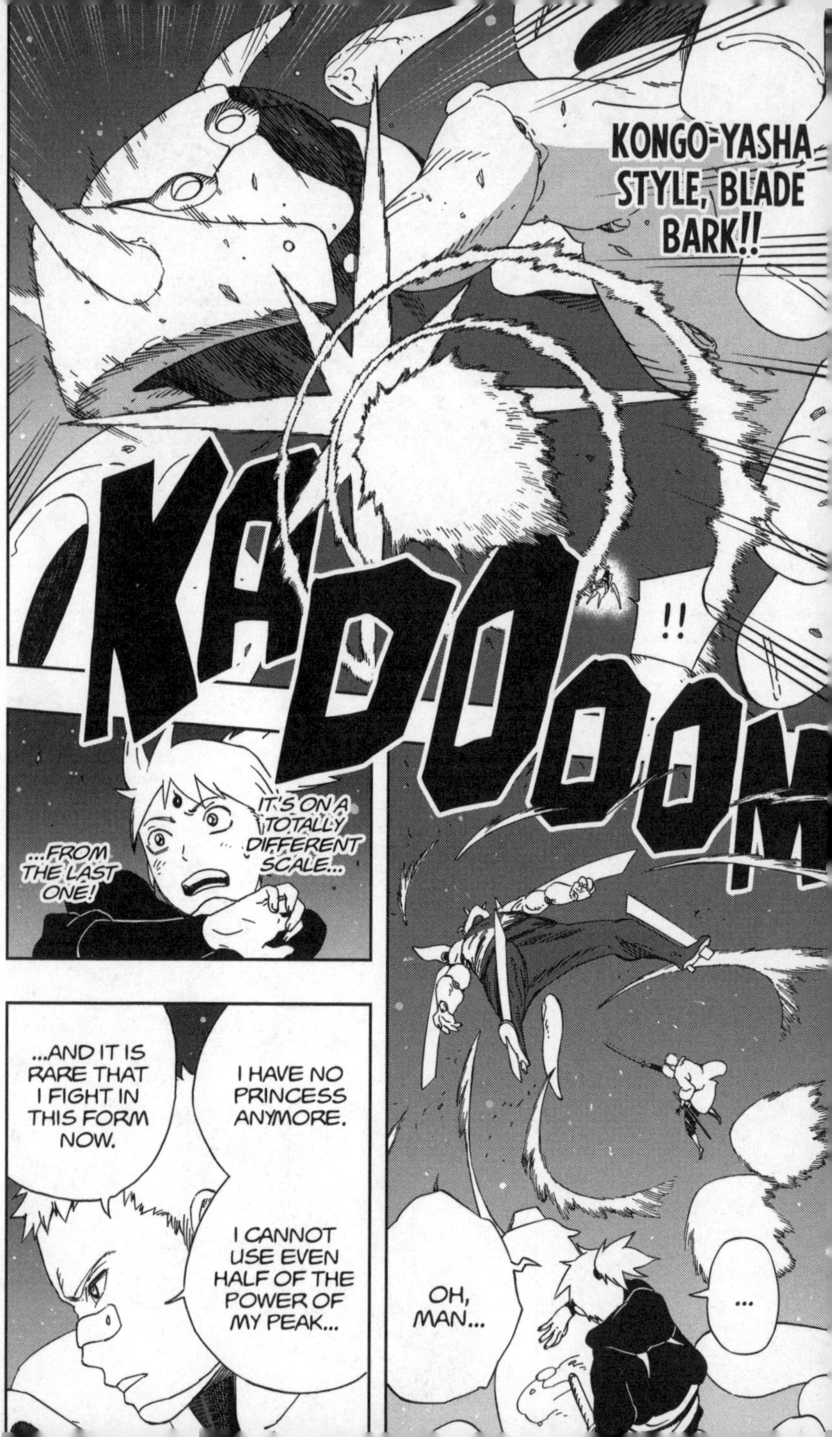
KONGO-YASHA STYLE, BLADE BARK!!
KADOOOOM
!!
...
OH, MAN...
IT'S ON A TOTALLY DIFFERENT SCALE...
...FROM THE LAST ONE!
I HAVE NO PRINCESS ANYMORE.
...AND IT IS RARE THAT I FIGHT IN THIS FORM NOW.
I CANNOT USE EVEN HALF OF THE POWER OF MY PEAK...

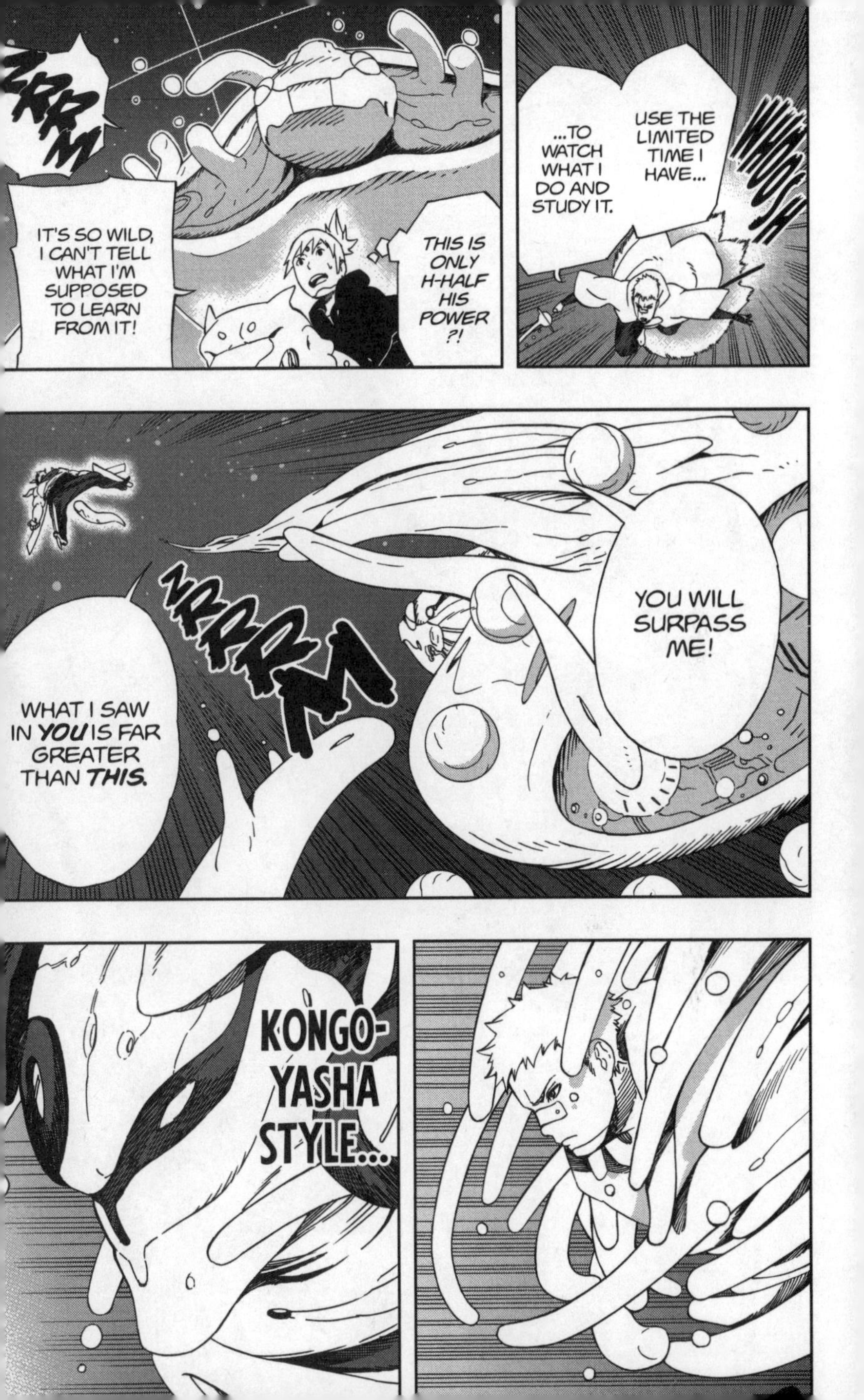

USE THE LIMITED TIME I HAVE...
...TO WATCH WHAT I DO AND STUDY IT.
WHOOSH
THIS IS ONLY H-HALF HIS POWER?!
IT'S SO WILD, I CAN'T TELL WHAT I'M SUPPOSED TO LEARN FROM IT!
YOU WILL SURPASS ME!
NRRRM
WHAT I SAW IN YOU IS FAR GREATER THAN THIS.
KONGO-YASHA STYLE...

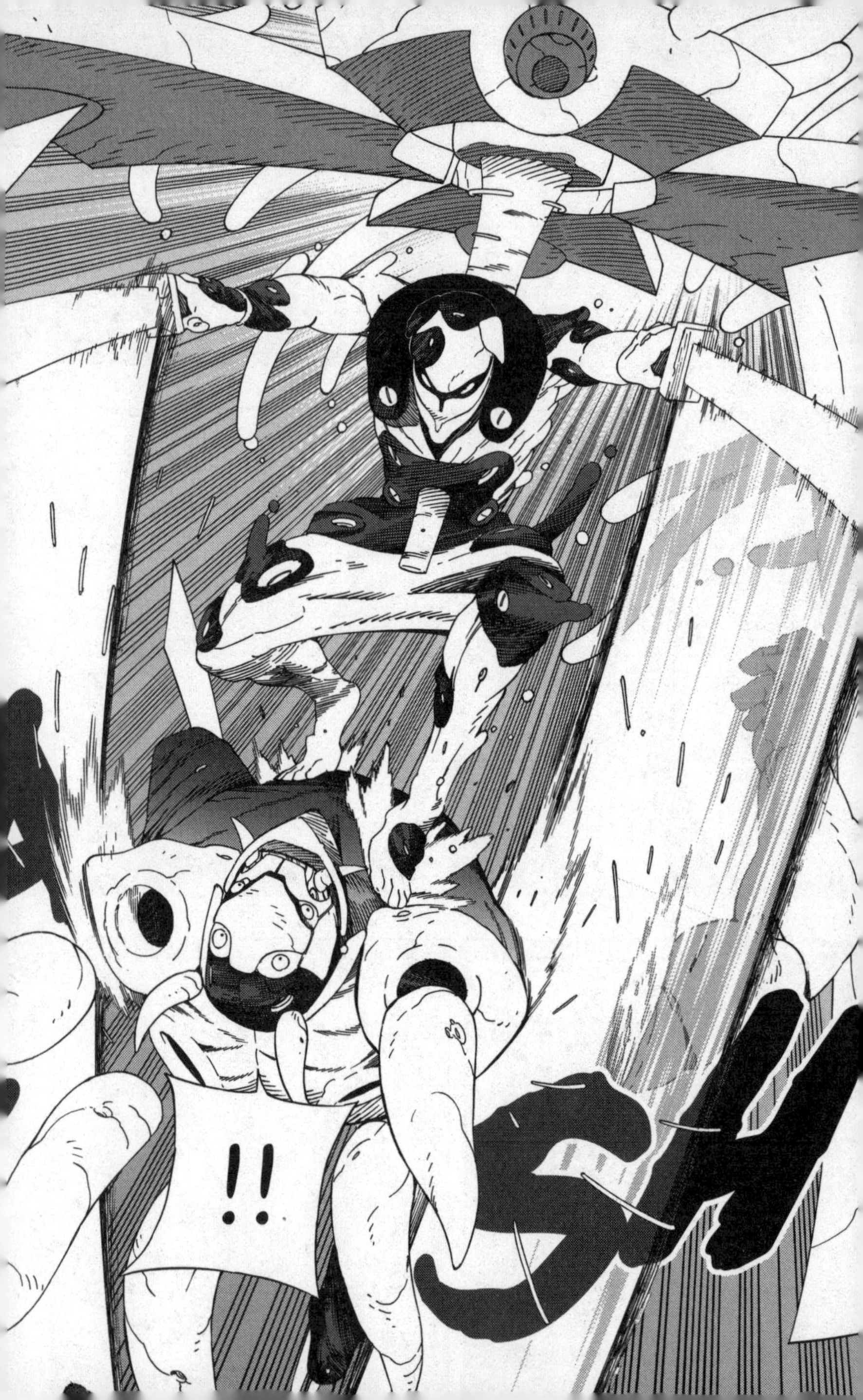
!!

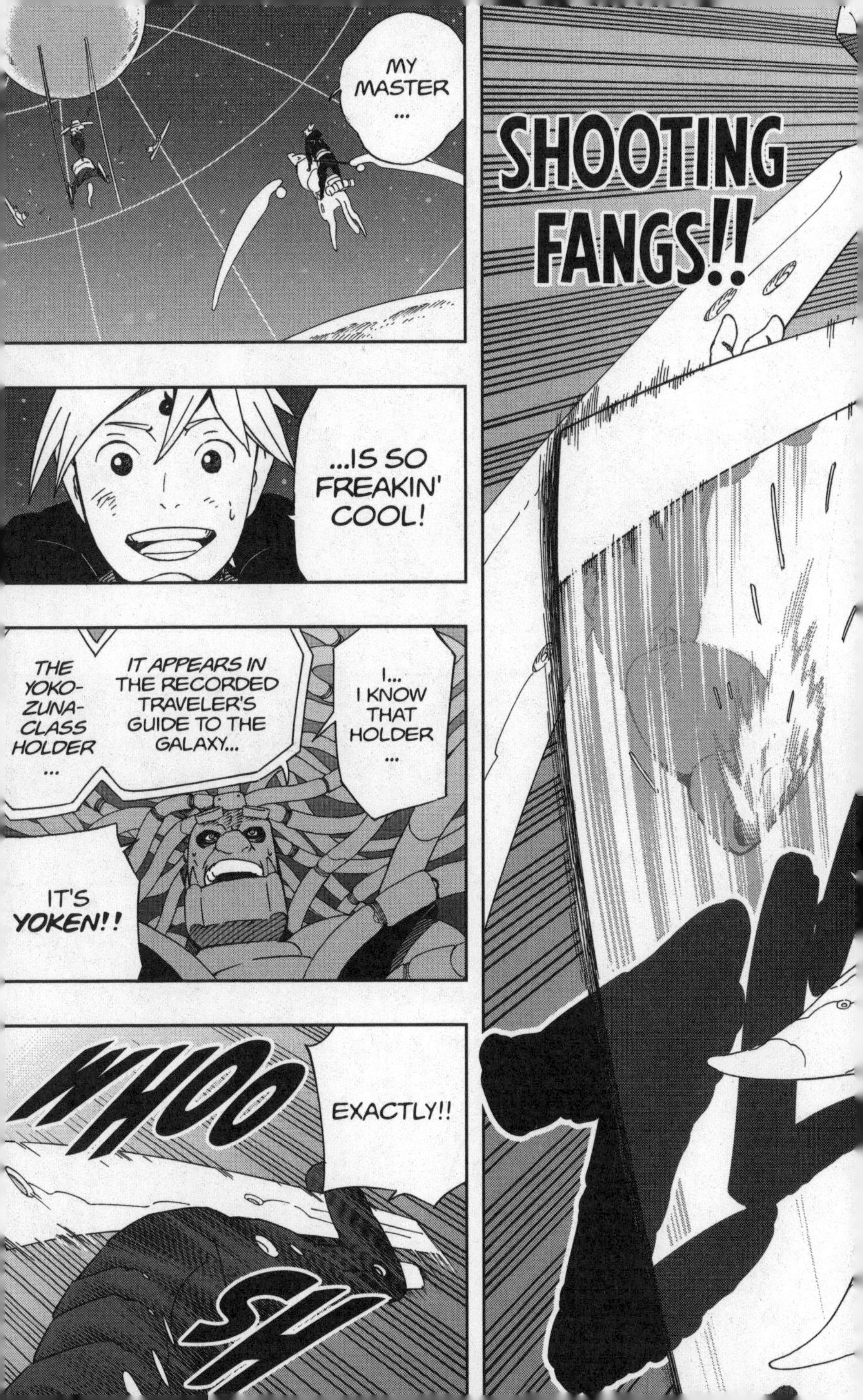
SHOOTING FANGS!!
MY MASTER ...
...IS SO FREAKIN' COOL!
I... I KNOW THAT HOLDER ...
IT APPEARS IN THE RECORDED TRAVELER'S GUIDE TO THE GALAXY...
THE YOKO-ZUNA-CLASS HOLDER ...
IT'S YOKEN!!
EXACTLY!!
WHOO
SH

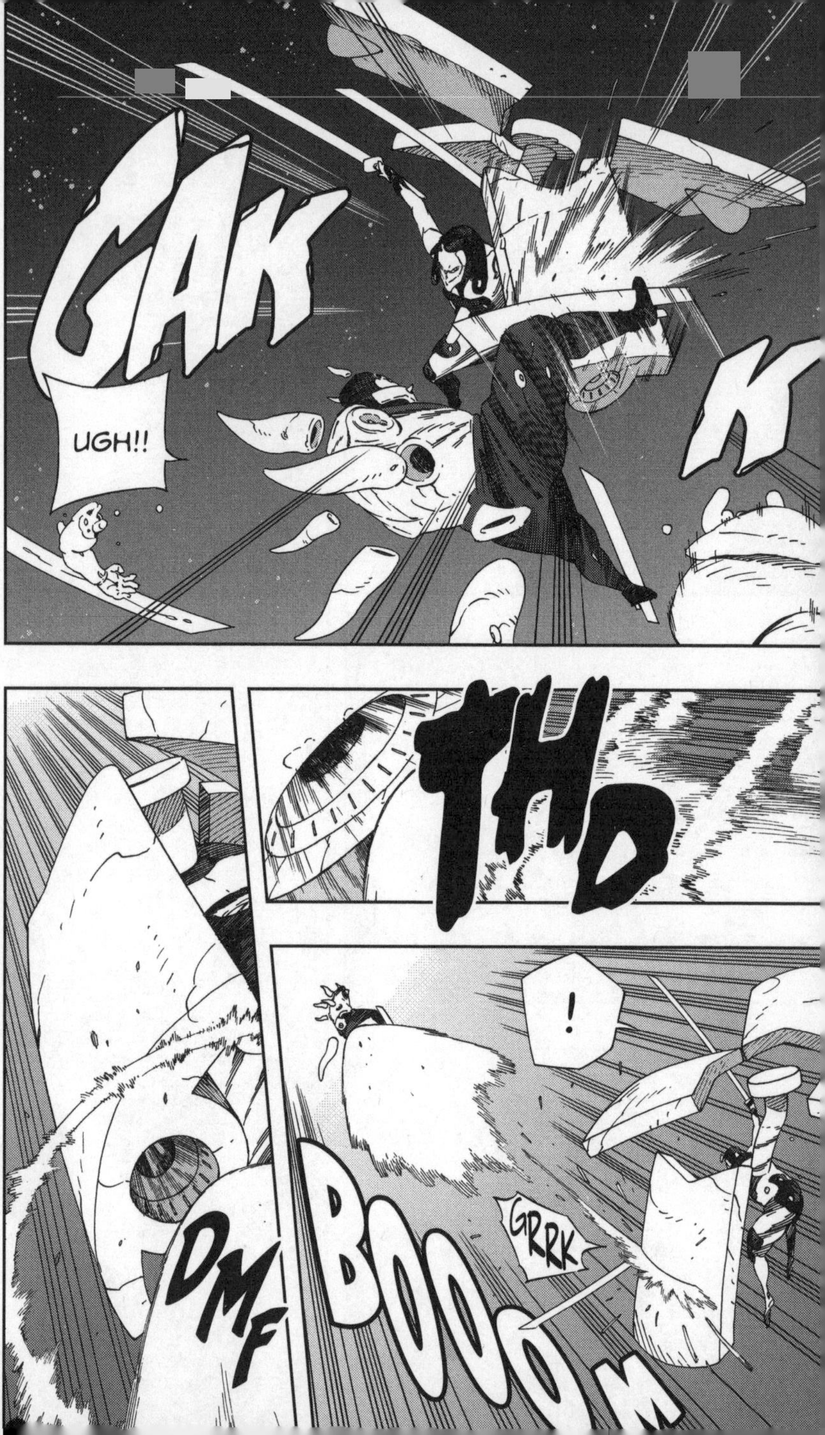
K
GAK
UGH!!
THD
!
GRRK
BOOOOM
DMF

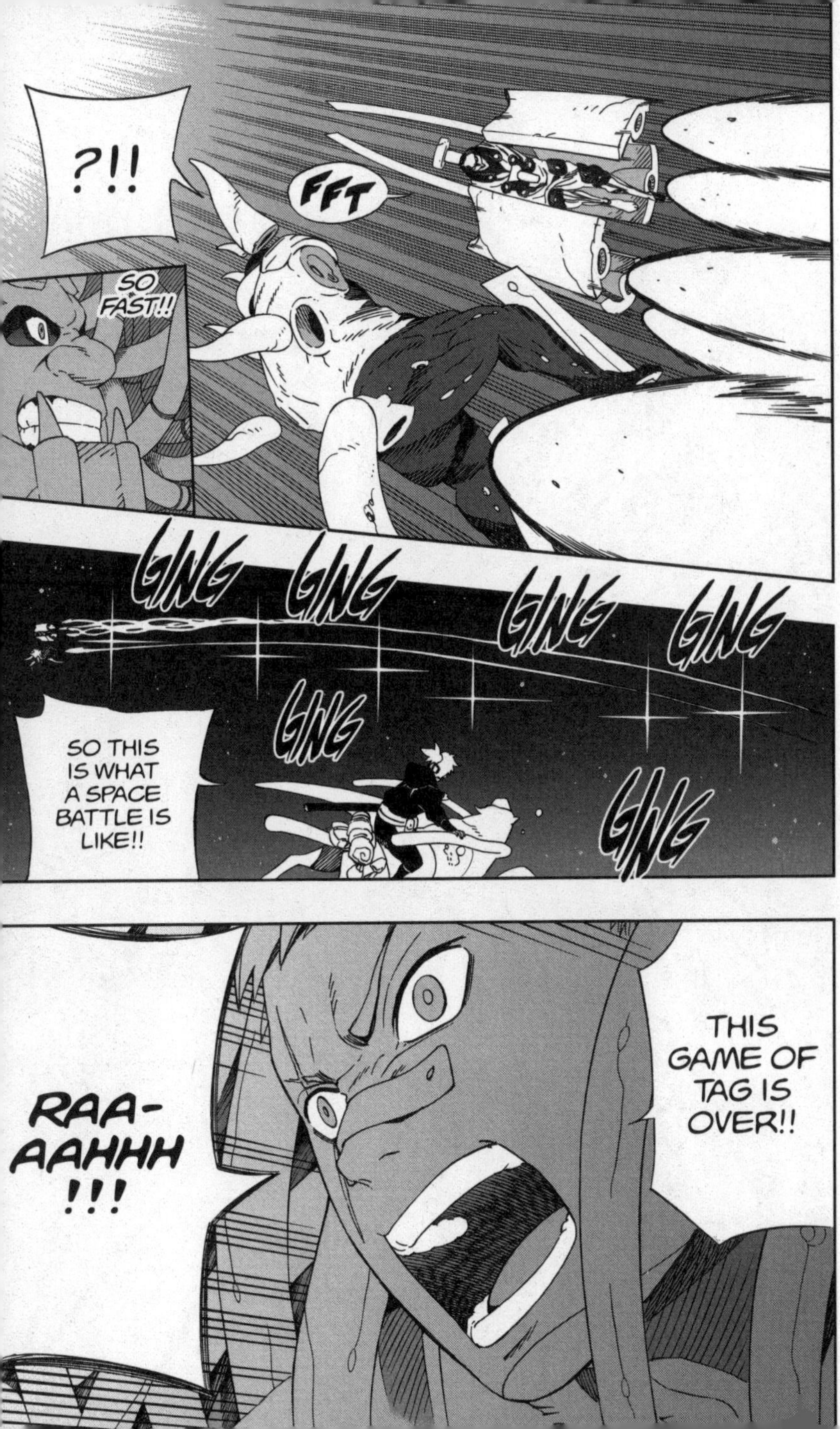
FFT
?!!
SO FAST!!
GNG GNG GNG GNG GNG GNG
SO THIS IS WHAT A SPACE BATTLE IS LIKE!!
THIS GAME OF TAG IS OVER!!
RAA-AAHHH!!!

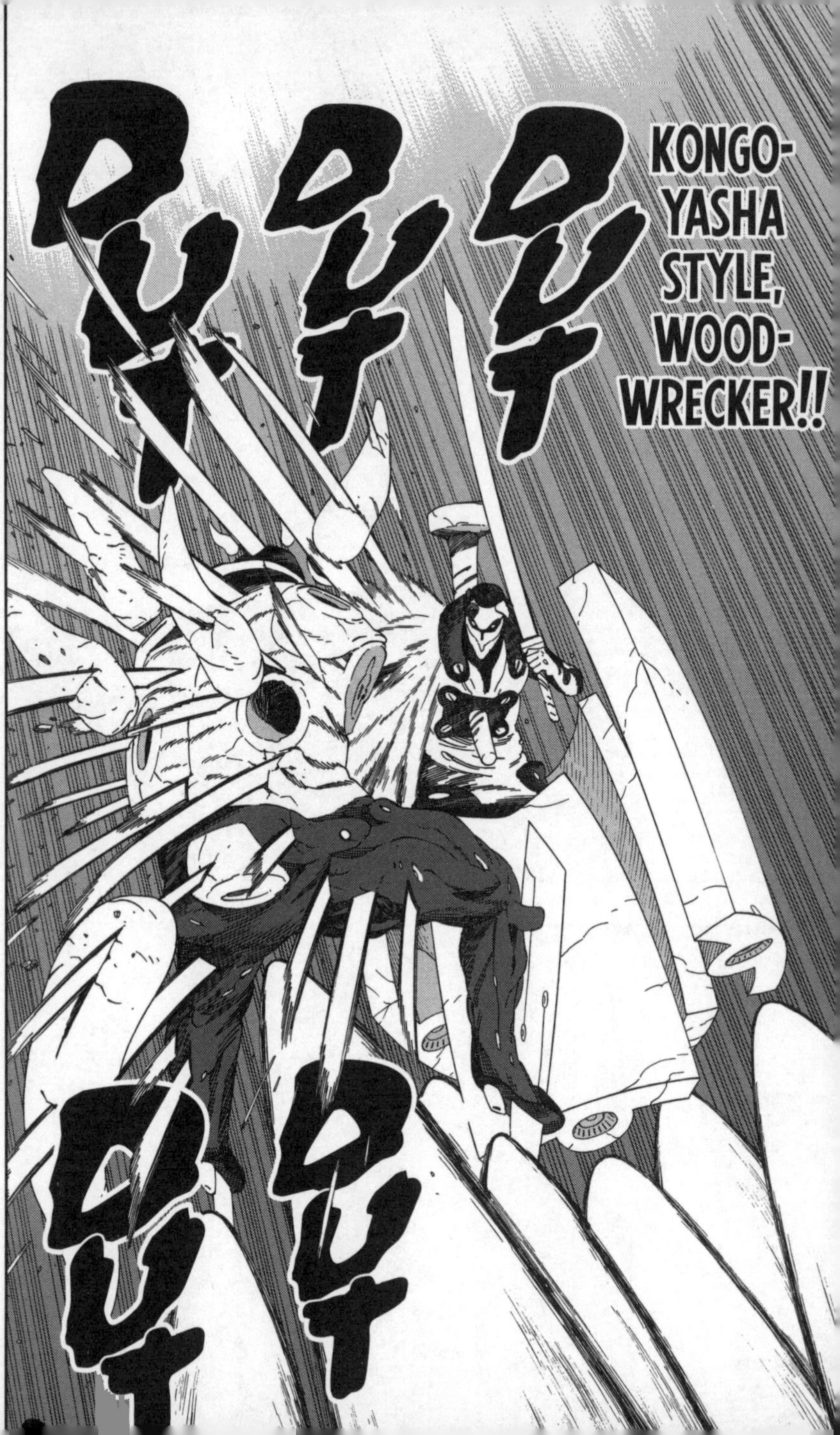
KONGO-YASHA STYLE, WOOD-WRECKER!!

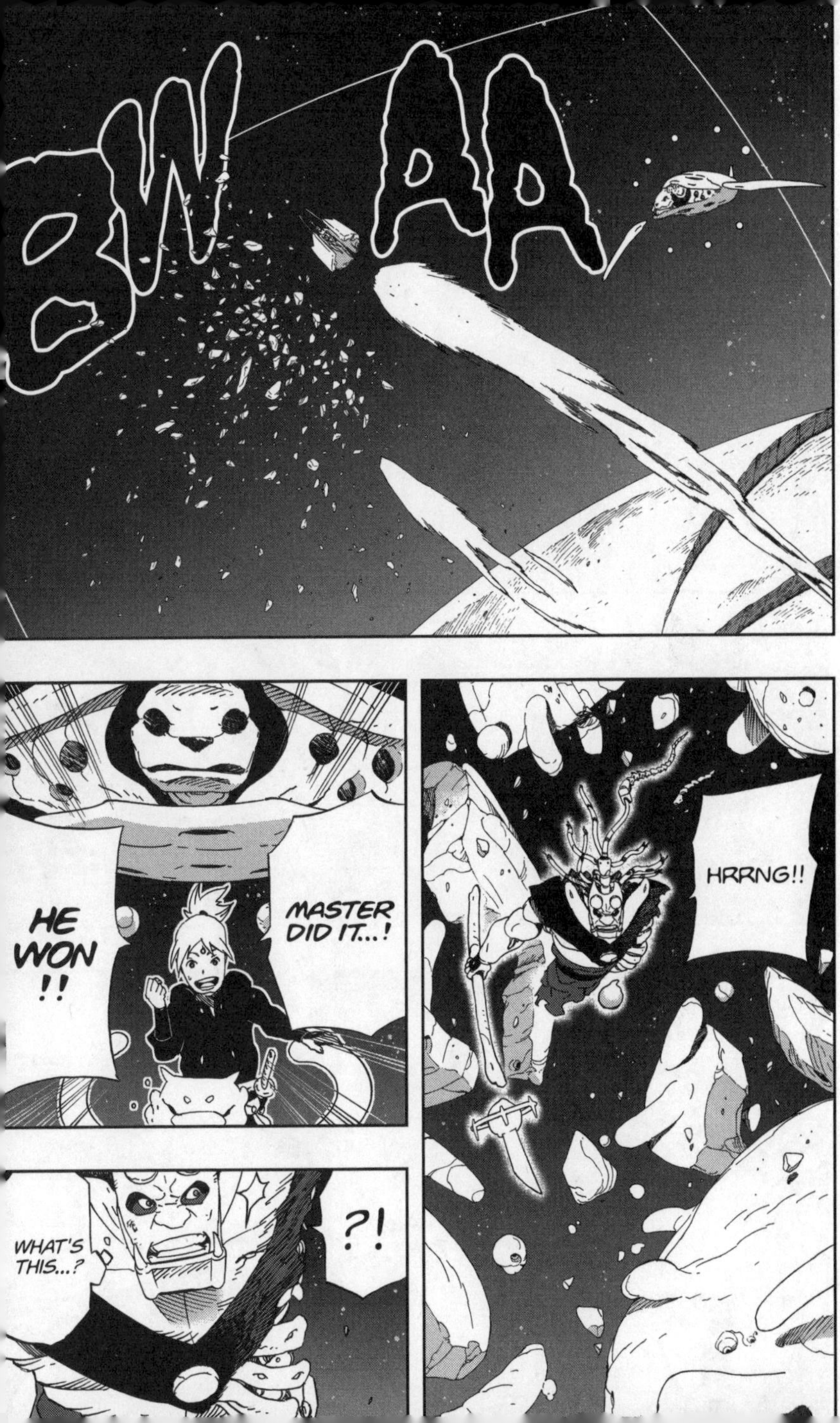
GWAA
HRRNG!!
MASTER DID IT...!
HE WON!!
?!
WHAT'S THIS...?

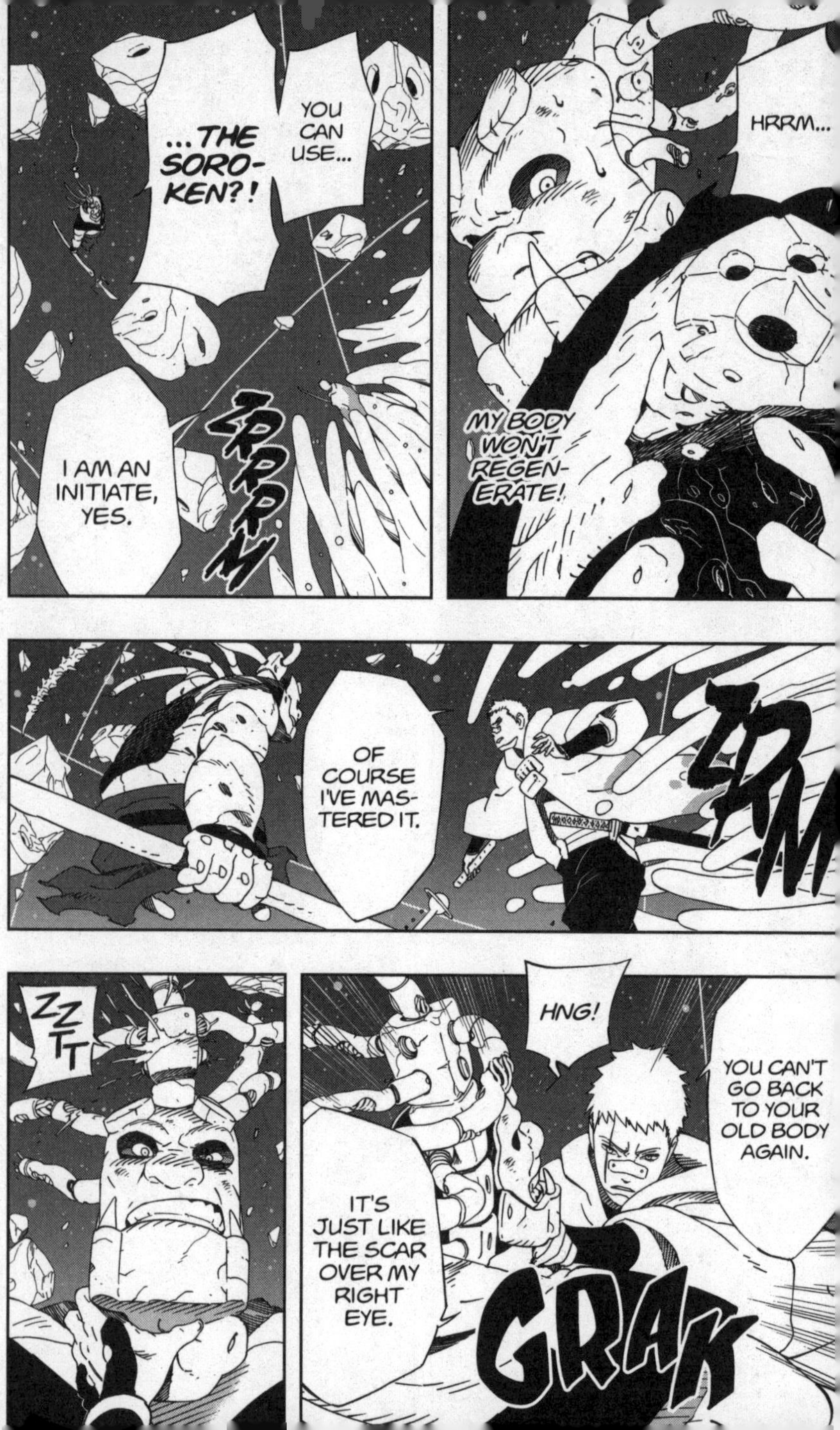
HRRM...
MY BODY WON'T REGEN-ERATE!
YOU CAN USE...
...THE SORO-KEN?!
ZRRRM
I AM AN INITIATE, YES.
ZRRM
OF COURSE I'VE MAS-TERED IT.
HNG!
YOU CAN'T GO BACK TO YOUR OLD BODY AGAIN.
IT'S JUST LIKE THE SCAR OVER MY RIGHT EYE.
GRAK
ZZTT

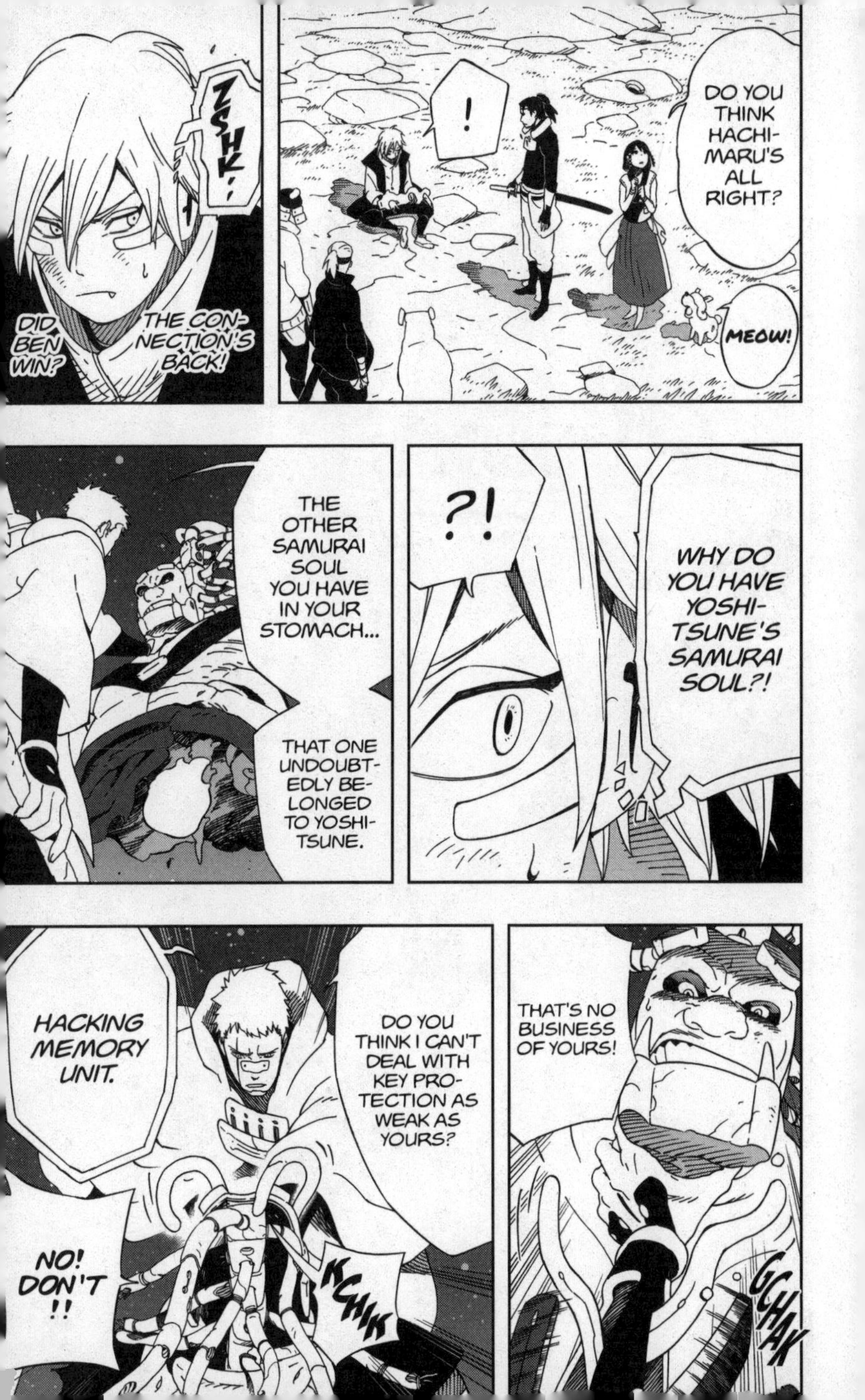
!
DO YOU THINK HACHIMARU'S ALL RIGHT?
MEOW!
ZSHK
THE CONNECTION'S BACK!
DID BEN WIN?
?!
WHY DO YOU HAVE YOSHITSUNE'S SAMURAI SOUL?!
THE OTHER SAMURAI SOUL YOU HAVE IN YOUR STOMACH...
THAT ONE UNDOUBTEDLY BELONGED TO YOSHITSUNE.
THAT'S NO BUSINESS OF YOURS!
GCHAK
DO YOU THINK I CAN'T DEAL WITH KEY PROTECTION AS WEAK AS YOURS?
HACKING MEMORY UNIT.
KCHIK
NO! DON'T!!

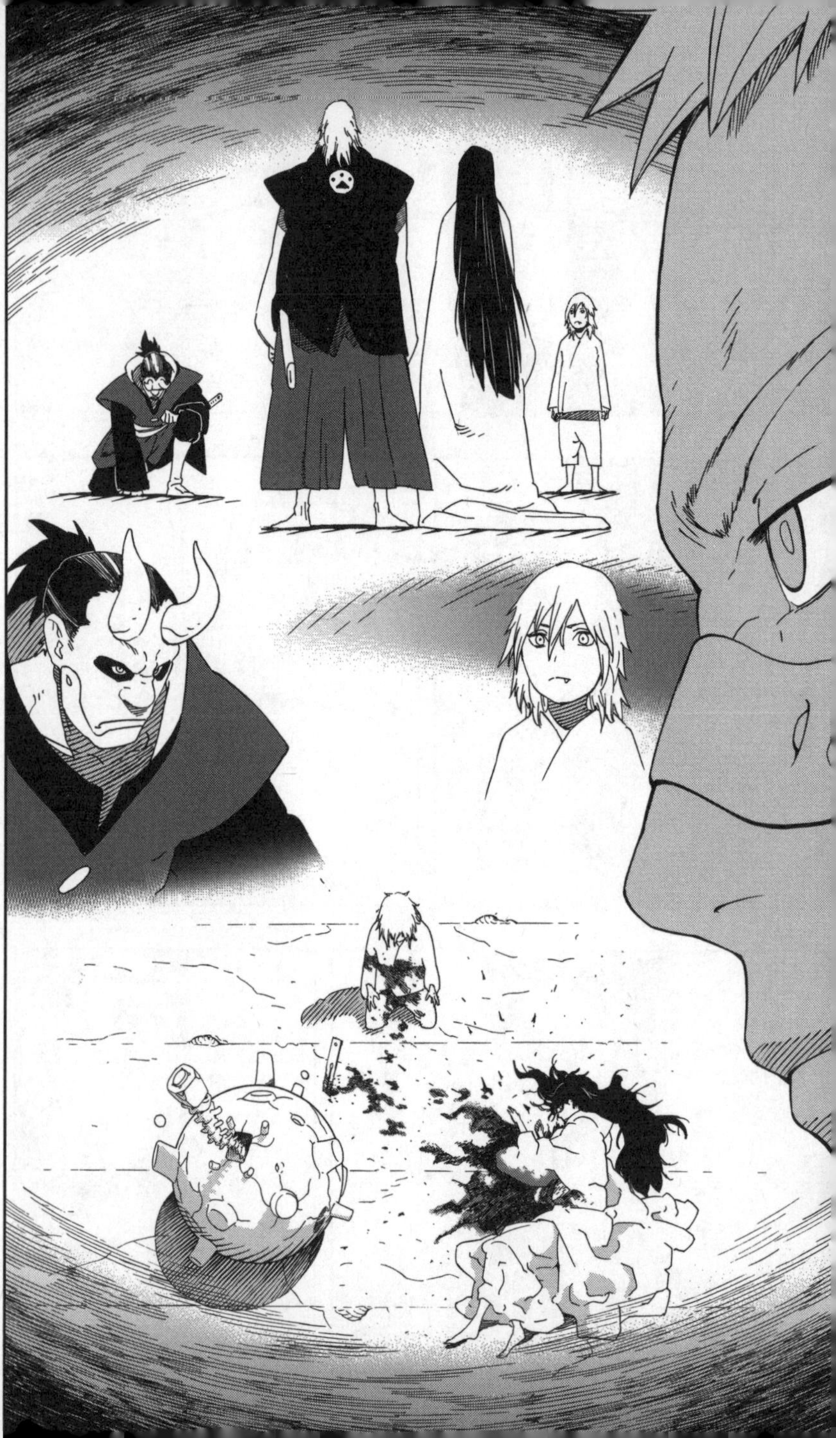

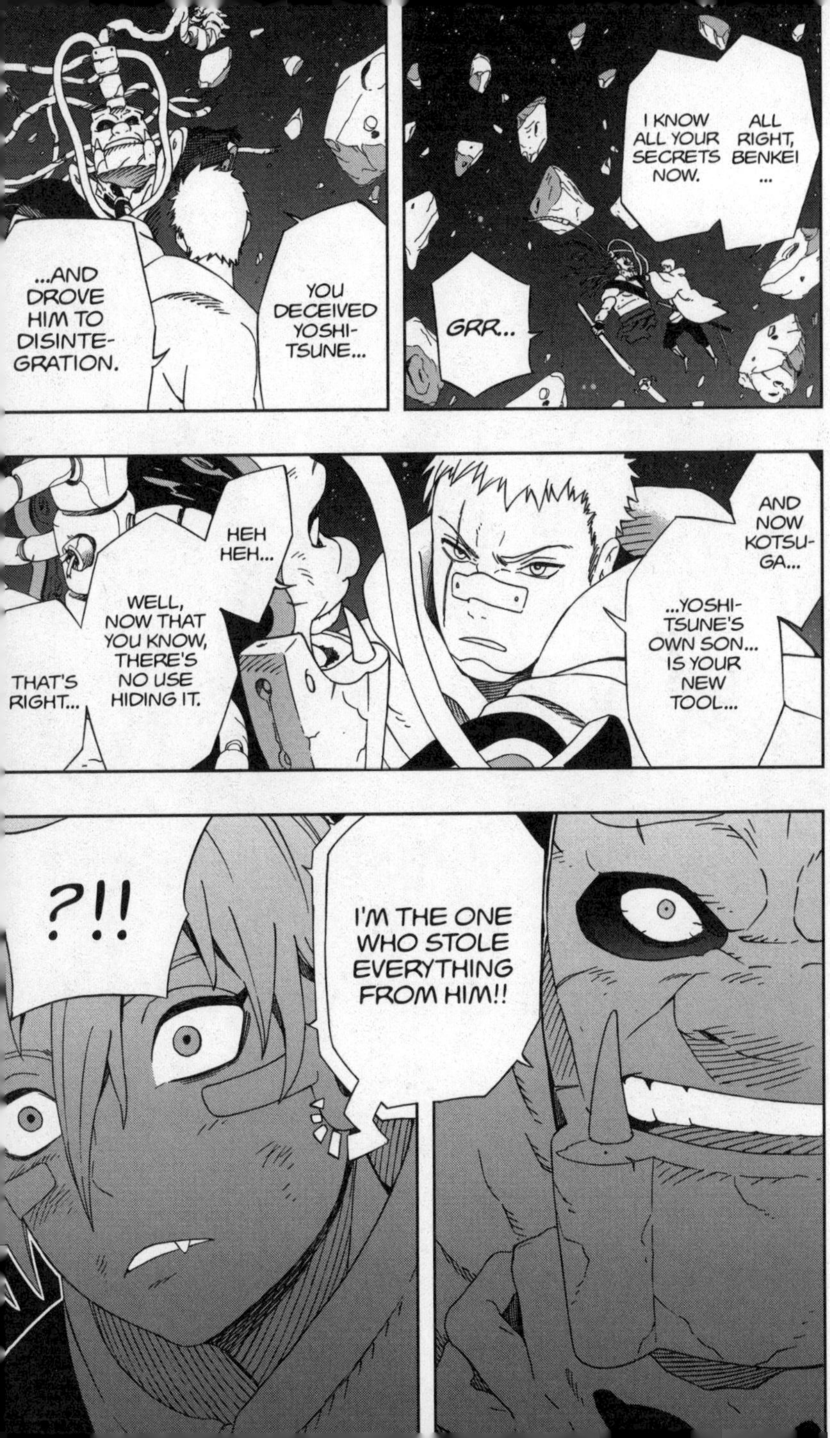
ALL RIGHT, BENKEI...
I KNOW ALL YOUR SECRETS NOW.
GRR...
YOU DECEIVED YOSHI-TSUNE...
...AND DROVE HIM TO DISINTE-GRATION.
AND NOW KOTSU-GA...
...YOSHI-TSUNE'S OWN SON... IS YOUR NEW TOOL...
HEH HEH...
WELL, NOW THAT YOU KNOW, THERE'S NO USE HIDING IT.
THAT'S RIGHT...
I'M THE ONE WHO STOLE EVERYTHING FROM HIM!!
?!!

Storyboard Reveal!
Chapter 28 (vol. 4, pg 67)

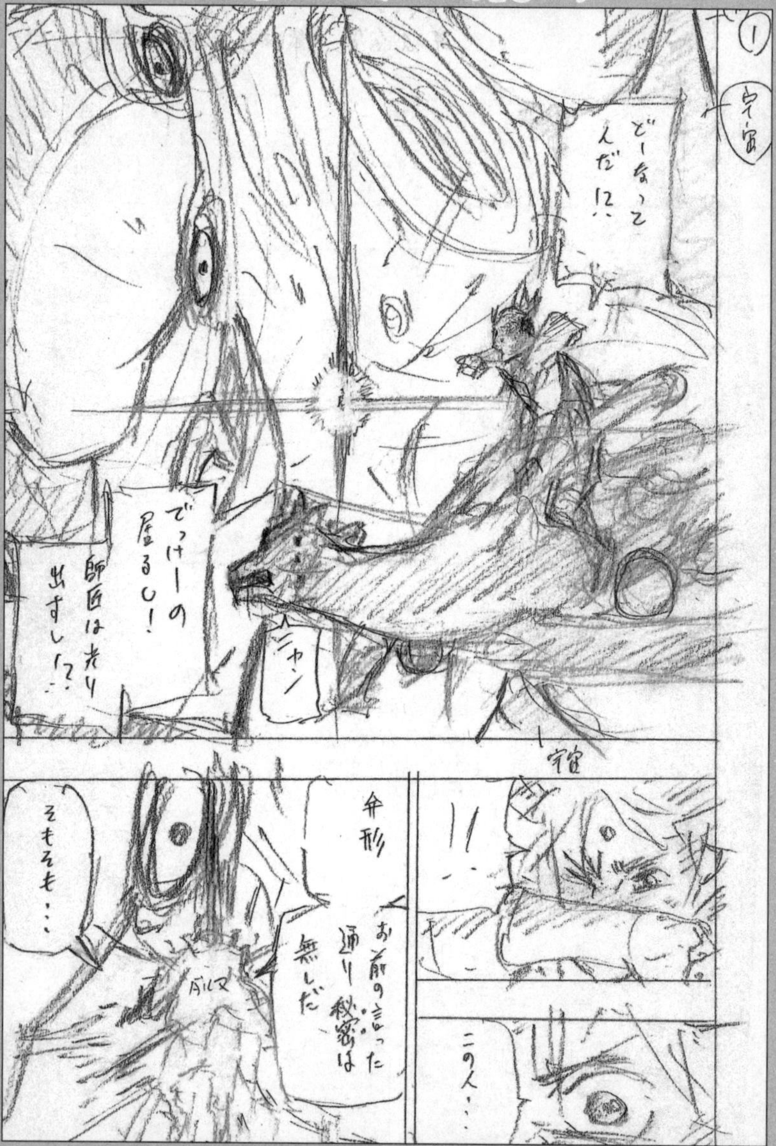
どーなってんだ!?
でっけーの居るし! 師匠は光り出すし!?…
ニャン
!!…
この人・・・
弁形
お前の言った通り秘密は無しだ
そもそも・・・

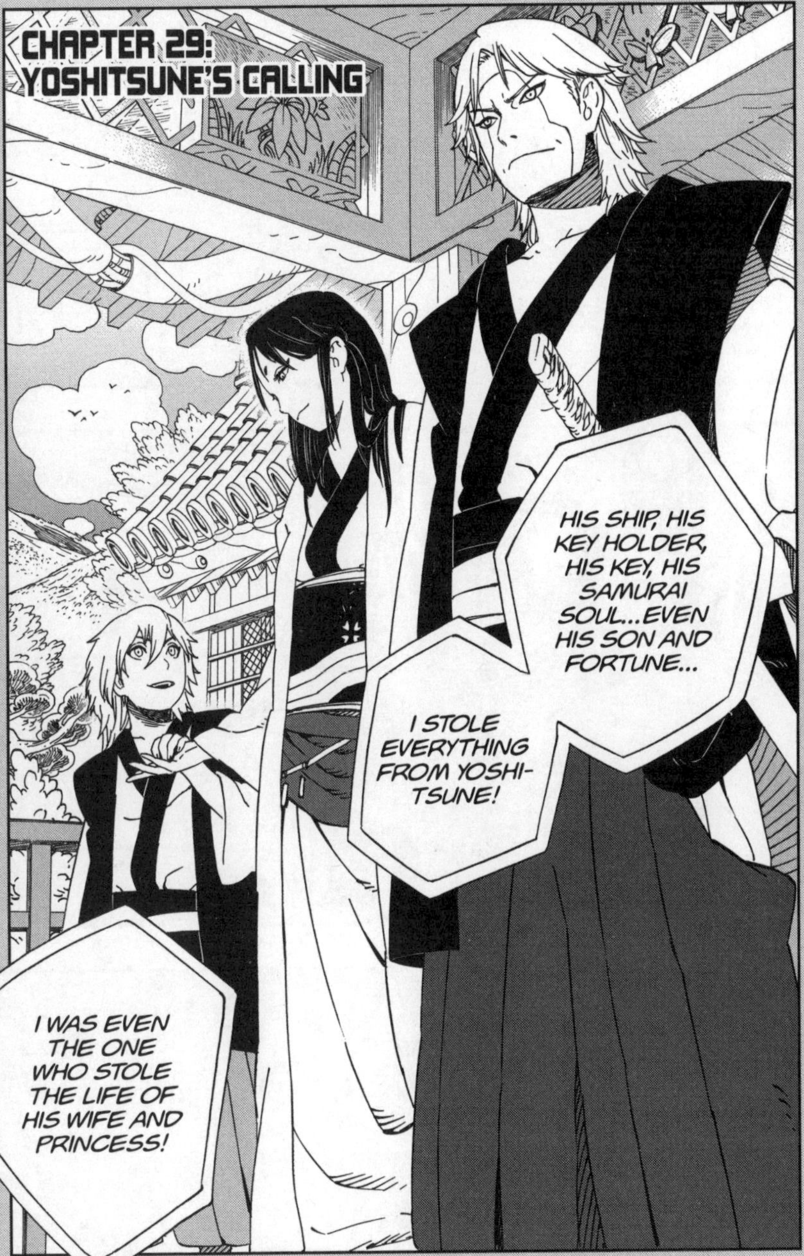
CHAPTER 29: YOSHITSUNE'S CALLING
HIS SHIP, HIS KEY HOLDER, HIS KEY, HIS SAMURAI SOUL...EVEN HIS SON AND FORTUNE...
I STOLE EVERYTHING FROM YOSHI-TSUNE!
I WAS EVEN THE ONE WHO STOLE THE LIFE OF HIS WIFE AND PRINCESS!

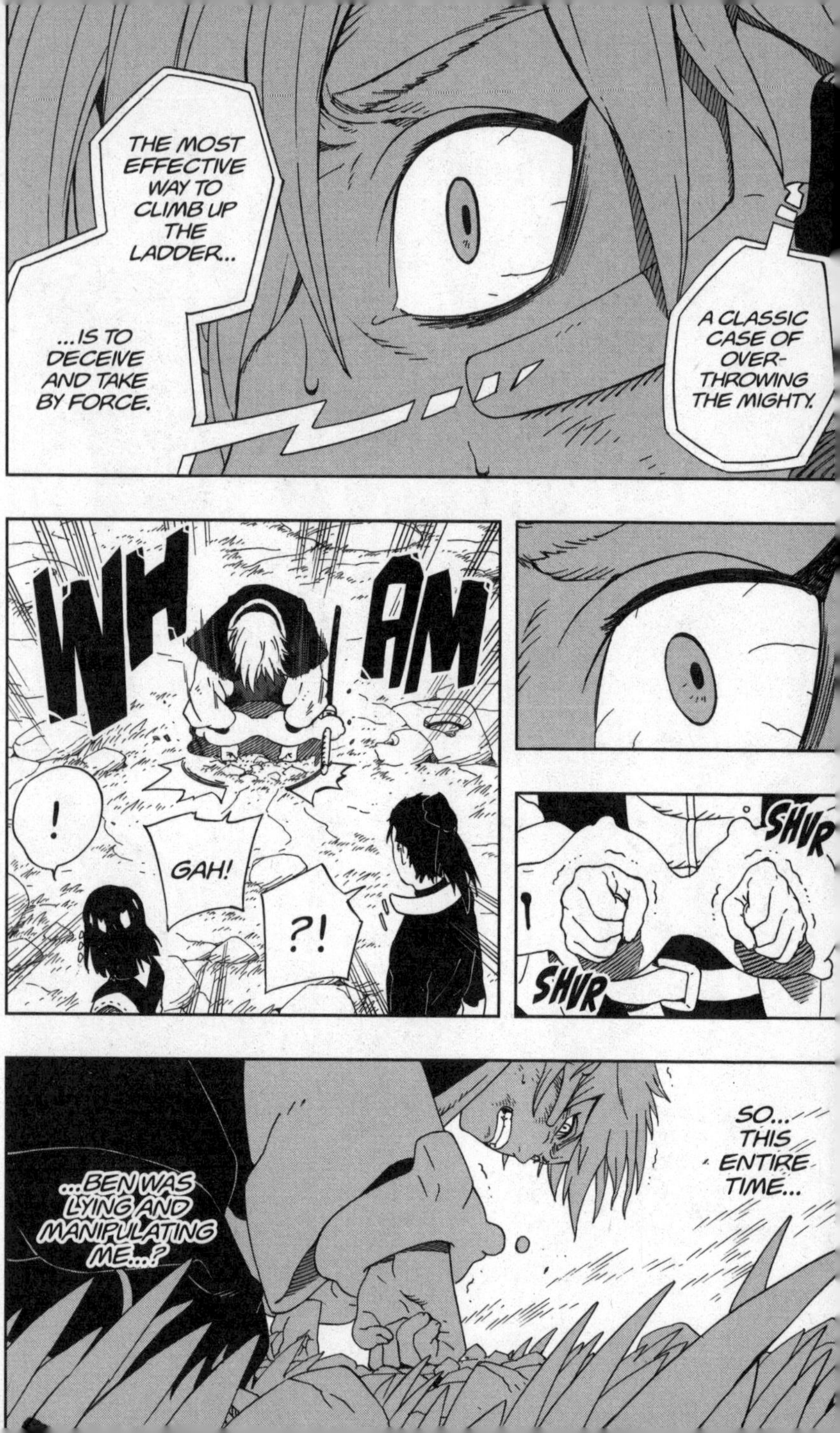
A CLASSIC CASE OF OVER-THROWING THE MIGHTY.
THE MOST EFFECTIVE WAY TO CLIMB UP THE LADDER...
...IS TO DECEIVE AND TAKE BY FORCE.
SHVR
SHVR
WHAM
!
GAH!
?!
SO... THIS ENTIRE TIME...
...BEN WAS LYING AND MANIPULATING ME...?

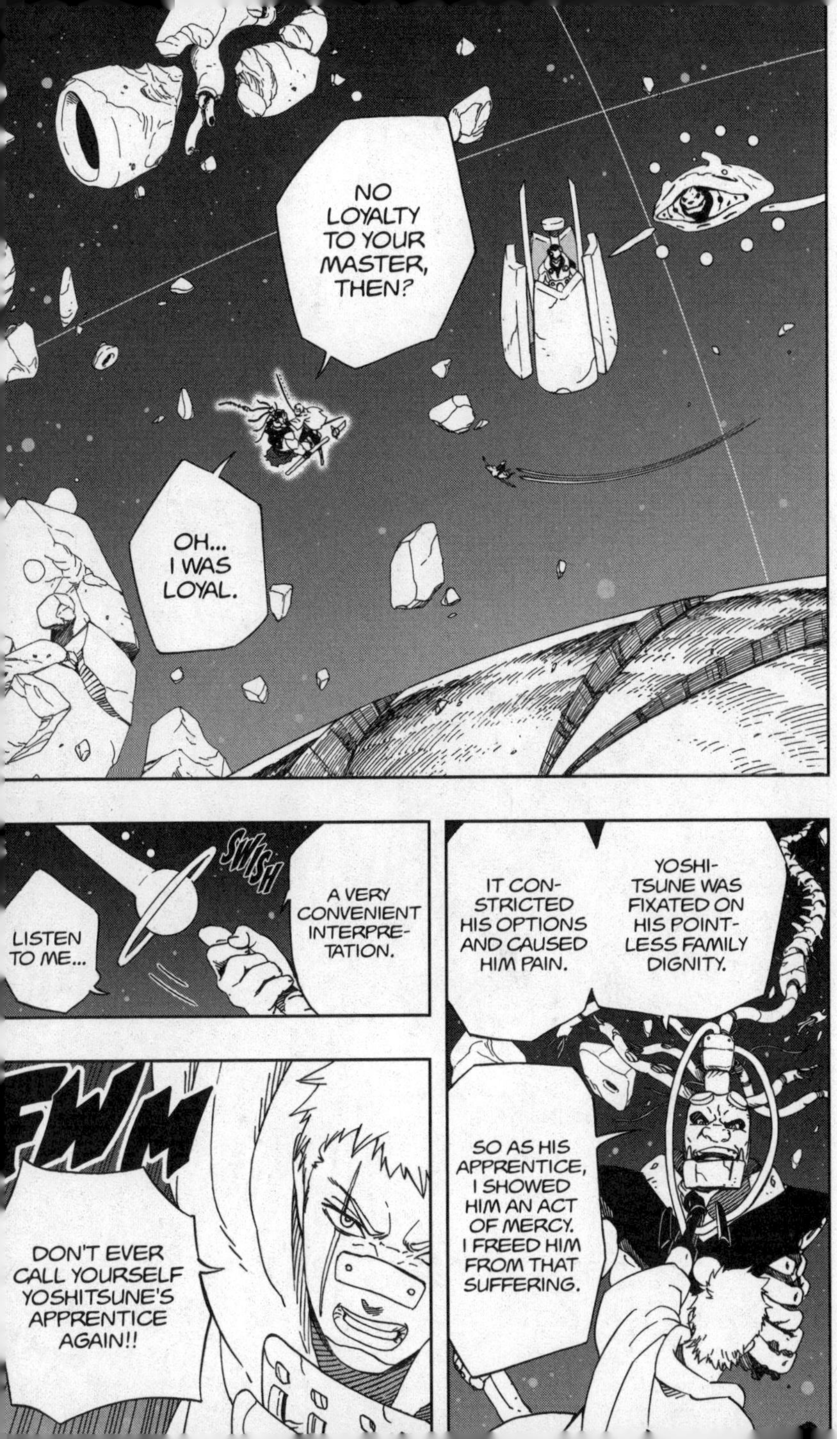
NO LOYALTY TO YOUR MASTER, THEN?
OH... I WAS LOYAL.
YOSHITSUNE WAS FIXATED ON HIS POINTLESS FAMILY DIGNITY.
IT CONSTRICTED HIS OPTIONS AND CAUSED HIM PAIN.
SO AS HIS APPRENTICE, I SHOWED HIM AN ACT OF MERCY. I FREED HIM FROM THAT SUFFERING.
SWISH
A VERY CONVENIENT INTERPRETATION.
LISTEN TO ME...
FWM
DON'T EVER CALL YOURSELF YOSHITSUNE'S APPRENTICE AGAIN!!

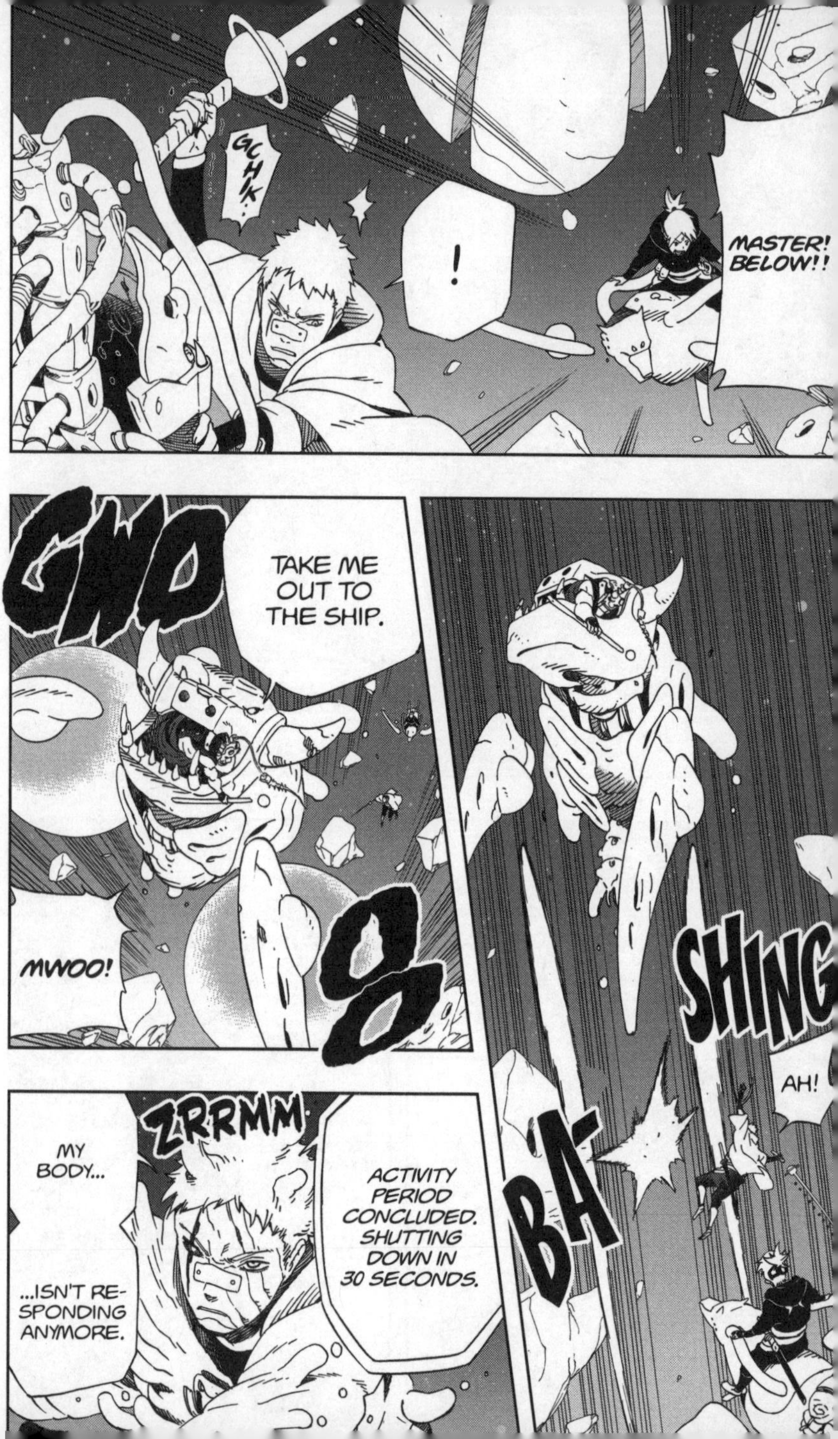
MASTER! BELOW!!
!
GCHIK..
SHING
AH!
BA
GWO
TAKE ME OUT TO THE SHIP.
MWOO!
O
ACTIVITY PERIOD CONCLUDED. SHUTTING DOWN IN 30 SECONDS.
ZRRMM
MY BODY...
...ISN'T RE-SPONDING ANYMORE.

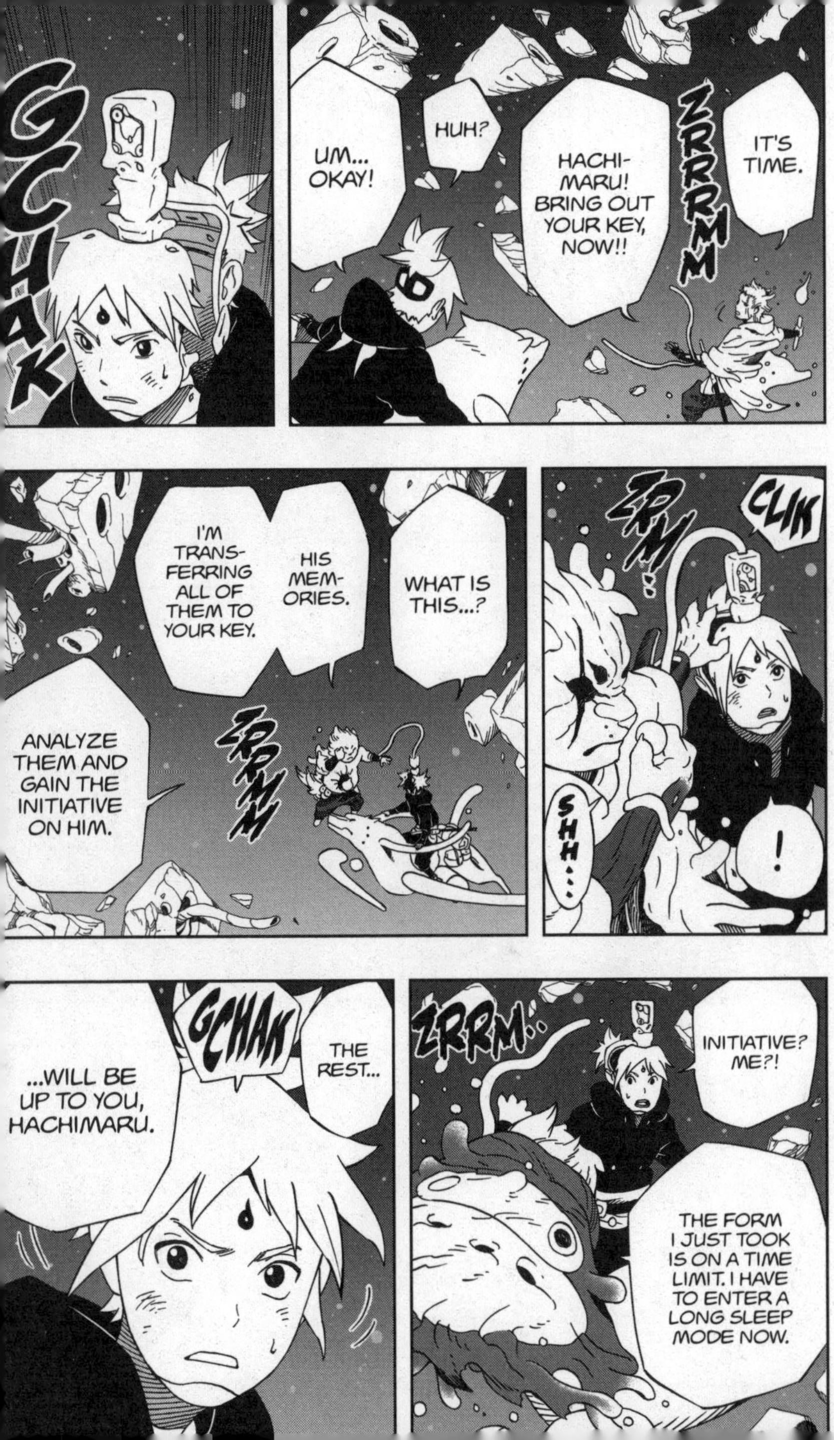
IT'S TIME.
ZRRRMM
HACHI-MARU! BRING OUT YOUR KEY, NOW!!
HUH?
UM... OKAY!
GCHAK
CLIK
ZRM
!
SHH...
WHAT IS THIS...?
HIS MEM-ORIES.
I'M TRANS-FERRING ALL OF THEM TO YOUR KEY.
ZRRMM
ANALYZE THEM AND GAIN THE INITIATIVE ON HIM.
INITIATIVE? ME?!
ZRRM
THE FORM I JUST TOOK IS ON A TIME LIMIT. I HAVE TO ENTER A LONG SLEEP MODE NOW.
THE REST...
GCHAK
...WILL BE UP TO YOU, HACHIMARU.

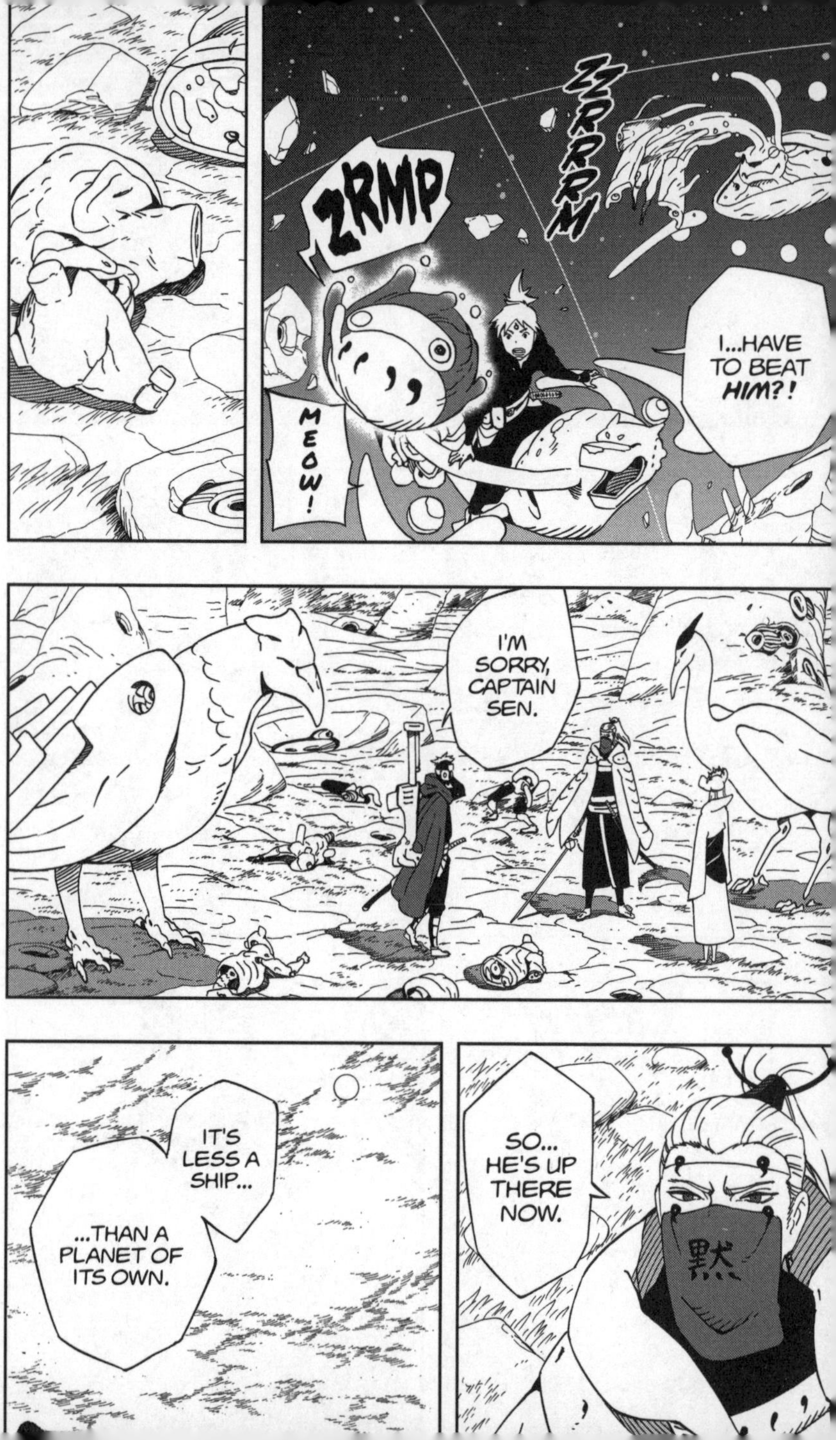
ZZRRRRM
ZRMP
I...HAVE TO BEAT HIM?!
MEOW!
I'M SORRY, CAPTAIN SEN.
SO... HE'S UP THERE NOW.
IT'S LESS A SHIP...
...THAN A PLANET OF ITS OWN.

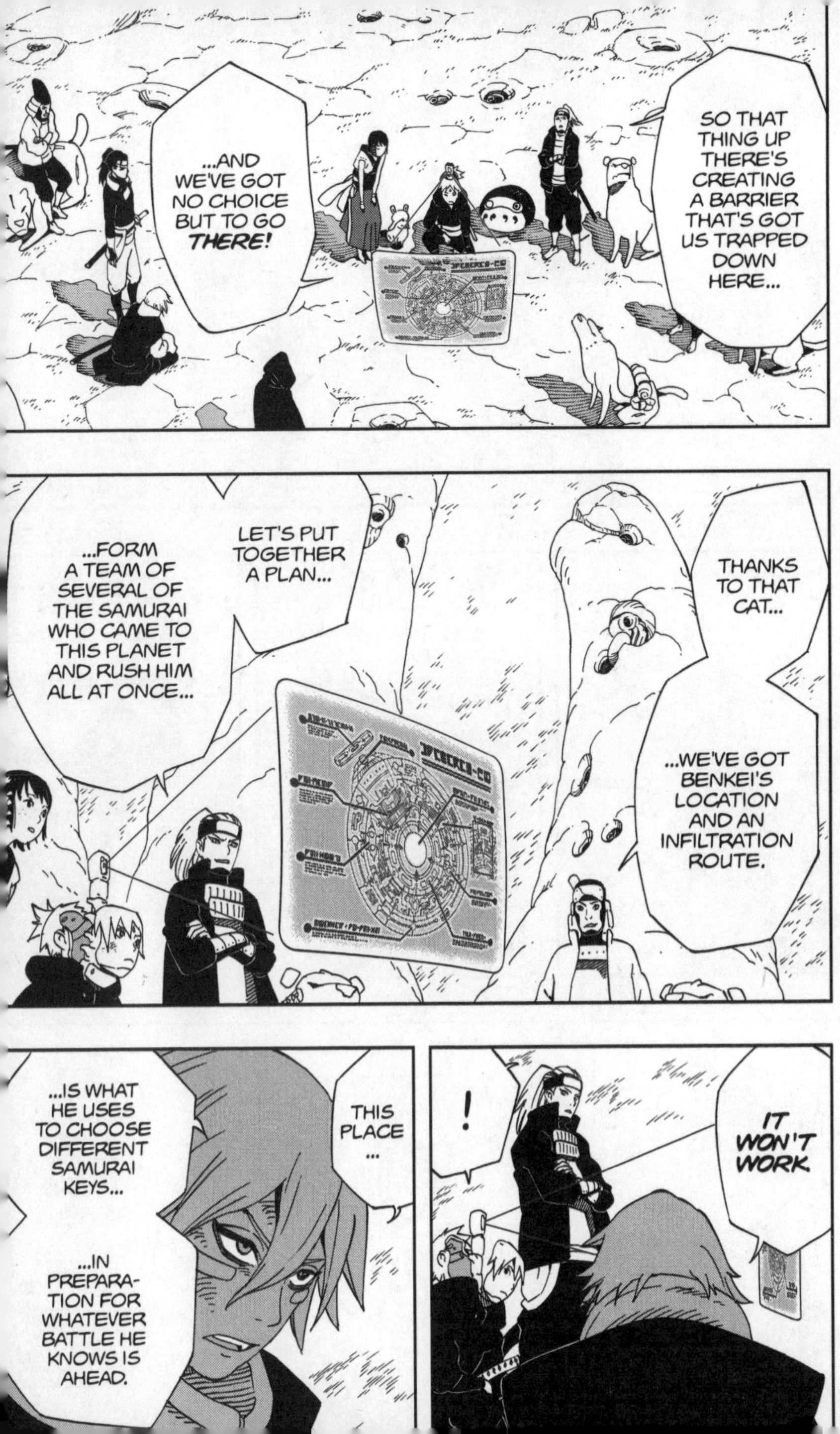
SO THAT THING UP THERE'S CREATING A BARRIER THAT'S GOT US TRAPPED DOWN HERE...
...AND WE'VE GOT NO CHOICE BUT TO GO *THERE!*
THANKS TO THAT CAT...
...WE'VE GOT BENKEI'S LOCATION AND AN INFILTRATION ROUTE.
LET'S PUT TOGETHER A PLAN...
...FORM A TEAM OF SEVERAL OF THE SAMURAI WHO CAME TO THIS PLANET AND RUSH HIM ALL AT ONCE...
IT WON'T WORK.
!
THIS PLACE ...
...IS WHAT HE USES TO CHOOSE DIFFERENT SAMURAI KEYS...
...IN PREPARATION FOR WHATEVER BATTLE HE KNOWS IS AHEAD.

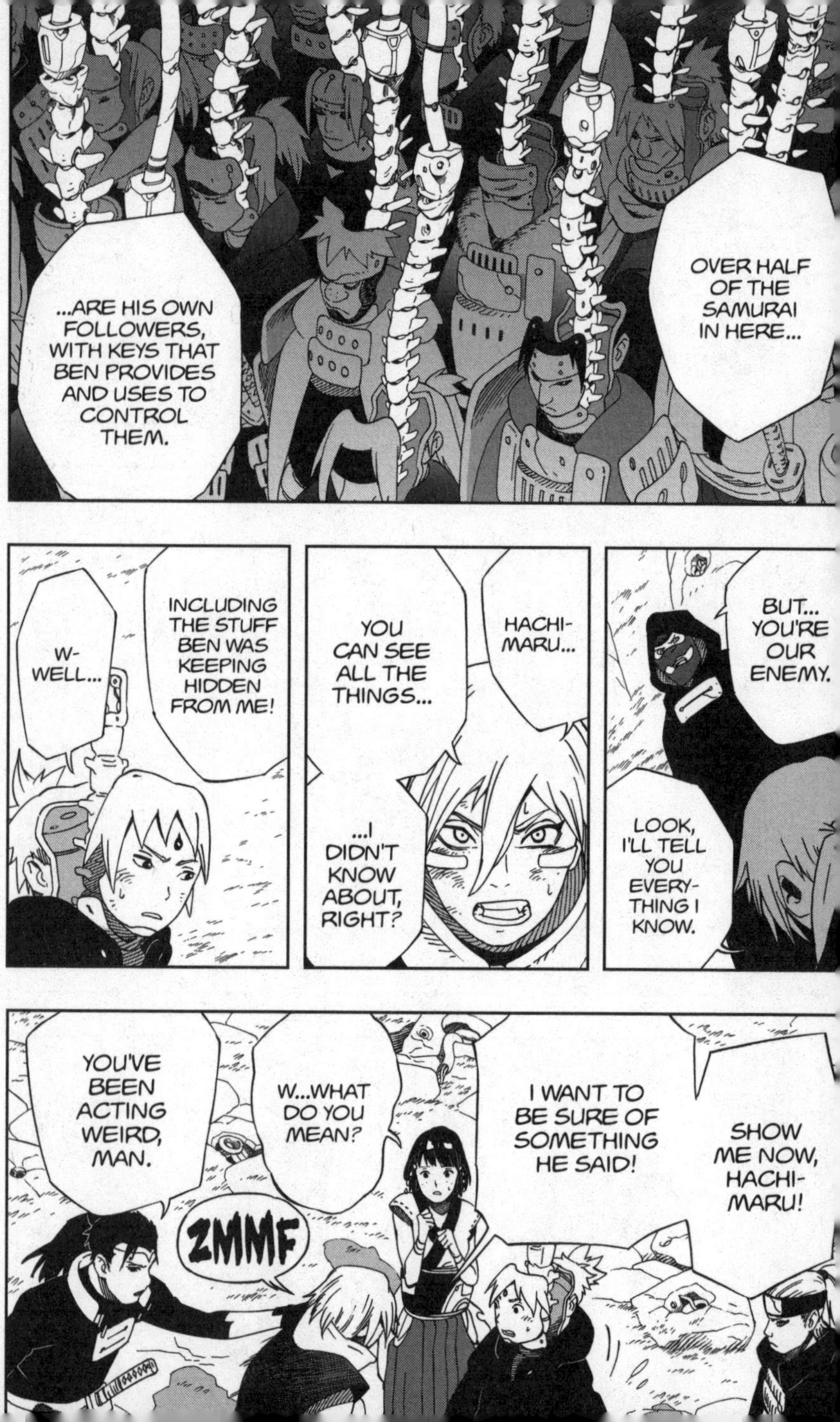
OVER HALF OF THE SAMURAI IN HERE...
...ARE HIS OWN FOLLOWERS, WITH KEYS THAT BEN PROVIDES AND USES TO CONTROL THEM.
BUT... YOU'RE OUR ENEMY.
LOOK, I'LL TELL YOU EVERY-THING I KNOW.
HACHI-MARU...
YOU CAN SEE ALL THE THINGS...
...I DIDN'T KNOW ABOUT, RIGHT?
INCLUDING THE STUFF BEN WAS KEEPING HIDDEN FROM ME!
W-WELL...
SHOW ME NOW, HACHI-MARU!
I WANT TO BE SURE OF SOMETHING HE SAID!
W...WHAT DO YOU MEAN?
YOU'VE BEEN ACTING WEIRD, MAN.
ZMMF

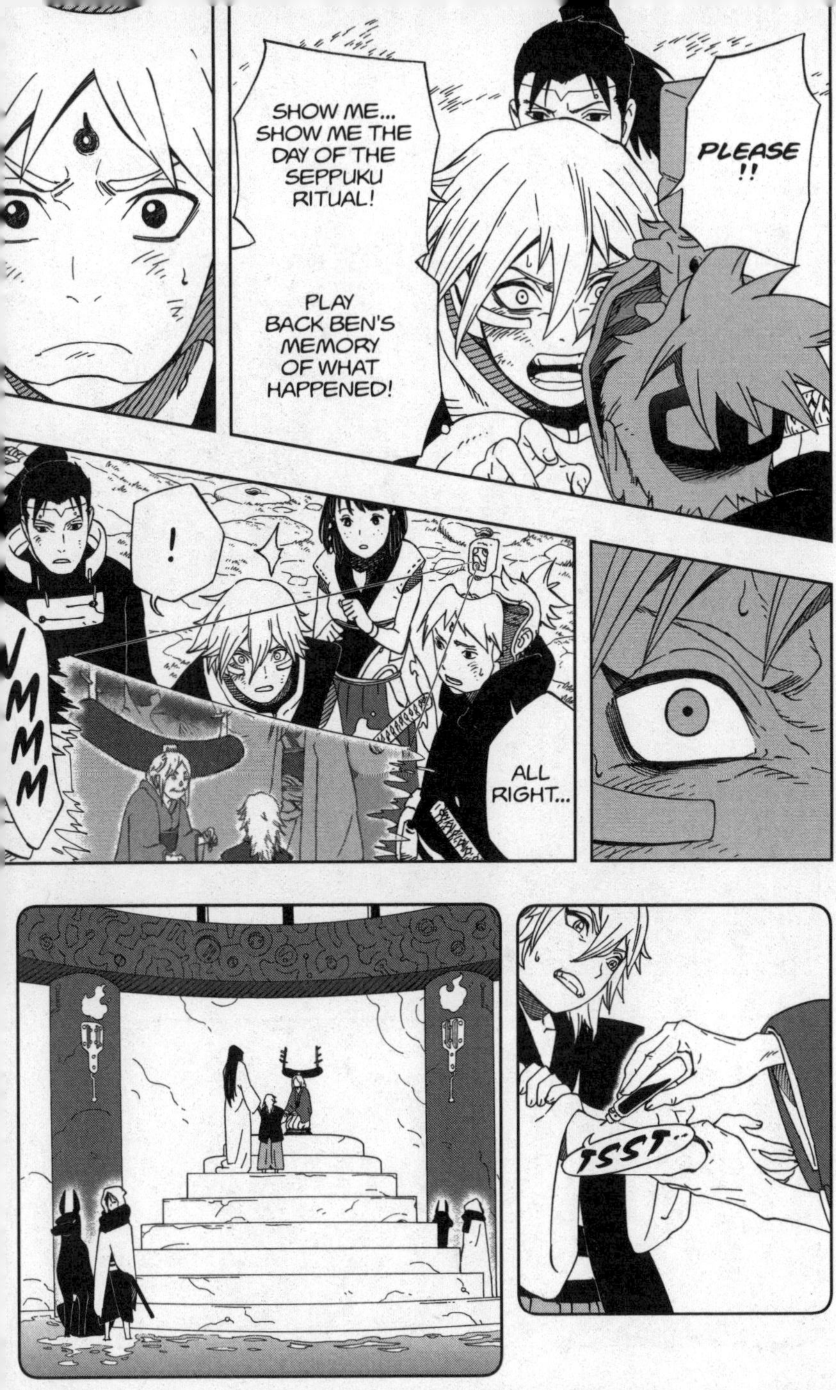
PLEASE !!
SHOW ME... SHOW ME THE DAY OF THE SEPPUKU RITUAL!
PLAY BACK BEN'S MEMORY OF WHAT HAPPENED!
ALL RIGHT...
!
VMMMM
TSST...

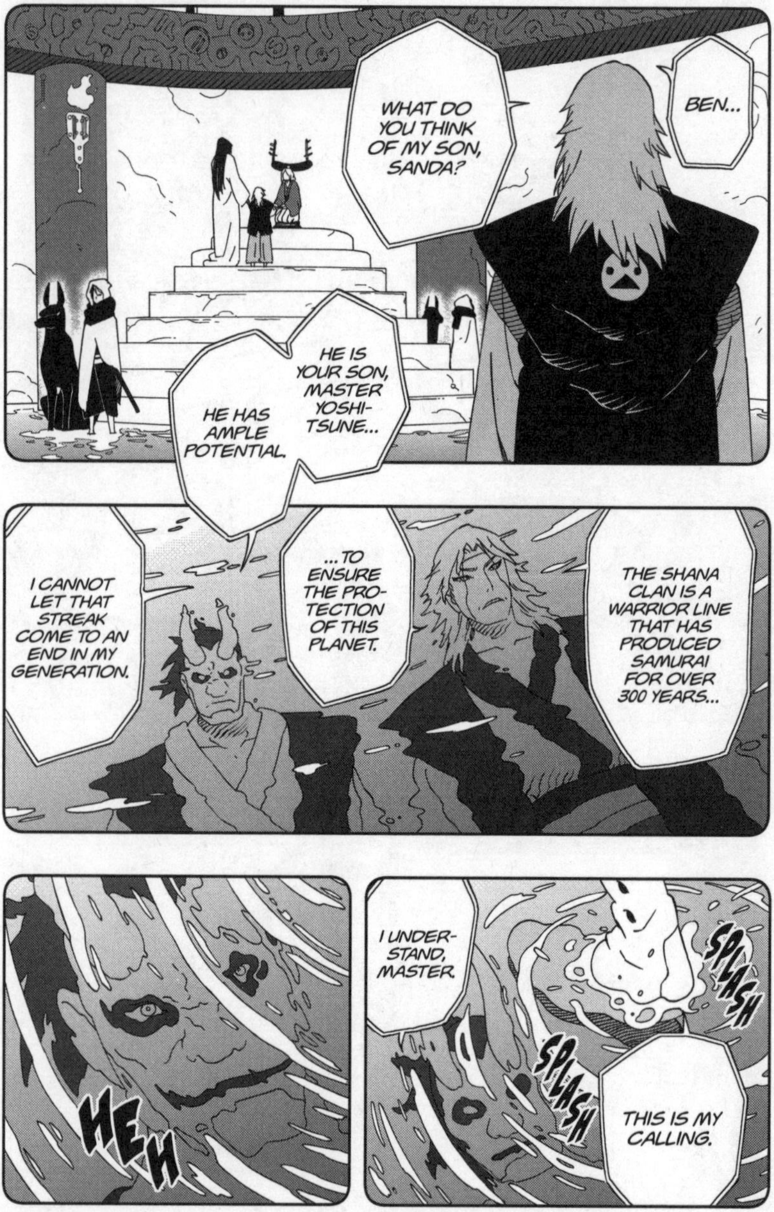
BEN...
WHAT DO YOU THINK OF MY SON, SANDA?
HE IS YOUR SON, MASTER YOSHI-TSUNE...
HE HAS AMPLE POTENTIAL.
THE SHANA CLAN IS A WARRIOR LINE THAT HAS PRODUCED SAMURAI FOR OVER 300 YEARS...
...TO ENSURE THE PRO-TECTION OF THIS PLANET.
I CANNOT LET THAT STREAK COME TO AN END IN MY GENERATION.
SPLASH
I UNDER-STAND, MASTER.
SPLASH
THIS IS MY CALLING.
HEH

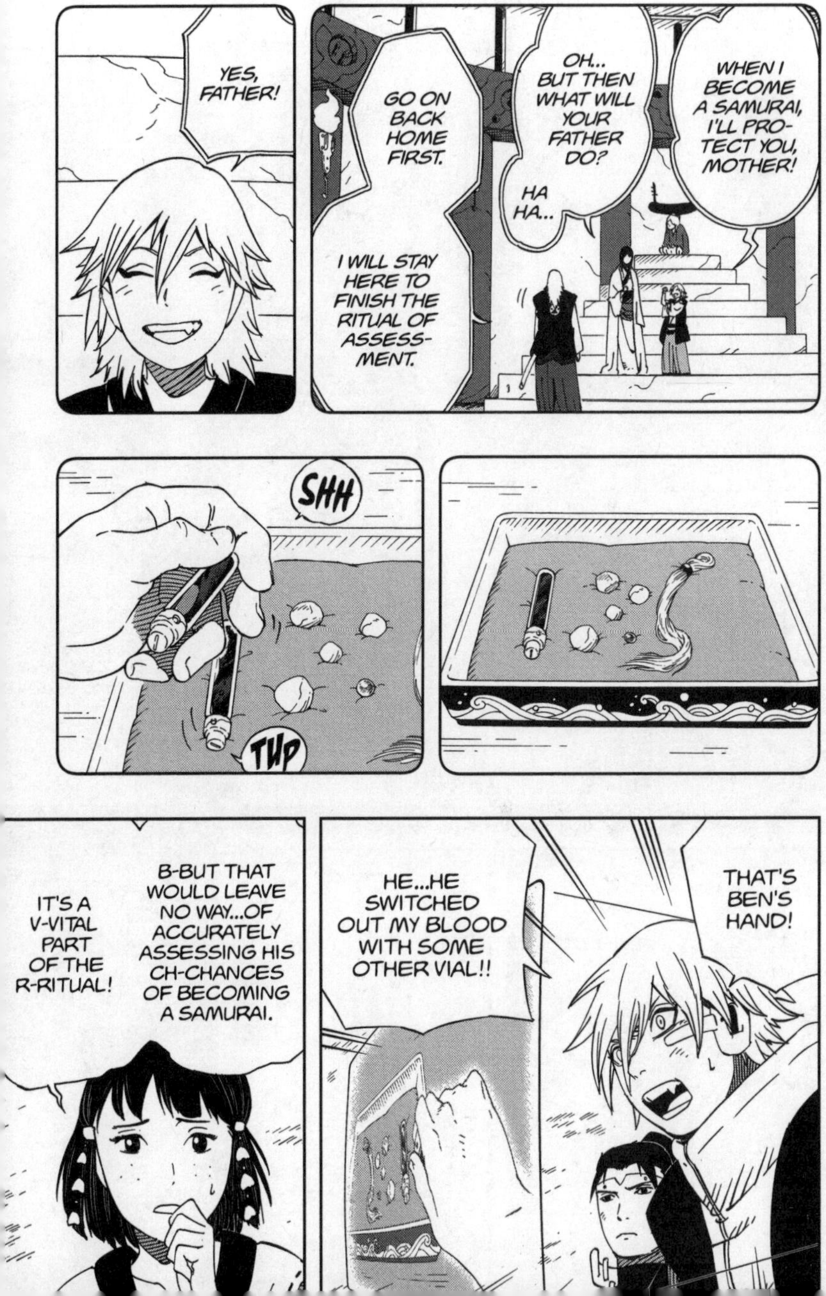
WHEN I BECOME A SAMURAI, I'LL PROTECT YOU, MOTHER!
OH... BUT THEN WHAT WILL YOUR FATHER DO?
HA HA...
GO ON BACK HOME FIRST.
I WILL STAY HERE TO FINISH THE RITUAL OF ASSESSMENT.
YES, FATHER!
SHH
THP
THAT'S BEN'S HAND!
HE...HE SWITCHED OUT MY BLOOD WITH SOME OTHER VIAL!!
B-BUT THAT WOULD LEAVE NO WAY...OF ACCURATELY ASSESSING HIS CH-CHANCES OF BECOMING A SAMURAI.
IT'S A V-VITAL PART OF THE R-RITUAL!

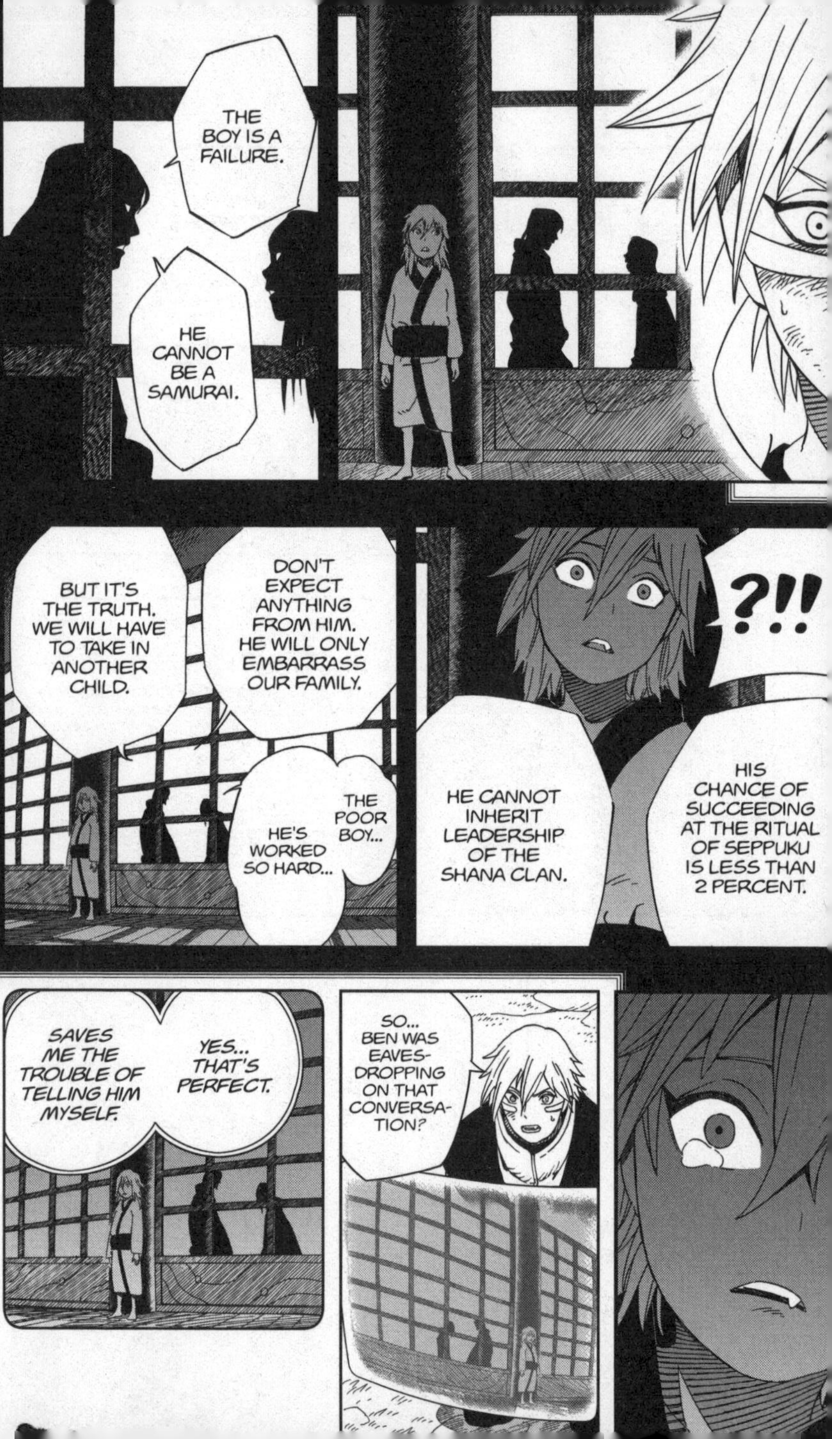
THE BOY IS A FAILURE.
HE CANNOT BE A SAMURAI.
?!!
HIS CHANCE OF SUCCEEDING AT THE RITUAL OF SEPPUKU IS LESS THAN 2 PERCENT.
HE CANNOT INHERIT LEADERSHIP OF THE SHANA CLAN.
DON'T EXPECT ANYTHING FROM HIM. HE WILL ONLY EMBARRASS OUR FAMILY.
BUT IT'S THE TRUTH. WE WILL HAVE TO TAKE IN ANOTHER CHILD.
THE POOR BOY...
HE'S WORKED SO HARD...
SO... BEN WAS EAVES-DROPPING ON THAT CONVERSA-TION?
YES... THAT'S PERFECT.
SAVES ME THE TROUBLE OF TELLING HIM MYSELF.

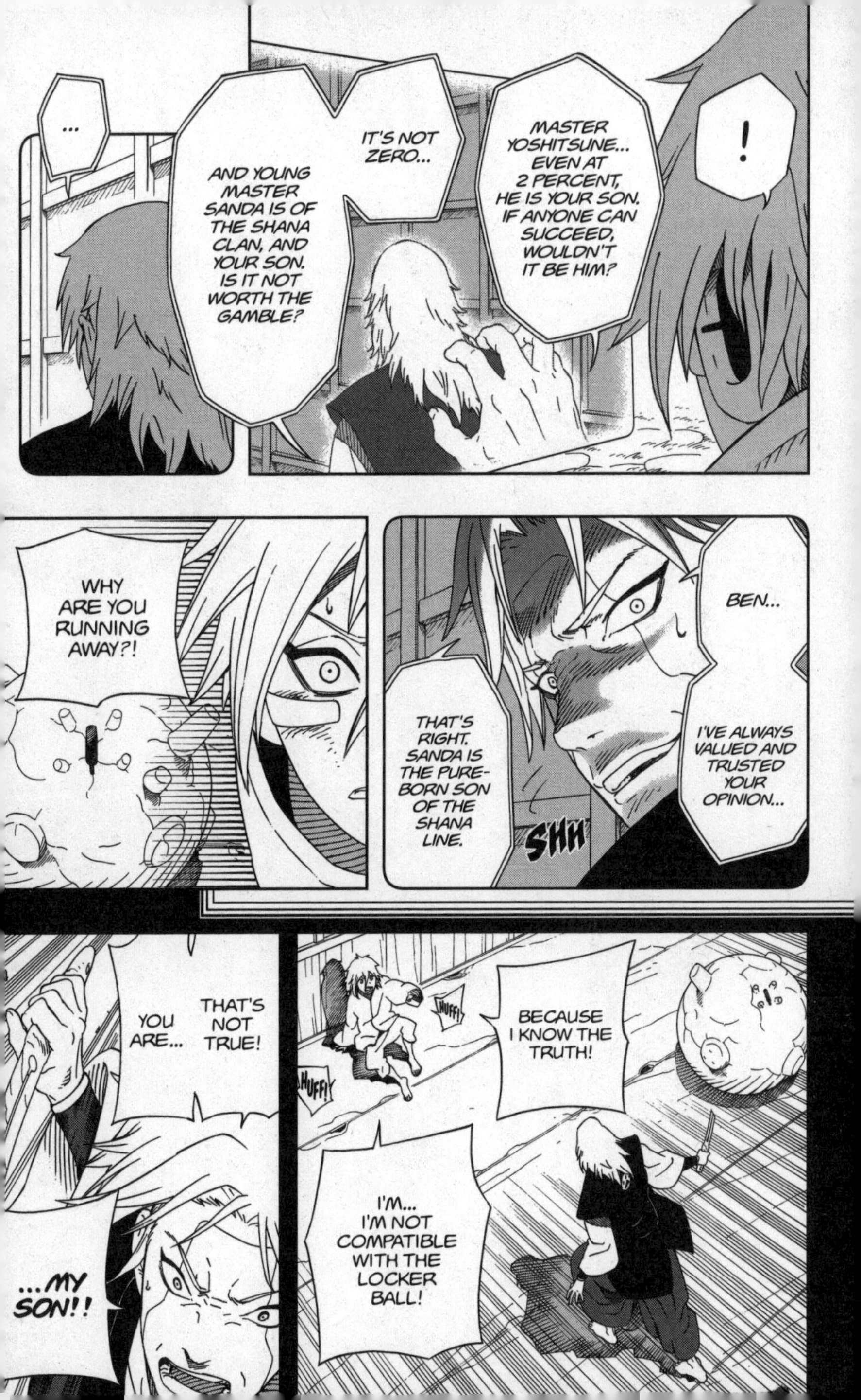
!
MASTER YOSHITSUNE... EVEN AT 2 PERCENT, HE IS YOUR SON. IF ANYONE CAN SUCCEED, WOULDN'T IT BE HIM?
IT'S NOT ZERO...
AND YOUNG MASTER SANDA IS OF THE SHANA CLAN, AND YOUR SON. IS IT NOT WORTH THE GAMBLE?
...
BEN...
I'VE ALWAYS VALUED AND TRUSTED YOUR OPINION...
THAT'S RIGHT. SANDA IS THE PURE-BORN SON OF THE SHANA LINE.
SHH
WHY ARE YOU RUNNING AWAY?!
BECAUSE I KNOW THE TRUTH!
HUFF!
HUFF!
I'M... I'M NOT COMPATIBLE WITH THE LOCKER BALL!
THAT'S NOT TRUE!
YOU ARE...
...MY SON!!

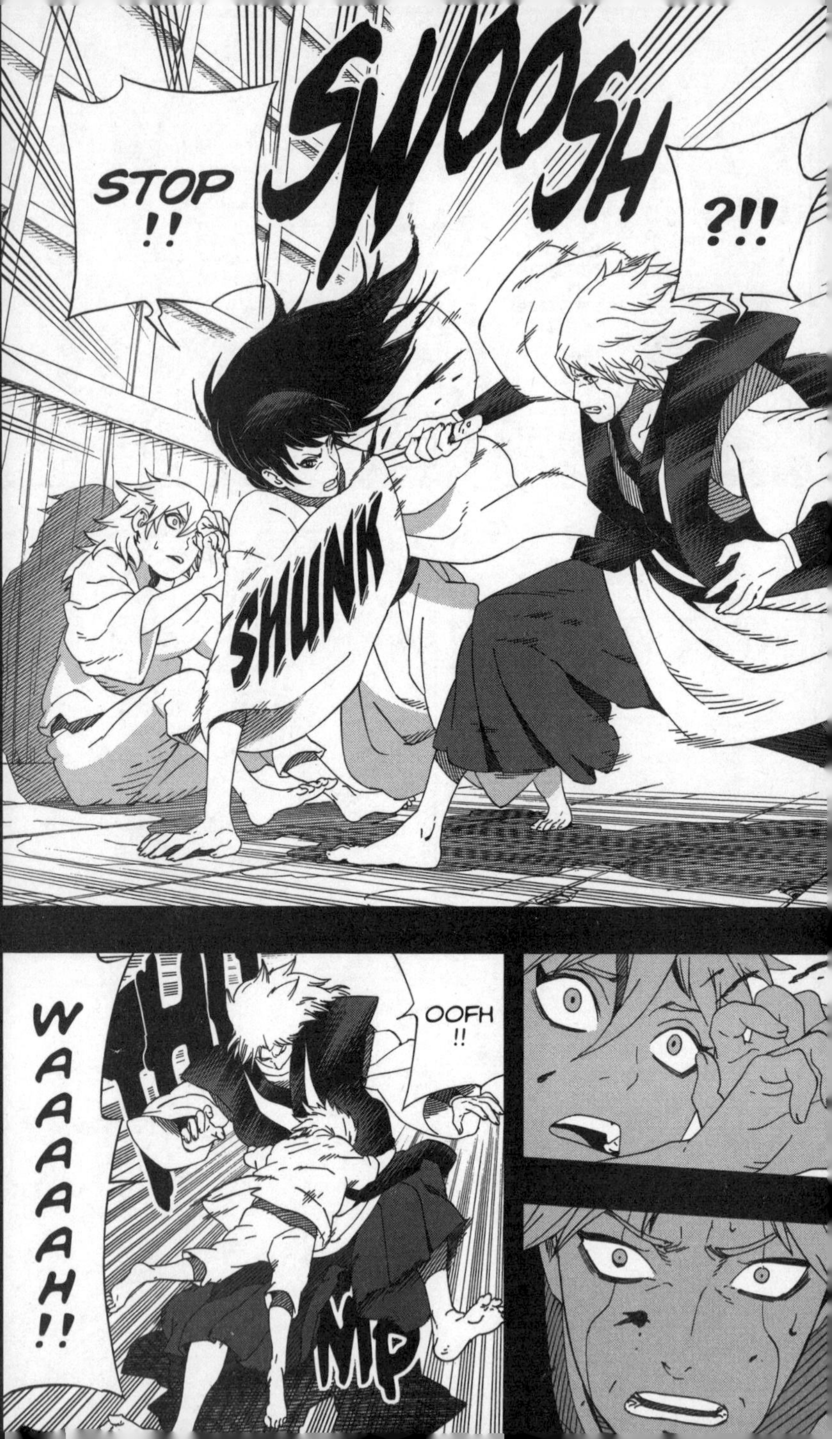
?!!
SWOOSH
SHUNK
STOP !!
OOFH !!
WAAAAAH!!

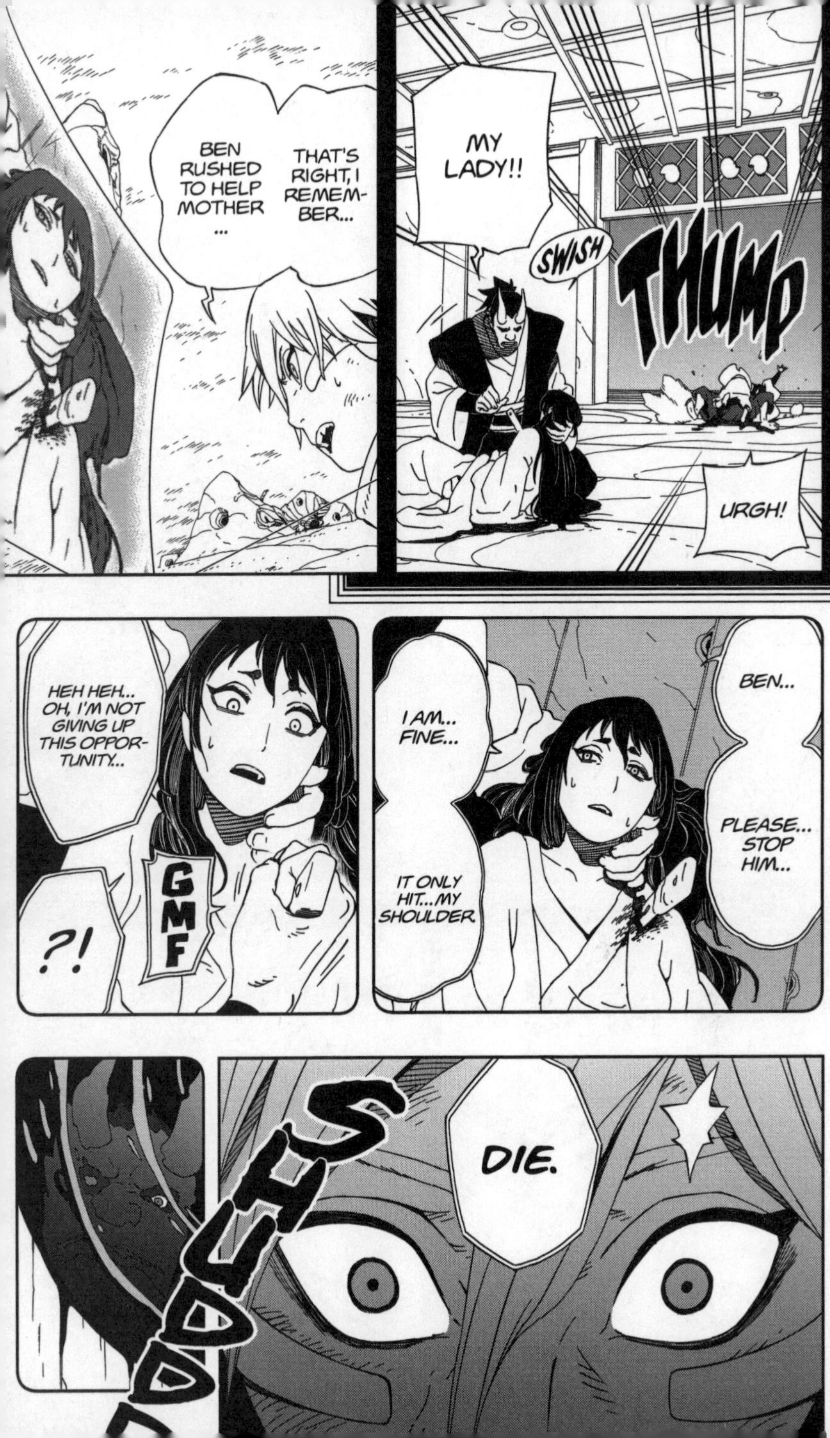
MY LADY!!
SWISH
THUMP
URGH!
THAT'S RIGHT, I REMEMBER...
BEN RUSHED TO HELP MOTHER ...
BEN... PLEASE... STOP HIM...
I AM... FINE...
IT ONLY HIT...MY SHOULDER
HEH HEH... OH, I'M NOT GIVING UP THIS OPPORTUNITY...
GMF
?!
DIE.
SHUDD

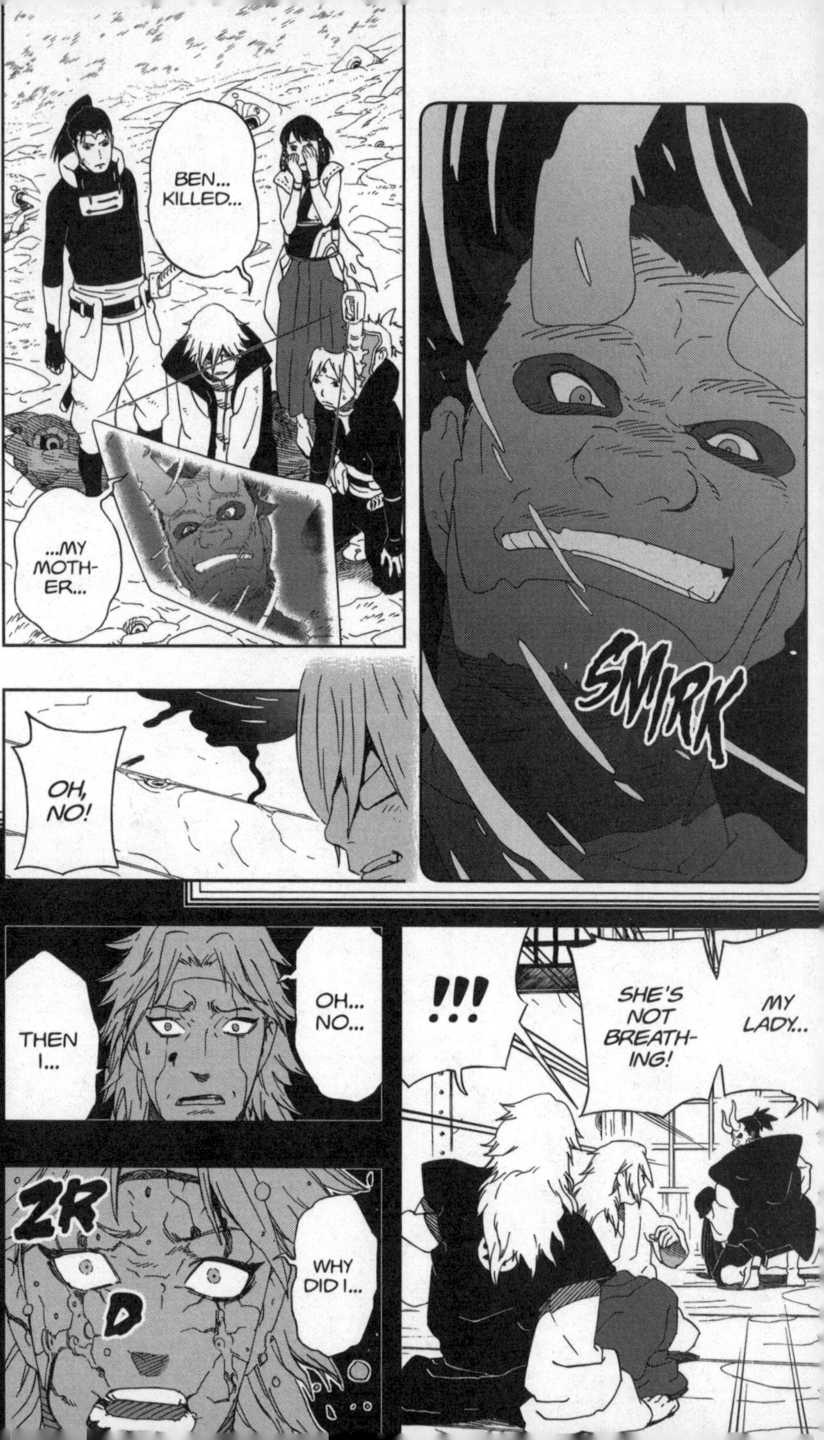
SMIRK
BEN... KILLED...
...MY MOTHER...
OH, NO!
MY LADY...
SHE'S NOT BREATHING!
!!!
OH... NO...
THEN I...
WHY DID I...
ZR D

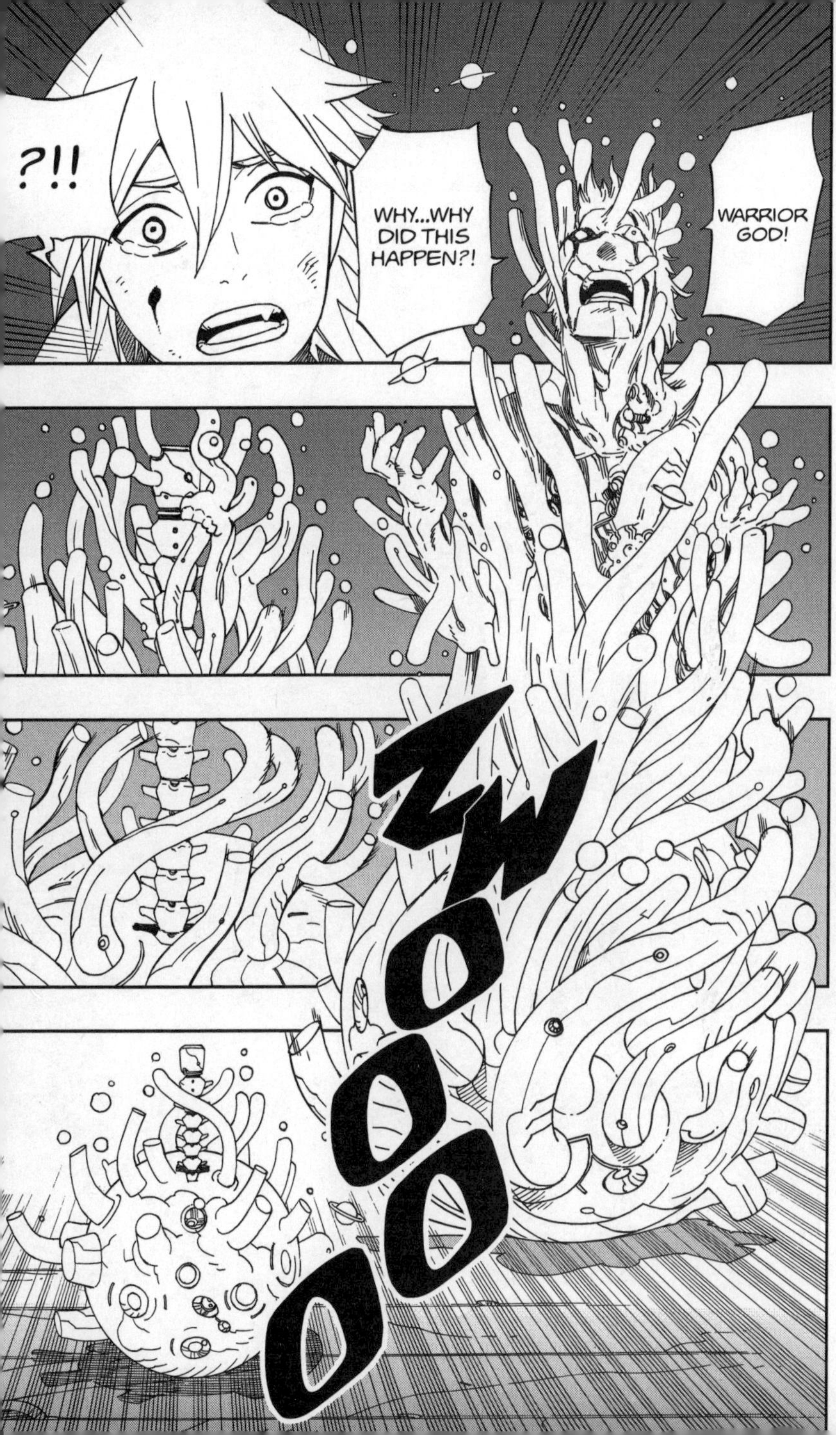
WARRIOR GOD!
WHY...WHY DID THIS HAPPEN?!
?!!
ZWOOOOOO

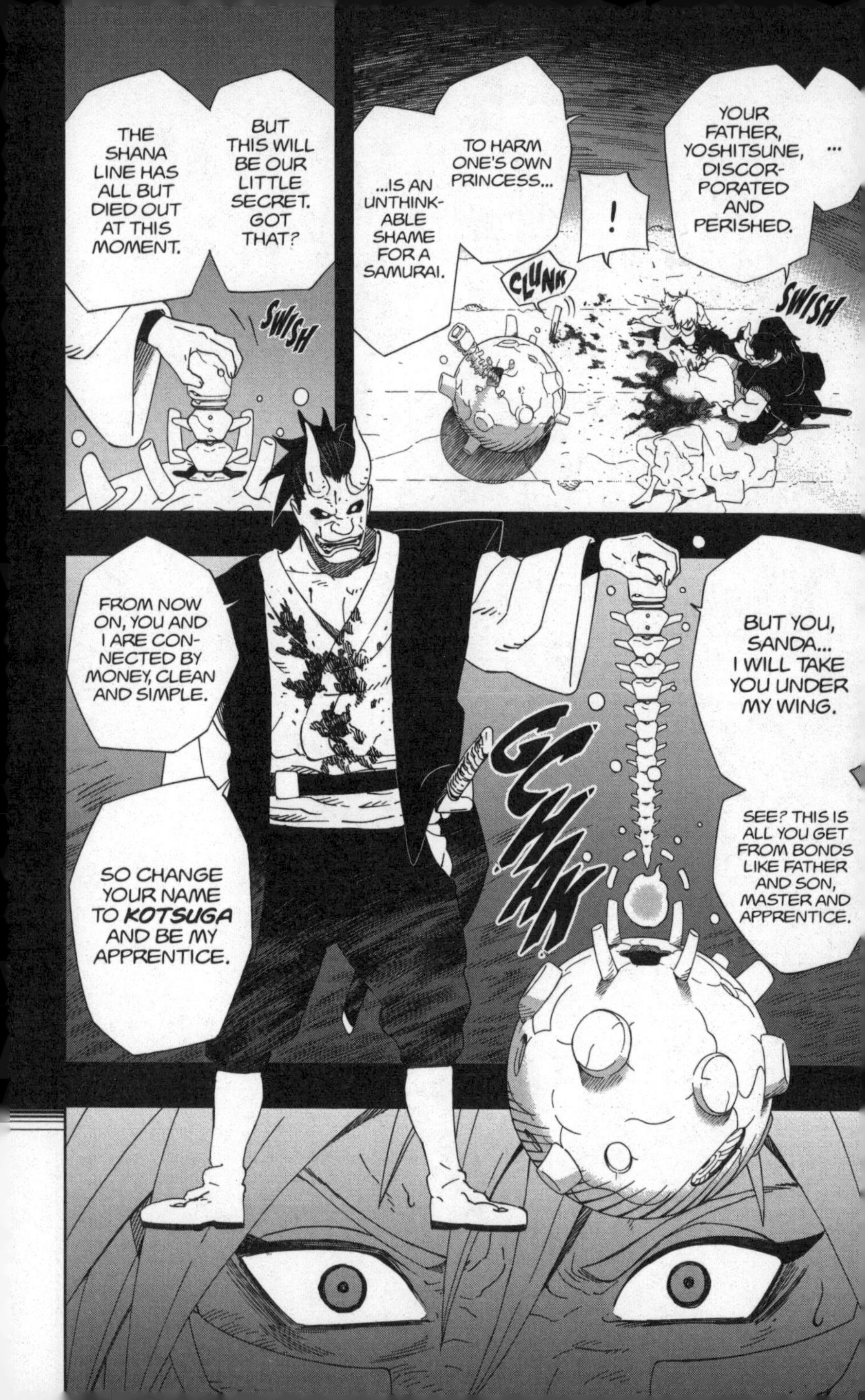
YOUR FATHER, YOSHITSUNE, DISCORPORATED AND PERISHED.
...
SWISH
!
CLUNK
TO HARM ONE'S OWN PRINCESS...
...IS AN UNTHINKABLE SHAME FOR A SAMURAI.
BUT THIS WILL BE OUR LITTLE SECRET. GOT THAT?
THE SHANA LINE HAS ALL BUT DIED OUT AT THIS MOMENT.
SWISH
BUT YOU, SANDA... I WILL TAKE YOU UNDER MY WING.
FROM NOW ON, YOU AND I ARE CONNECTED BY MONEY, CLEAN AND SIMPLE.
GCHAK
SEE? THIS IS ALL YOU GET FROM BONDS LIKE FATHER AND SON, MASTER AND APPRENTICE.
SO CHANGE YOUR NAME TO ***KOTSUGA*** AND BE MY APPRENTICE.

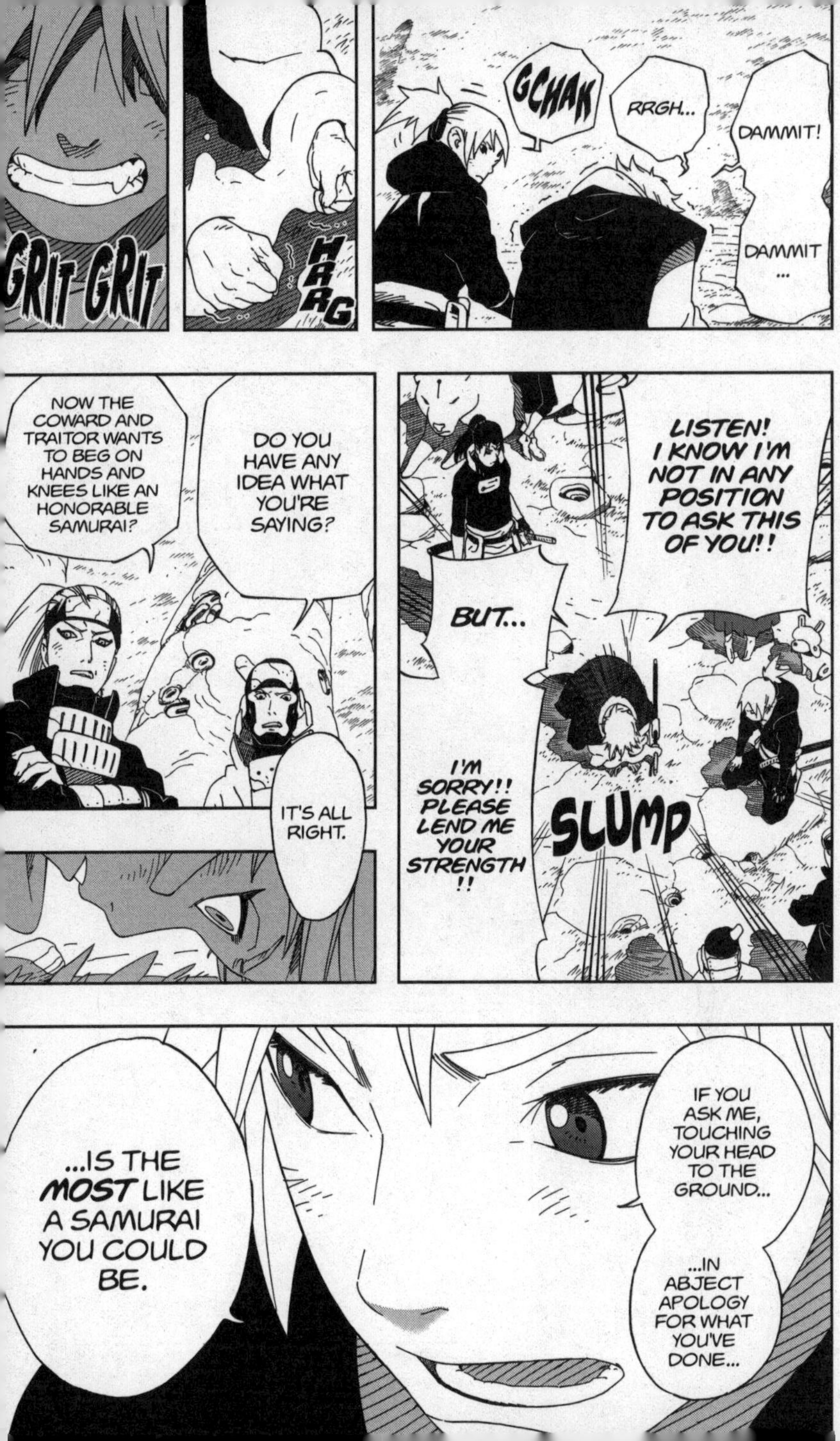
DAMMIT!
RRGH...
GCHAK
DAMMIT ...
HRRG
GRIT GRIT
LISTEN! I KNOW I'M NOT IN ANY POSITION TO ASK THIS OF YOU!!
BUT...
SLUMP
I'M SORRY!! PLEASE LEND ME YOUR STRENGTH!!
DO YOU HAVE ANY IDEA WHAT YOU'RE SAYING?
NOW THE COWARD AND TRAITOR WANTS TO BEG ON HANDS AND KNEES LIKE AN HONORABLE SAMURAI?
IT'S ALL RIGHT.
IF YOU ASK ME, TOUCHING YOUR HEAD TO THE GROUND...
...IN ABJECT APOLOGY FOR WHAT YOU'VE DONE...
...IS THE MOST LIKE A SAMURAI YOU COULD BE.

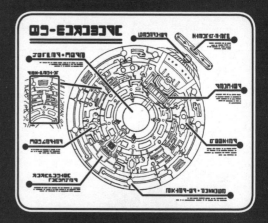

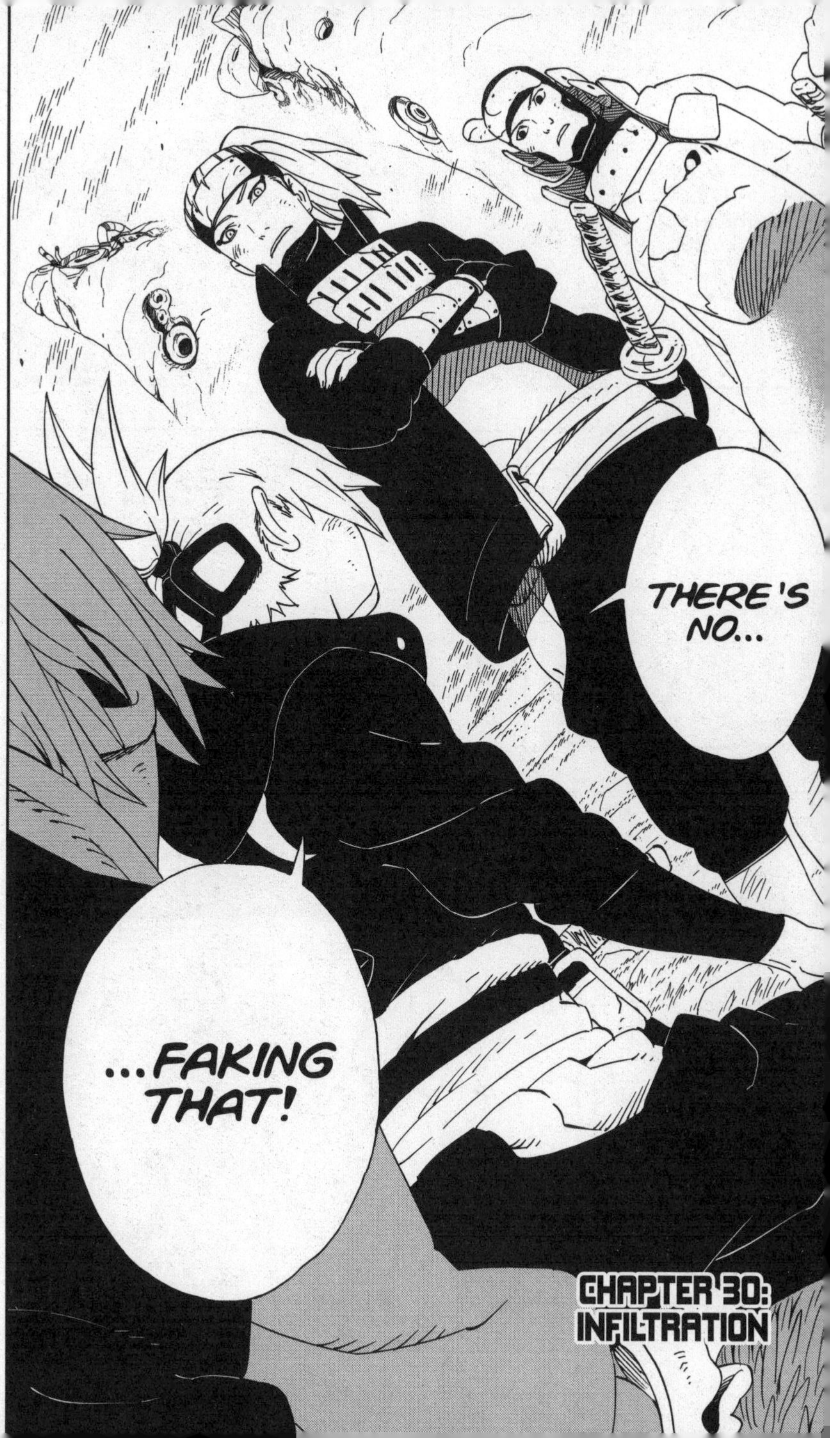

THERE'S NO...
...FAKING THAT!
CHAPTER 30: INFILTRATION

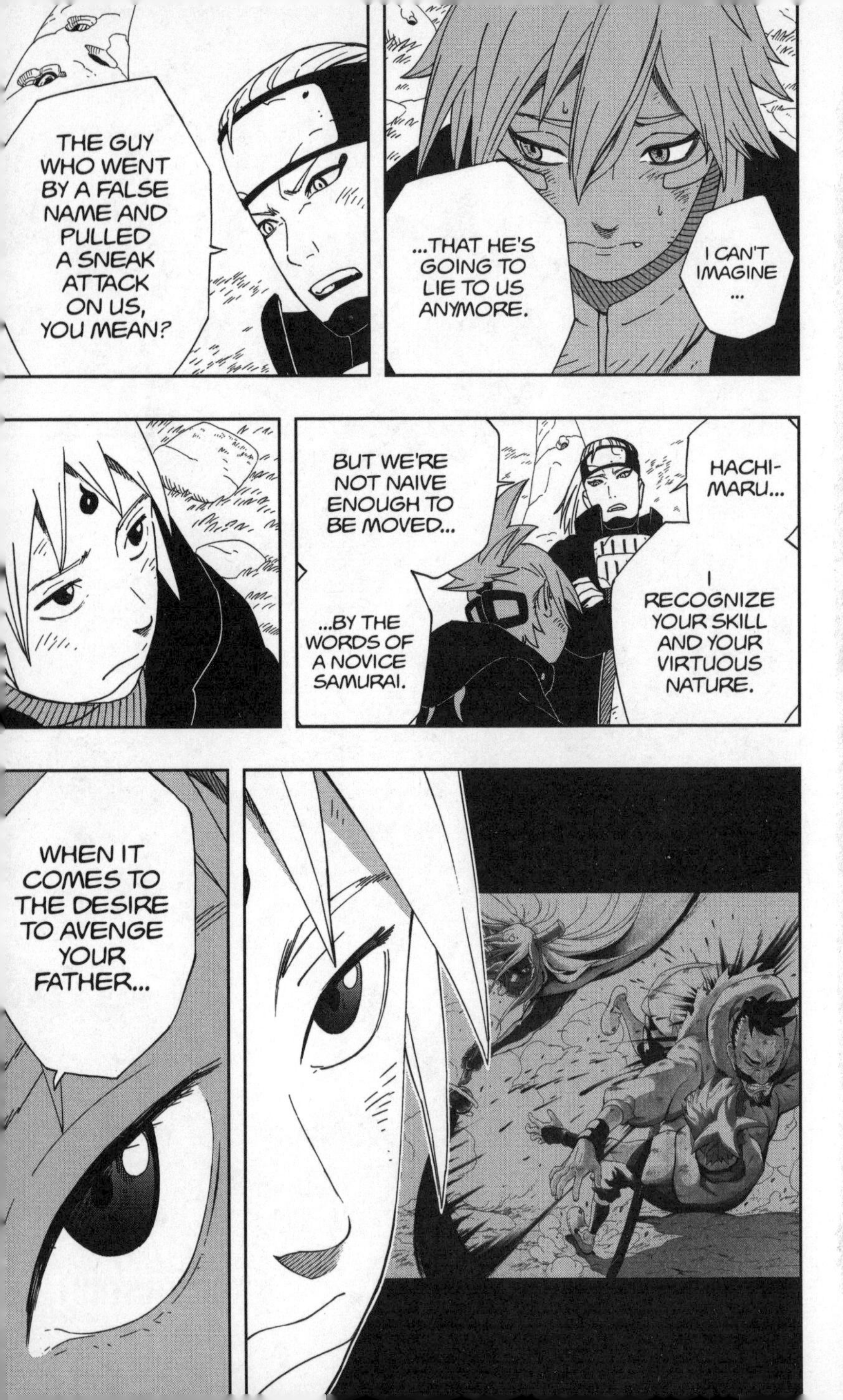
I CAN'T IMAGINE ...
...THAT HE'S GOING TO LIE TO US ANYMORE.
THE GUY WHO WENT BY A FALSE NAME AND PULLED A SNEAK ATTACK ON US, YOU MEAN?
HACHI-MARU...
I RECOGNIZE YOUR SKILL AND YOUR VIRTUOUS NATURE.
BUT WE'RE NOT NAIVE ENOUGH TO BE MOVED...
...BY THE WORDS OF A NOVICE SAMURAI.
WHEN IT COMES TO THE DESIRE TO AVENGE YOUR FATHER...

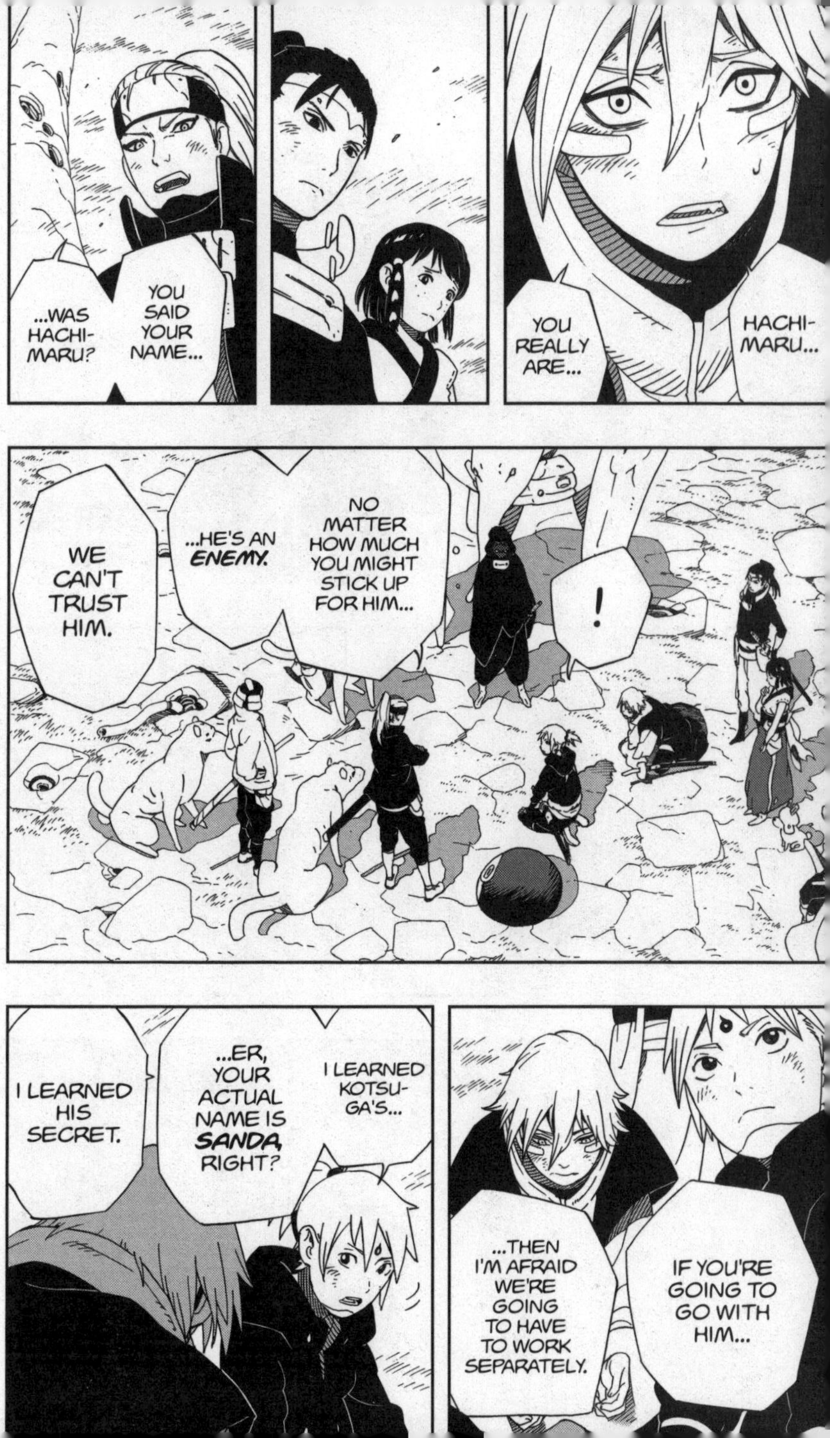
HACHI-MARU...
YOU REALLY ARE...
YOU SAID YOUR NAME...
...WAS HACHI-MARU?
!
NO MATTER HOW MUCH YOU MIGHT STICK UP FOR HIM...
...HE'S AN *ENEMY.*
WE CAN'T TRUST HIM.
IF YOU'RE GOING TO GO WITH HIM...
...THEN I'M AFRAID WE'RE GOING TO HAVE TO WORK SEPARATELY.
I LEARNED KOTSUGA'S...
...ER, YOUR ACTUAL NAME IS *SANDA,* RIGHT?
I LEARNED HIS SECRET.

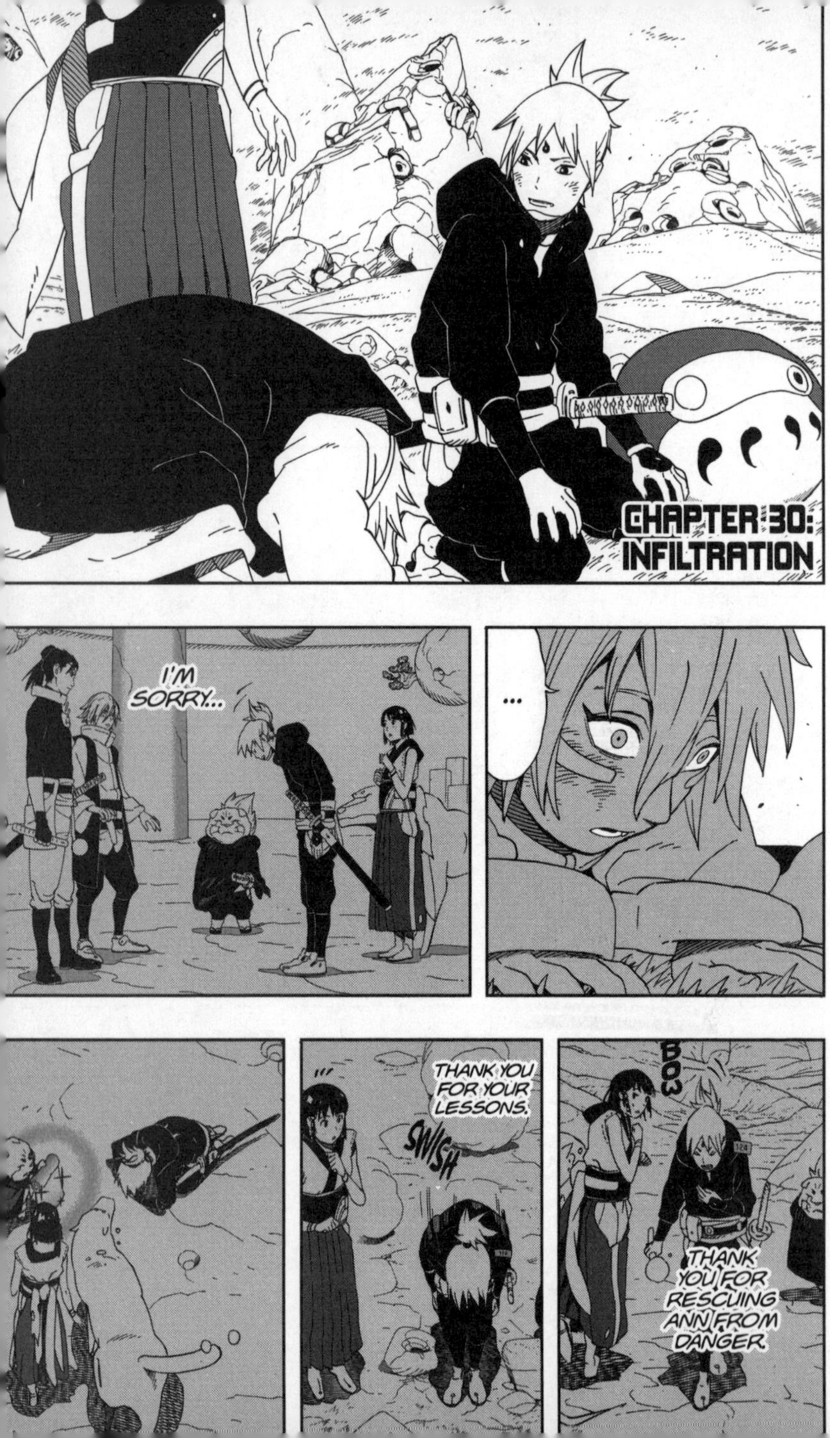
CHAPTER 30:
INFILTRATION
...
I'M SORRY...
THANK YOU FOR RESCUING ANN FROM DANGER.
THANK YOU FOR YOUR LESSONS.
SWISH

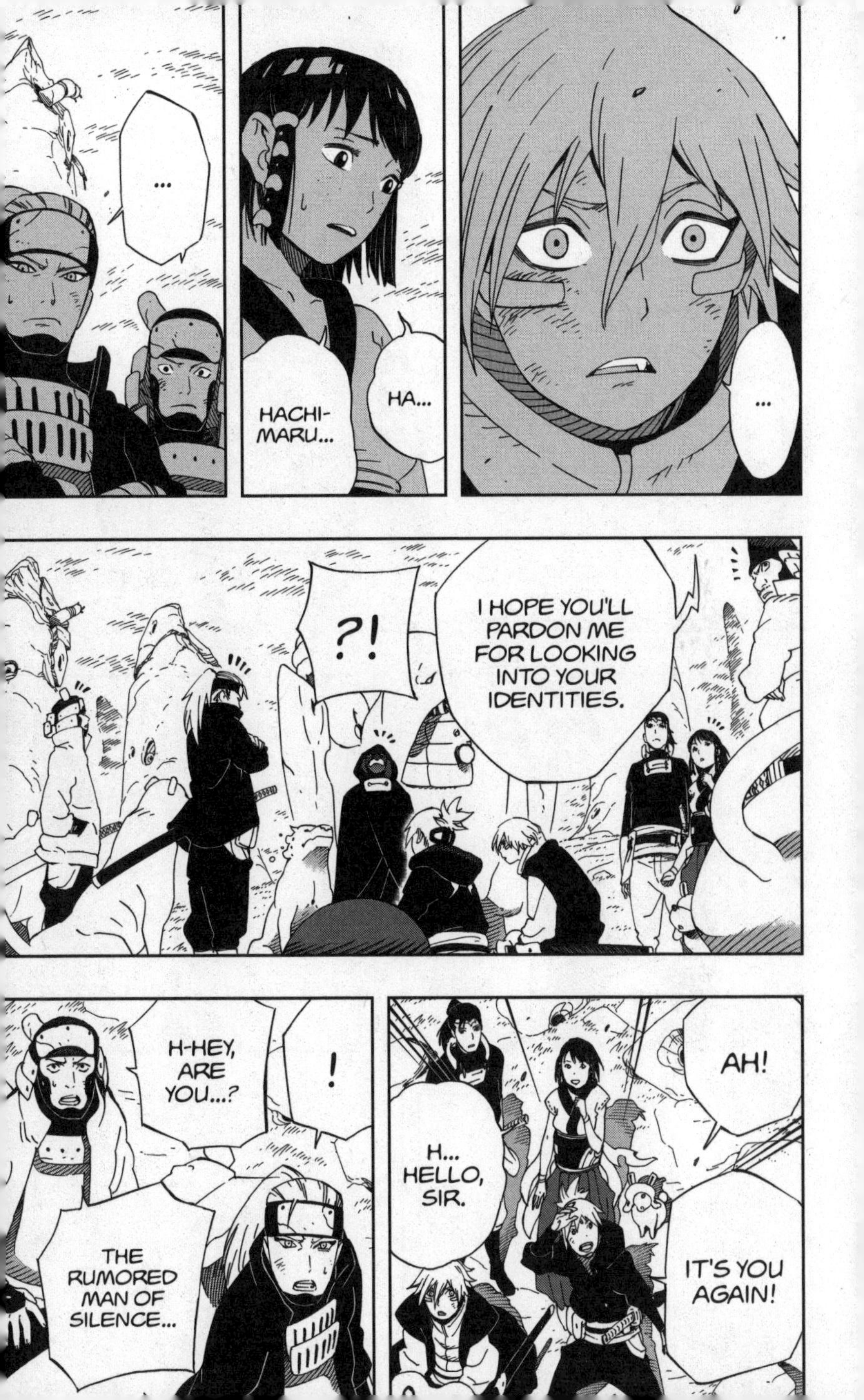
...
HA...
HACHI-MARU...
...
I HOPE YOU'LL PARDON ME FOR LOOKING INTO YOUR IDENTITIES.
?!
AH!
H... HELLO, SIR.
IT'S YOU AGAIN!
!
H-HEY, ARE YOU...?
THE RUMORED MAN OF SILENCE...

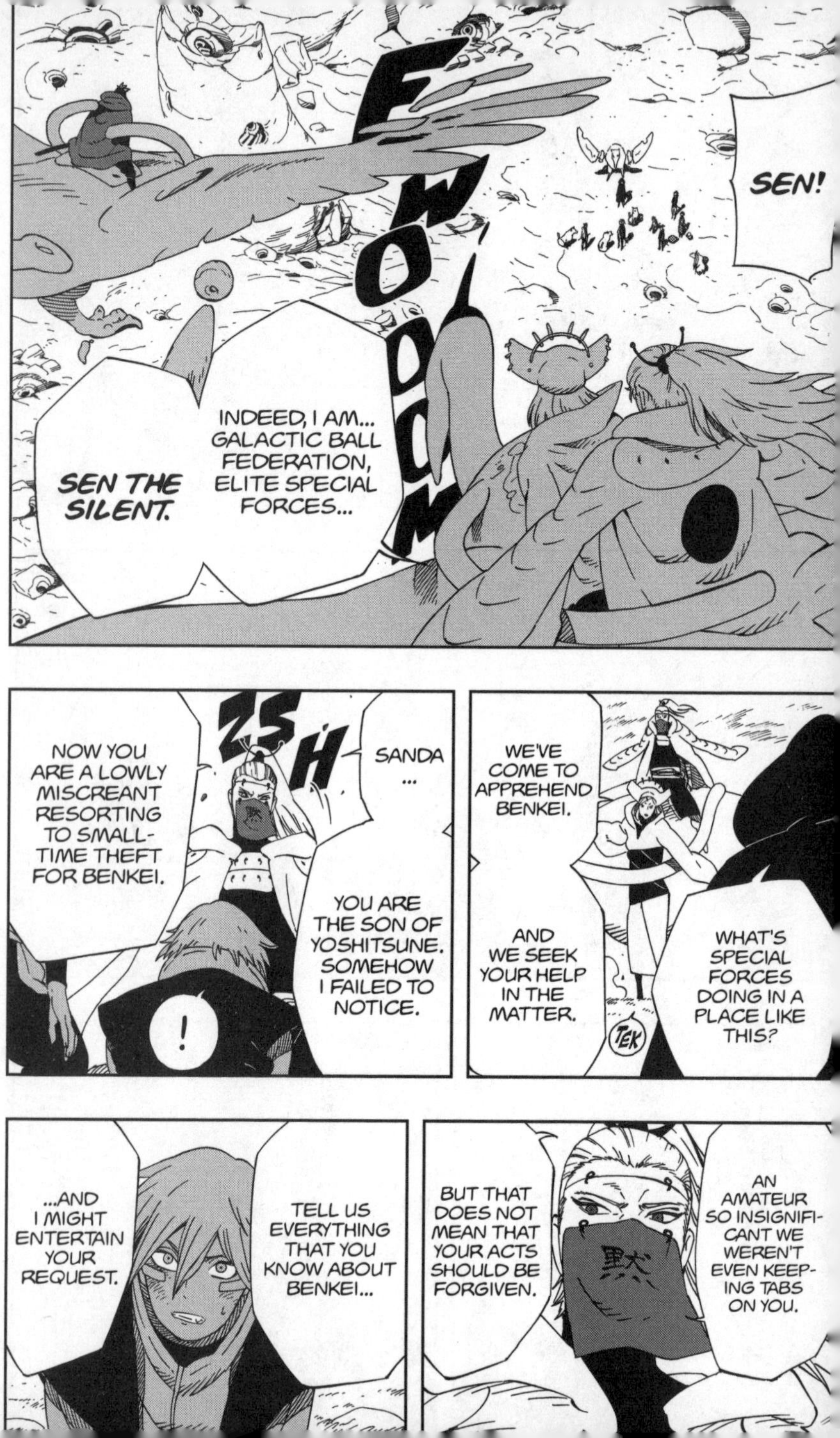
SEN!
FWOOOM
INDEED, I AM... GALACTIC BALL FEDERATION, ELITE SPECIAL FORCES...
SEN THE SILENT.
WHAT'S SPECIAL FORCES DOING IN A PLACE LIKE THIS?
WE'VE COME TO APPREHEND BENKEI.
AND WE SEEK YOUR HELP IN THE MATTER.
TEK
SANDA ...
YOU ARE THE SON OF YOSHITSUNE. SOMEHOW I FAILED TO NOTICE.
ZSH
NOW YOU ARE A LOWLY MISCREANT RESORTING TO SMALL-TIME THEFT FOR BENKEI.
!
AN AMATEUR SO INSIGNIFICANT WE WEREN'T EVEN KEEPING TABS ON YOU.
BUT THAT DOES NOT MEAN THAT YOUR ACTS SHOULD BE FORGIVEN.
TELL US EVERYTHING THAT YOU KNOW ABOUT BENKEI...
...AND I MIGHT ENTERTAIN YOUR REQUEST.

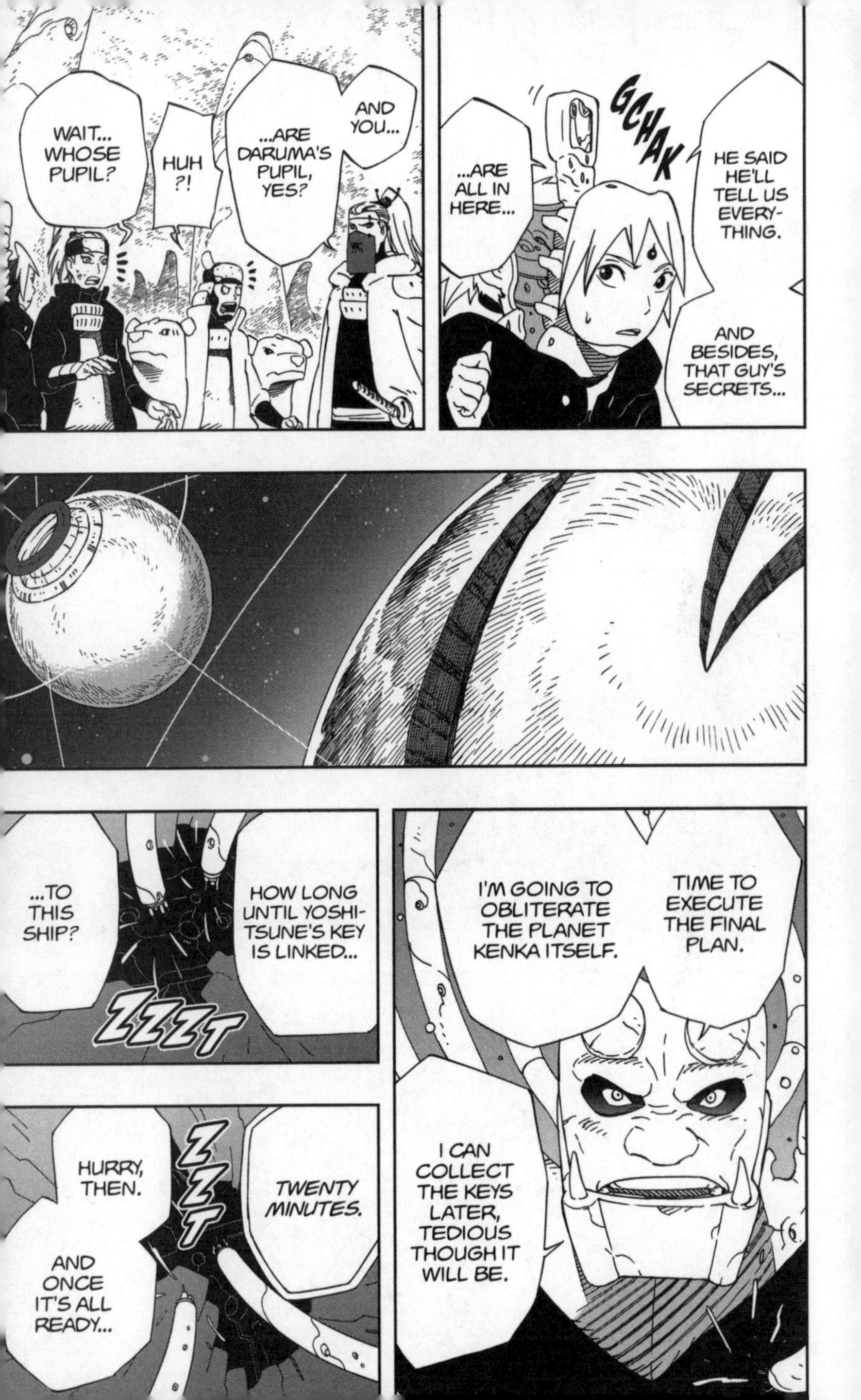
HE SAID HE'LL TELL US EVERY-THING.
GCHAK
AND BESIDES, THAT GUY'S SECRETS...
...ARE ALL IN HERE...
AND YOU...
...ARE DARUMA'S PUPIL, YES?
HUH ?!
WAIT... WHOSE PUPIL?
TIME TO EXECUTE THE FINAL PLAN.
I'M GOING TO OBLITERATE THE PLANET KENKA ITSELF.
I CAN COLLECT THE KEYS LATER, TEDIOUS THOUGH IT WILL BE.
HOW LONG UNTIL YOSHI-TSUNE'S KEY IS LINKED...
...TO THIS SHIP?
ZZZT
TWENTY MINUTES.
ZZZT
HURRY, THEN.
AND ONCE IT'S ALL READY...

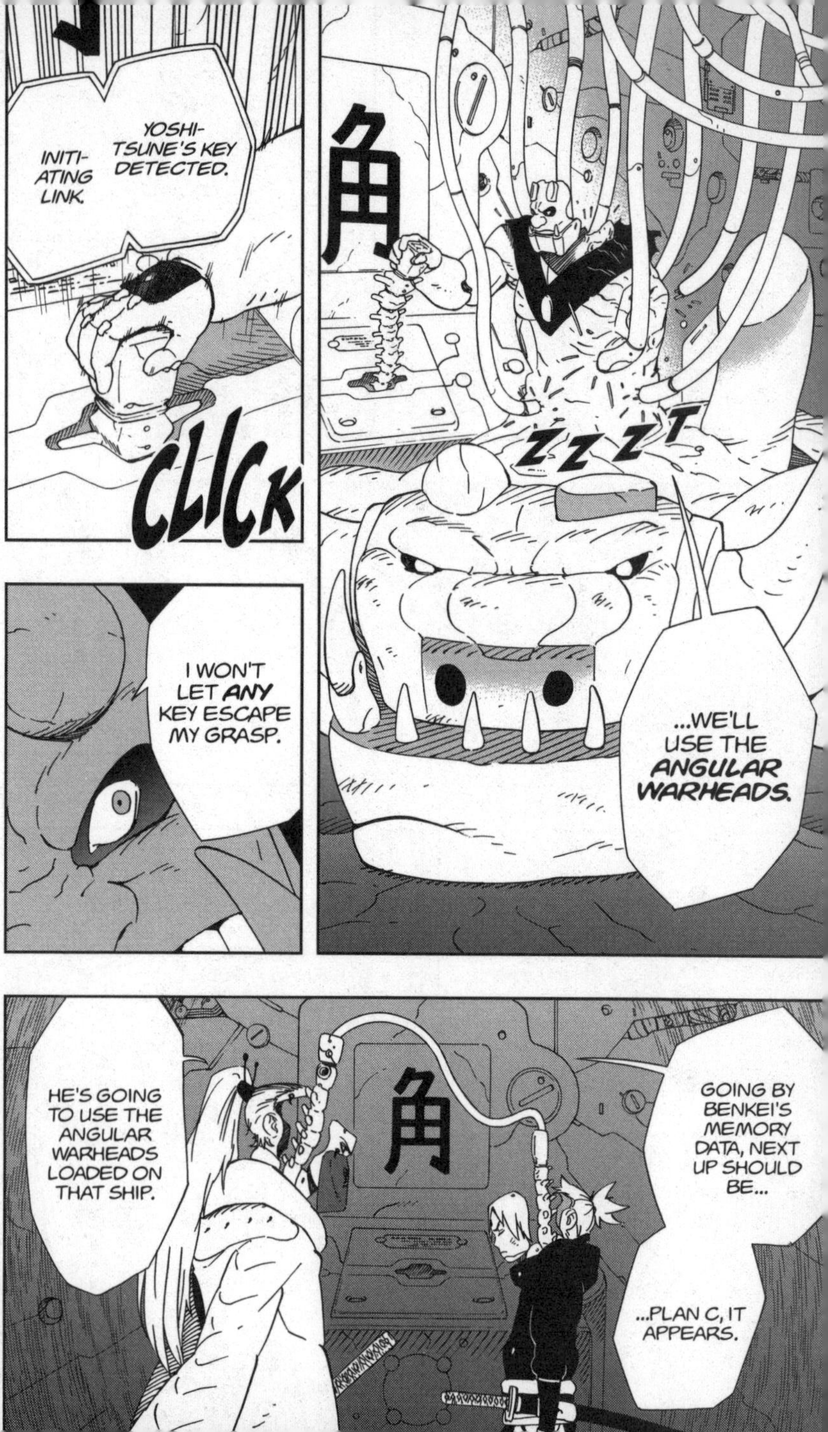
角
ZZZZT
...WE'LL USE THE ANGULAR WARHEADS.
YOSHI-TSUNE'S KEY DETECTED.
INITI-ATING LINK.
CLICK
I WON'T LET ANY KEY ESCAPE MY GRASP.
GOING BY BENKEI'S MEMORY DATA, NEXT UP SHOULD BE...
...PLAN C, IT APPEARS.
角
HE'S GOING TO USE THE ANGULAR WARHEADS LOADED ON THAT SHIP.

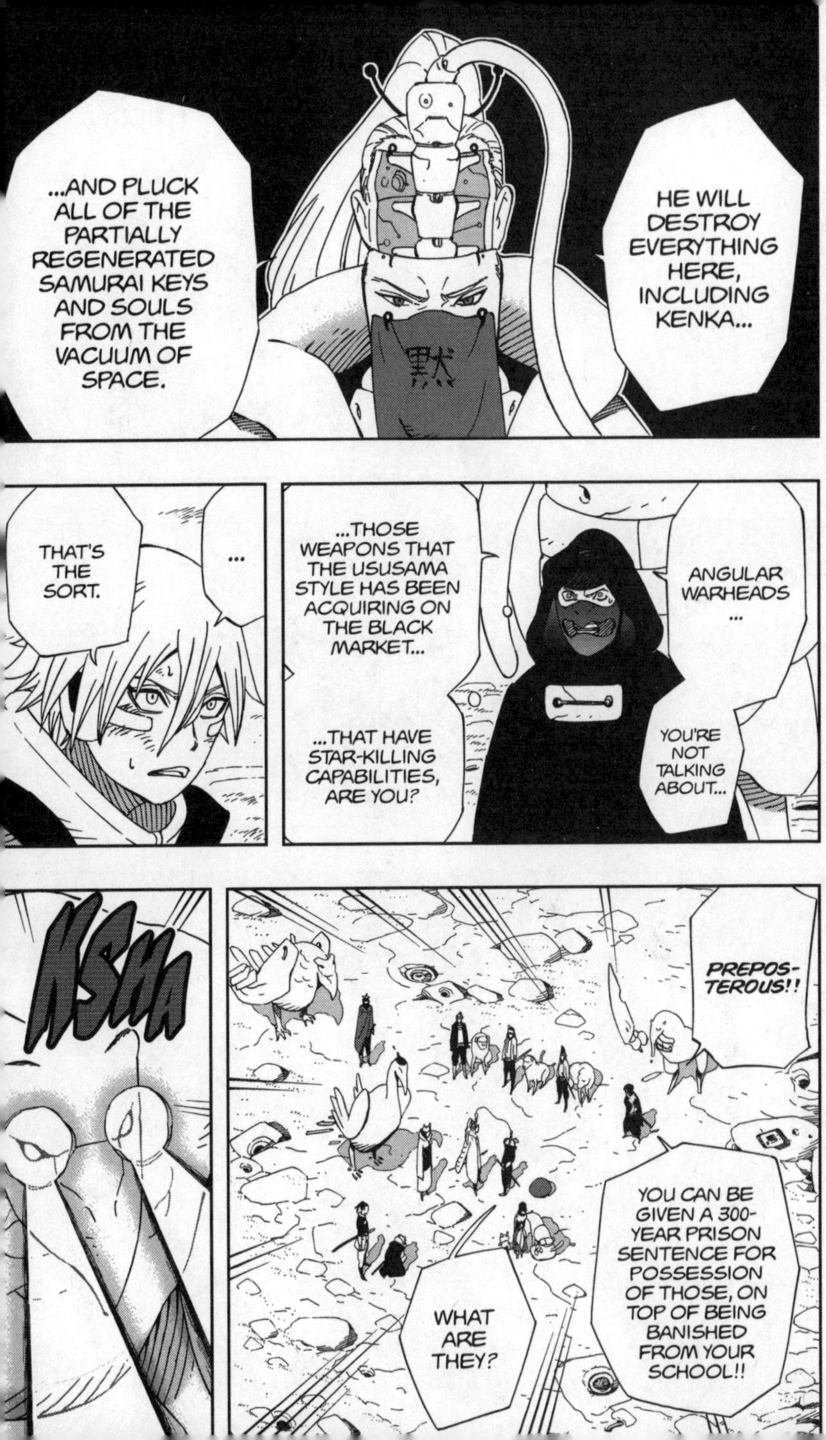
HE WILL DESTROY EVERYTHING HERE, INCLUDING KENKA...
...AND PLUCK ALL OF THE PARTIALLY REGENERATED SAMURAI KEYS AND SOULS FROM THE VACUUM OF SPACE.
ANGULAR WARHEADS ...
...THOSE WEAPONS THAT THE USUSAMA STYLE HAS BEEN ACQUIRING ON THE BLACK MARKET...
YOU'RE NOT TALKING ABOUT...
...THAT HAVE STAR-KILLING CAPABILITIES, ARE YOU?
...
THAT'S THE SORT.
PREPOSTEROUS!!
YOU CAN BE GIVEN A 300-YEAR PRISON SENTENCE FOR POSSESSION OF THOSE, ON TOP OF BEING BANISHED FROM YOUR SCHOOL!!
WHAT ARE THEY?
KSHA

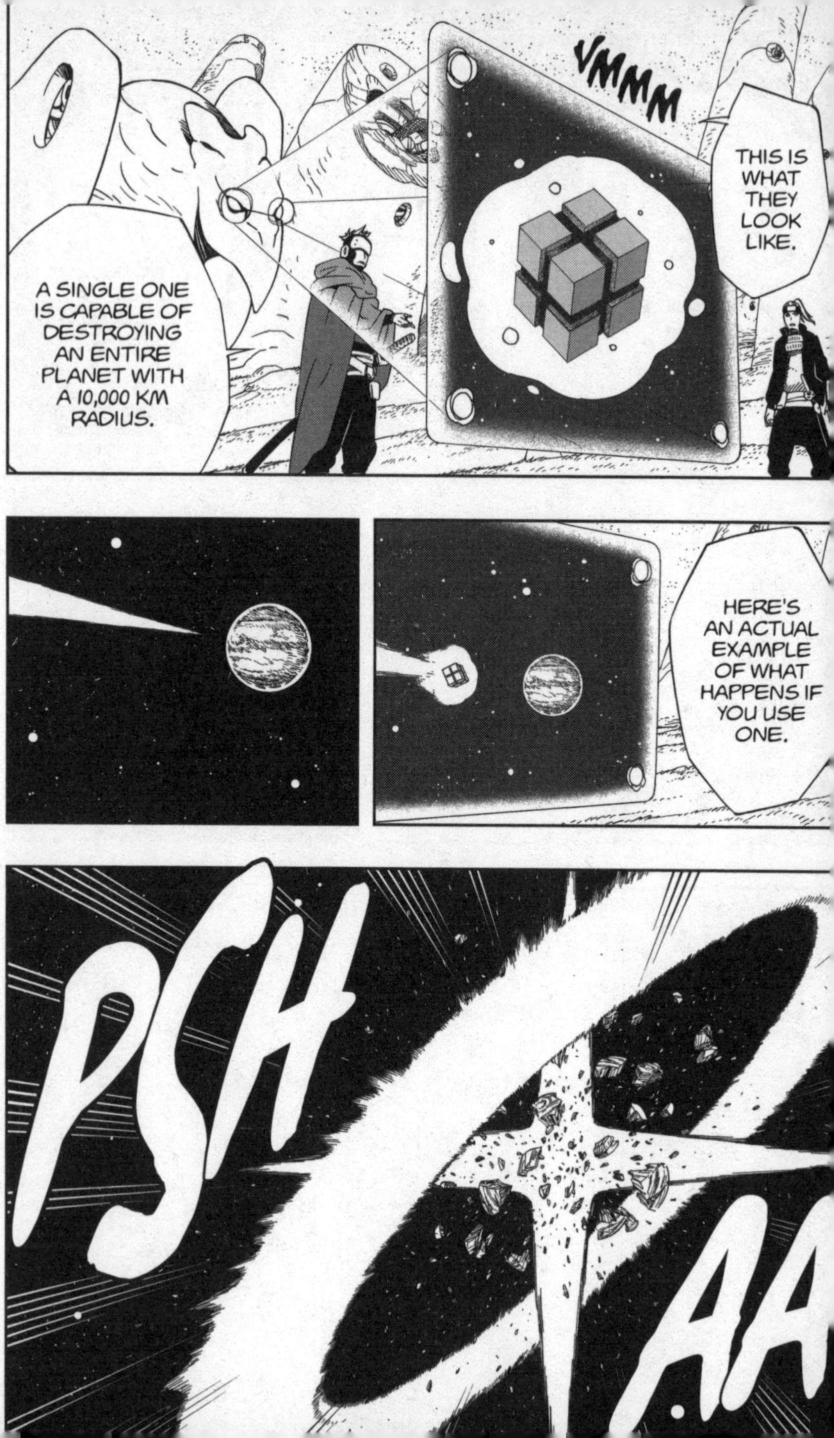
VMMM
THIS IS WHAT THEY LOOK LIKE.
A SINGLE ONE IS CAPABLE OF DESTROYING AN ENTIRE PLANET WITH A 10,000 KM RADIUS.
HERE'S AN ACTUAL EXAMPLE OF WHAT HAPPENS IF YOU USE ONE.
PSH
AA

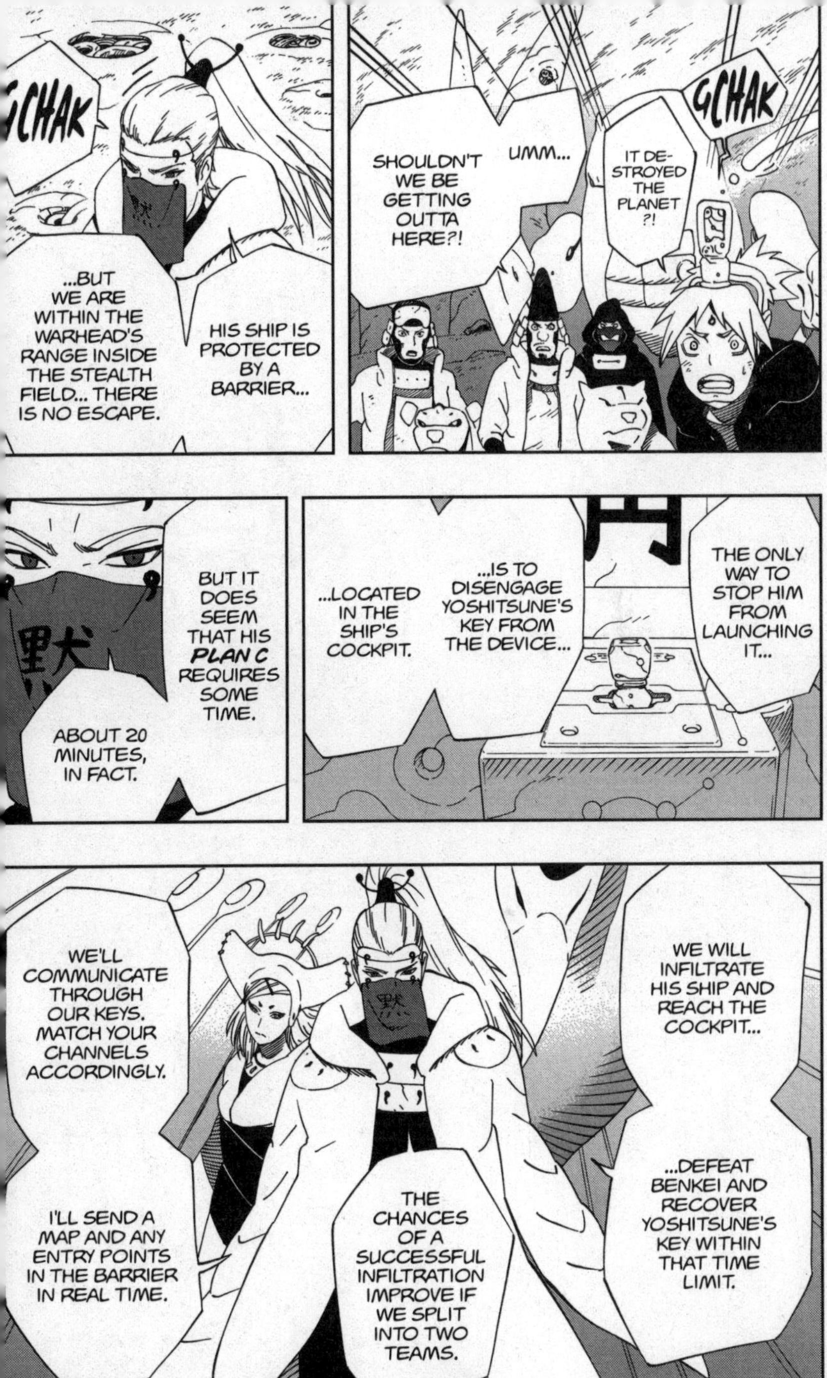
GCHAK
IT DESTROYED THE PLANET?!
UMM...
SHOULDN'T WE BE GETTING OUTTA HERE?!
GCHAK
HIS SHIP IS PROTECTED BY A BARRIER...
...BUT WE ARE WITHIN THE WARHEAD'S RANGE INSIDE THE STEALTH FIELD... THERE IS NO ESCAPE.
THE ONLY WAY TO STOP HIM FROM LAUNCHING IT...
...IS TO DISENGAGE YOSHITSUNE'S KEY FROM THE DEVICE...
...LOCATED IN THE SHIP'S COCKPIT.
BUT IT DOES SEEM THAT HIS **PLAN C** REQUIRES SOME TIME.
ABOUT 20 MINUTES, IN FACT.
WE WILL INFILTRATE HIS SHIP AND REACH THE COCKPIT...
...DEFEAT BENKEI AND RECOVER YOSHITSUNE'S KEY WITHIN THAT TIME LIMIT.
THE CHANCES OF A SUCCESSFUL INFILTRATION IMPROVE IF WE SPLIT INTO TWO TEAMS.
WE'LL COMMUNICATE THROUGH OUR KEYS. MATCH YOUR CHANNELS ACCORDINGLY.
I'LL SEND A MAP AND ANY ENTRY POINTS IN THE BARRIER IN REAL TIME.

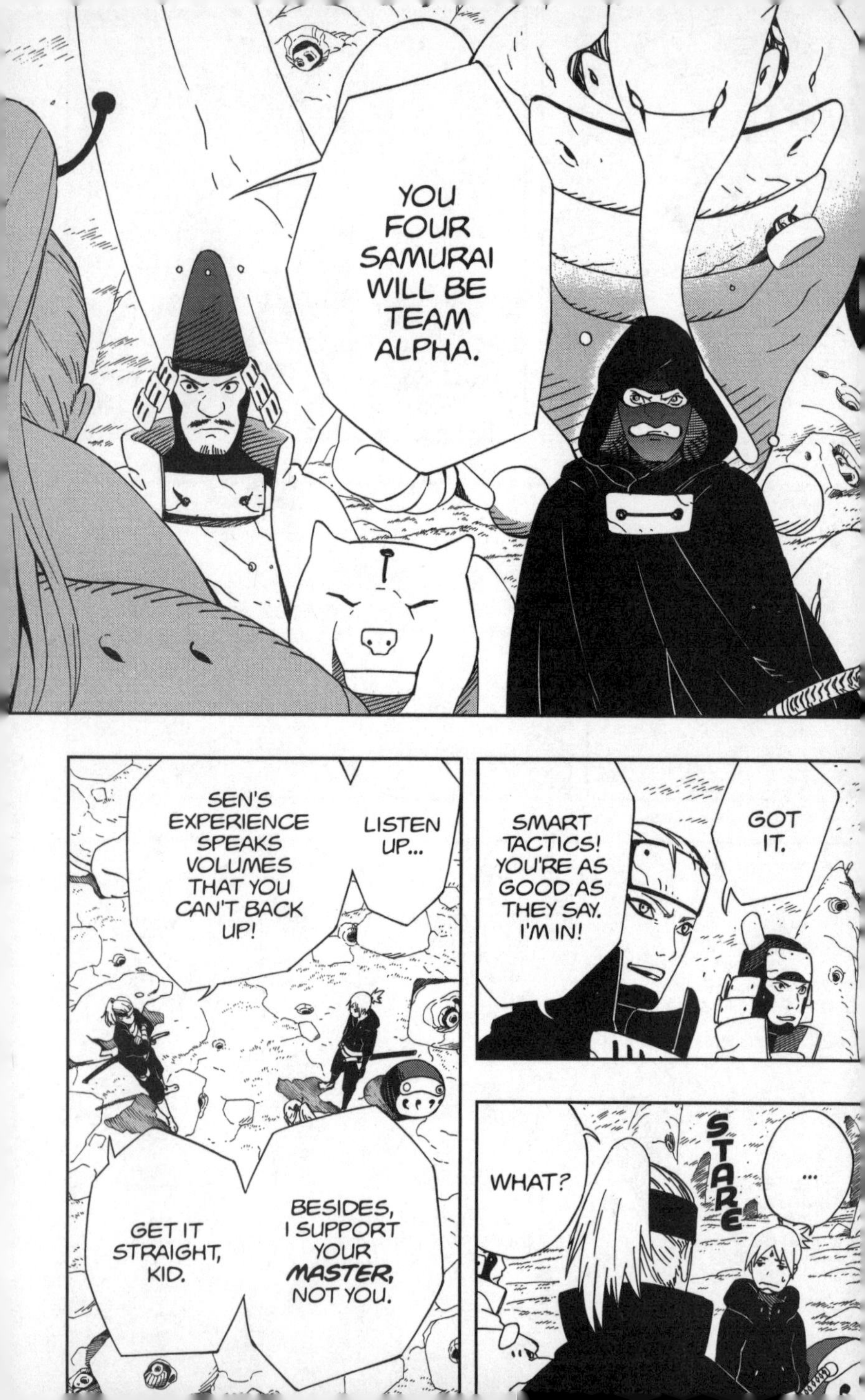
YOU FOUR SAMURAI WILL BE TEAM ALPHA.
GOT IT.
SMART TACTICS! YOU'RE AS GOOD AS THEY SAY. I'M IN!
...
STARE
WHAT?
LISTEN UP...
SEN'S EXPERIENCE SPEAKS VOLUMES THAT YOU CAN'T BACK UP!
BESIDES, I SUPPORT YOUR *MASTER,* NOT YOU.
GET IT STRAIGHT, KID.

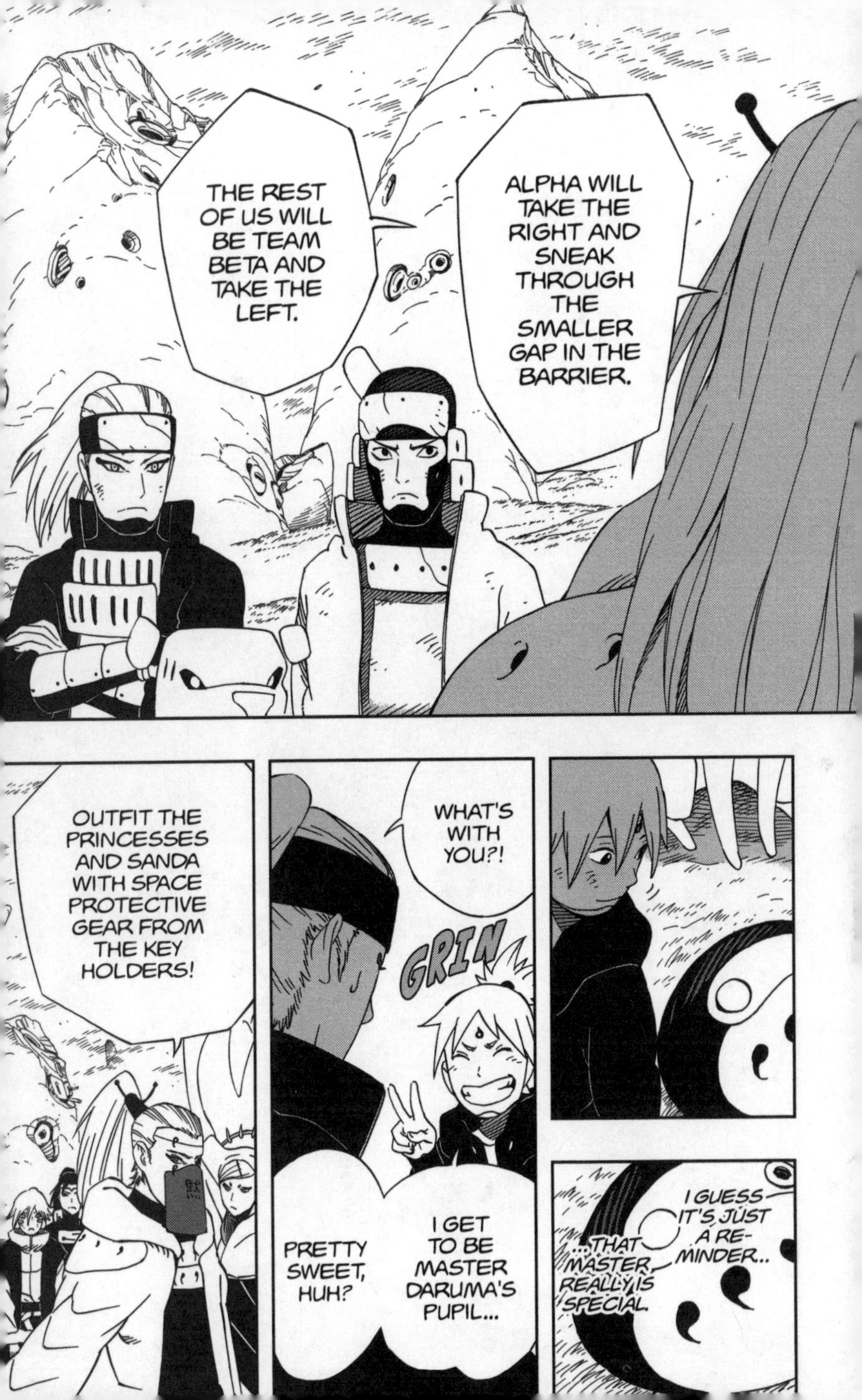
ALPHA WILL TAKE THE RIGHT AND SNEAK THROUGH THE SMALLER GAP IN THE BARRIER.
THE REST OF US WILL BE TEAM BETA AND TAKE THE LEFT.
I GUESS IT'S JUST A RE-MINDER...
...THAT MASTER REALLY IS SPECIAL.
WHAT'S WITH YOU?!
GRIN
I GET TO BE MASTER DARUMA'S PUPIL...
PRETTY SWEET, HUH?
OUTFIT THE PRINCESSES AND SANDA WITH SPACE PROTECTIVE GEAR FROM THE KEY HOLDERS!

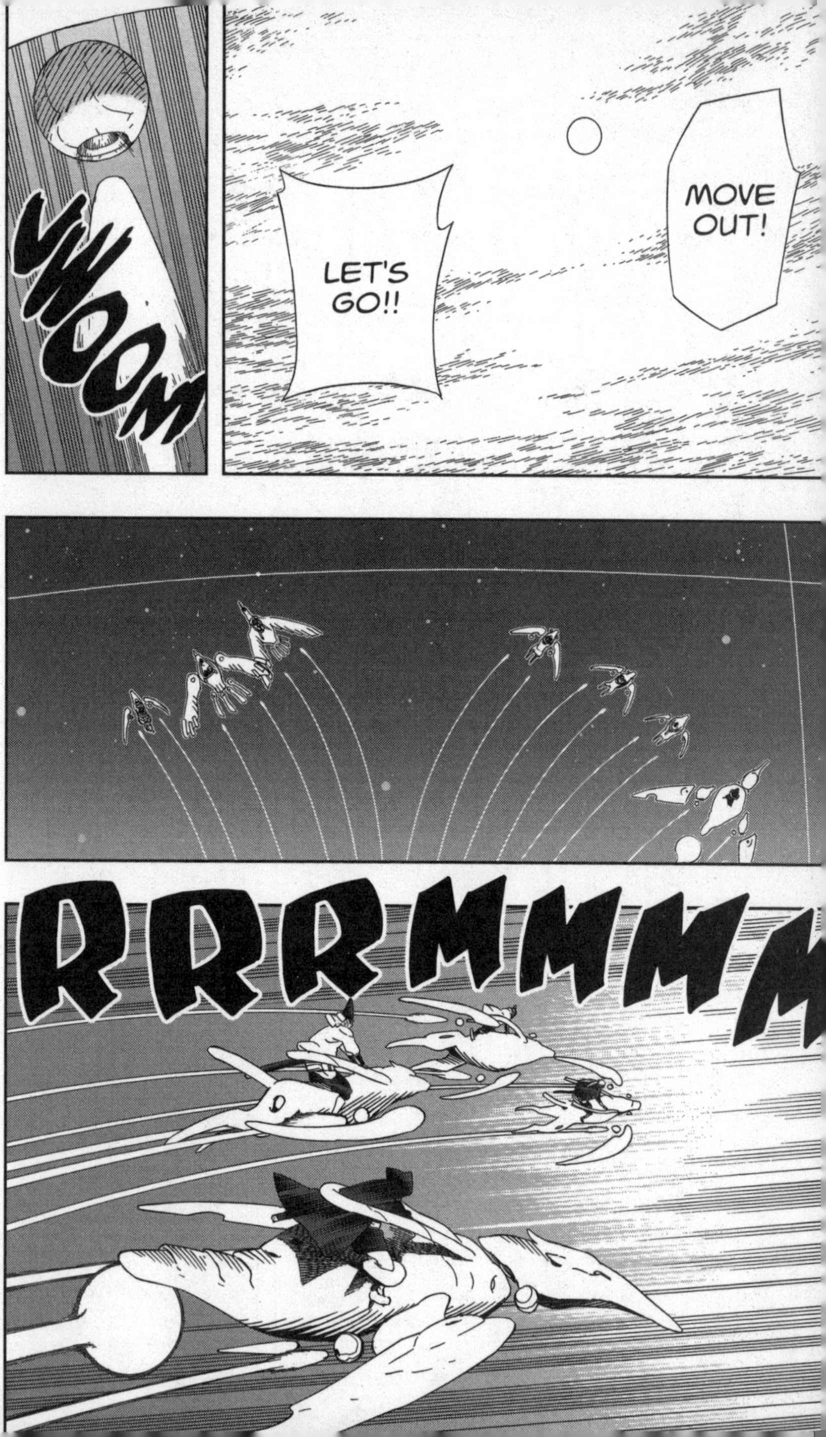
MOVE OUT!
LET'S GO!!
VWOOM
RRRMMMMM

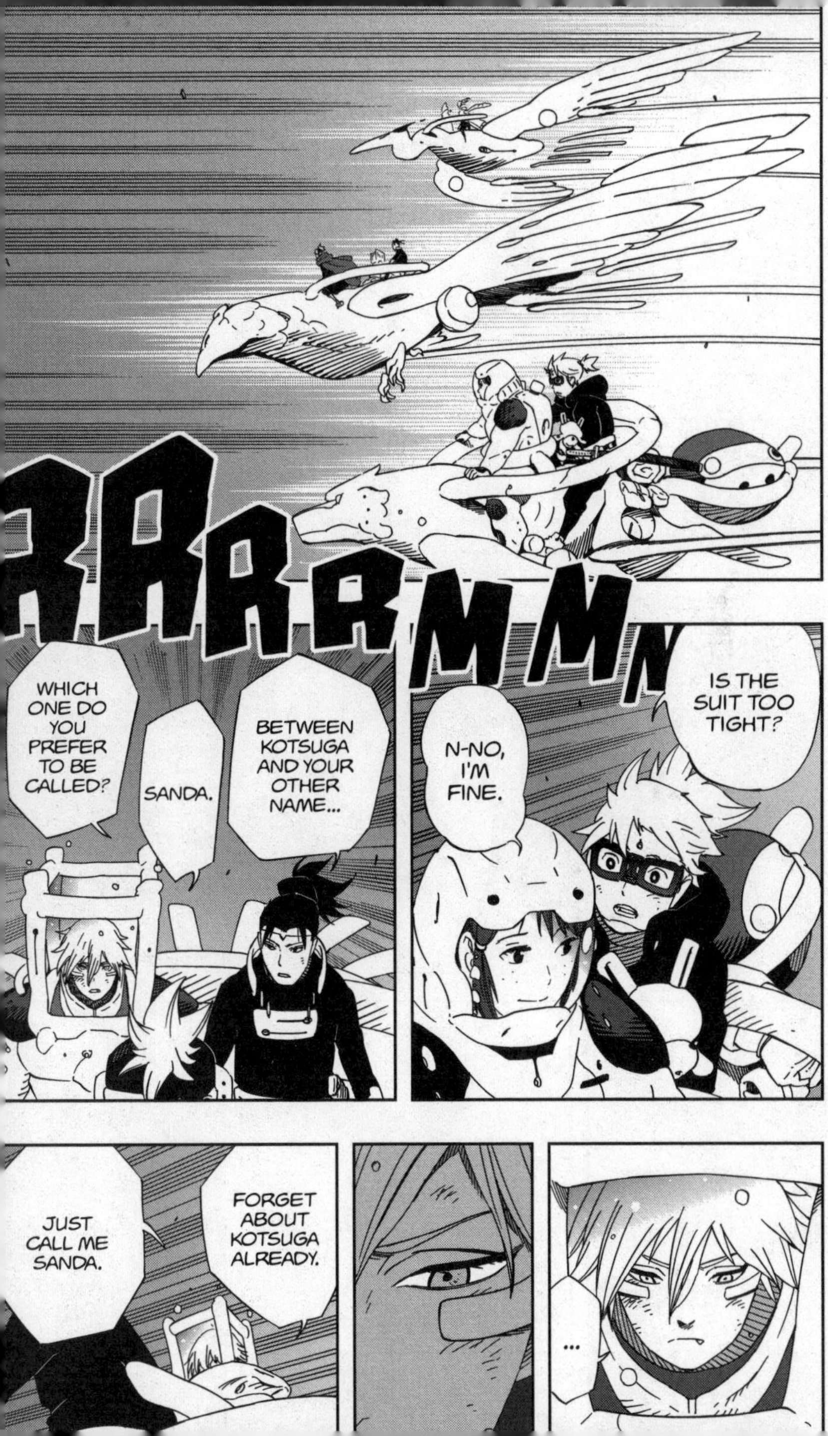
RRRRRMMMN
IS THE SUIT TOO TIGHT?
N-NO, I'M FINE.
BETWEEN KOTSUGA AND YOUR OTHER NAME...
WHICH ONE DO YOU PREFER TO BE CALLED?
SANDA.
...
FORGET ABOUT KOTSUGA ALREADY.
JUST CALL ME SANDA.

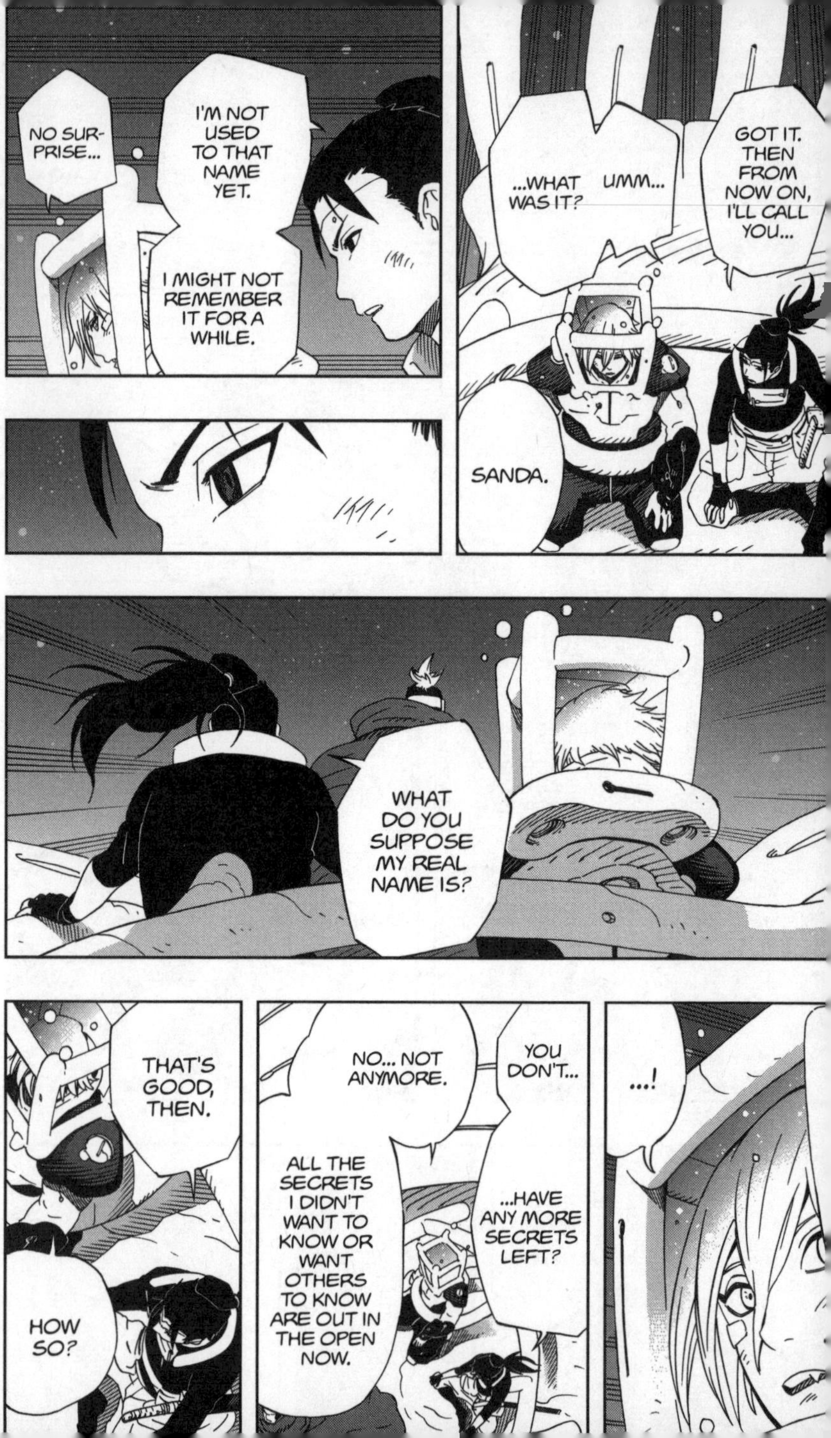
GOT IT. THEN FROM NOW ON, I'LL CALL YOU...
UMM...
...WHAT WAS IT?
SANDA.
I'M NOT USED TO THAT NAME YET.
I MIGHT NOT REMEMBER IT FOR A WHILE.
NO SURPRISE...
WHAT DO YOU SUPPOSE MY REAL NAME IS?
...!
YOU DON'T...
...HAVE ANY MORE SECRETS LEFT?
NO... NOT ANYMORE.
ALL THE SECRETS I DIDN'T WANT TO KNOW OR WANT OTHERS TO KNOW ARE OUT IN THE OPEN NOW.
THAT'S GOOD, THEN.
HOW SO?

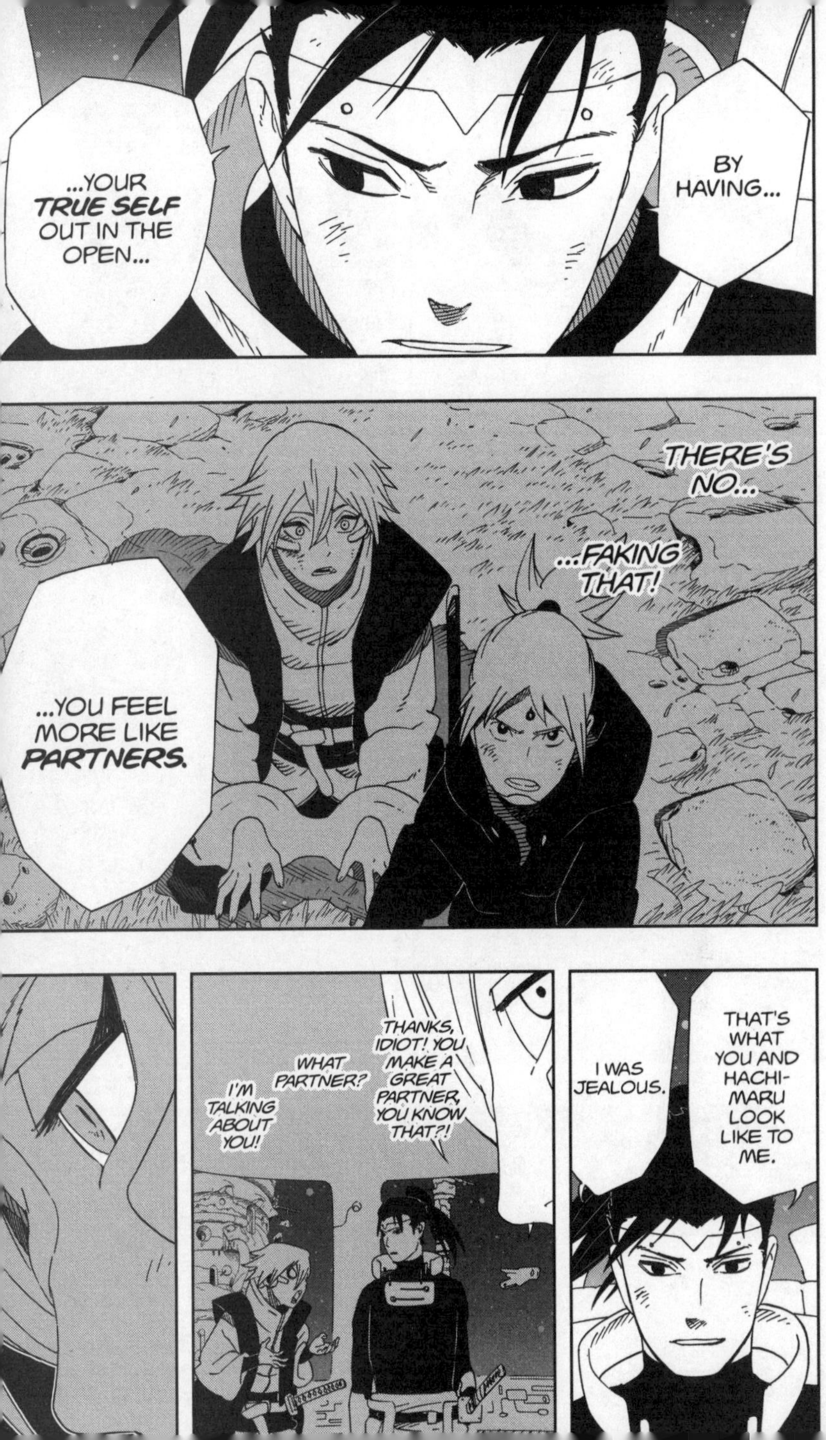
BY HAVING...
...YOUR TRUE SELF OUT IN THE OPEN...
THERE'S NO...
...FAKING THAT!
...YOU FEEL MORE LIKE PARTNERS.
THAT'S WHAT YOU AND HACHI-MARU LOOK LIKE TO ME.
I WAS JEALOUS.
THANKS, IDIOT! YOU MAKE A GREAT PARTNER, YOU KNOW THAT?!
WHAT PARTNER?
I'M TALKING ABOUT YOU!

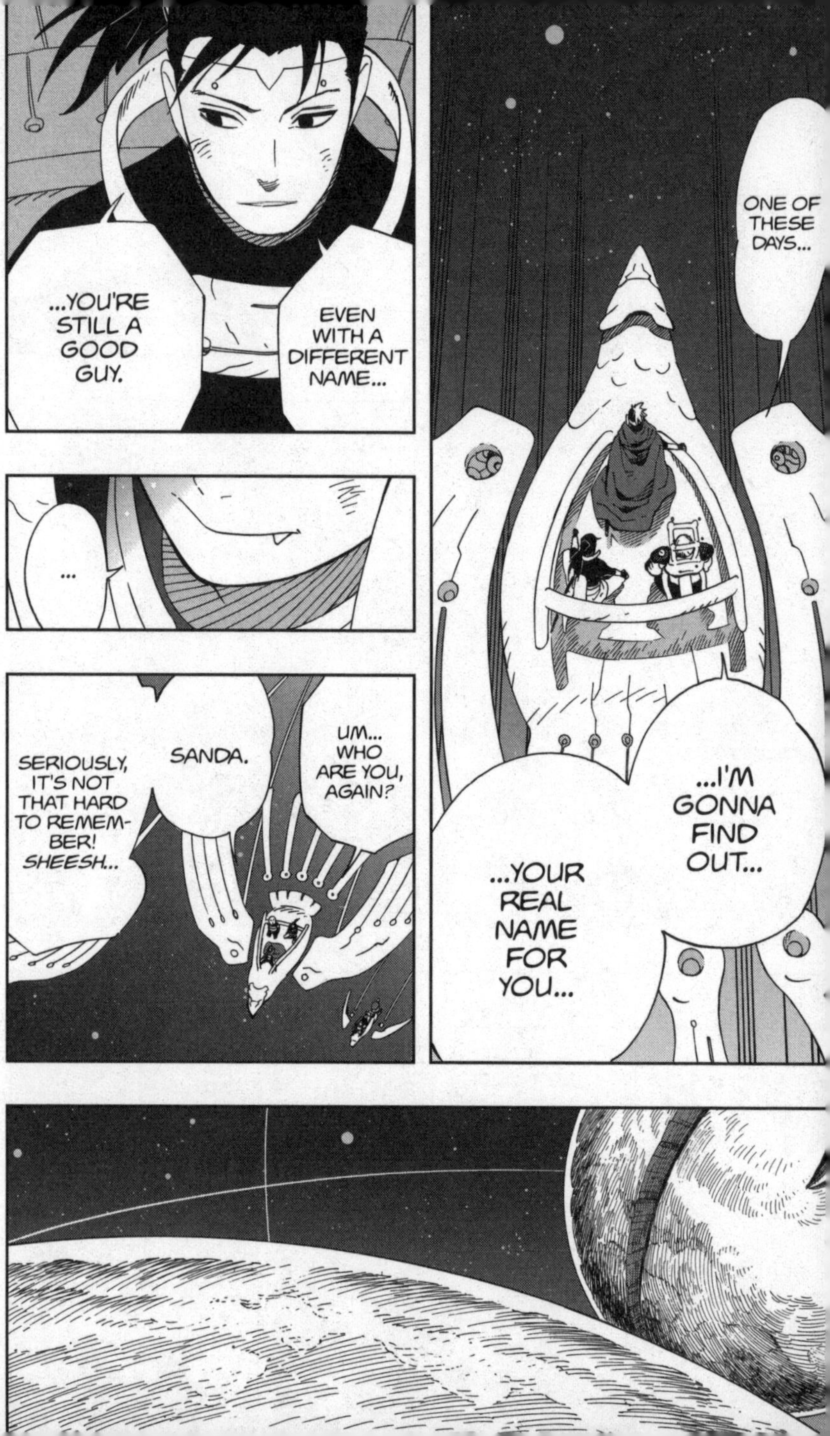
ONE OF THESE DAYS...
...I'M GONNA FIND OUT...
...YOUR REAL NAME FOR YOU...
EVEN WITH A DIFFERENT NAME...
...YOU'RE STILL A GOOD GUY.
...
UM... WHO ARE YOU, AGAIN?
SANDA.
SERIOUSLY, IT'S NOT THAT HARD TO REMEMBER! SHEESH...

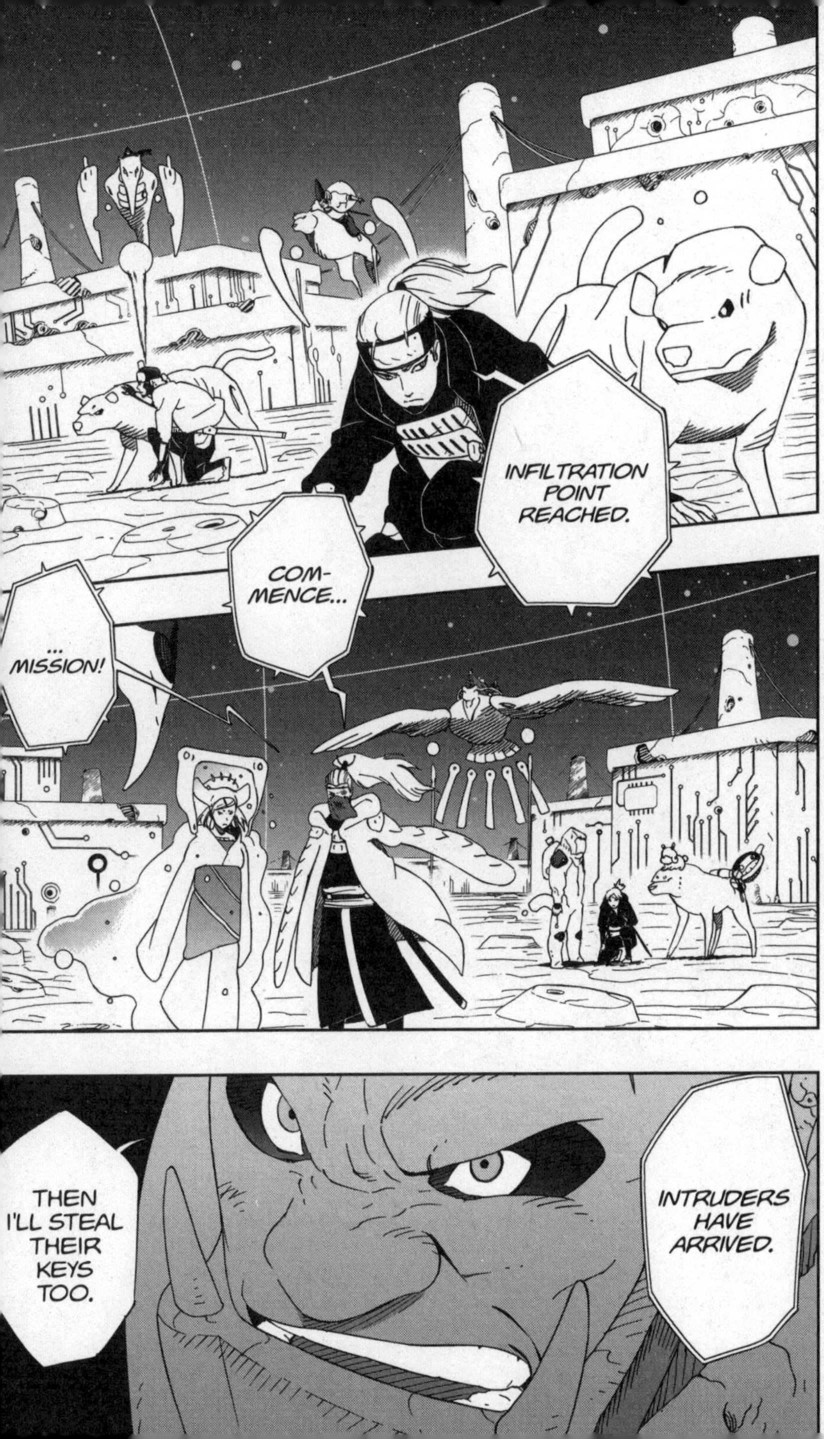

INFILTRATION POINT REACHED.
COM-MENCE...
... MISSION!
INTRUDERS HAVE ARRIVED.
THEN I'LL STEAL THEIR KEYS TOO.

Character Design Sketches: Yoken

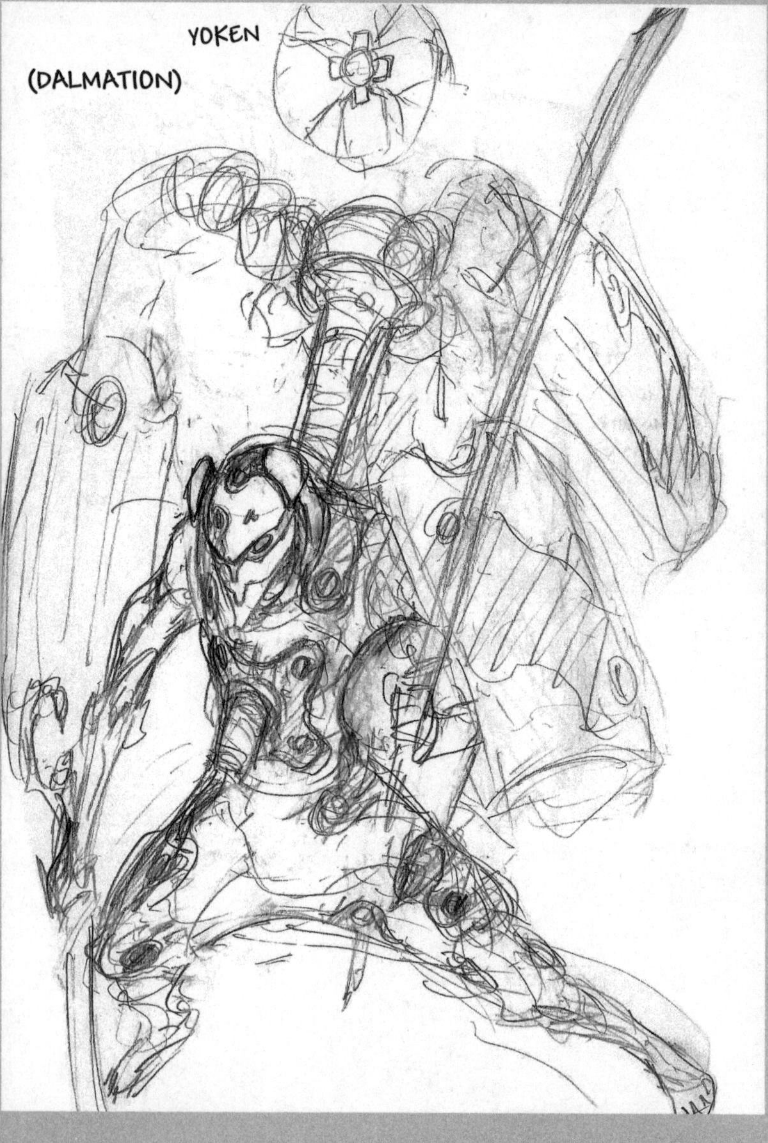
YOKEN
(DALMATION)

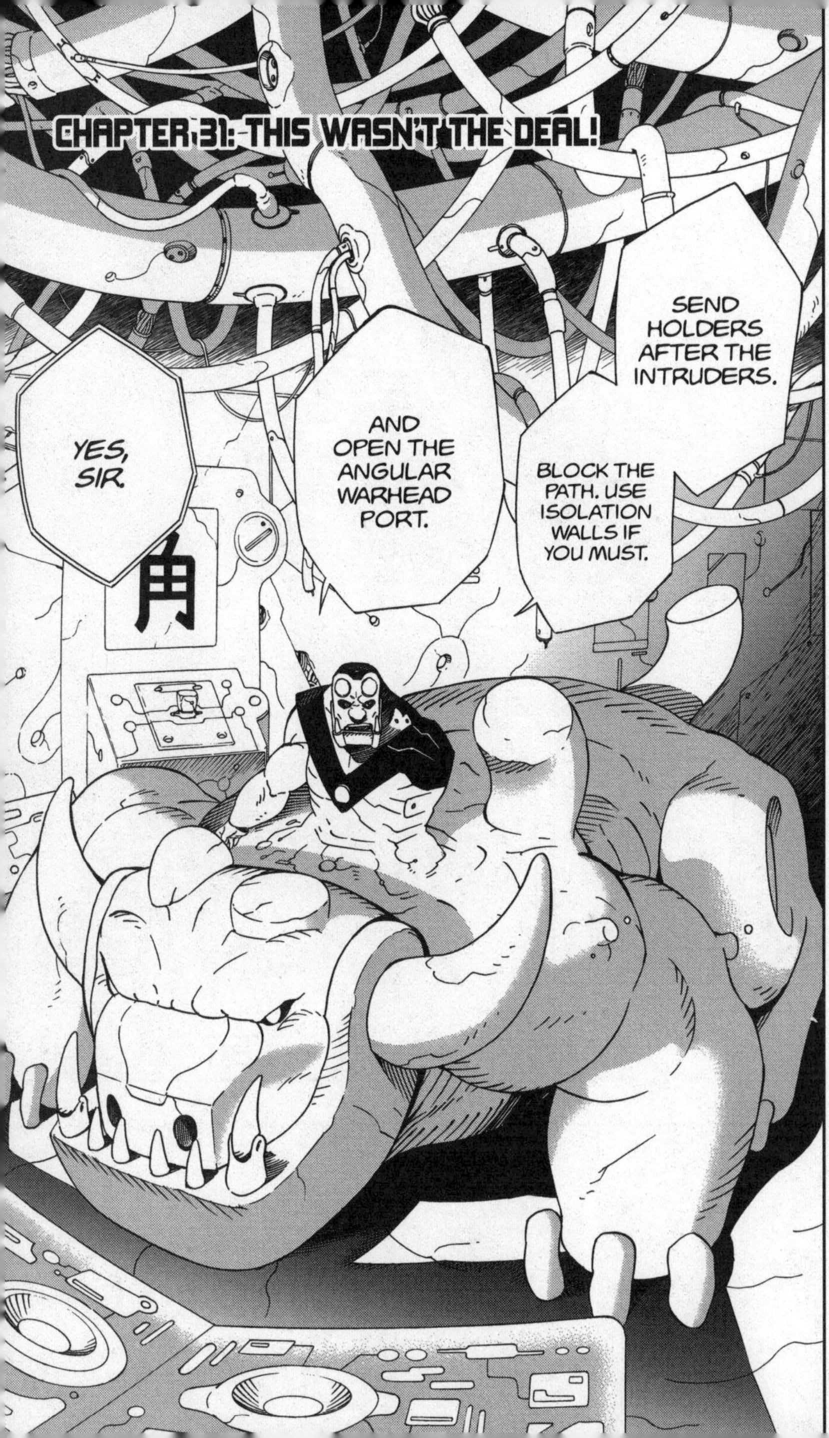
CHAPTER 31: THIS WASN'T THE DEAL!
SEND HOLDERS AFTER THE INTRUDERS.
BLOCK THE PATH. USE ISOLATION WALLS IF YOU MUST.
AND OPEN THE ANGULAR WARHEAD PORT.
YES, SIR.
角

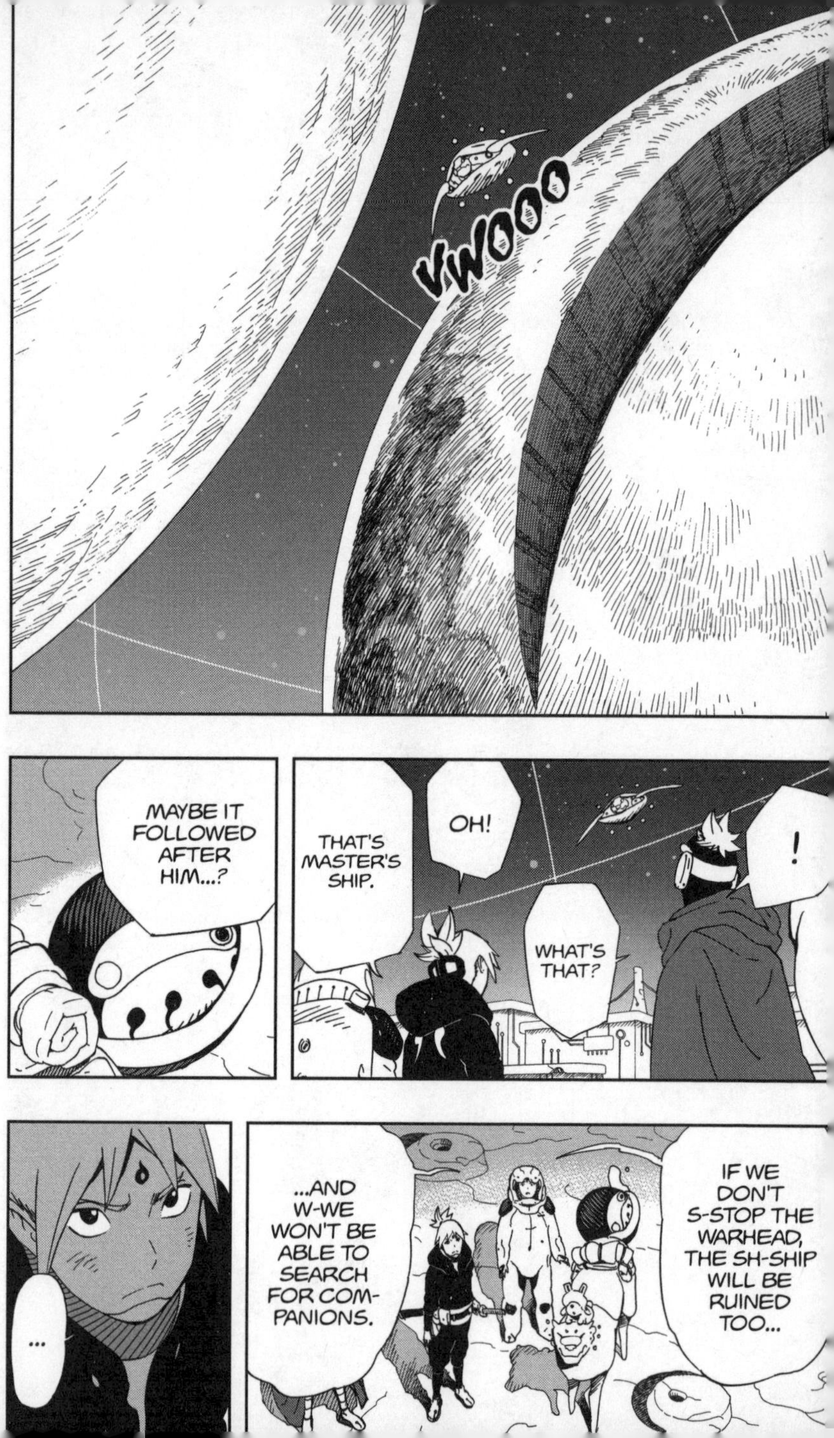
VWOOO
!
WHAT'S THAT?
OH!
THAT'S MASTER'S SHIP.
MAYBE IT FOLLOWED AFTER HIM...?
IF WE DON'T S-STOP THE WARHEAD, THE SH-SHIP WILL BE RUINED TOO...
...AND W-WE WON'T BE ABLE TO SEARCH FOR COM-PANIONS.
...

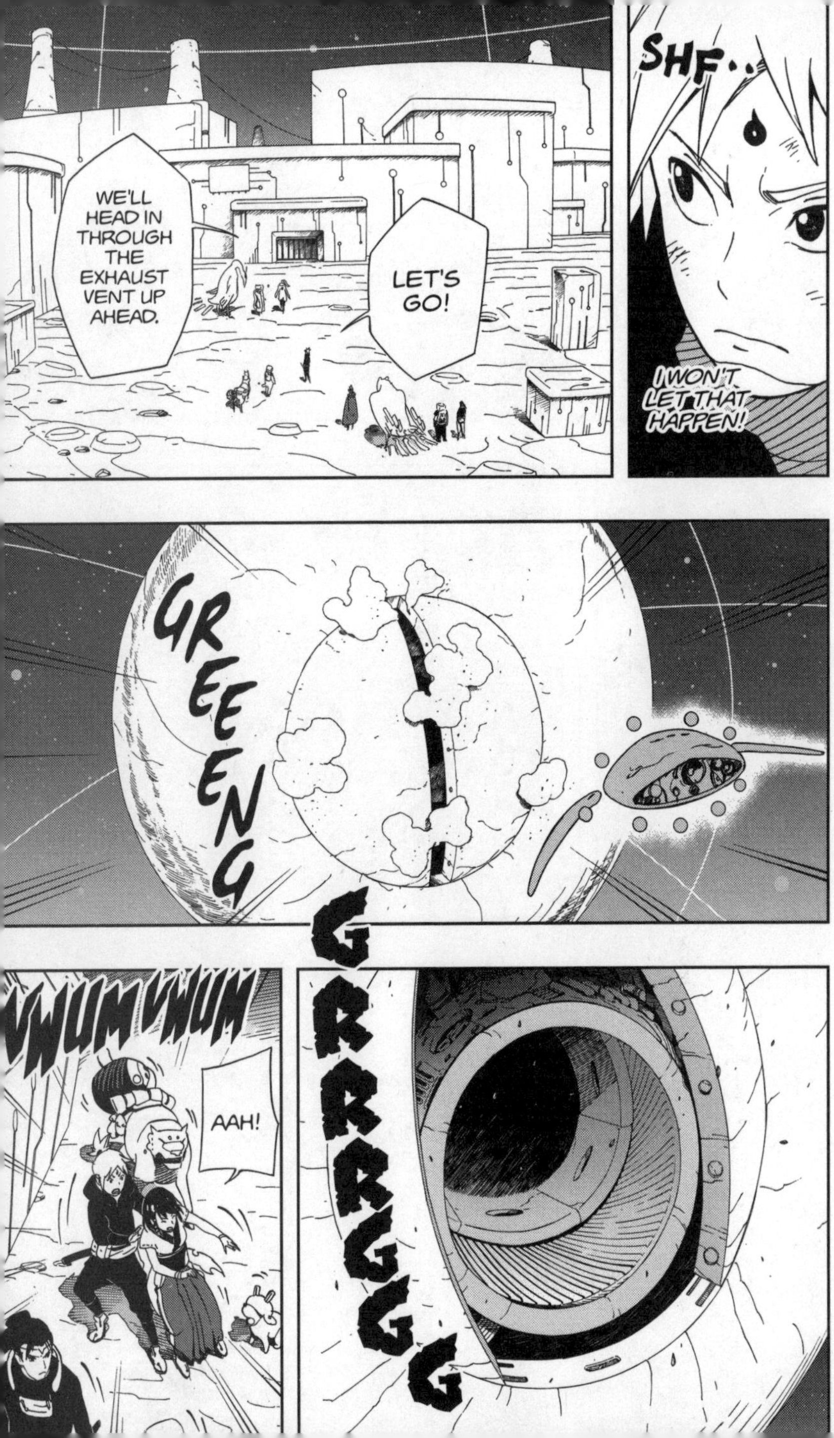
SHF..
I WON'T LET THAT HAPPEN!
WE'LL HEAD IN THROUGH THE EXHAUST VENT UP AHEAD.
LET'S GO!
GREEENG
GRRRGGG
VHUM VHUM
AAH!

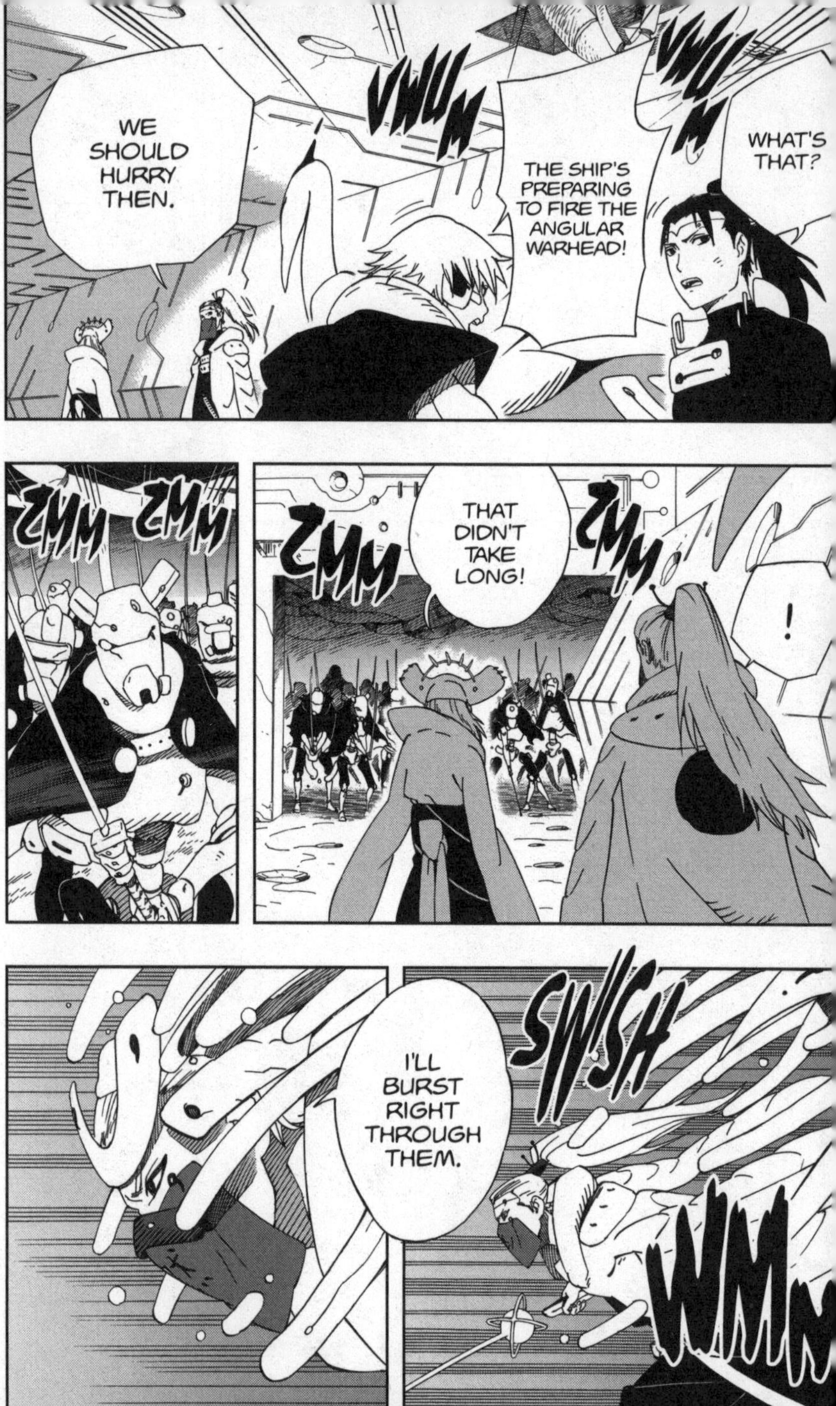
WHAT'S THAT?
VWUM
THE SHIP'S PREPARING TO FIRE THE ANGULAR WARHEAD!
VWUM
WE SHOULD HURRY THEN.
!
ZMM
THAT DIDN'T TAKE LONG!
ZMM
ZMM ZMM
SWISH
I'LL BURST RIGHT THROUGH THEM.
WMM

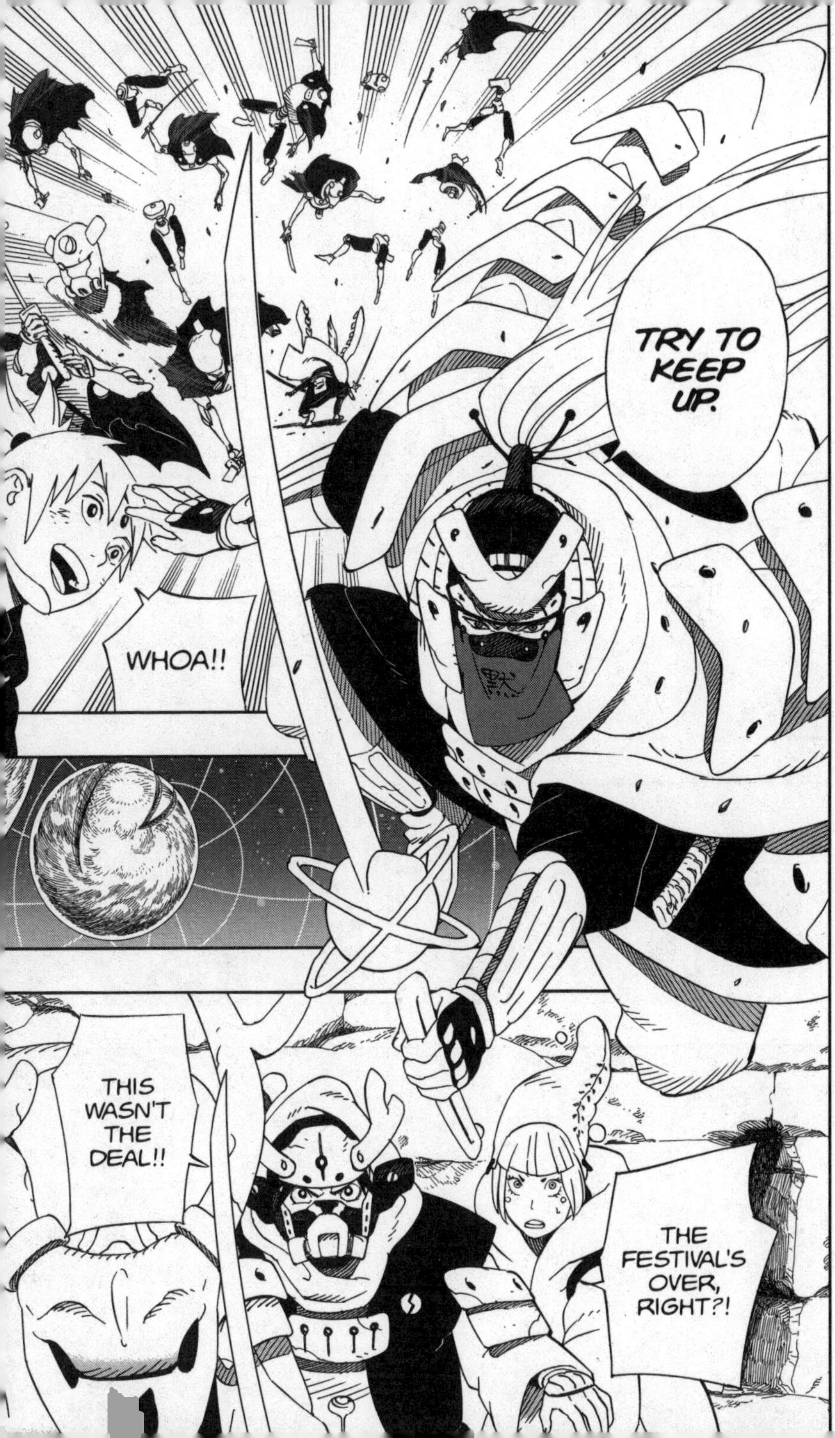
TRY TO KEEP UP.
WHOA!!
THE FESTIVAL'S OVER, RIGHT?!
THIS WASN'T THE DEAL!!

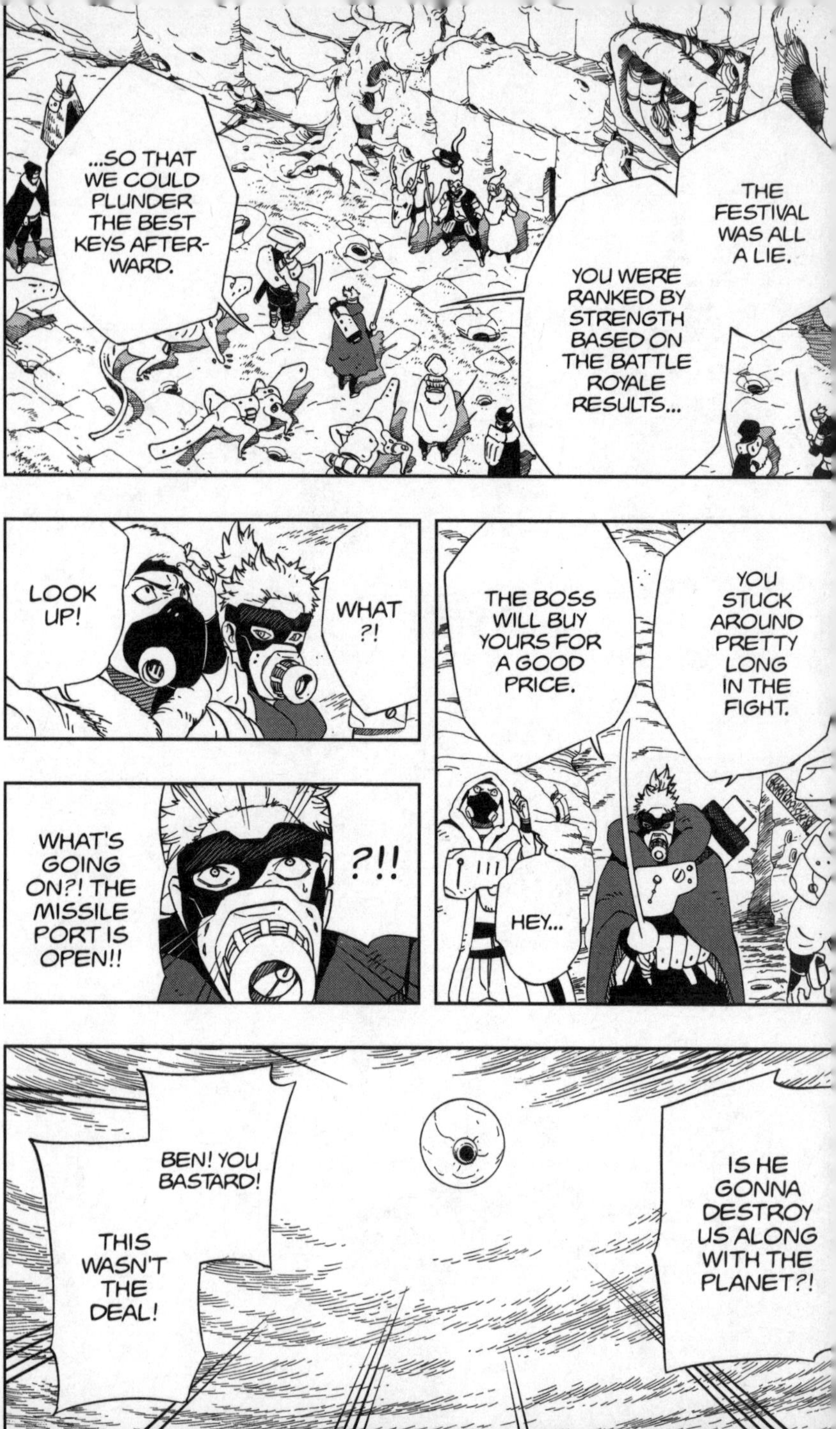
THE FESTIVAL WAS ALL A LIE.
YOU WERE RANKED BY STRENGTH BASED ON THE BATTLE ROYALE RESULTS...
...SO THAT WE COULD PLUNDER THE BEST KEYS AFTER-WARD.
YOU STUCK AROUND PRETTY LONG IN THE FIGHT.
THE BOSS WILL BUY YOURS FOR A GOOD PRICE.
HEY...
WHAT ?!
LOOK UP!
?!!
WHAT'S GOING ON?! THE MISSILE PORT IS OPEN!!
IS HE GONNA DESTROY US ALONG WITH THE PLANET?!
BEN! YOU BASTARD!
THIS WASN'T THE DEAL!

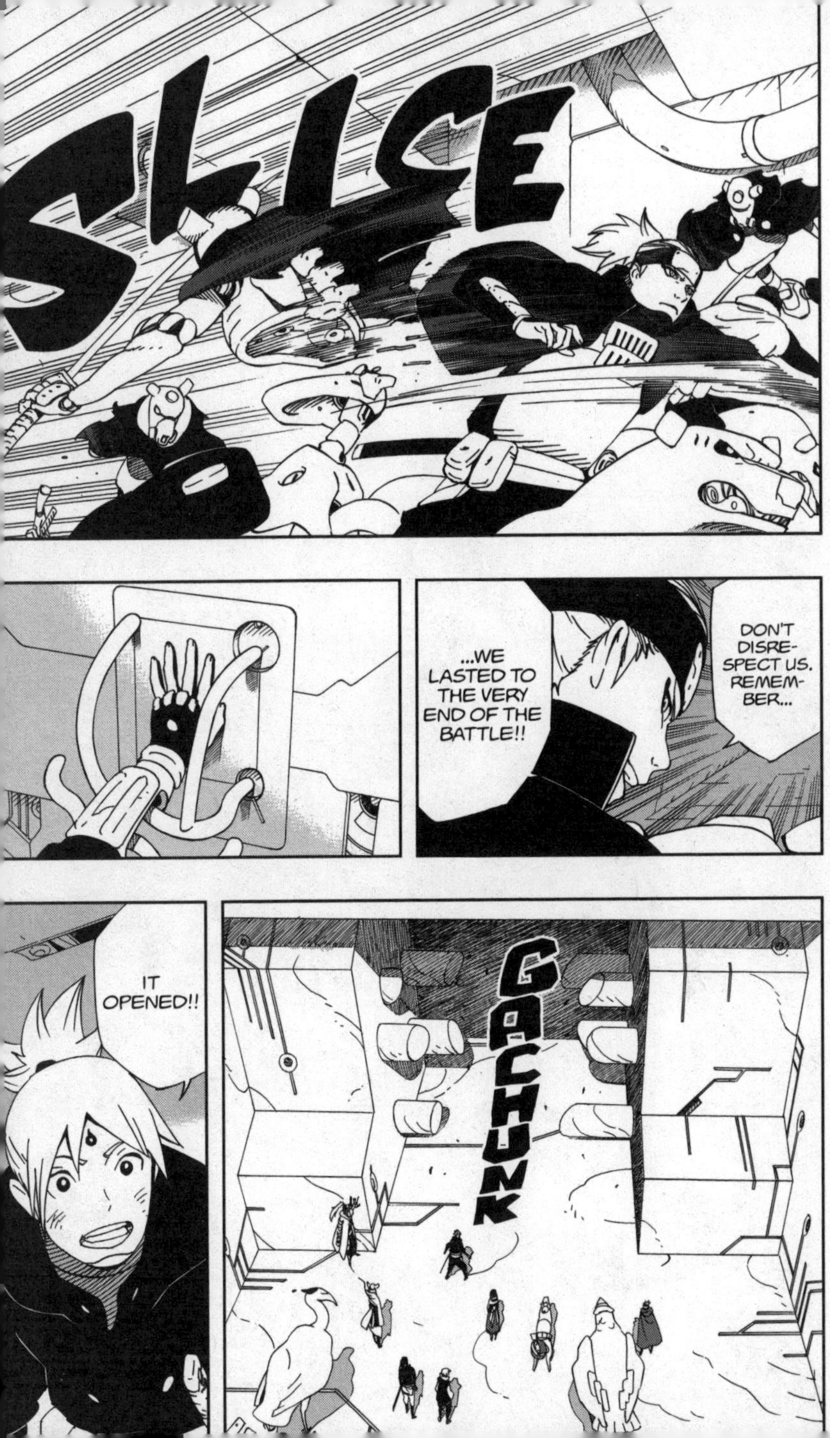
SLICE
DON'T DISRESPECT US. REMEMBER...
...WE LASTED TO THE VERY END OF THE BATTLE!!
GACHUNK
IT OPENED!!

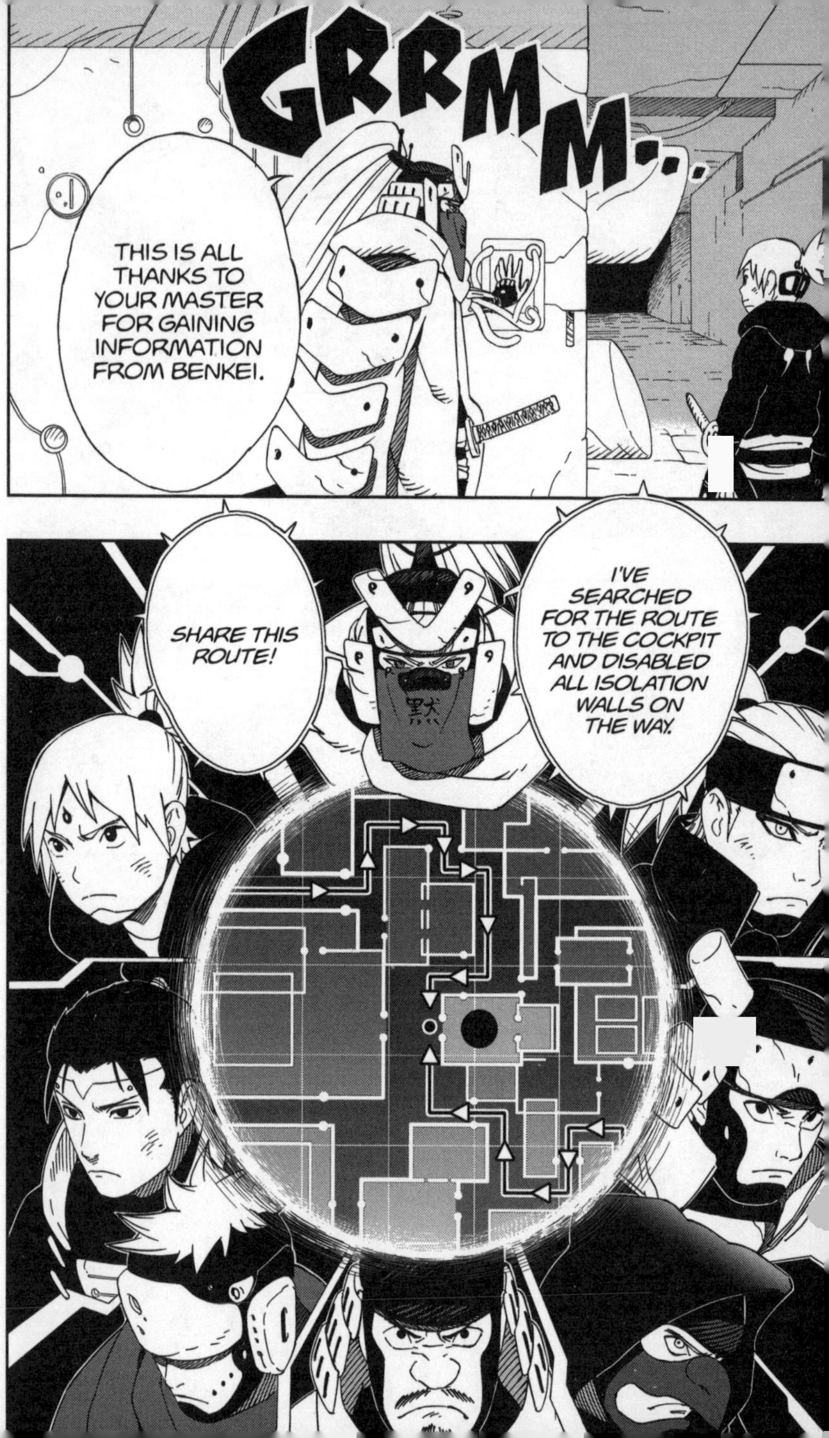
GRRMM...
THIS IS ALL THANKS TO YOUR MASTER FOR GAINING INFORMATION FROM BENKEI.
I'VE SEARCHED FOR THE ROUTE TO THE COCKPIT AND DISABLED ALL ISOLATION WALLS ON THE WAY.
SHARE THIS ROUTE!

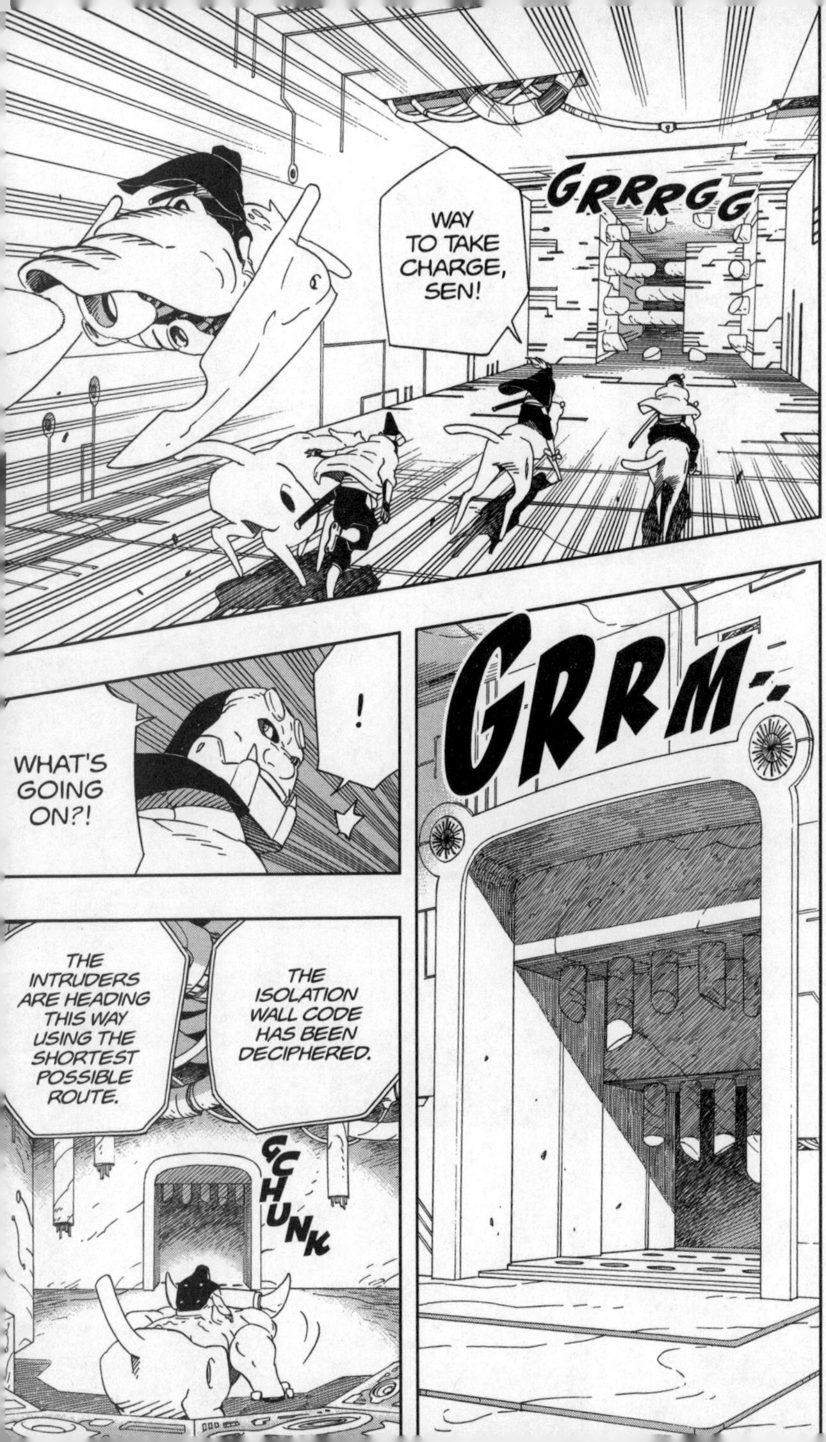
GRRRGG
WAY TO TAKE CHARGE, SEN!
GRRM
!
WHAT'S GOING ON?!
THE ISOLATION WALL CODE HAS BEEN DECIPHERED.
THE INTRUDERS ARE HEADING THIS WAY USING THE SHORTEST POSSIBLE ROUTE.
GCHUNK

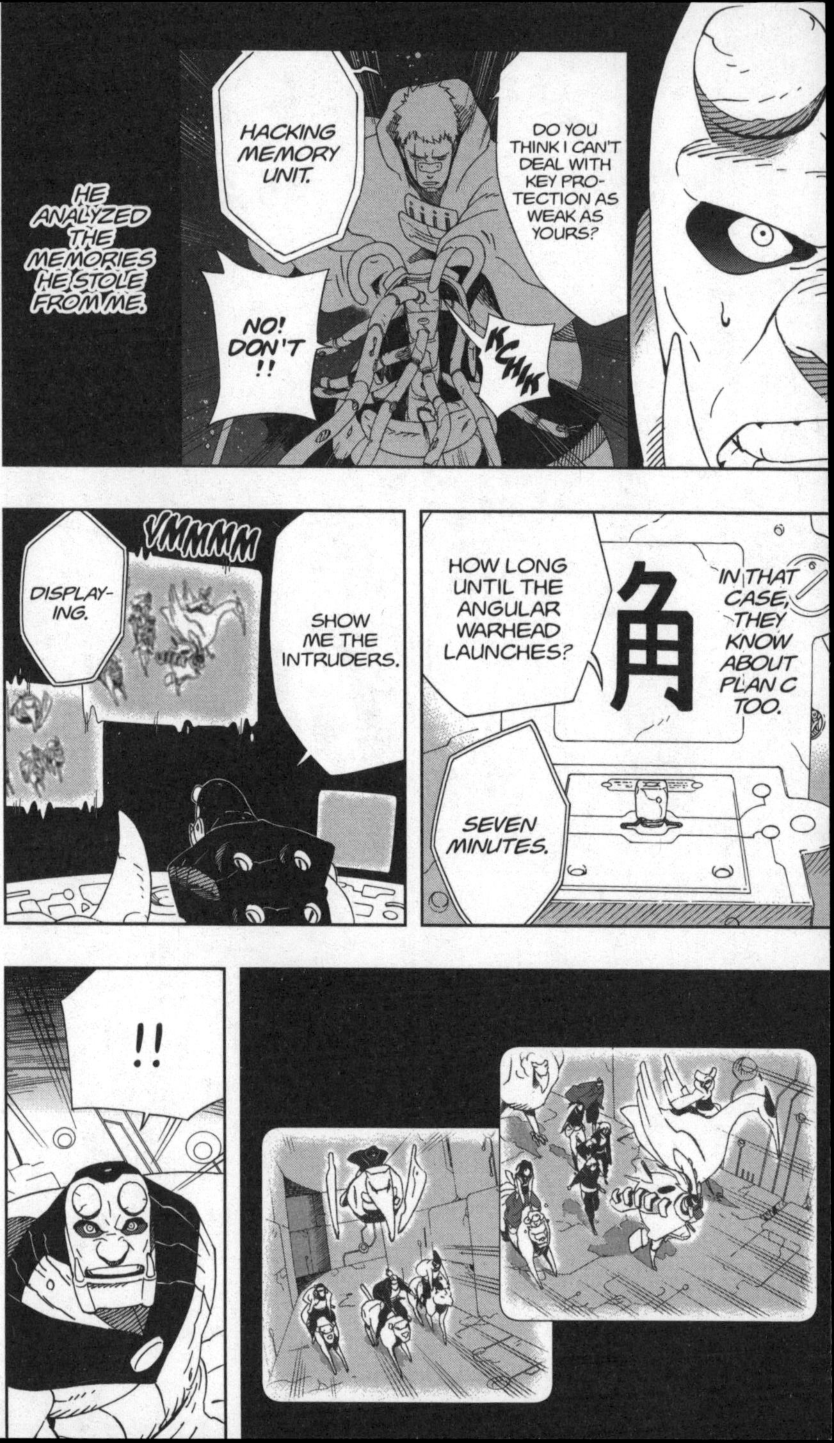
DO YOU THINK I CAN'T DEAL WITH KEY PROTECTION AS WEAK AS YOURS?
HACKING MEMORY UNIT.
KCHIK
NO! DON'T !!
HE ANALYZED THE MEMORIES HE STOLE FROM ME.
IN THAT CASE, THEY KNOW ABOUT PLAN C TOO.
HOW LONG UNTIL THE ANGULAR WARHEAD LAUNCHES?
角
SEVEN MINUTES.
SHOW ME THE INTRUDERS.
VMMMM
DISPLAYING.
!!

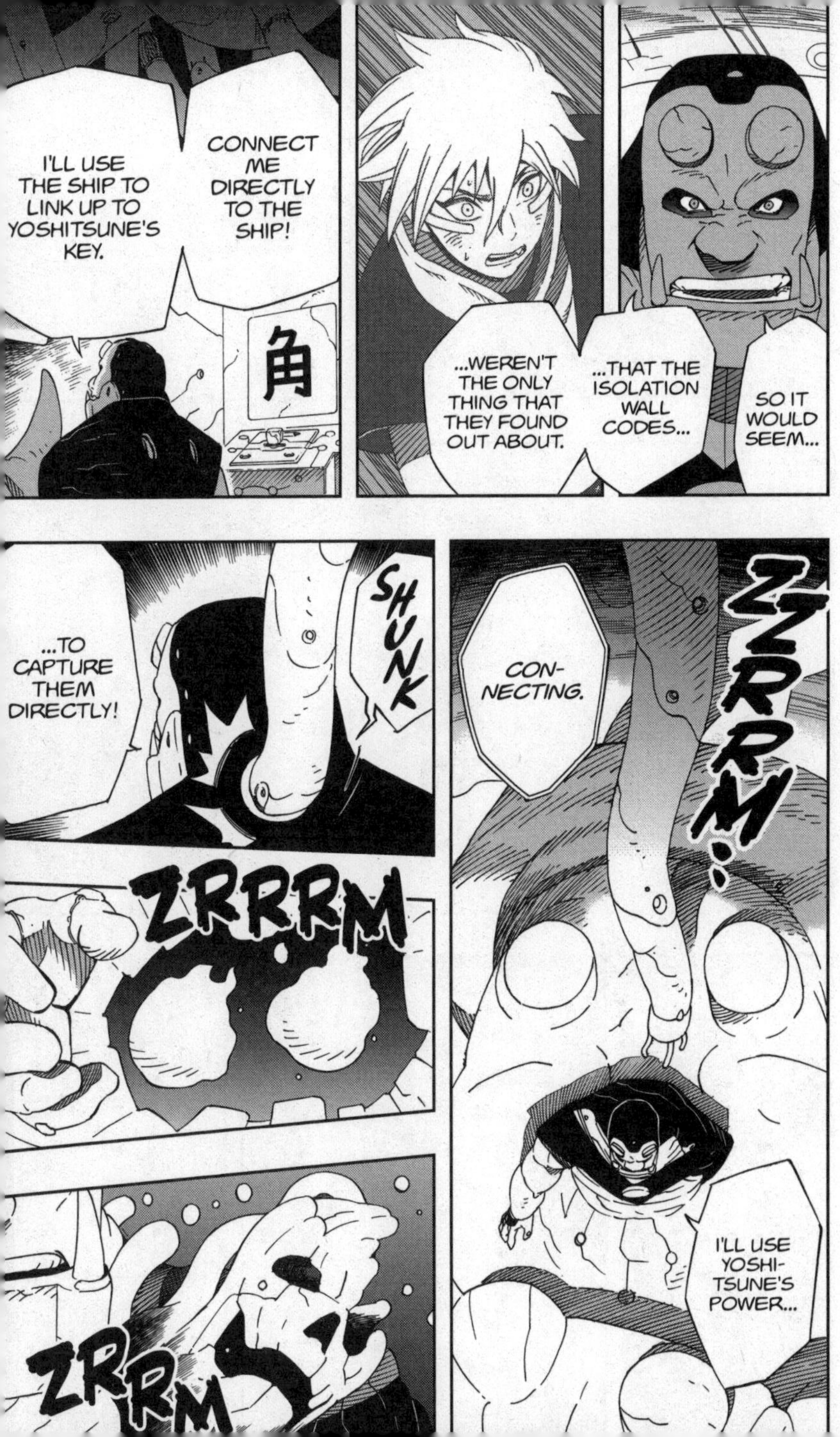
SO IT WOULD SEEM...
...THAT THE ISOLATION WALL CODES...
...WEREN'T THE ONLY THING THAT THEY FOUND OUT ABOUT.
CONNECT ME DIRECTLY TO THE SHIP!
I'LL USE THE SHIP TO LINK UP TO YOSHITSUNE'S KEY.
角
ZZRRRM...
CON-NECTING.
I'LL USE YOSHI-TSUNE'S POWER...
SHUNK
...TO CAPTURE THEM DIRECTLY!
ZRRRM
ZRRM

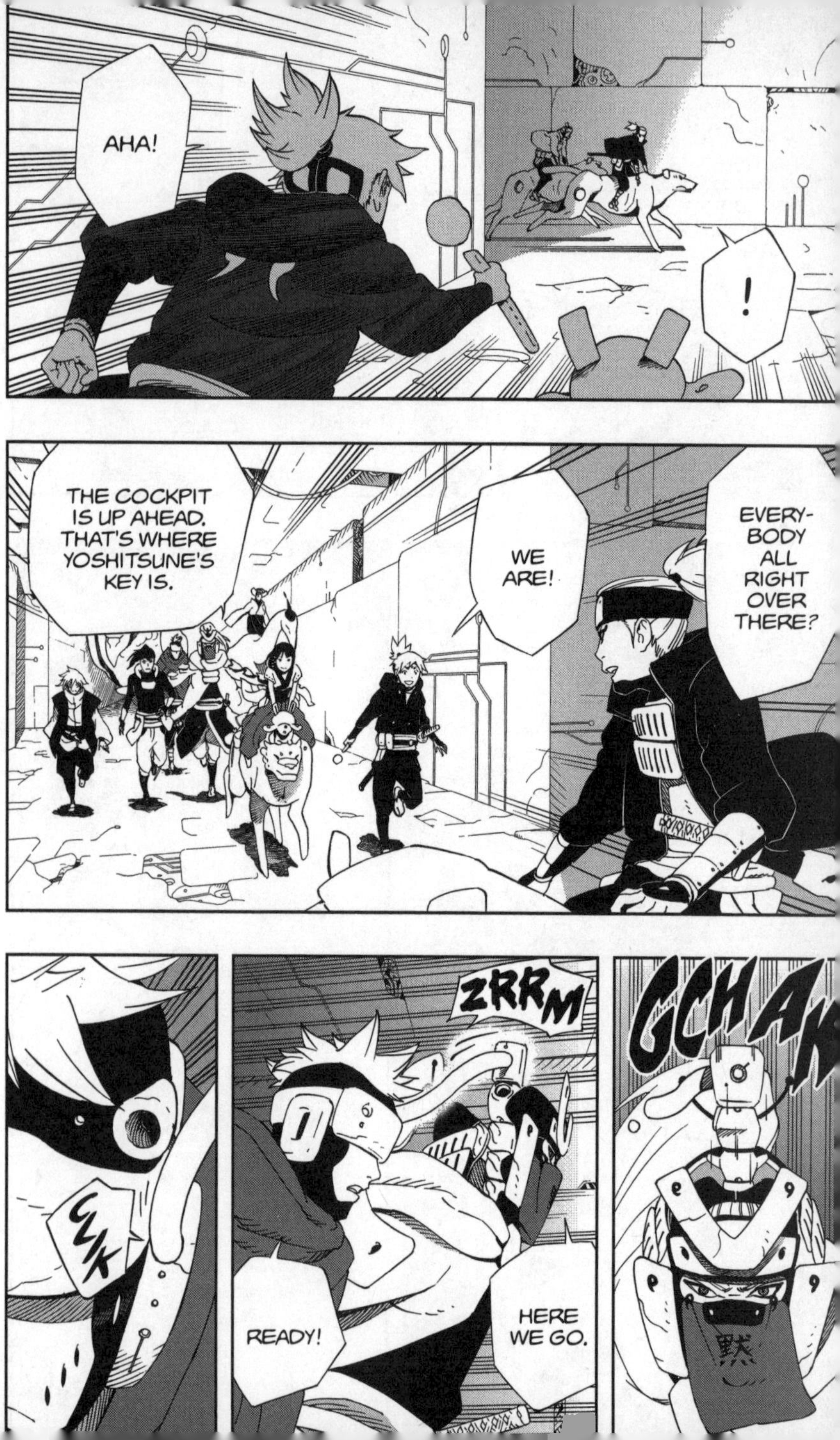
!
AHA!
EVERY-BODY ALL RIGHT OVER THERE?
WE ARE!
THE COCKPIT IS UP AHEAD. THAT'S WHERE YOSHITSUNE'S KEY IS.
ZRRM
HERE WE GO.
READY!
EEK

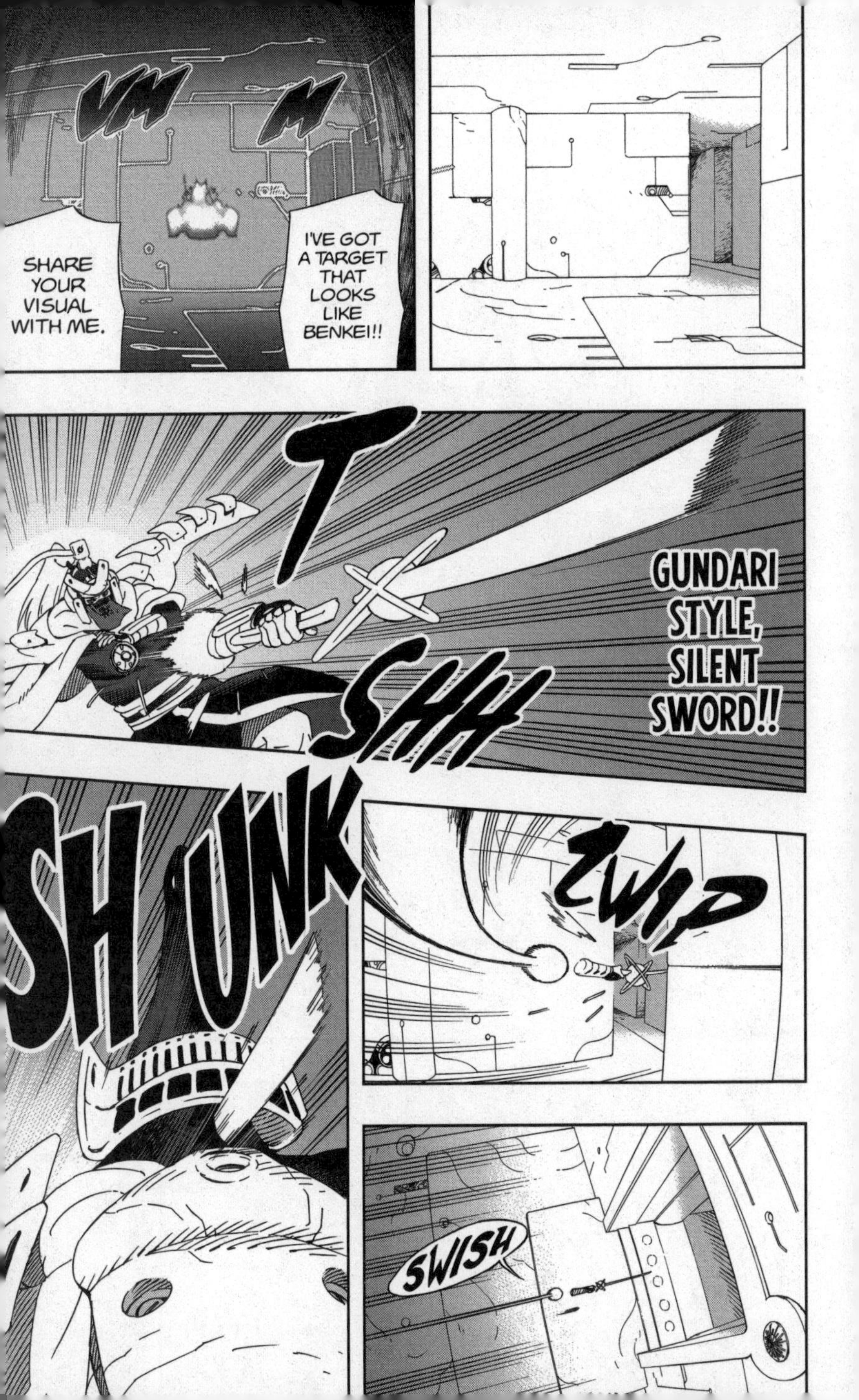
VMM
I'VE GOT A TARGET THAT LOOKS LIKE BENKEI!!
SHARE YOUR VISUAL WITH ME.
GUNDARI STYLE, SILENT SWORD!!
T
SHH
ZWIP
SWISH
SHUNK

YOUR
AIM WAS
JUST A
BIT OFF,
SEN...

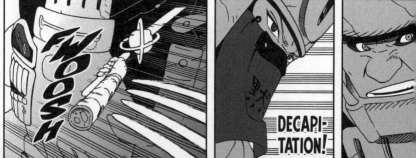

FWOOSH

DECAPI-
TATION!

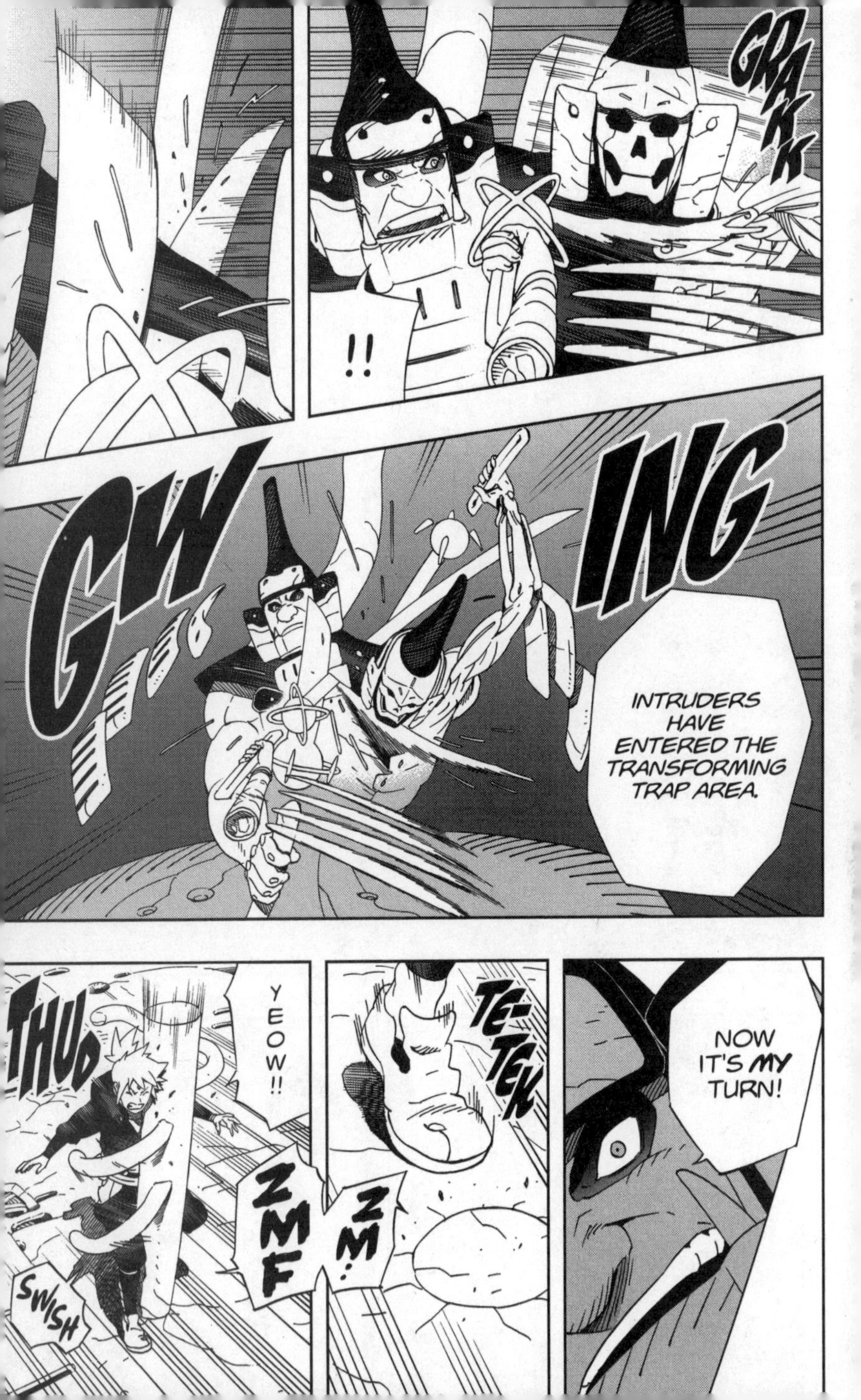
GRAKK
!!
GW ING
INTRUDERS HAVE ENTERED THE TRANSFORMING TRAP AREA.
NOW IT'S MY TURN!
TE-TEK
ZMF
ZMF
YEOW!!
THUD
SWISH

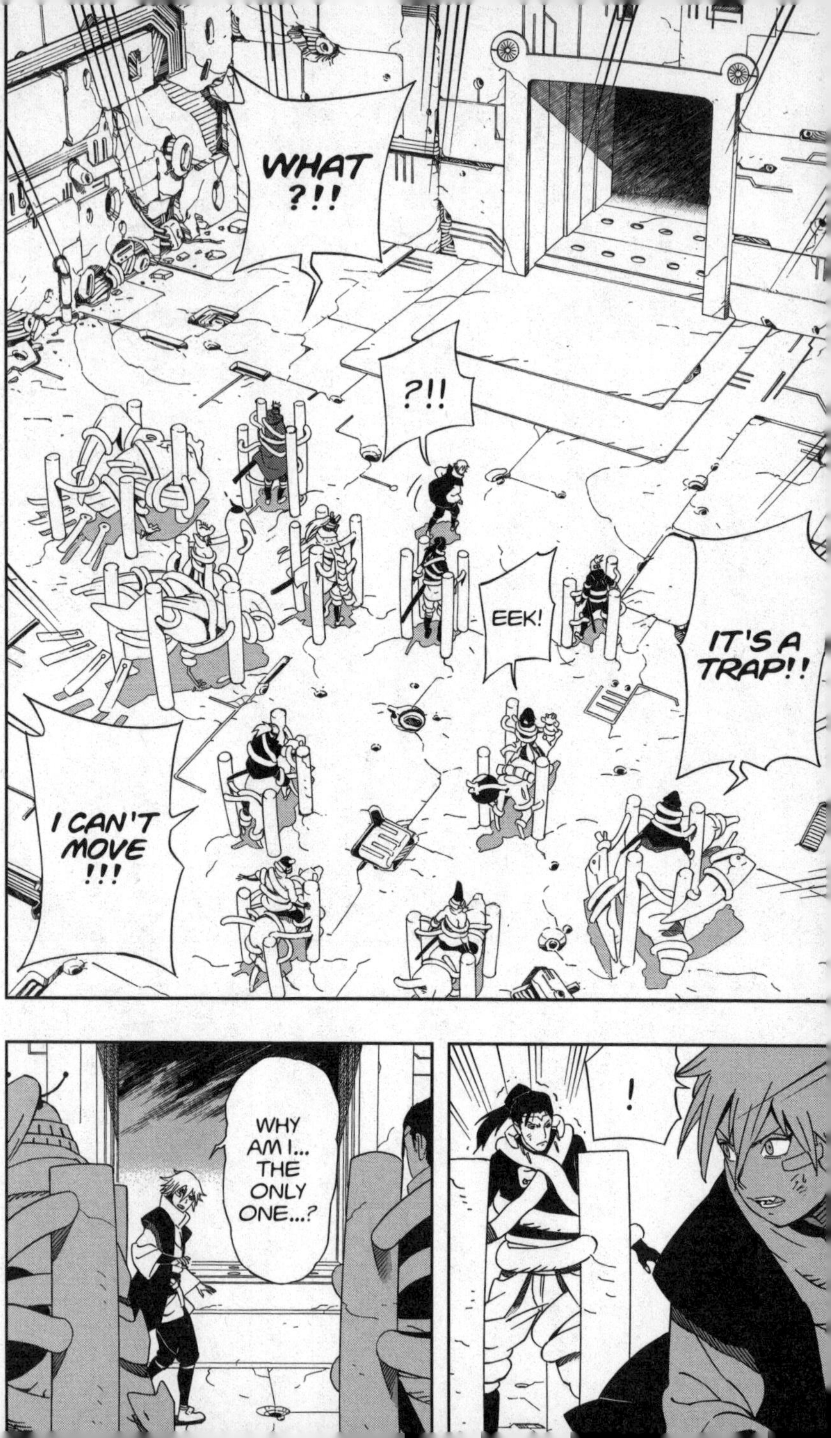
WHAT?!!
?!!
IT'S A TRAP!!
EEK!
I CAN'T MOVE!!!
!
WHY AM I... THE ONLY ONE...?

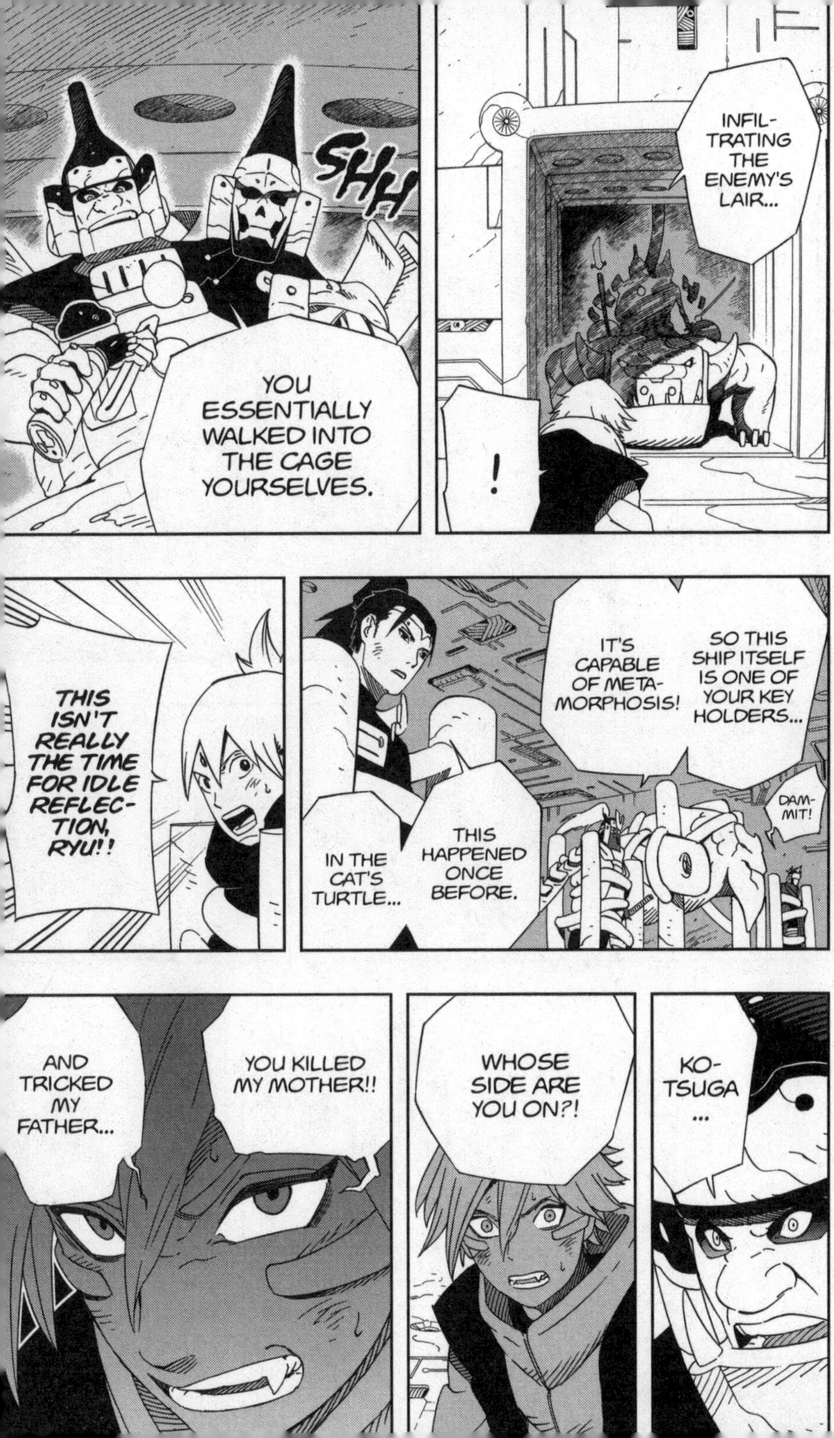
INFIL-TRATING THE ENEMY'S LAIR...
!
SHH
YOU ESSENTIALLY WALKED INTO THE CAGE YOURSELVES.
SO THIS SHIP ITSELF IS ONE OF YOUR KEY HOLDERS...
IT'S CAPABLE OF META-MORPHOSIS!
DAM-MIT!
THIS HAPPENED ONCE BEFORE.
IN THE CAT'S TURTLE...
THIS ISN'T REALLY THE TIME FOR IDLE REFLEC-TION, RYU!!
KO-TSUGA ...
WHOSE SIDE ARE YOU ON?!
YOU KILLED MY MOTHER!!
AND TRICKED MY FATHER...

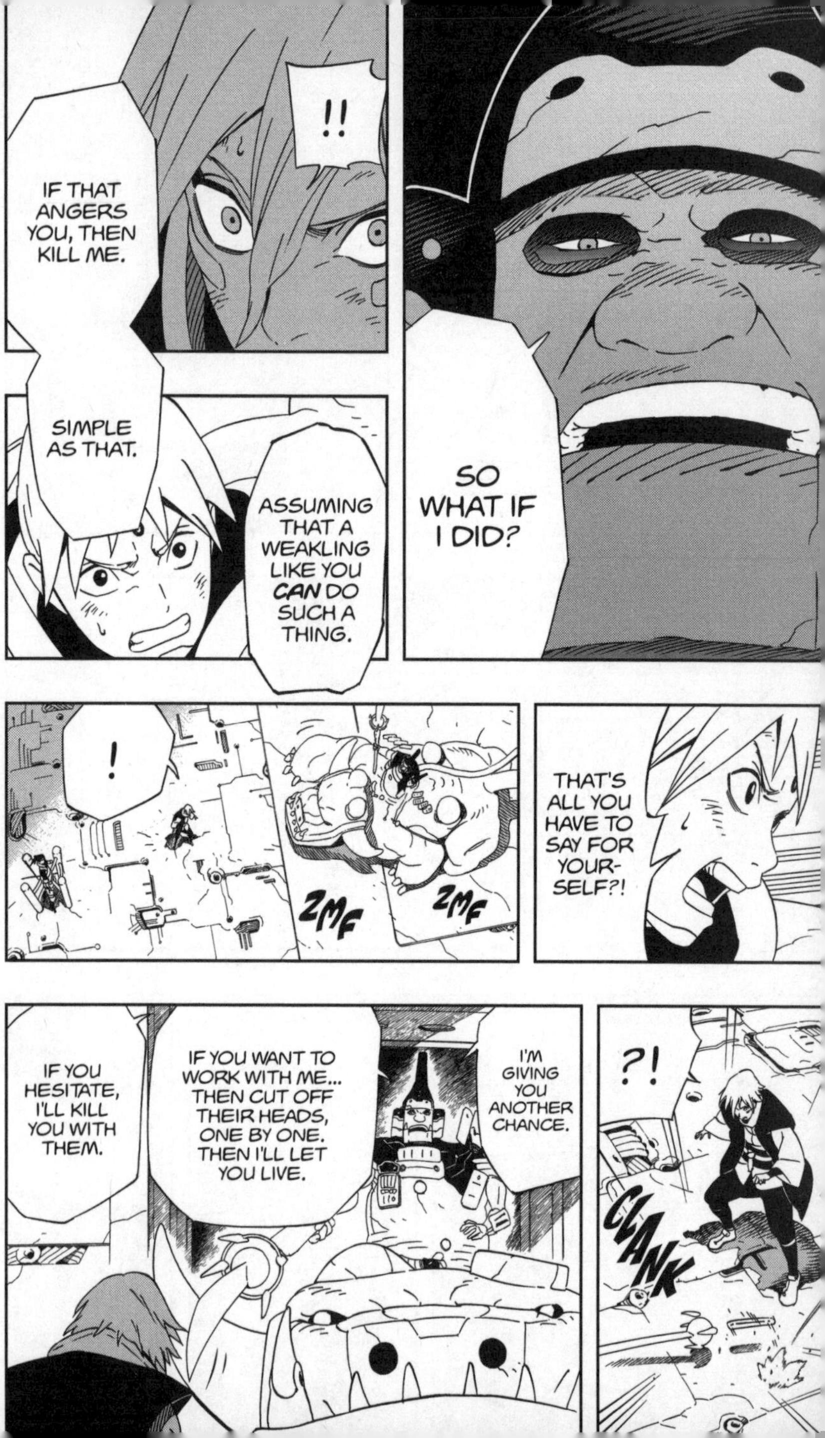
SO WHAT IF I DID?
!!
IF THAT ANGERS YOU, THEN KILL ME.
SIMPLE AS THAT.
ASSUMING THAT A WEAKLING LIKE YOU CAN DO SUCH A THING.
THAT'S ALL YOU HAVE TO SAY FOR YOUR-SELF?!
ZMF
ZMF
!
?!
CLANK
I'M GIVING YOU ANOTHER CHANCE.
IF YOU WANT TO WORK WITH ME... THEN CUT OFF THEIR HEADS, ONE BY ONE. THEN I'LL LET YOU LIVE.
IF YOU HESITATE, I'LL KILL YOU WITH THEM.

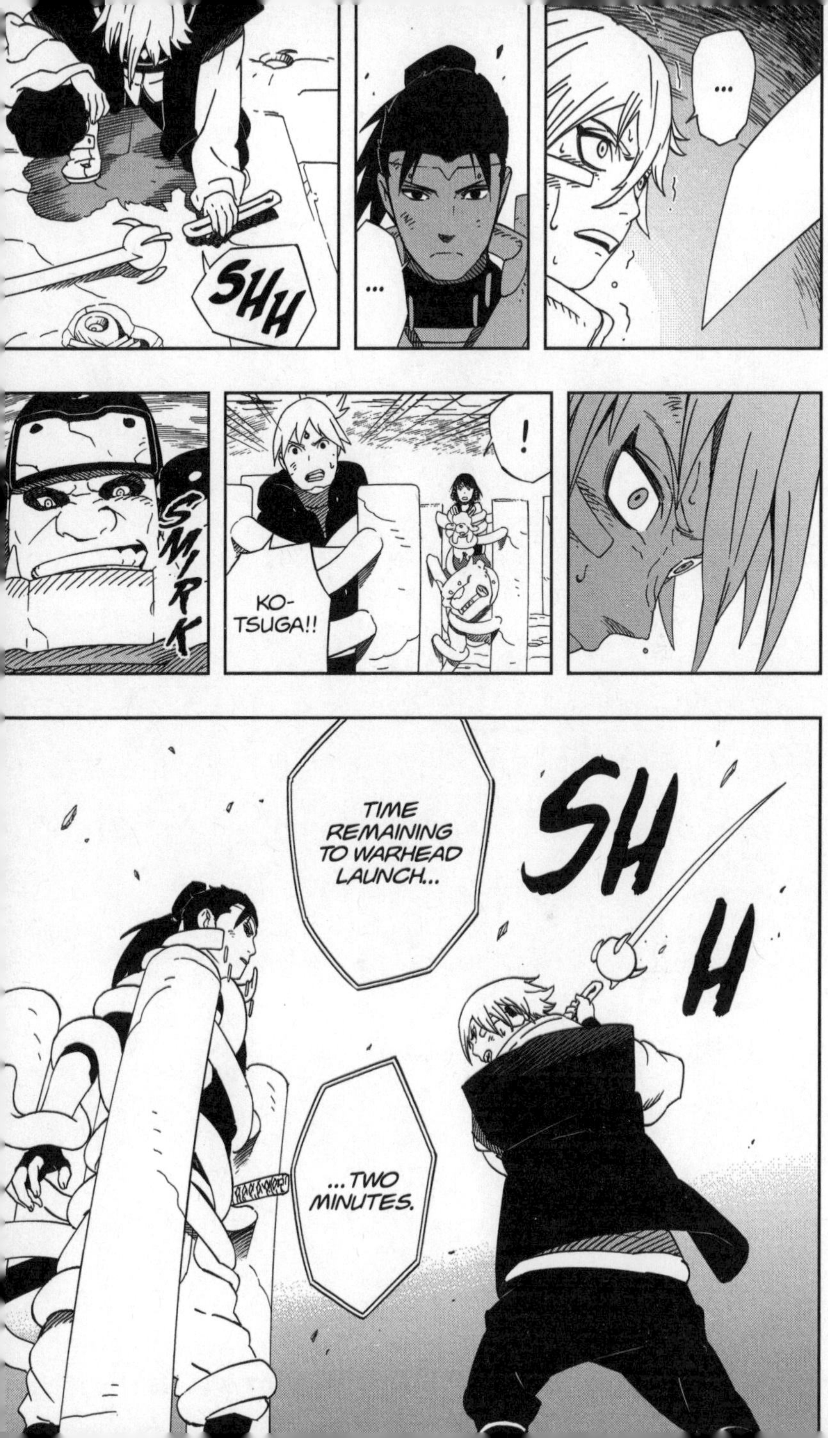
...
...
SHH
!
KO-TSUGA!!
SMIRK
SHH
TIME REMAINING TO WARHEAD LAUNCH...
...TWO MINUTES.

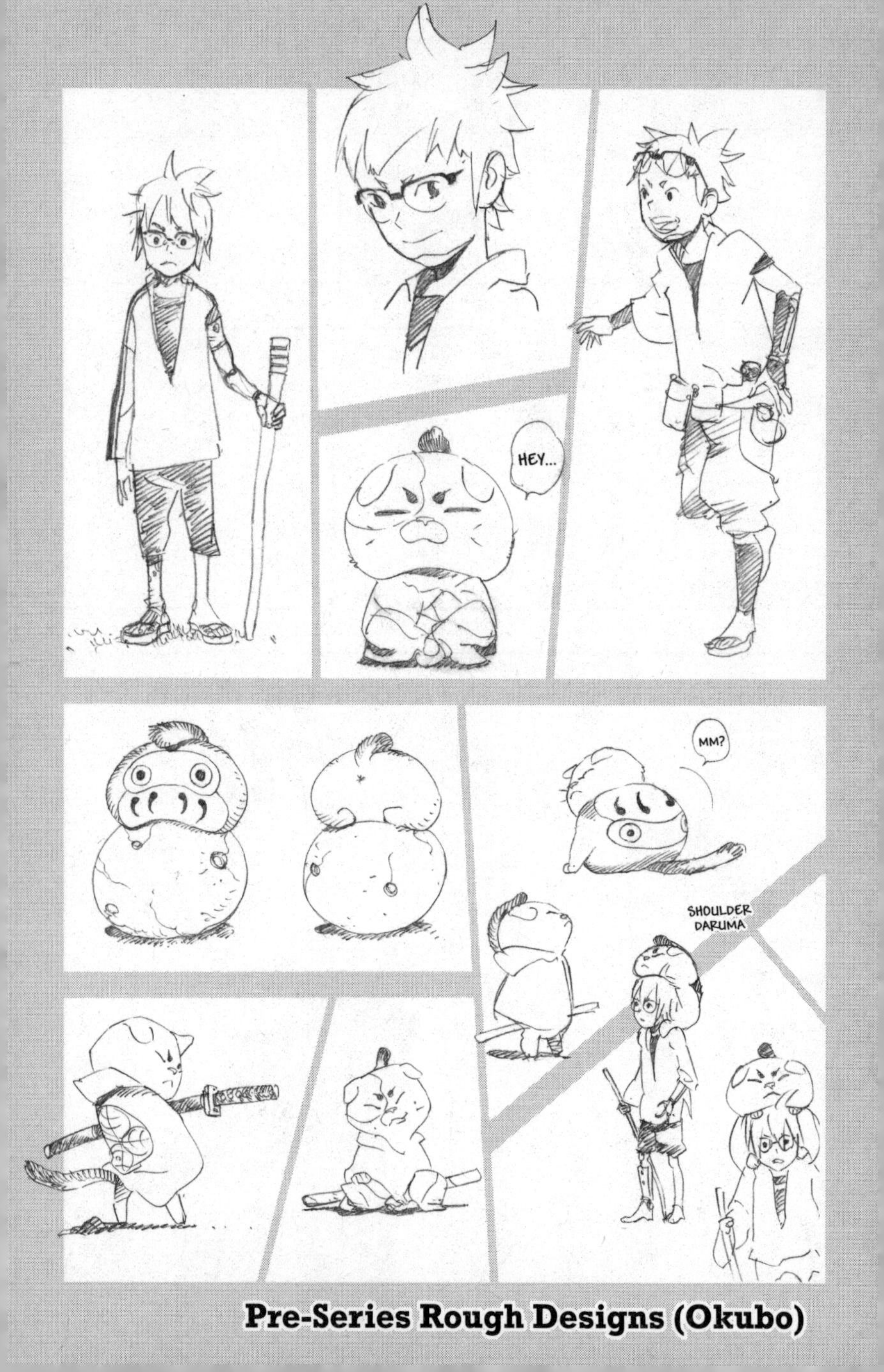
HEY...
MM?
SHOULDER DARUMA

Pre-Series Rough Designs (Okubo)

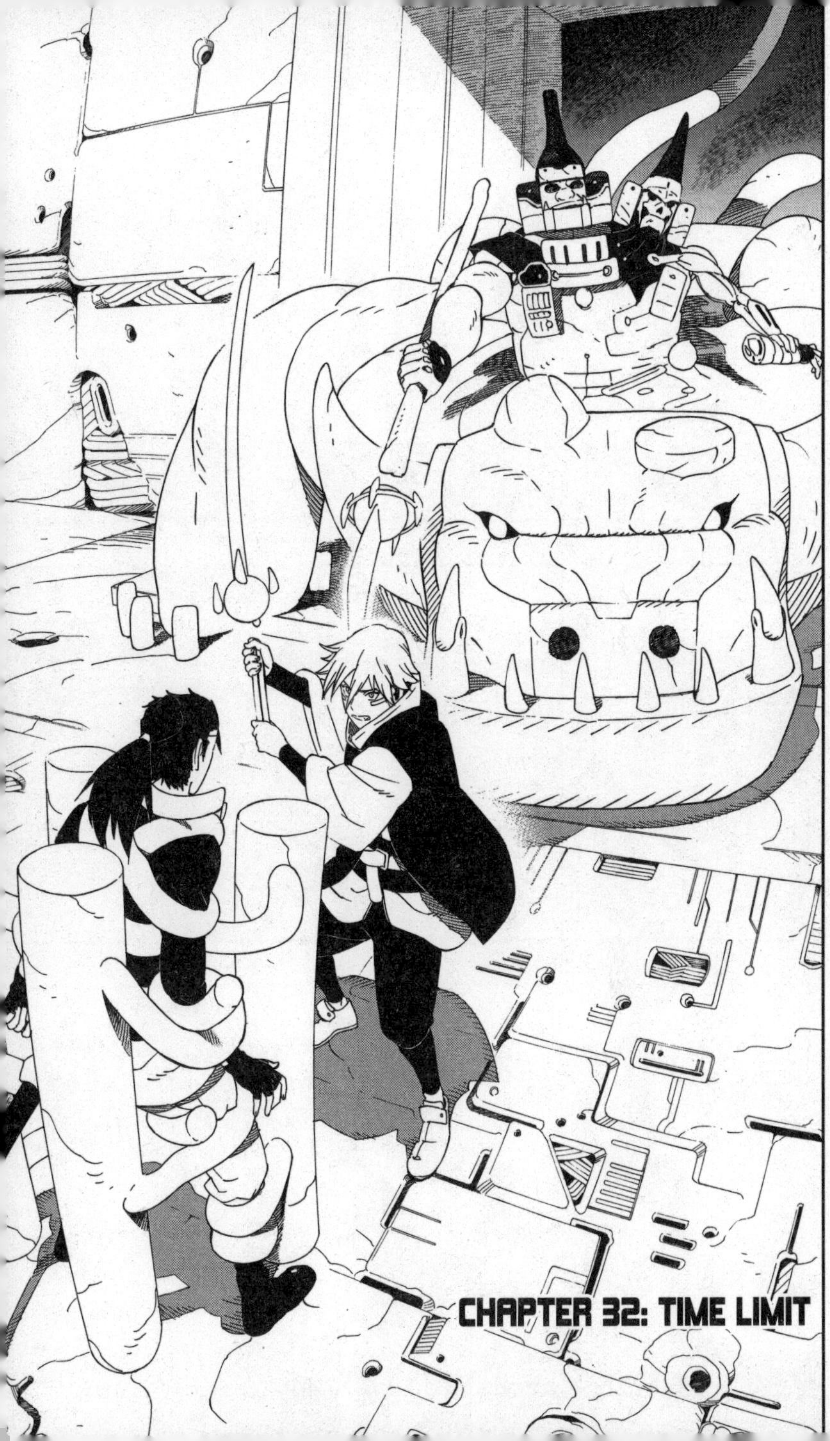
CHAPTER 32: TIME LIMIT

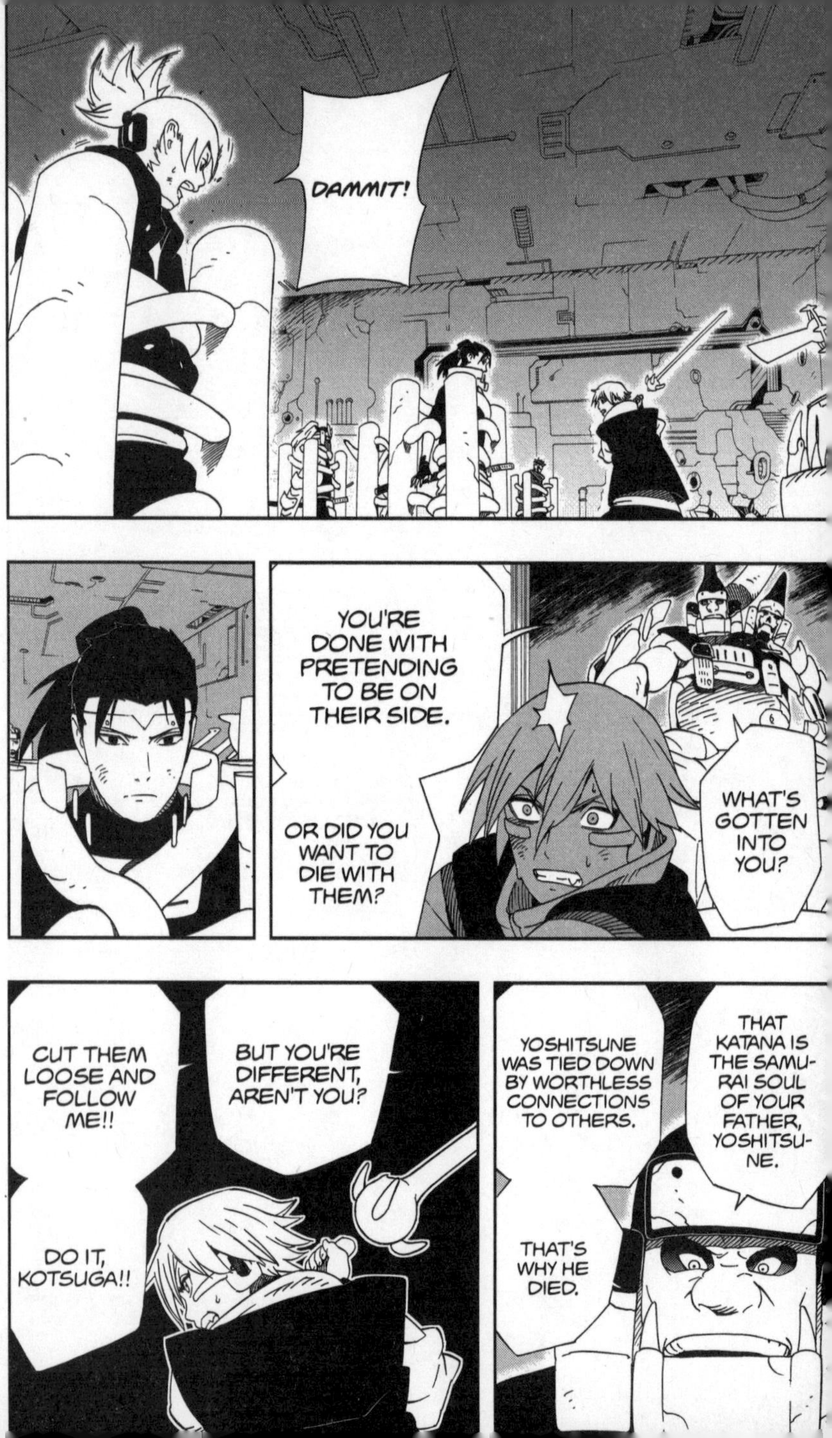
DAMMIT!
WHAT'S GOTTEN INTO YOU?
YOU'RE DONE WITH PRETENDING TO BE ON THEIR SIDE.
OR DID YOU WANT TO DIE WITH THEM?
THAT KATANA IS THE SAMURAI SOUL OF YOUR FATHER, YOSHITSUNE.
YOSHITSUNE WAS TIED DOWN BY WORTHLESS CONNECTIONS TO OTHERS.
THAT'S WHY HE DIED.
BUT YOU'RE DIFFERENT, AREN'T YOU?
CUT THEM LOOSE AND FOLLOW ME!!
DO IT, KOTSUGA!!

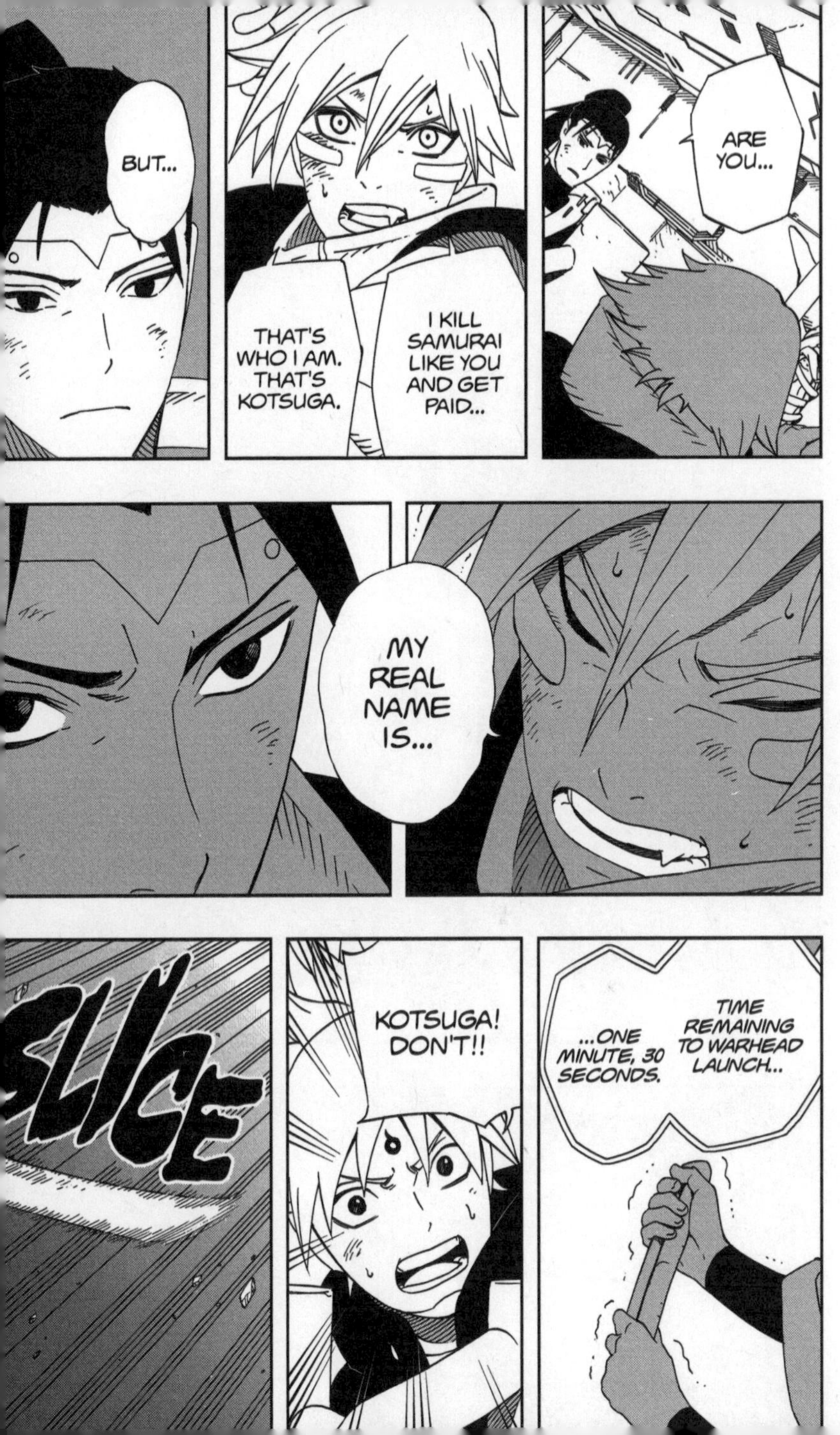
ARE YOU...
I KILL SAMURAI LIKE YOU AND GET PAID...
THAT'S WHO I AM. THAT'S KOTSUGA.
BUT...
MY REAL NAME IS...
TIME REMAINING TO WARHEAD LAUNCH...
...ONE MINUTE, 30 SECONDS.
KOTSUGA! DON'T!!
SLICE

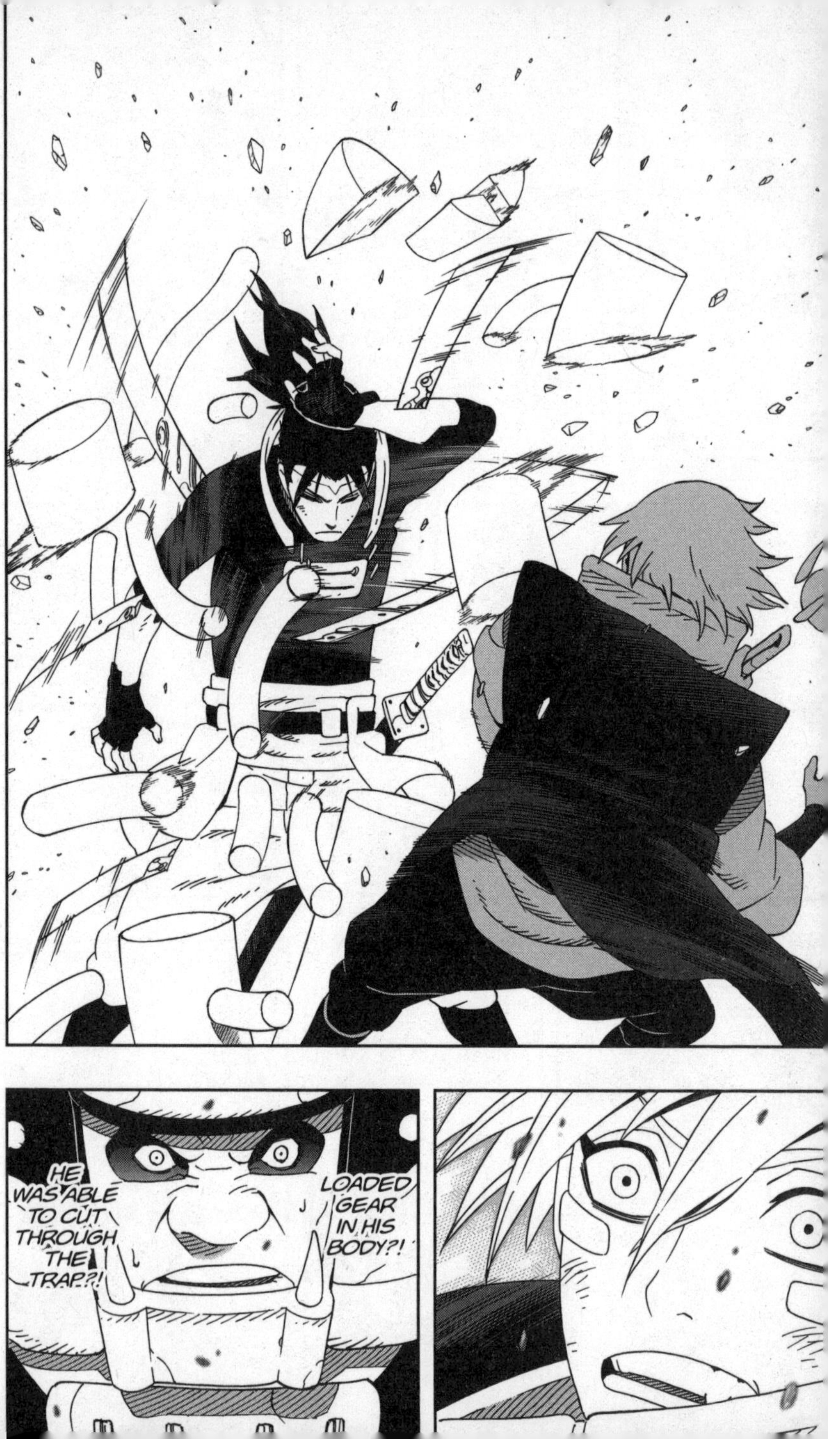
LOADED GEAR IN HIS BODY?!
HE WAS ABLE TO CUT THROUGH THE TRAP?!

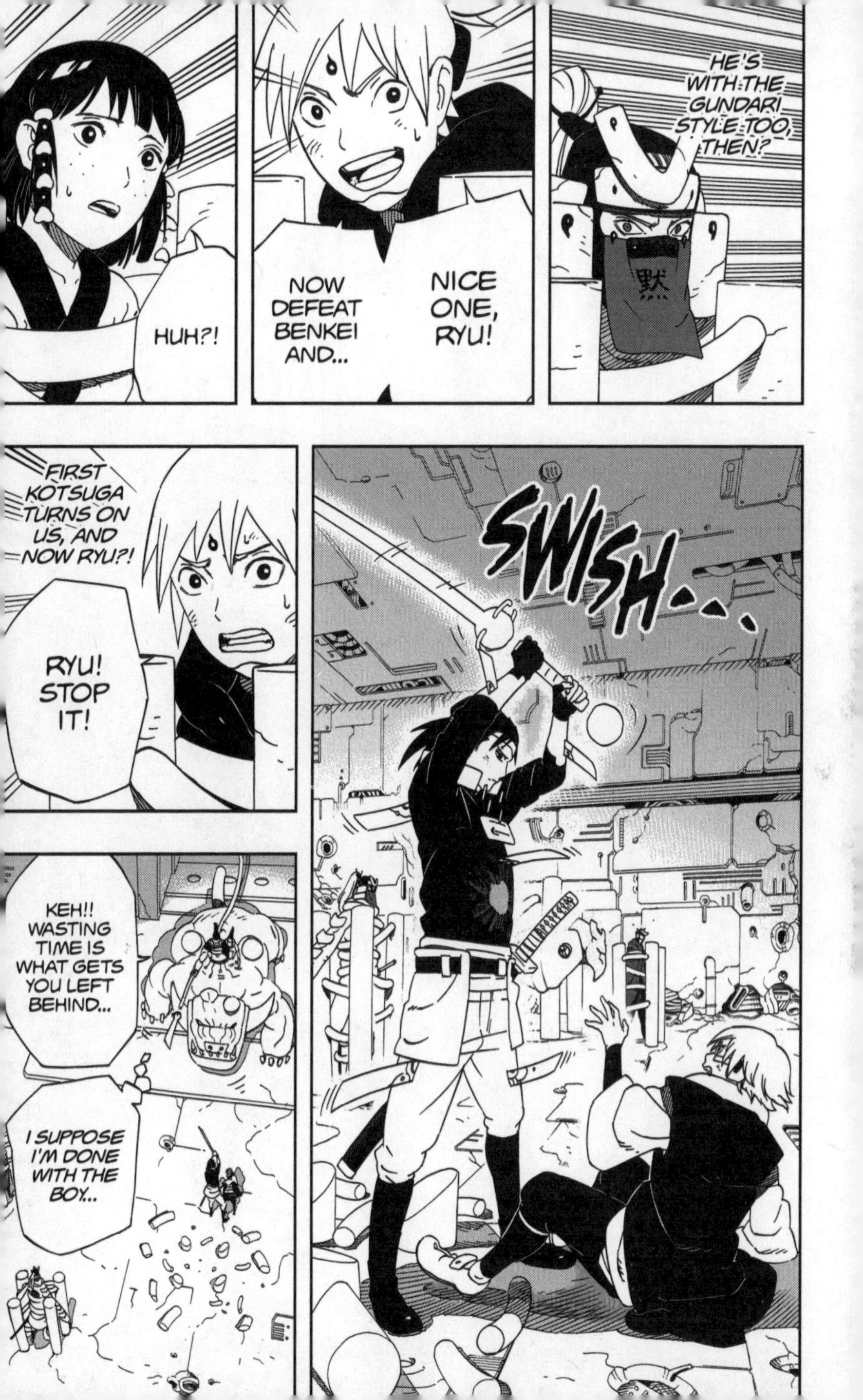
HE'S WITH THE GUNDARI STYLE TOO, THEN?
NICE ONE, RYU!
NOW DEFEAT BENKEI AND...
HUH?!
SWISH...
FIRST KOTSUGA TURNS ON US, AND NOW RYU?!
RYU! STOP IT!
KEH!! WASTING TIME IS WHAT GETS YOU LEFT BEHIND...
I SUPPOSE I'M DONE WITH THE BOY...

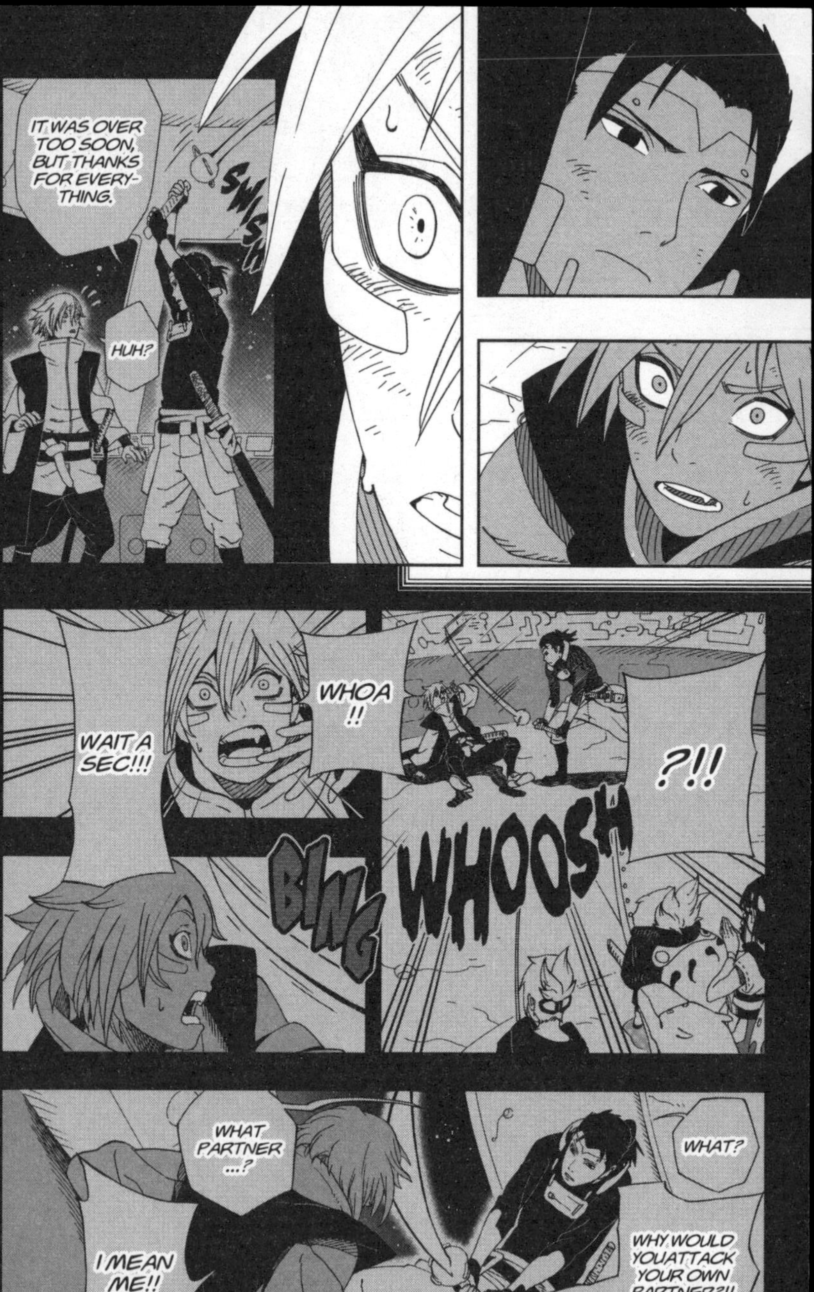
IT WAS OVER TOO SOON, BUT THANKS FOR EVERY-THING.
SWISH
HUH?
?!!
WHOOSH
WHOA !!
WAIT A SEC!!!
BING
WHAT?
WHY WOULD YOU ATTACK YOUR OWN PARTNER?!!
WHAT PARTNER ...?
I MEAN ME!!

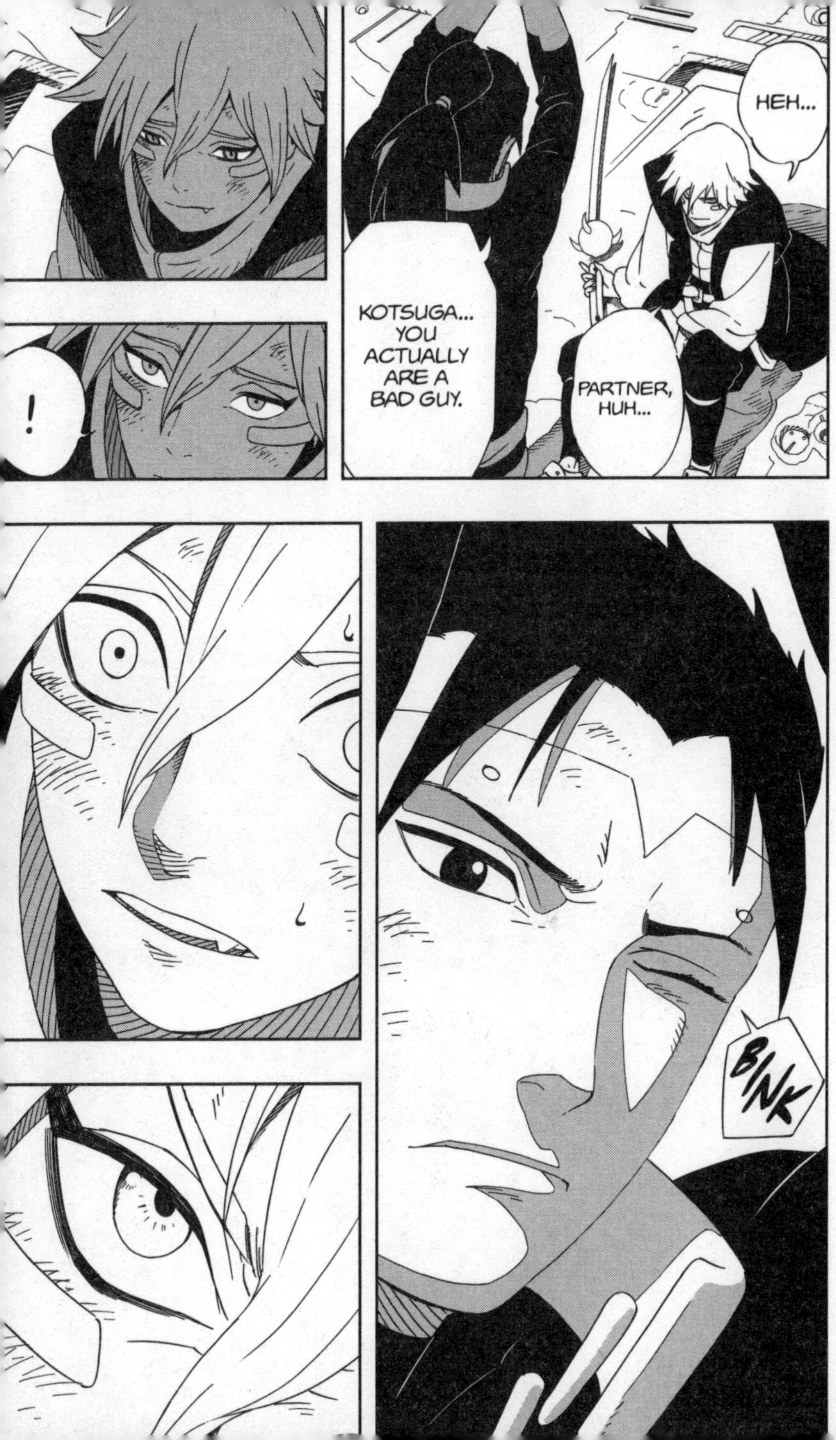
HEH...
PARTNER, HUH...
KOTSUGA... YOU ACTUALLY ARE A BAD GUY.
!
BINK

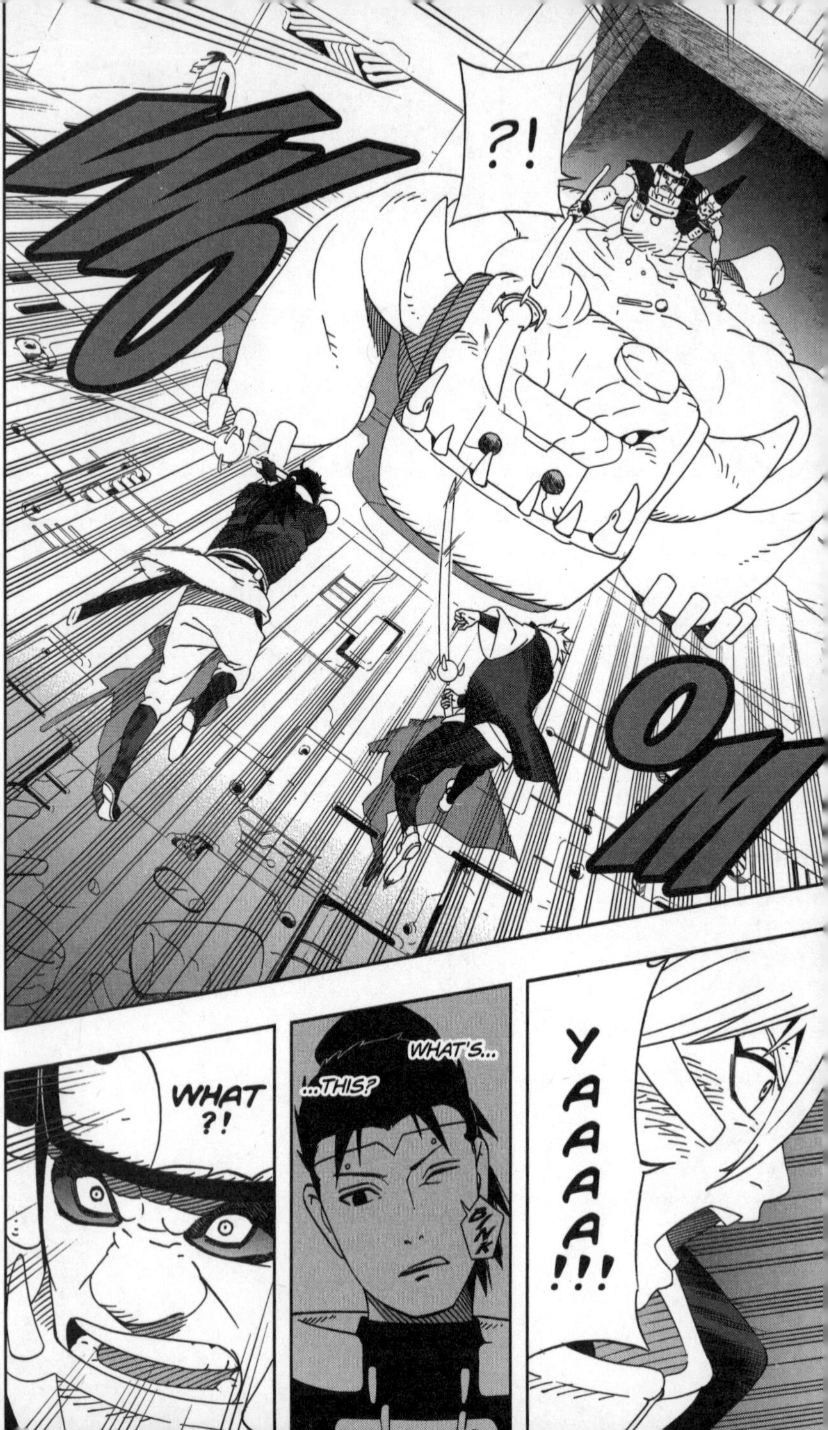
?!
YAAAAA!!!
WHAT'S...
...THIS?
BLINK
WHAT ?!

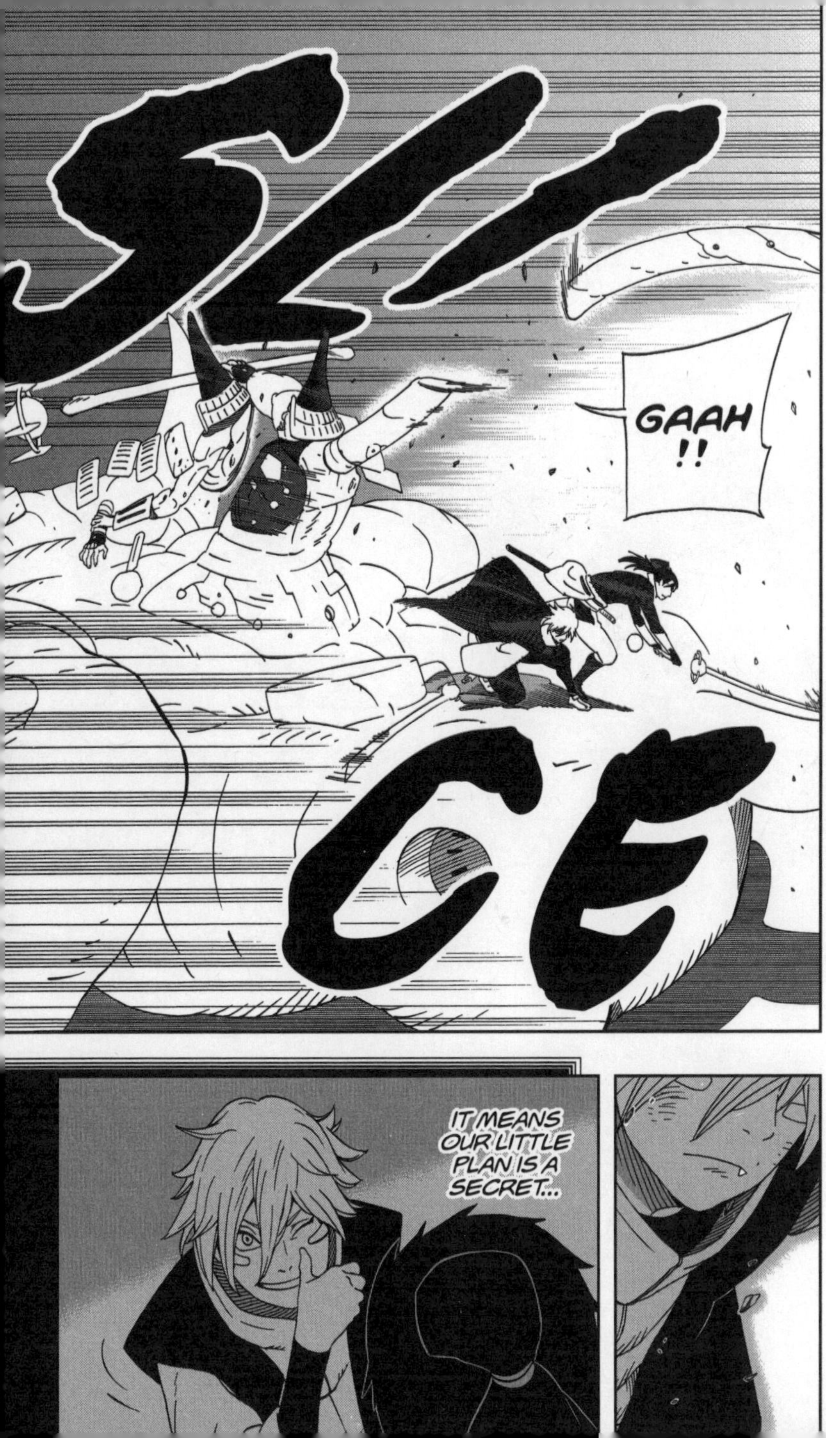
SLI
GAAH !!
CE
IT MEANS OUR LITTLE PLAN IS A SECRET...

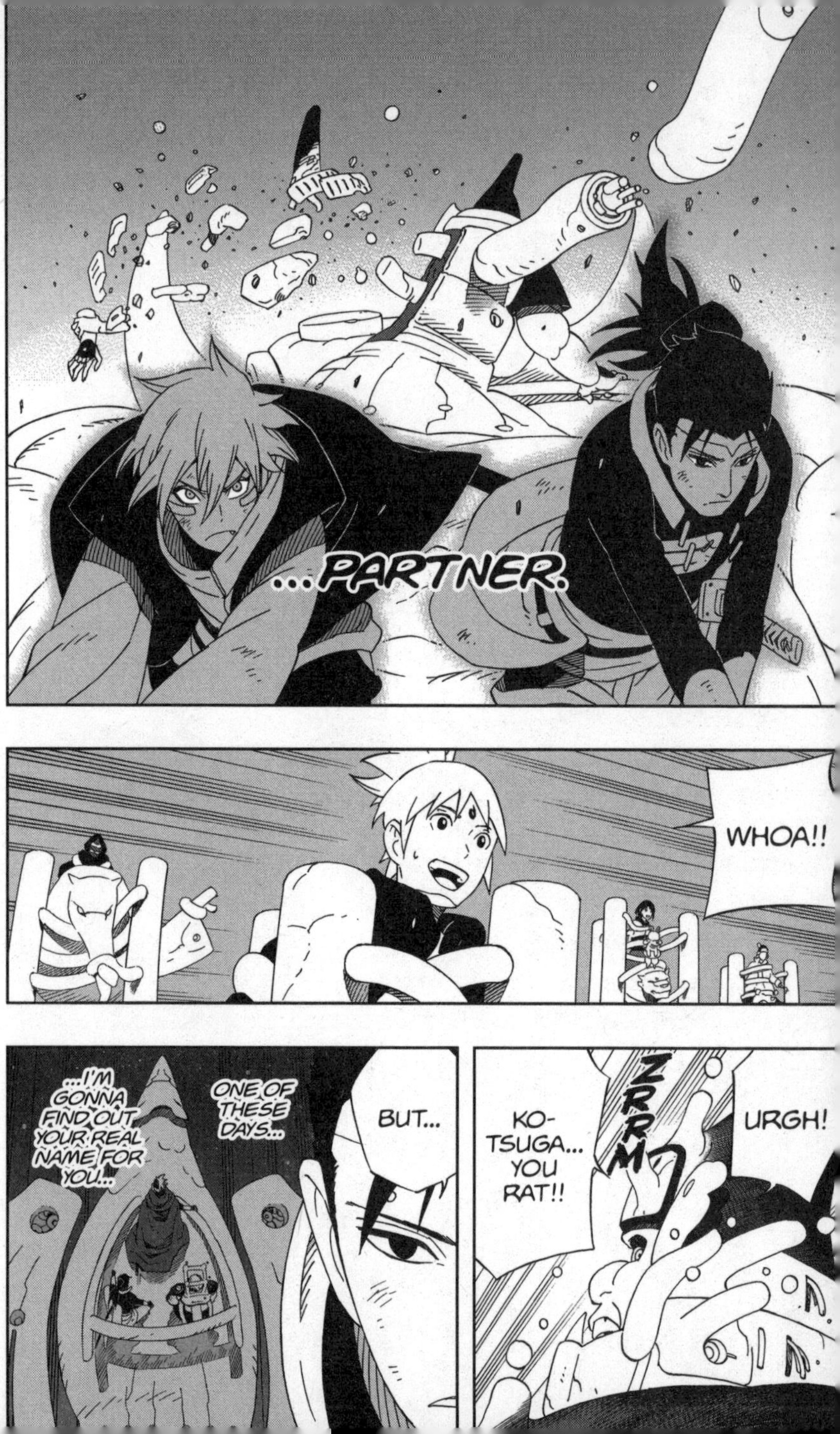
...PARTNER.
WHOA!!
URGH!
ZRRM
KO-TSUGA... YOU RAT!!
BUT...
ONE OF THESE DAYS...
...I'M GONNA FIND OUT YOUR REAL NAME FOR YOU...

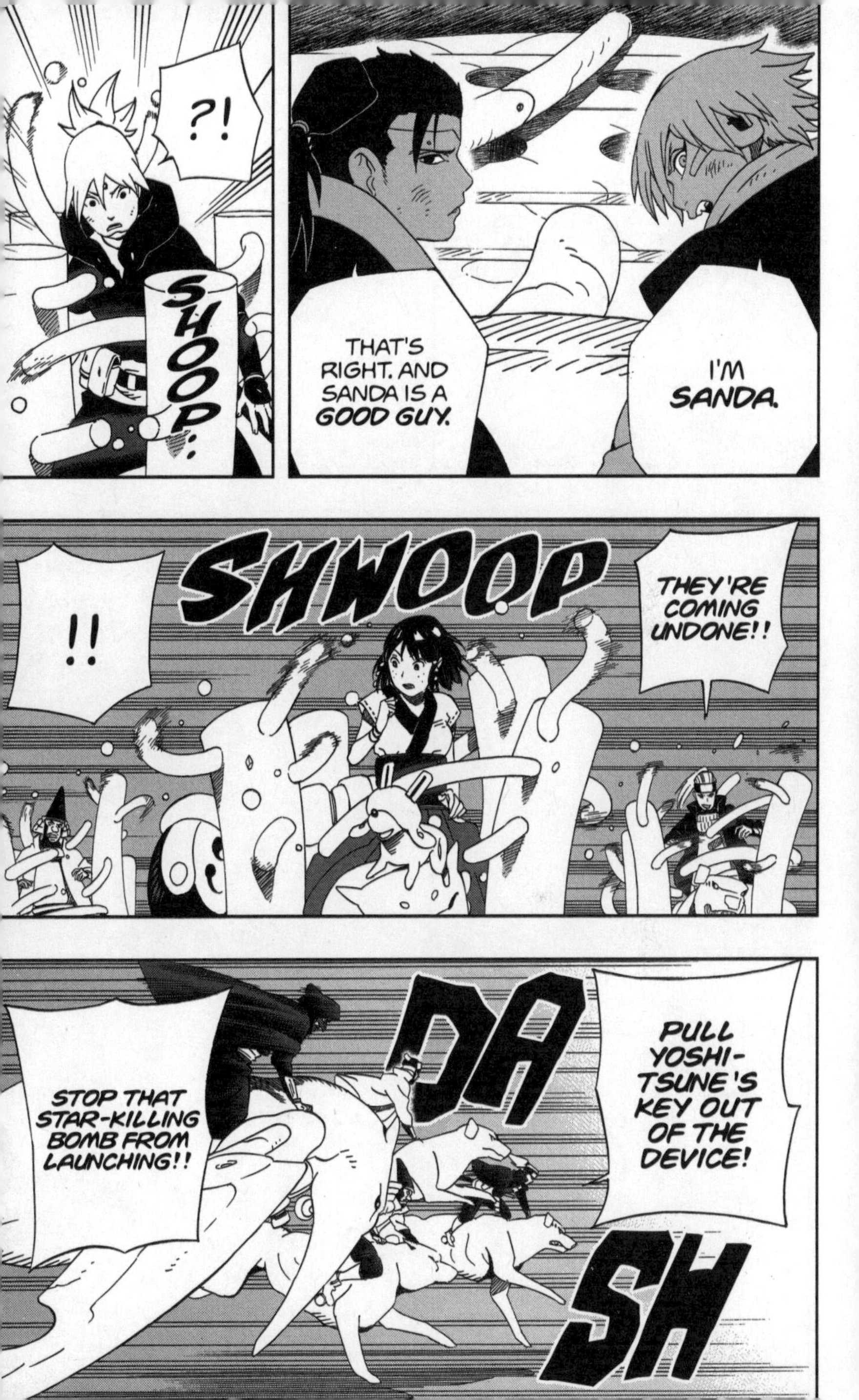
I'M SANDA.
THAT'S RIGHT. AND SANDA IS A GOOD GUY.
?!
SHOOP
THEY'RE COMING UNDONE!!
SHWOOP
!!
PULL YOSHI-TSUNE'S KEY OUT OF THE DEVICE!
DA
SH
STOP THAT STAR-KILLING BOMB FROM LAUNCHING!!

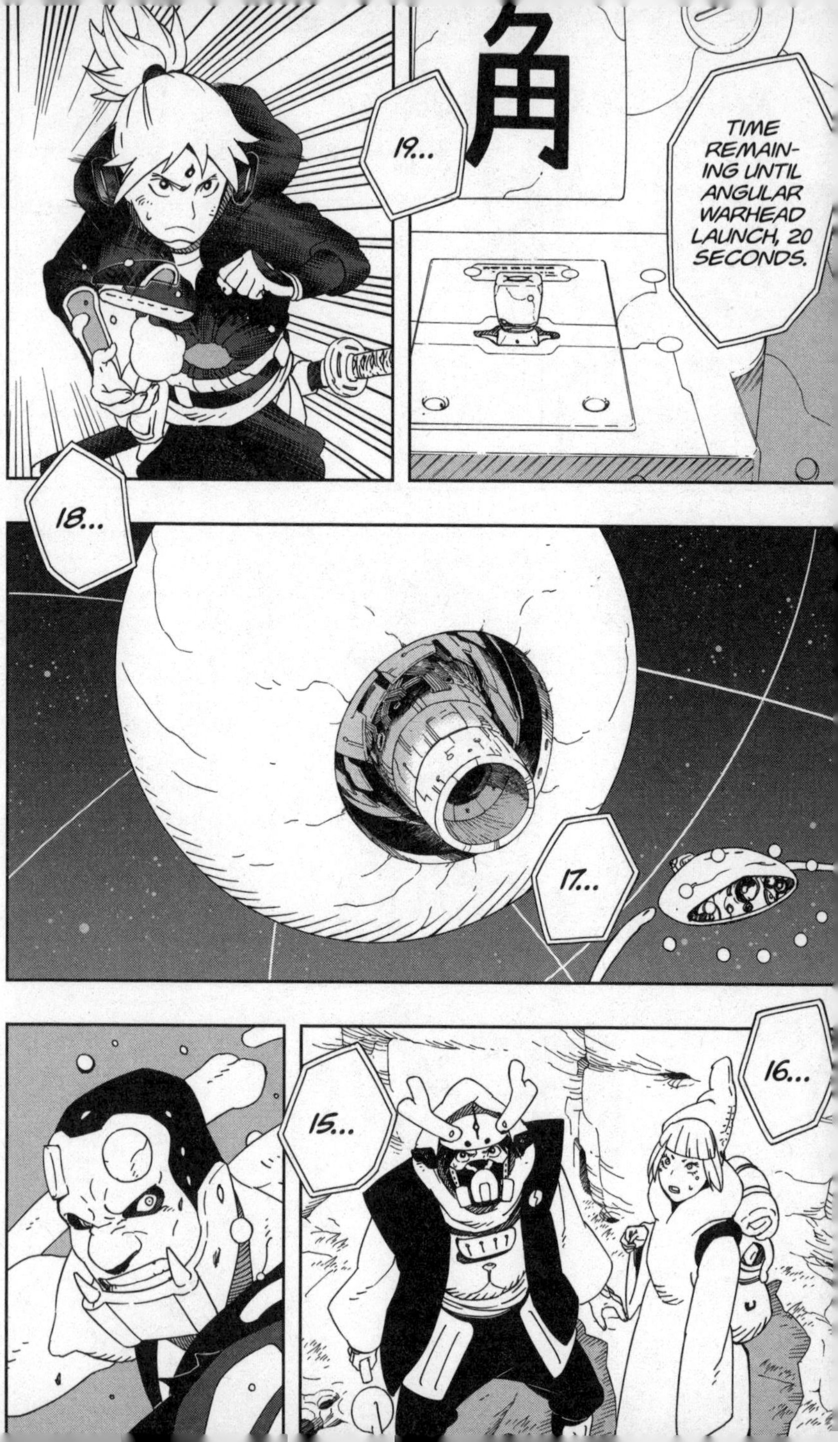
TIME REMAIN-ING UNTIL ANGULAR WARHEAD LAUNCH, 20 SECONDS.
角
19...
18...
17...
16...
15...

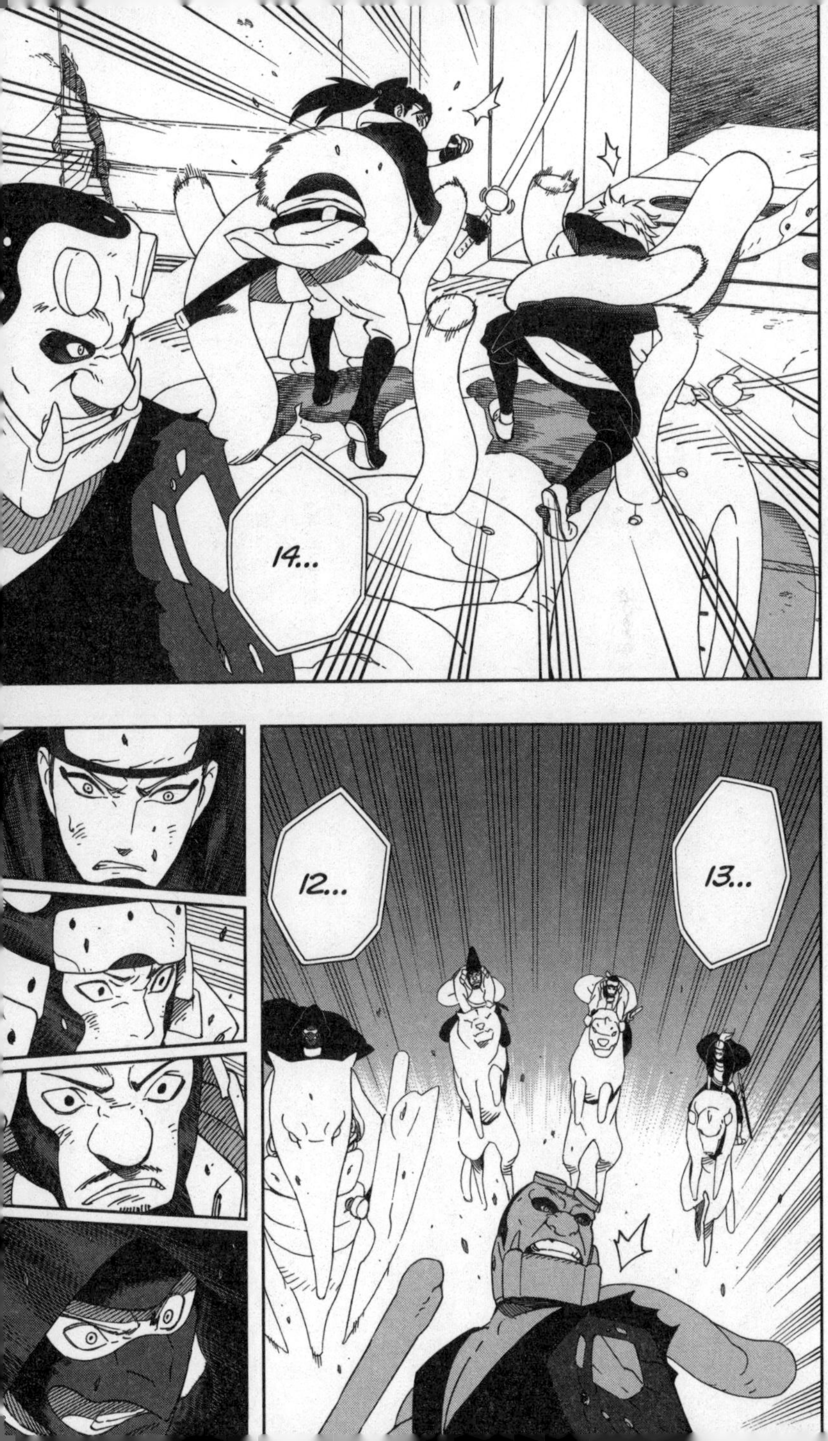
14...
13...
12...

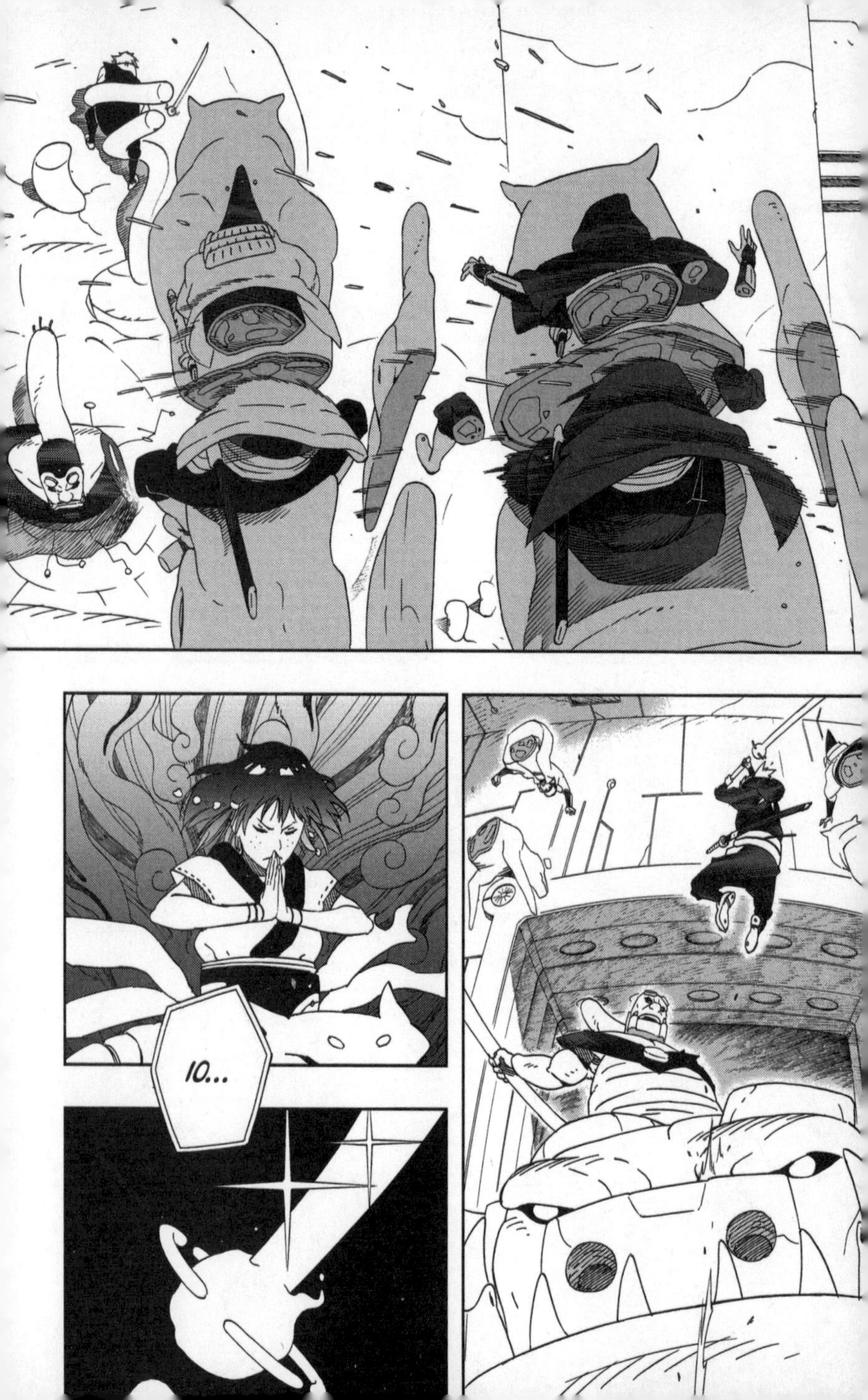
10...

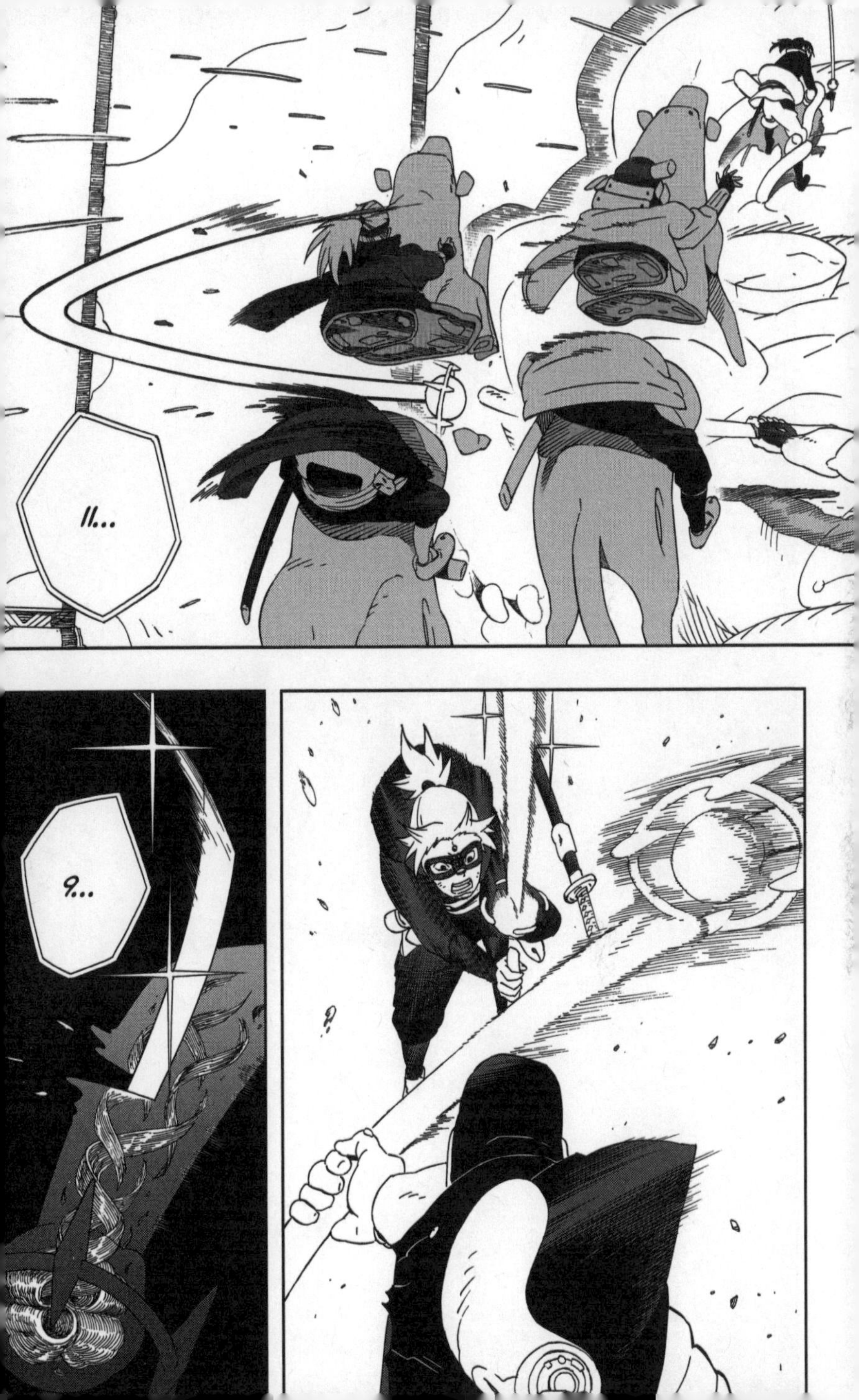
11...
9...

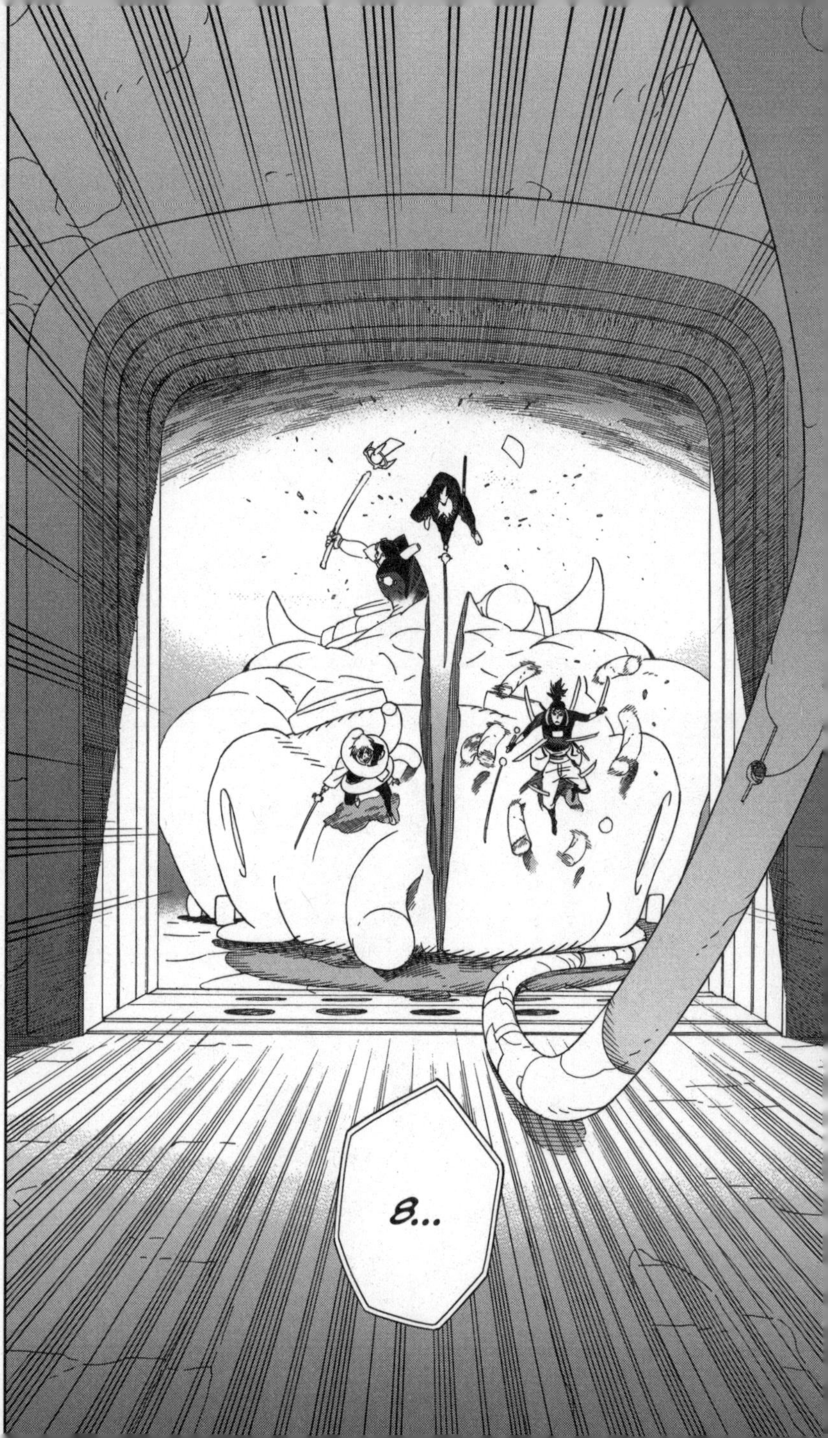
8...

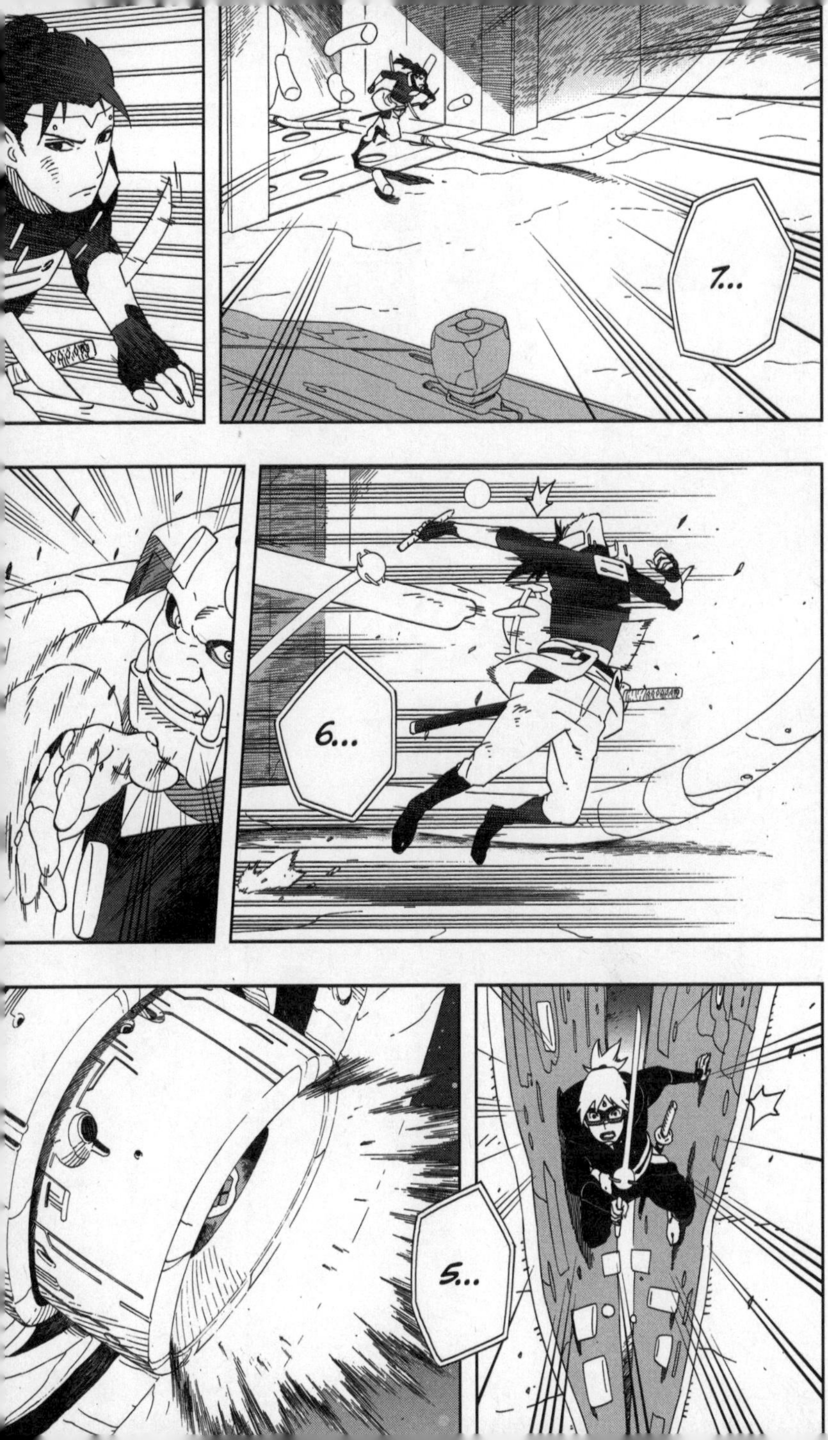
7...
6...
5...

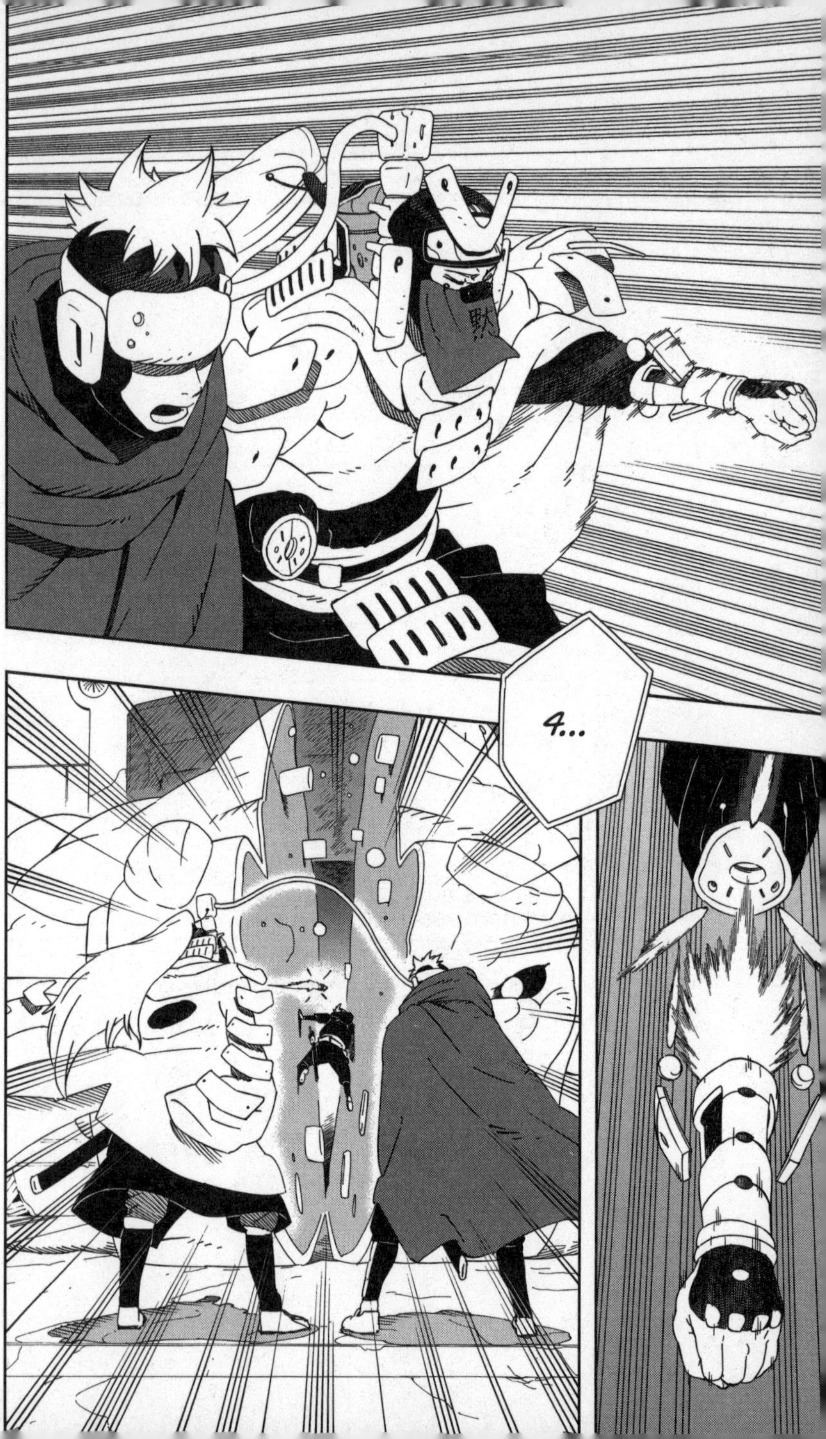
4...

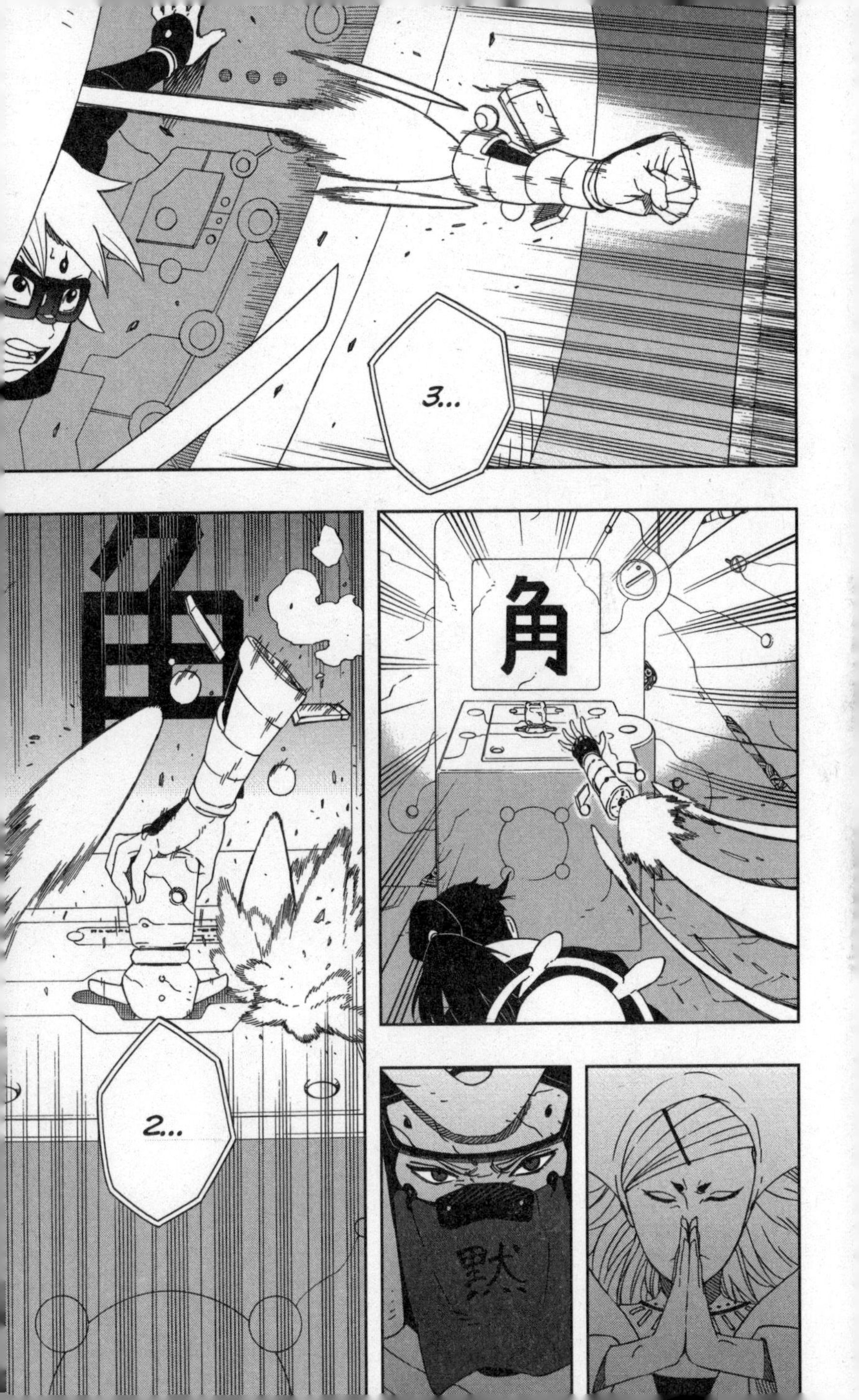
3...
角
2...

Pre-Series Rough Designs (Okubo)

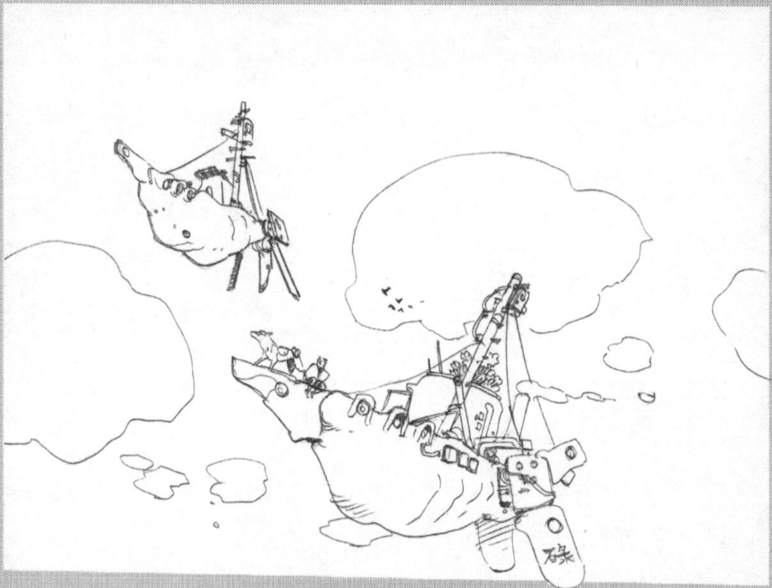

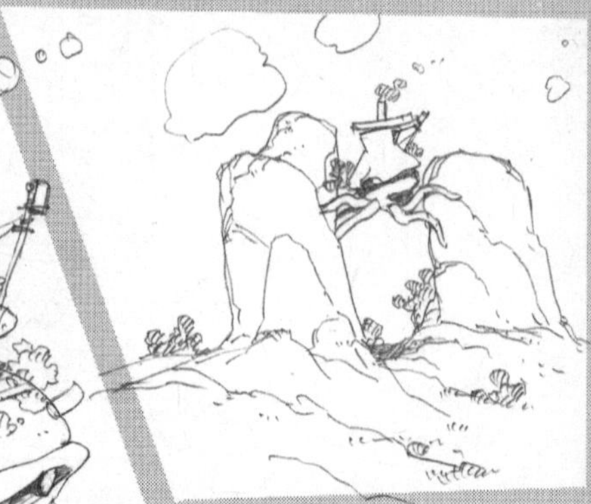

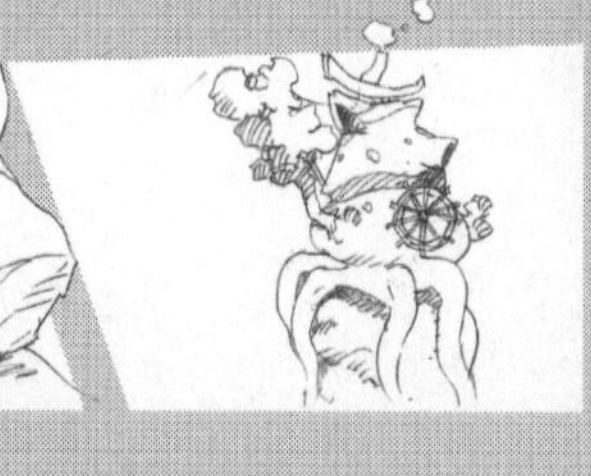

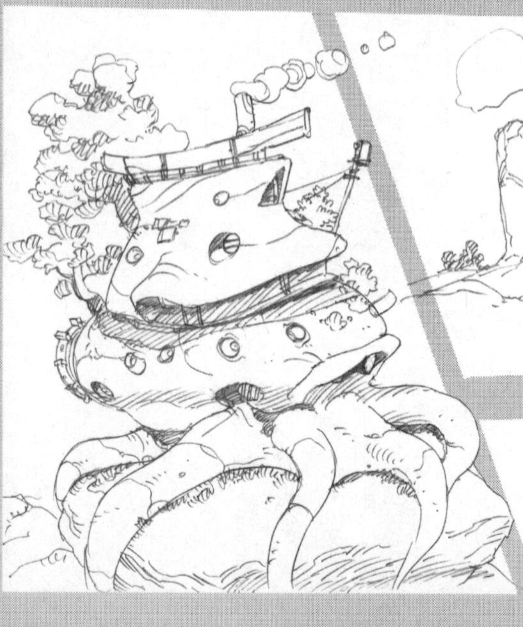

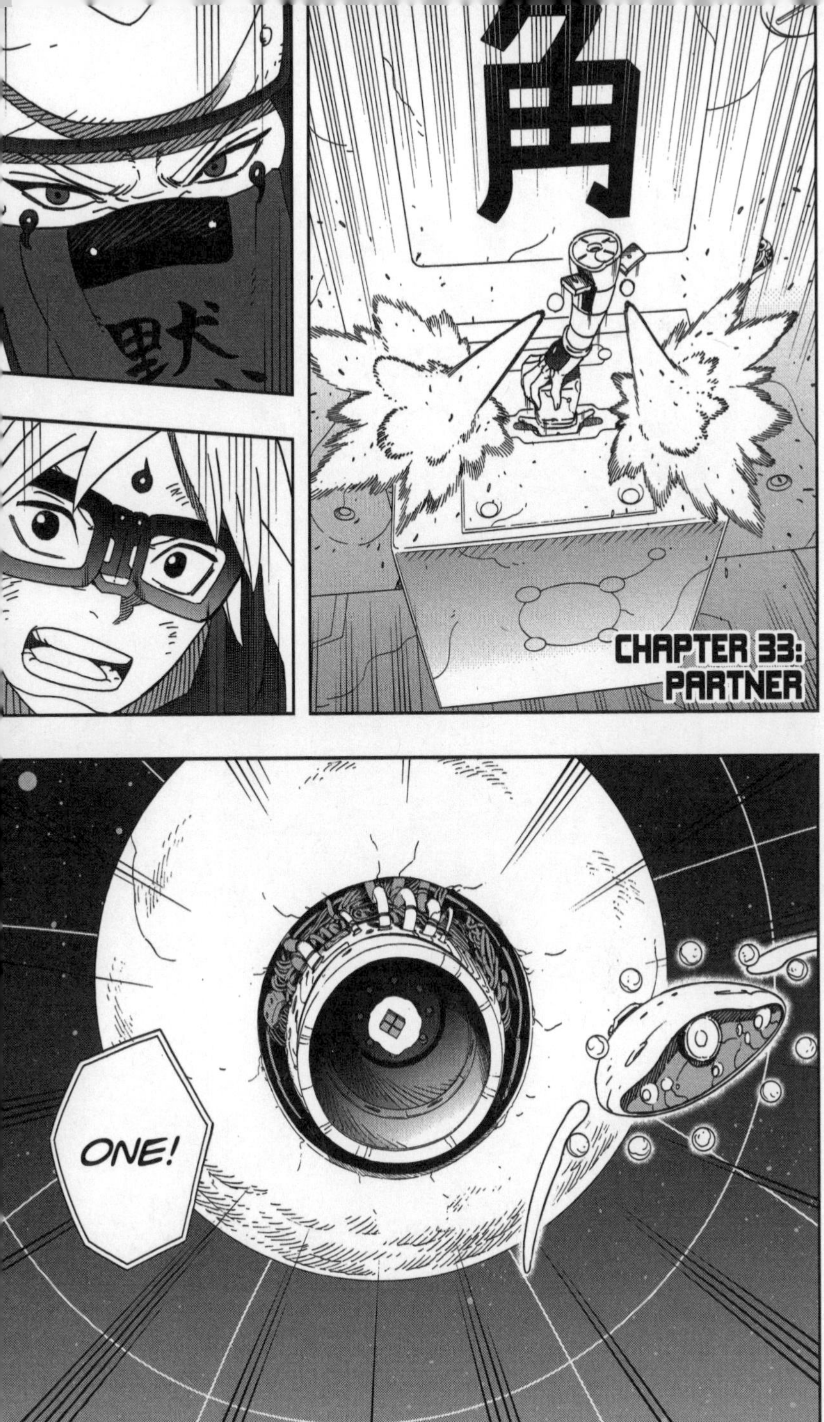
角
CHAPTER 33:
PARTNER
默
ONE!

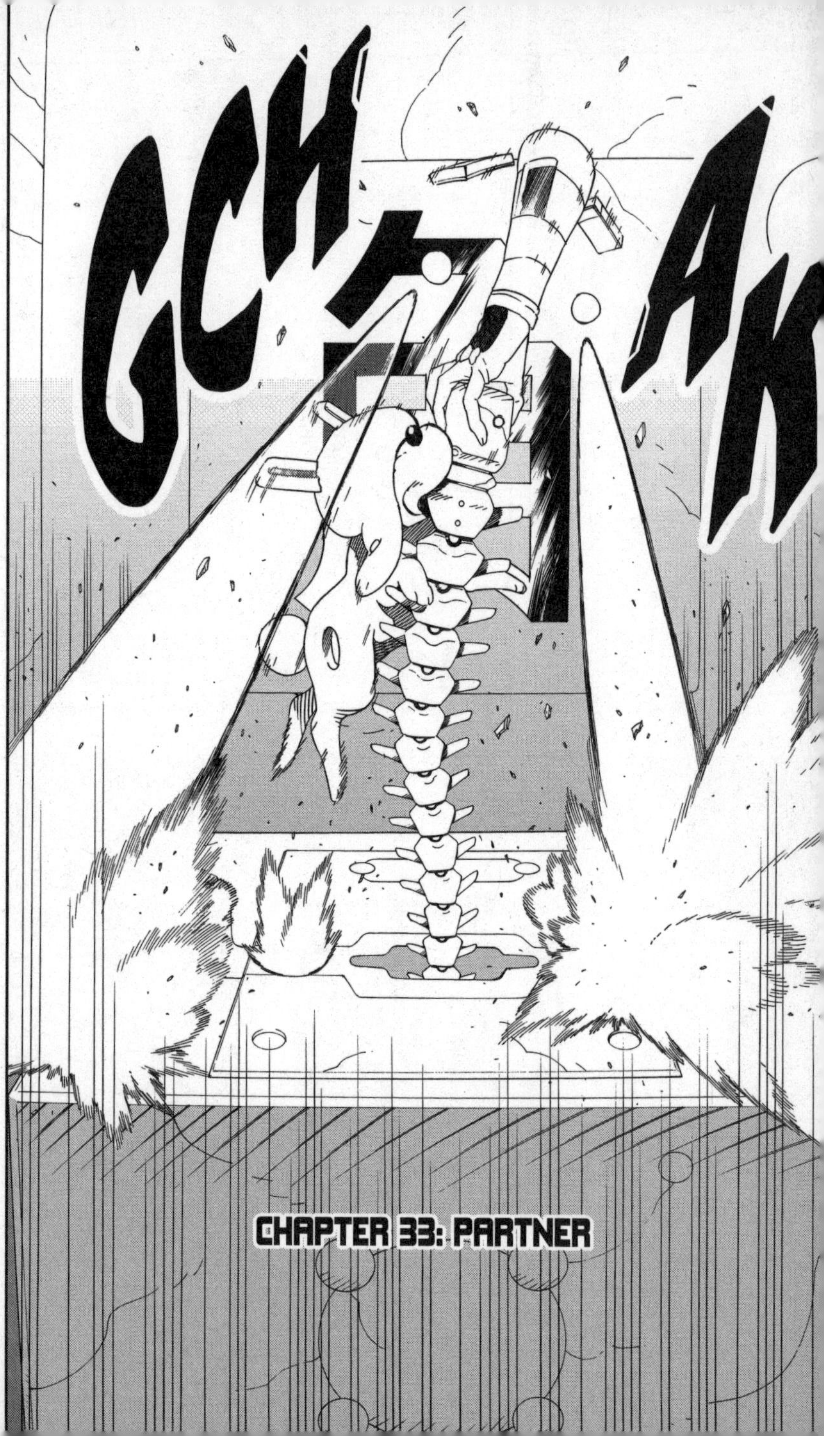
GCH-AK
CHAPTER 33: PARTNER

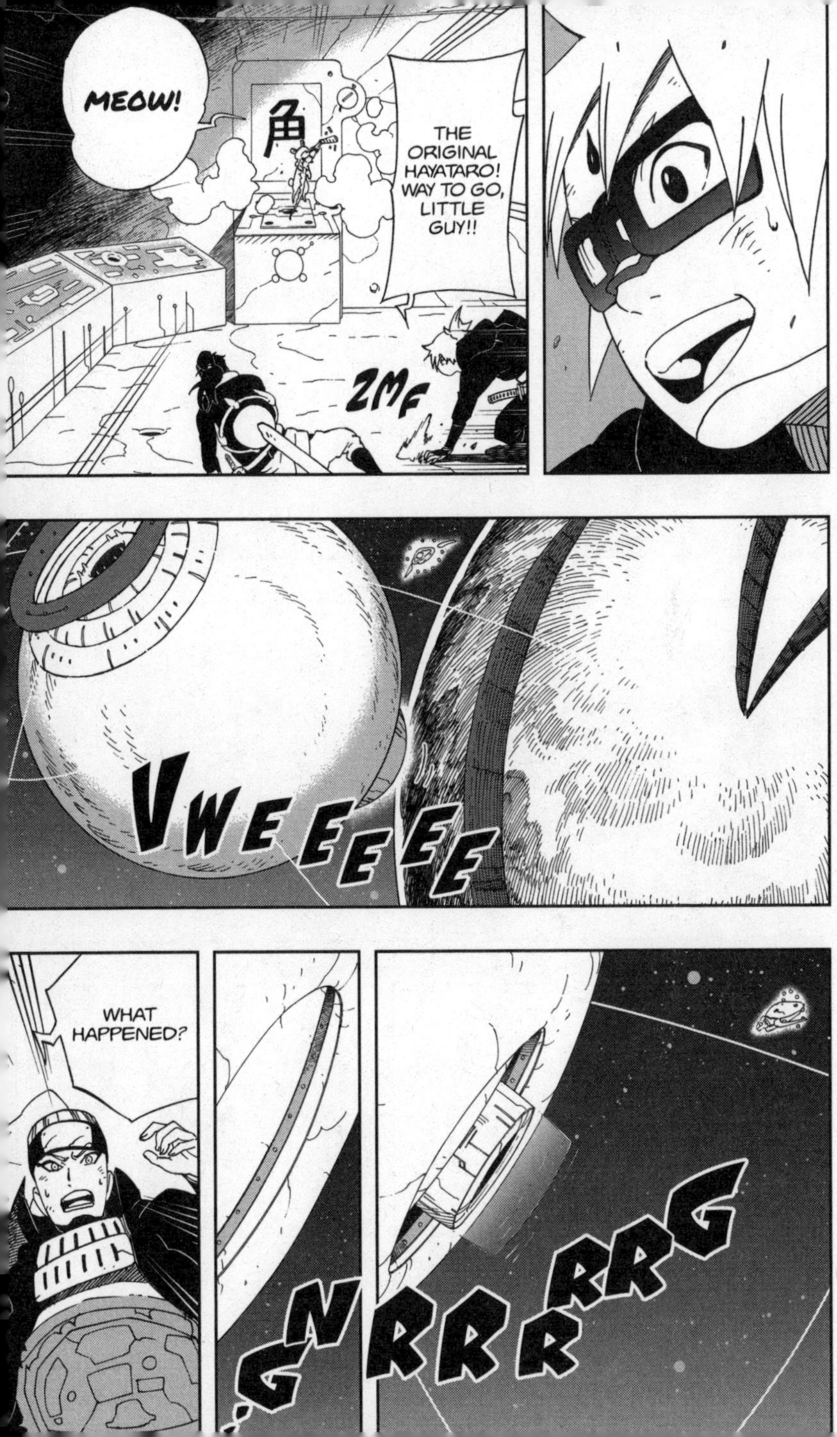
MEOW!
THE ORIGINAL HAYATARO! WAY TO GO, LITTLE GUY!!
ZMF
VWEEEEE
GNRRRRRG
WHAT HAPPENED?

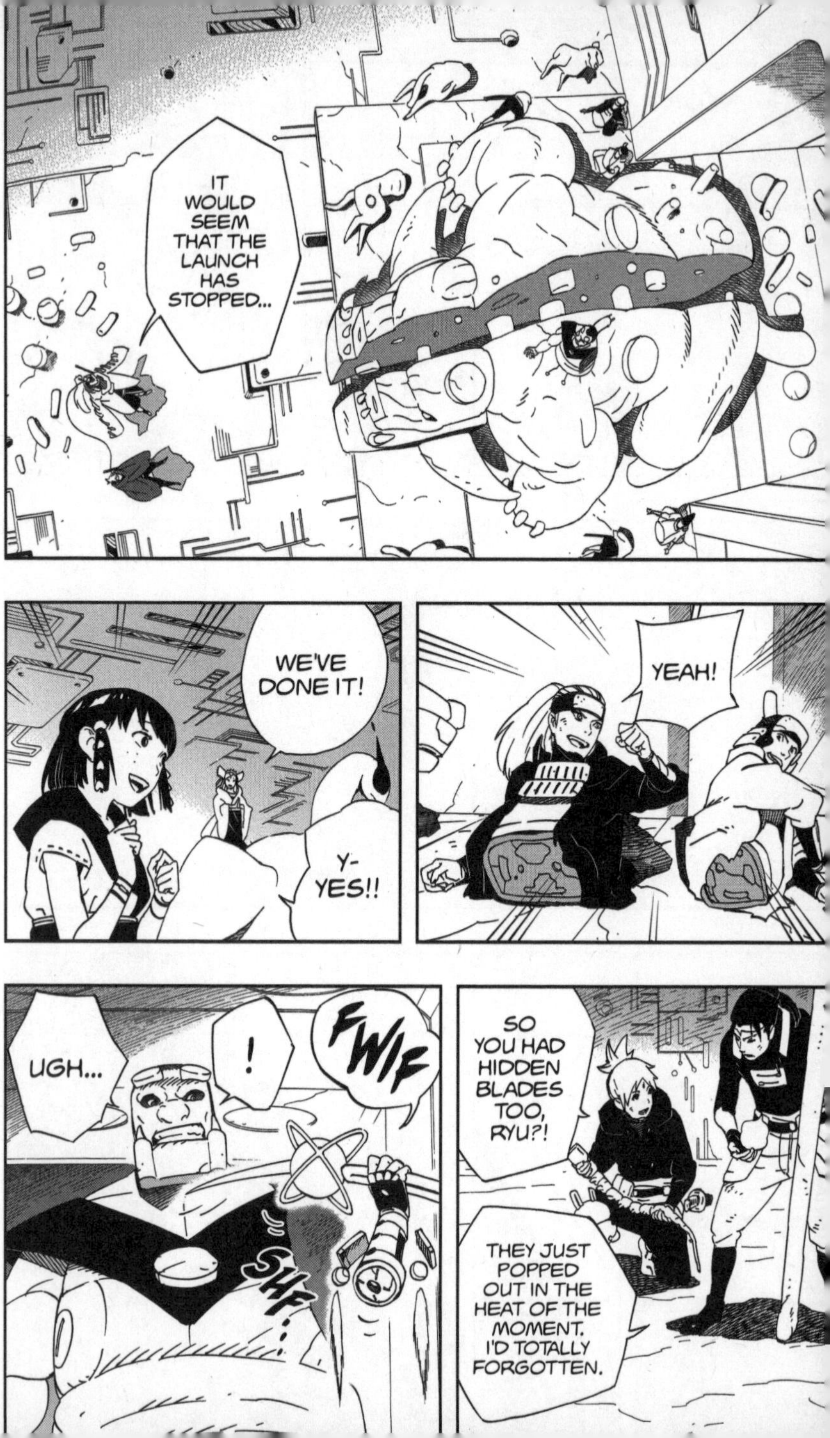
IT WOULD SEEM THAT THE LAUNCH HAS STOPPED...
YEAH!
WE'VE DONE IT!
Y- YES!!
SO YOU HAD HIDDEN BLADES TOO, RYU?!
THEY JUST POPPED OUT IN THE HEAT OF THE MOMENT. I'D TOTALLY FORGOTTEN.
FWIF
!
UGH...
SHF...

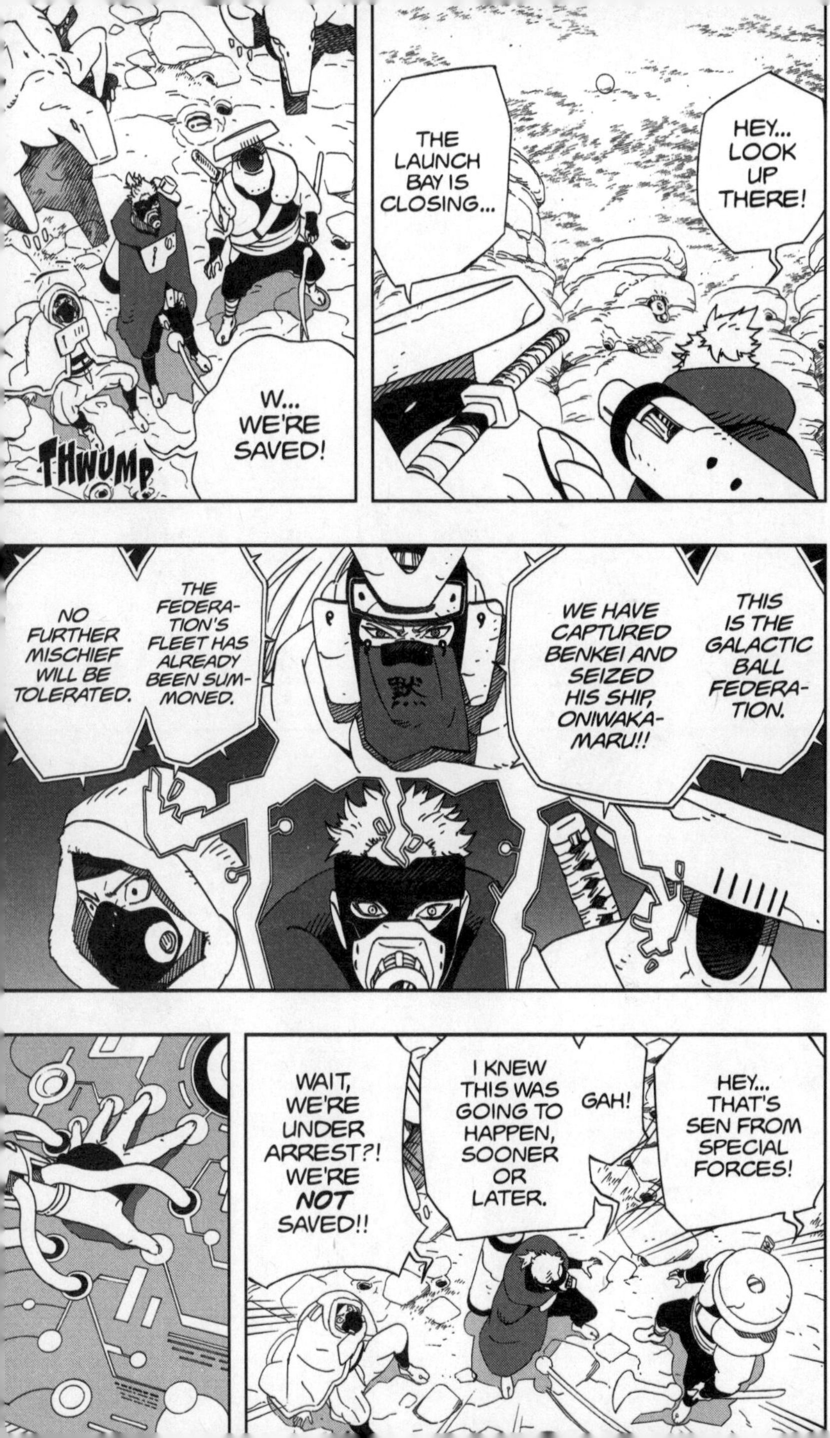
HEY... LOOK UP THERE!
THE LAUNCH BAY IS CLOSING...
W... WE'RE SAVED!
THWUMP
THIS IS THE GALACTIC BALL FEDERATION.
WE HAVE CAPTURED BENKEI AND SEIZED HIS SHIP, ONIWAKAMARU!!
THE FEDERATION'S FLEET HAS ALREADY BEEN SUMMONED.
NO FURTHER MISCHIEF WILL BE TOLERATED.
HEY... THAT'S SEN FROM SPECIAL FORCES!
GAH!
I KNEW THIS WAS GOING TO HAPPEN, SOONER OR LATER.
WAIT, WE'RE UNDER ARREST?! WE'RE ***NOT*** SAVED!!

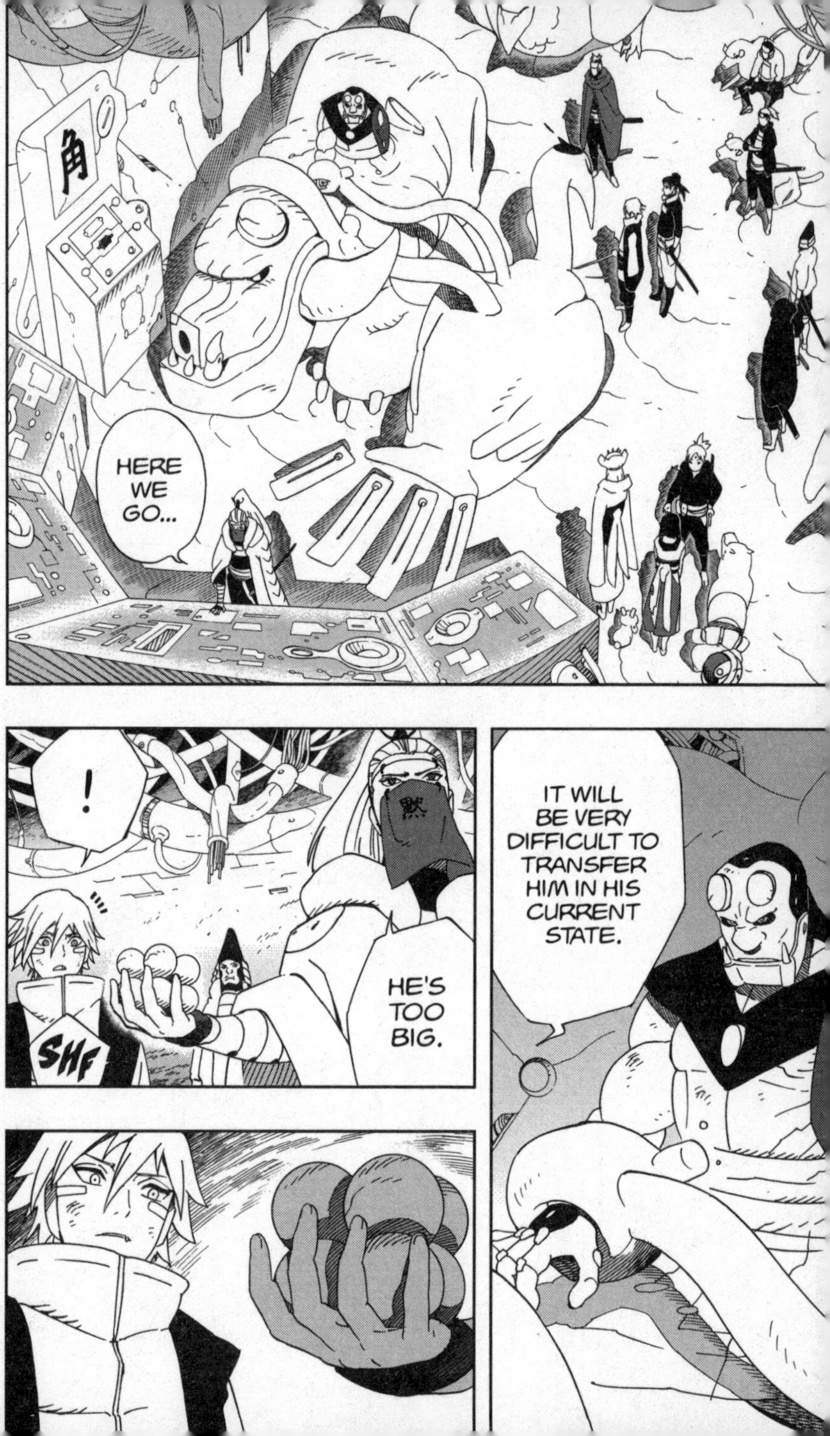
角
HERE WE GO...
IT WILL BE VERY DIFFICULT TO TRANSFER HIM IN HIS CURRENT STATE.
!
HE'S TOO BIG.
SHF

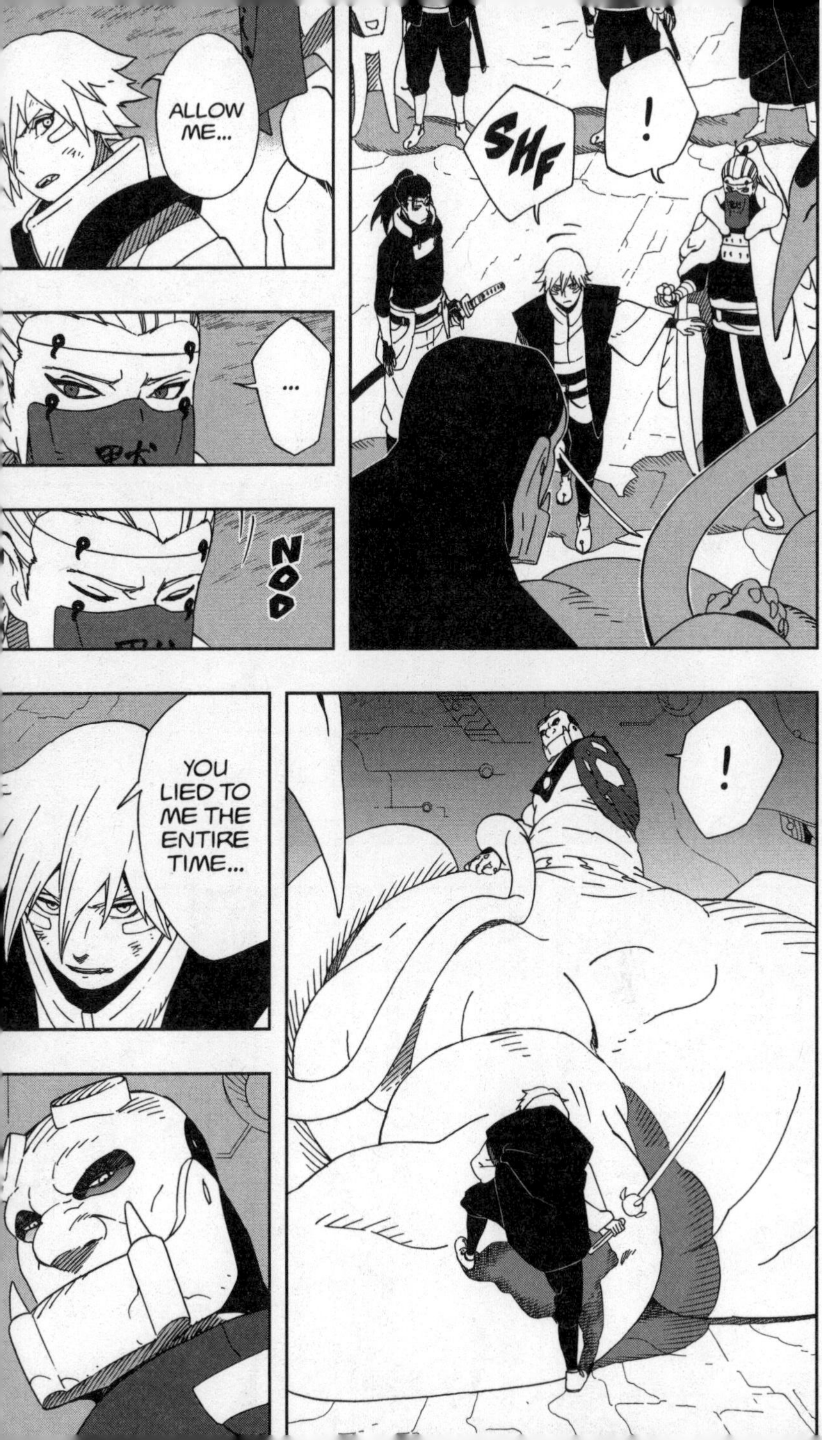
!
SHF
ALLOW ME...
...
NOD
!
YOU LIED TO ME THE ENTIRE TIME...

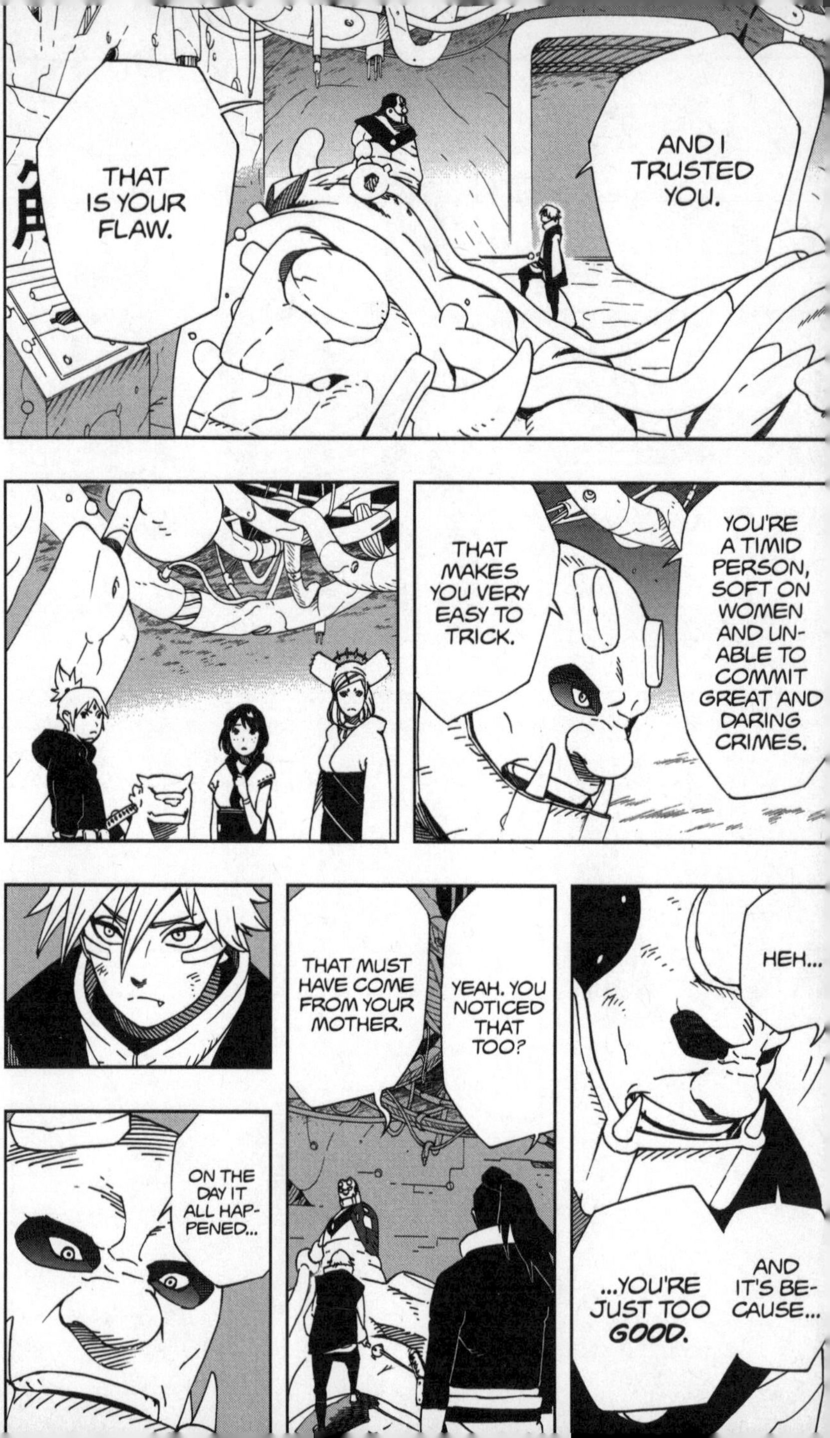
AND I TRUSTED YOU.
THAT IS YOUR FLAW.
YOU'RE A TIMID PERSON, SOFT ON WOMEN AND UN-ABLE TO COMMIT GREAT AND DARING CRIMES.
THAT MAKES YOU VERY EASY TO TRICK.
HEH...
AND IT'S BE-CAUSE...
...YOU'RE JUST TOO GOOD.
THAT MUST HAVE COME FROM YOUR MOTHER.
YEAH. YOU NOTICED THAT TOO?
ON THE DAY IT ALL HAP-PENED...

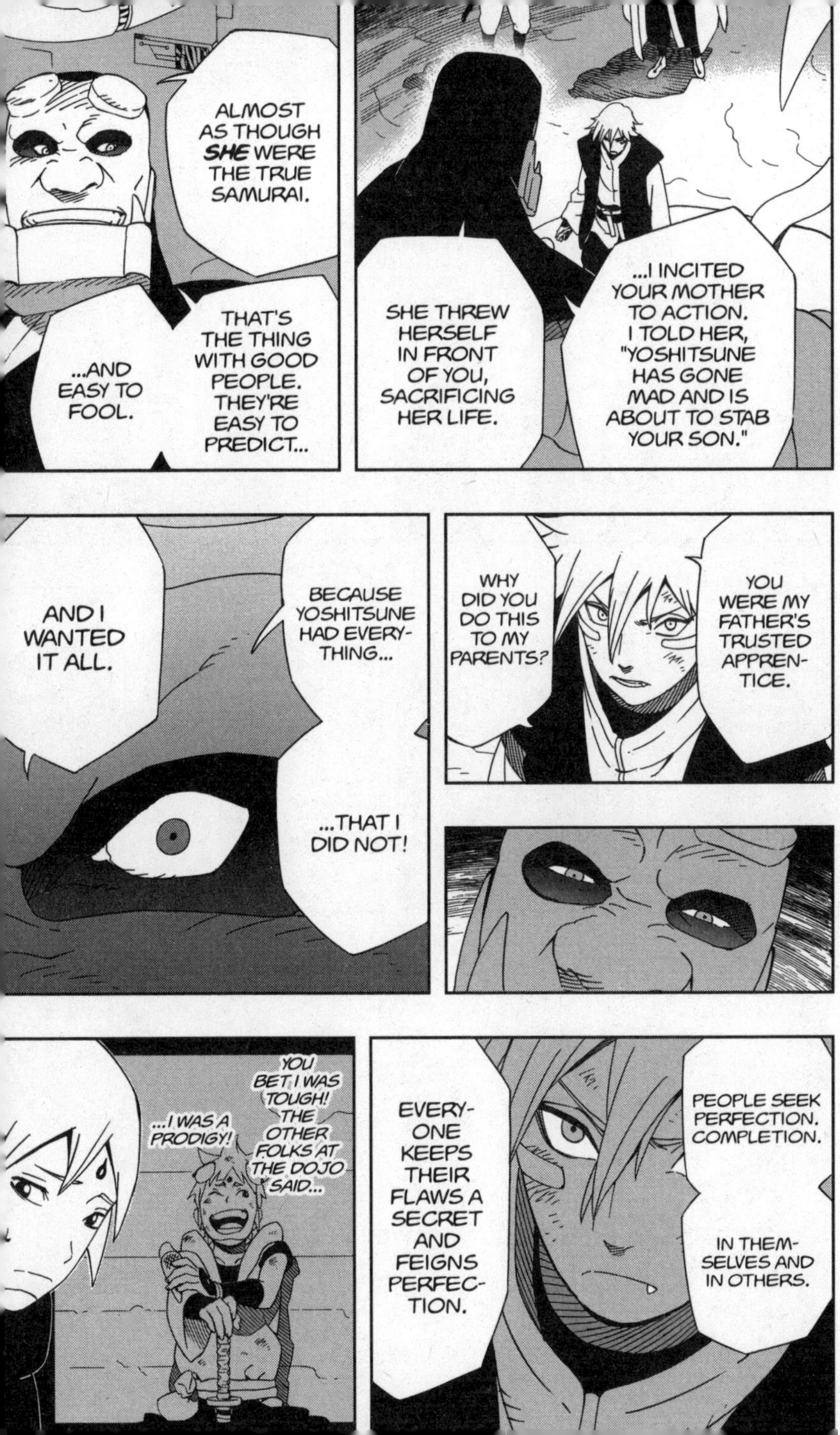
...I INCITED YOUR MOTHER TO ACTION. I TOLD HER, "YOSHITSUNE HAS GONE MAD AND IS ABOUT TO STAB YOUR SON."
SHE THREW HERSELF IN FRONT OF YOU, SACRIFICING HER LIFE.
ALMOST AS THOUGH *SHE* WERE THE TRUE SAMURAI.
THAT'S THE THING WITH GOOD PEOPLE. THEY'RE EASY TO PREDICT...
...AND EASY TO FOOL.
YOU WERE MY FATHER'S TRUSTED APPRENTICE.
WHY DID YOU DO THIS TO MY PARENTS?
BECAUSE YOSHITSUNE HAD EVERYTHING...
...THAT I DID NOT!
AND I WANTED IT ALL.
PEOPLE SEEK PERFECTION. COMPLETION.
IN THEMSELVES AND IN OTHERS.
EVERYONE KEEPS THEIR FLAWS A SECRET AND FEIGNS PERFECTION.
YOU BET I WAS TOUGH! THE OTHER FOLKS AT THE DOJO SAID...
...I WAS A PRODIGY!

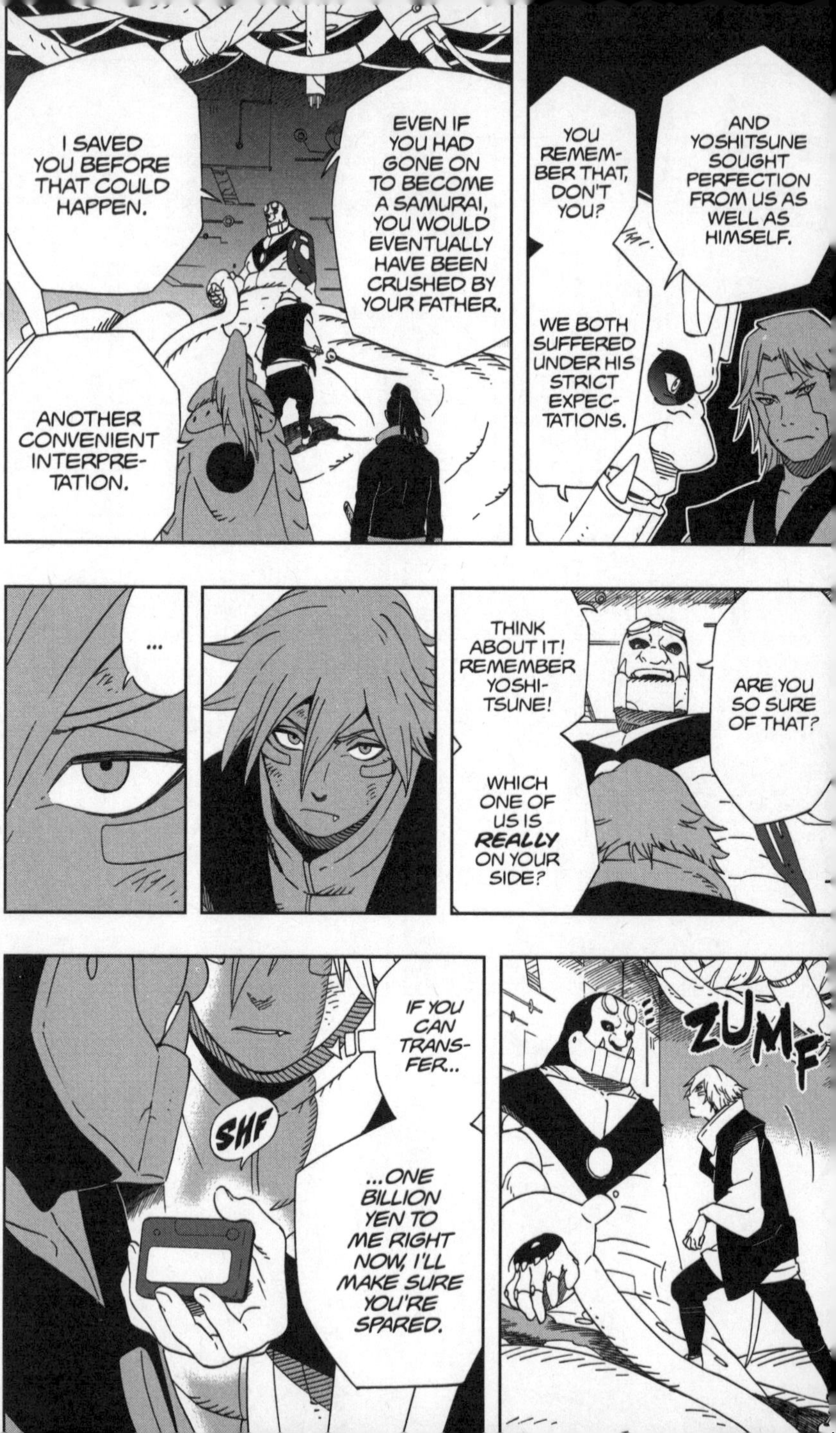
AND YOSHITSUNE SOUGHT PERFECTION FROM US AS WELL AS HIMSELF.
YOU REMEMBER THAT, DON'T YOU?
WE BOTH SUFFERED UNDER HIS STRICT EXPECTATIONS.
EVEN IF YOU HAD GONE ON TO BECOME A SAMURAI, YOU WOULD EVENTUALLY HAVE BEEN CRUSHED BY YOUR FATHER.
I SAVED YOU BEFORE THAT COULD HAPPEN.
ANOTHER CONVENIENT INTERPRETATION.
ARE YOU SO SURE OF THAT?
THINK ABOUT IT! REMEMBER YOSHITSUNE!
WHICH ONE OF US IS REALLY ON YOUR SIDE?
...
ZUMF
IF YOU CAN TRANSFER...
SHF
...ONE BILLION YEN TO ME RIGHT NOW, I'LL MAKE SURE YOU'RE SPARED.

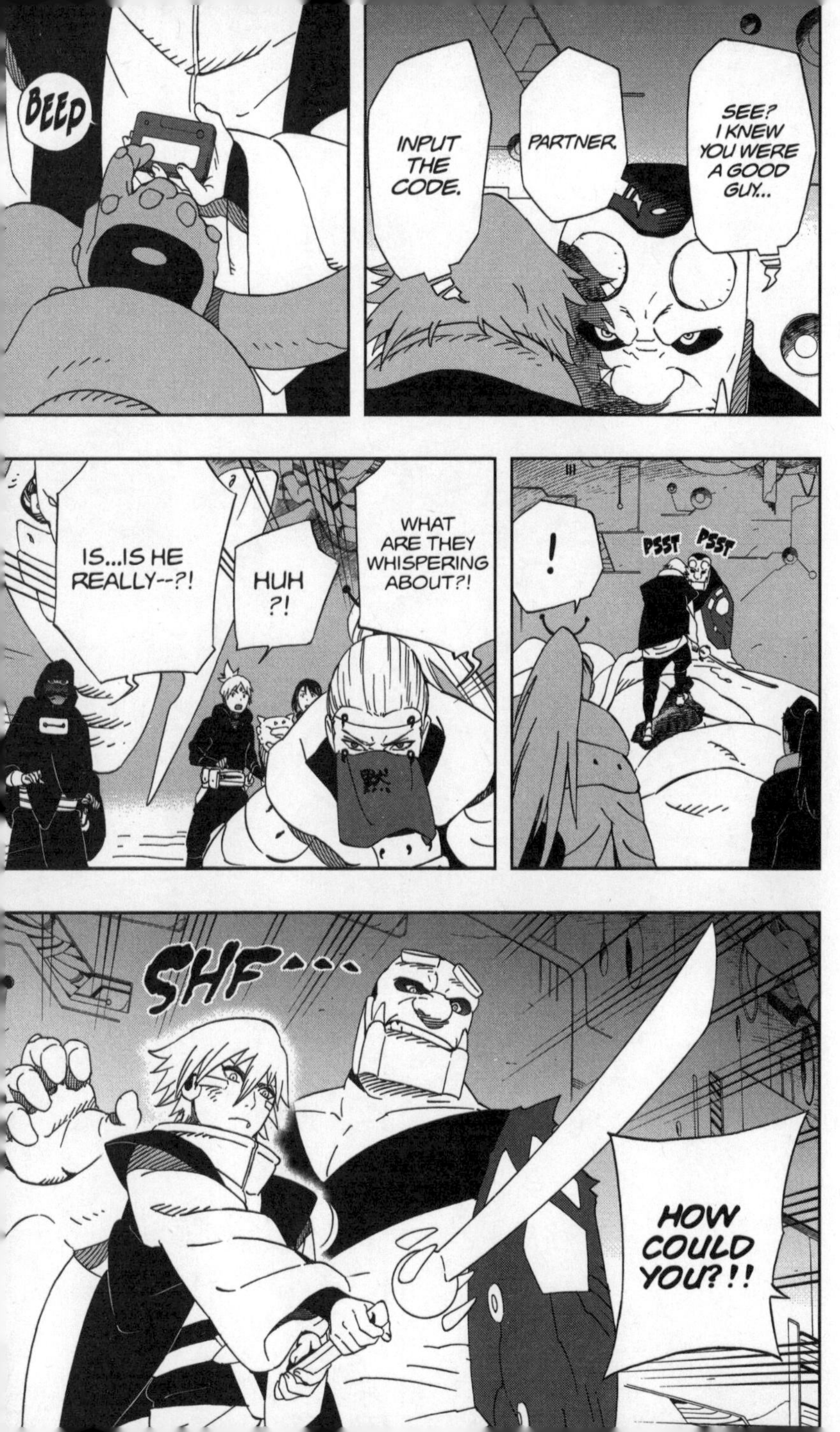
SEE? I KNEW YOU WERE A GOOD GUY...
PARTNER.
INPUT THE CODE.
BEEP
PSST
PSST
!
WHAT ARE THEY WHISPERING ABOUT?!
HUH ?!
IS...IS HE REALLY--?!
HOW COULD YOU?!!
SHF...

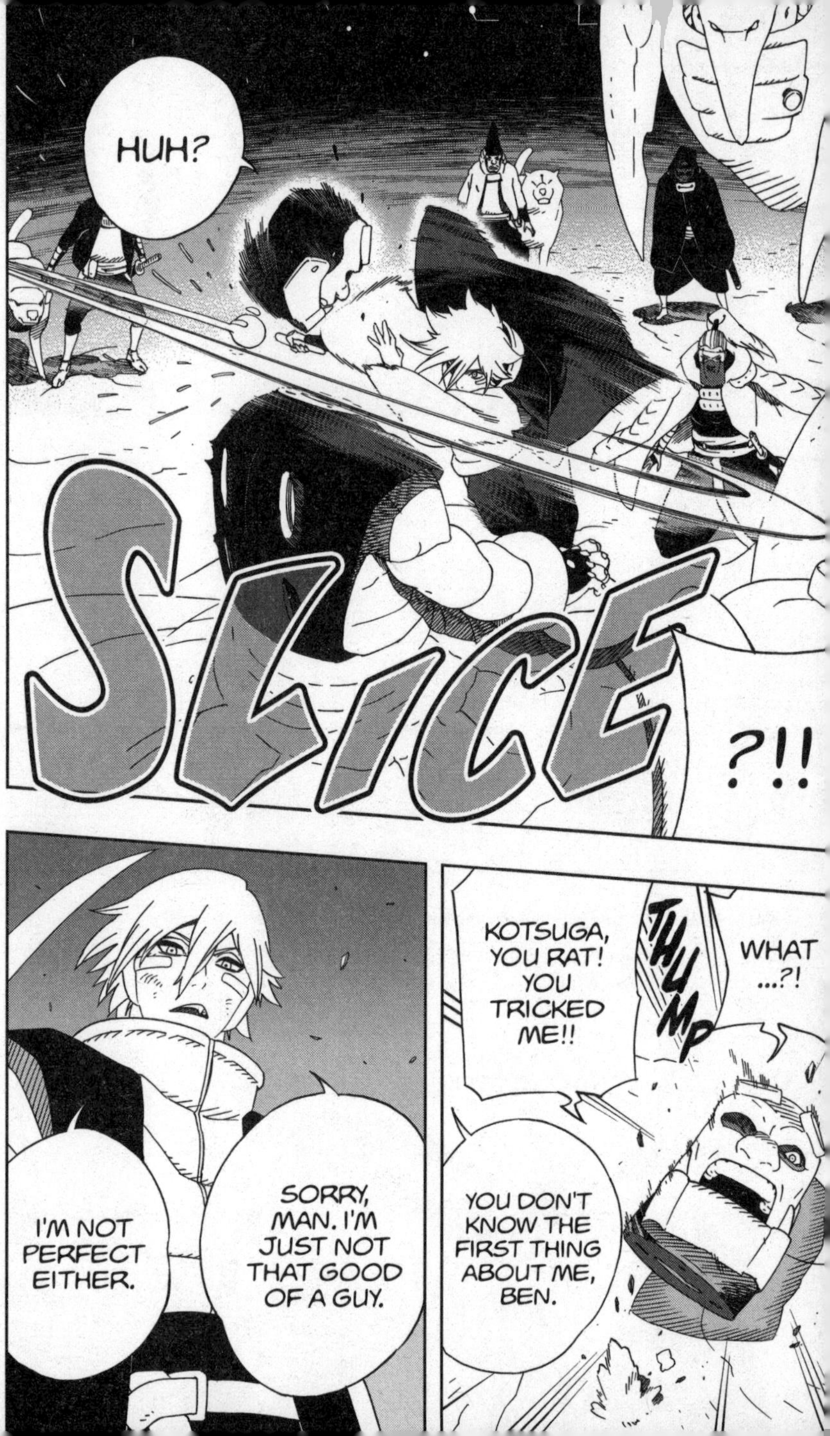
HUH?
SLICE
?!!
WHAT ...?!
KOTSUGA, YOU RAT! YOU TRICKED ME!!
THUMP
YOU DON'T KNOW THE FIRST THING ABOUT ME, BEN.
SORRY, MAN. I'M JUST NOT THAT GOOD OF A GUY.
I'M NOT PERFECT EITHER.

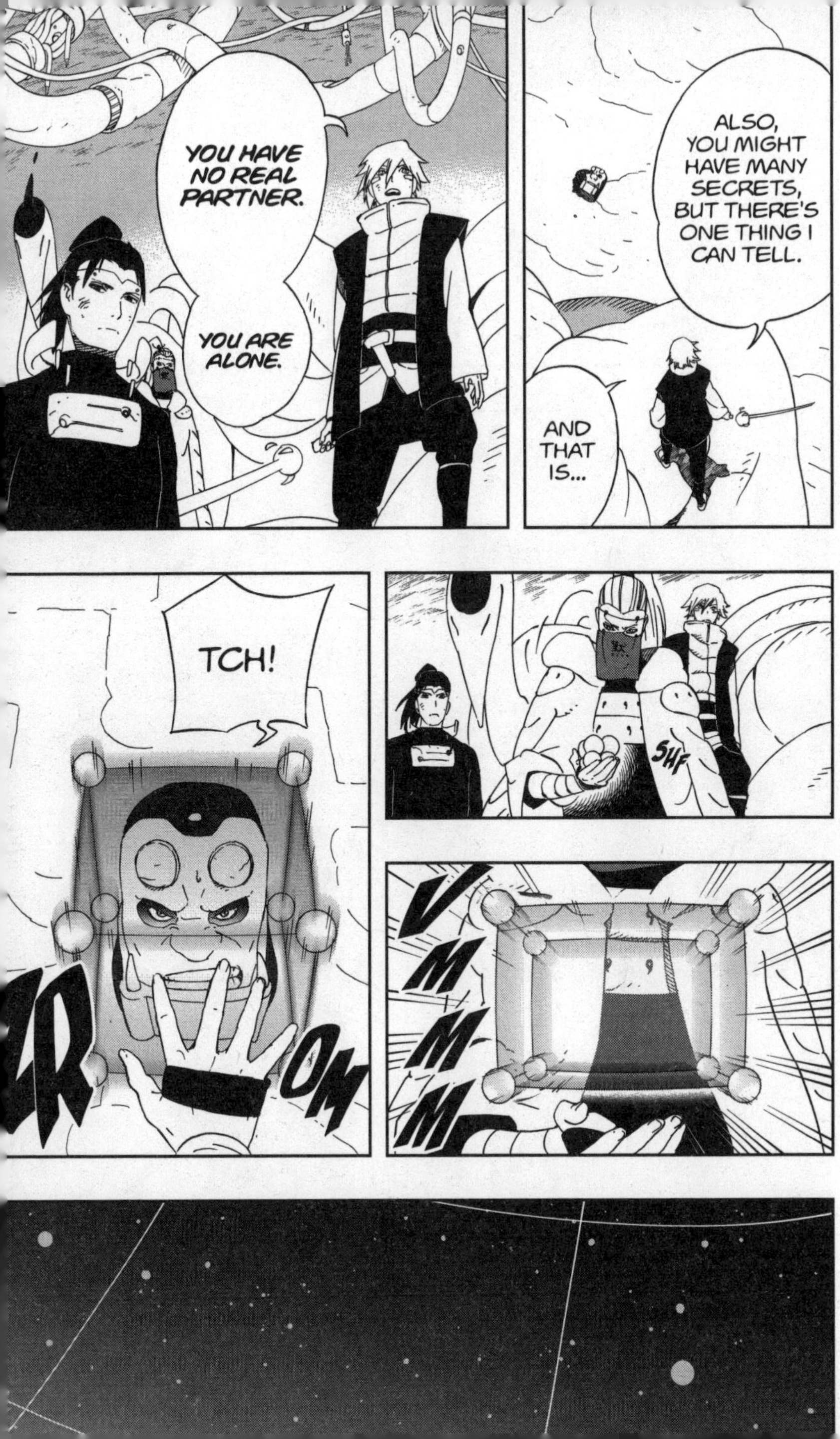
ALSO, YOU MIGHT HAVE MANY SECRETS, BUT THERE'S ONE THING I CAN TELL.
AND THAT IS...
YOU HAVE NO REAL PARTNER.
YOU ARE ALONE.
SHF
VMMMM
TCH!
ZR
OM

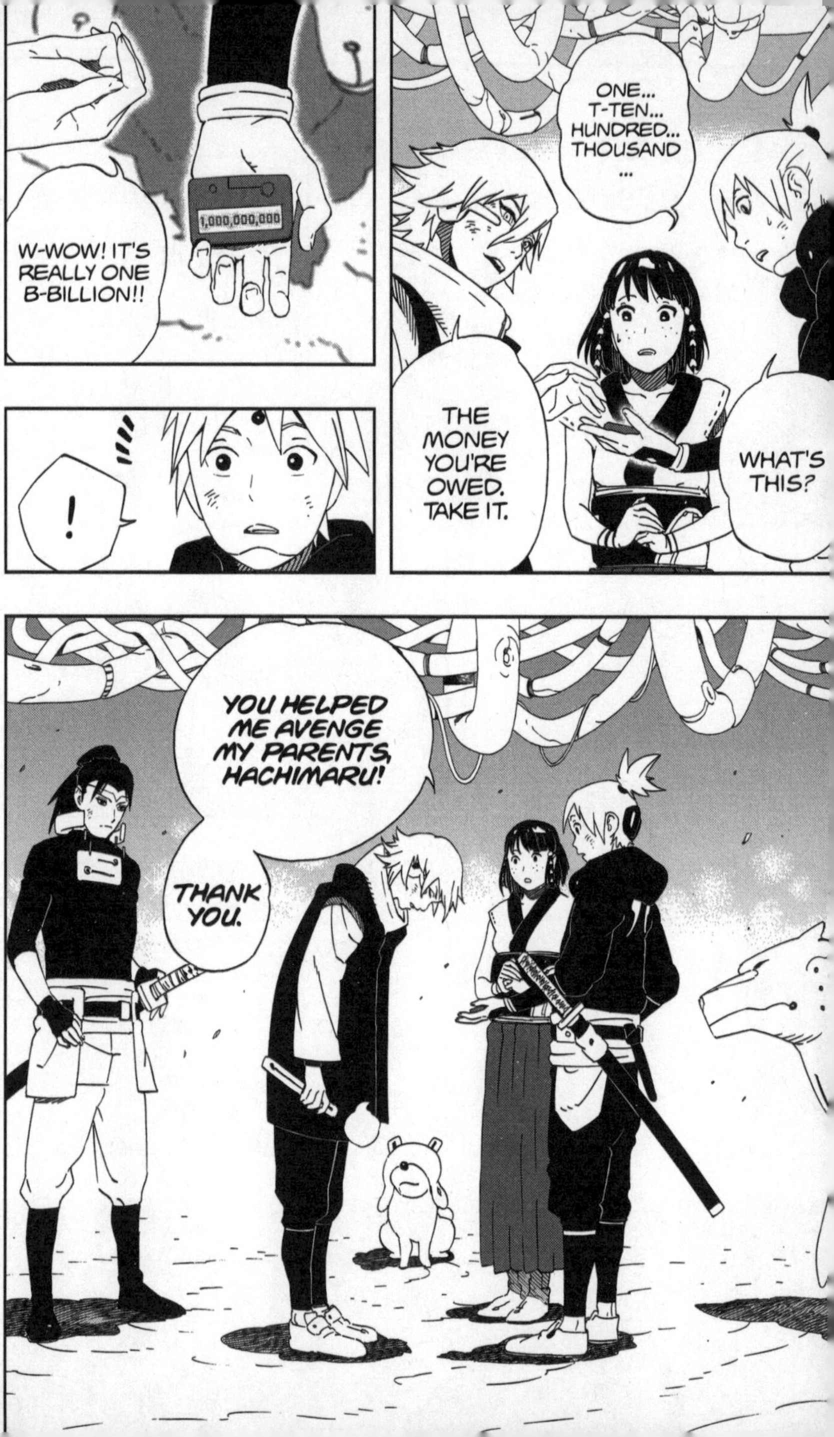
WHAT'S THIS?
THE MONEY YOU'RE OWED. TAKE IT.
ONE... T-TEN... HUNDRED... THOUSAND ...
1,000,000,000
W-WOW! IT'S REALLY ONE B-BILLION!!
!
YOU HELPED ME AVENGE MY PARENTS, HACHIMARU!
THANK YOU.

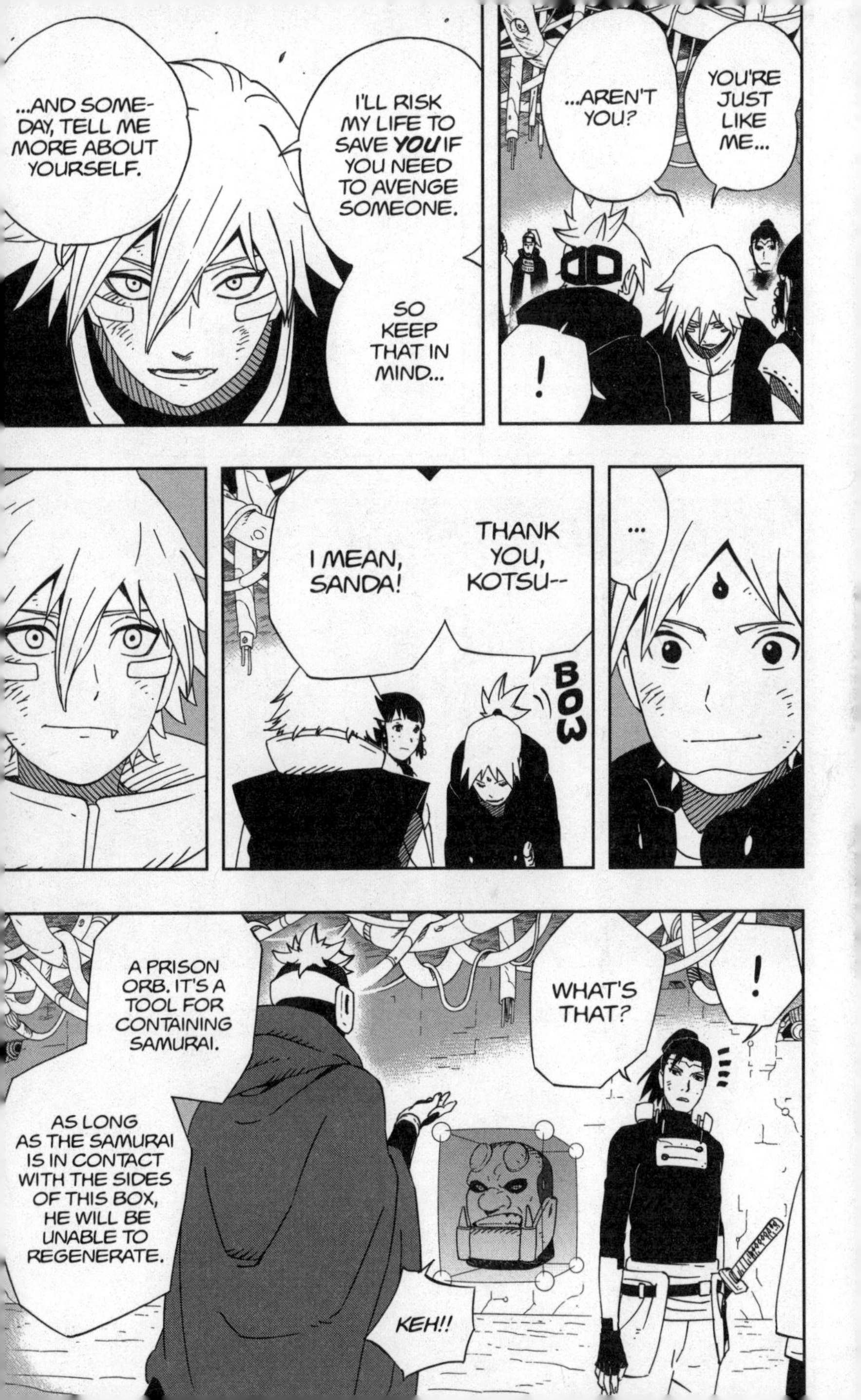
YOU'RE JUST LIKE ME...
...AREN'T YOU?
!
I'LL RISK MY LIFE TO SAVE *YOU* IF YOU NEED TO AVENGE SOMEONE.
SO KEEP THAT IN MIND...
...AND SOME-DAY, TELL ME MORE ABOUT YOURSELF.
...
THANK YOU, KOTSU--
I MEAN, SANDA!
BOW
!
WHAT'S THAT?
A PRISON ORB. IT'S A TOOL FOR CONTAINING SAMURAI.
AS LONG AS THE SAMURAI IS IN CONTACT WITH THE SIDES OF THIS BOX, HE WILL BE UNABLE TO REGENERATE.
KEH!!

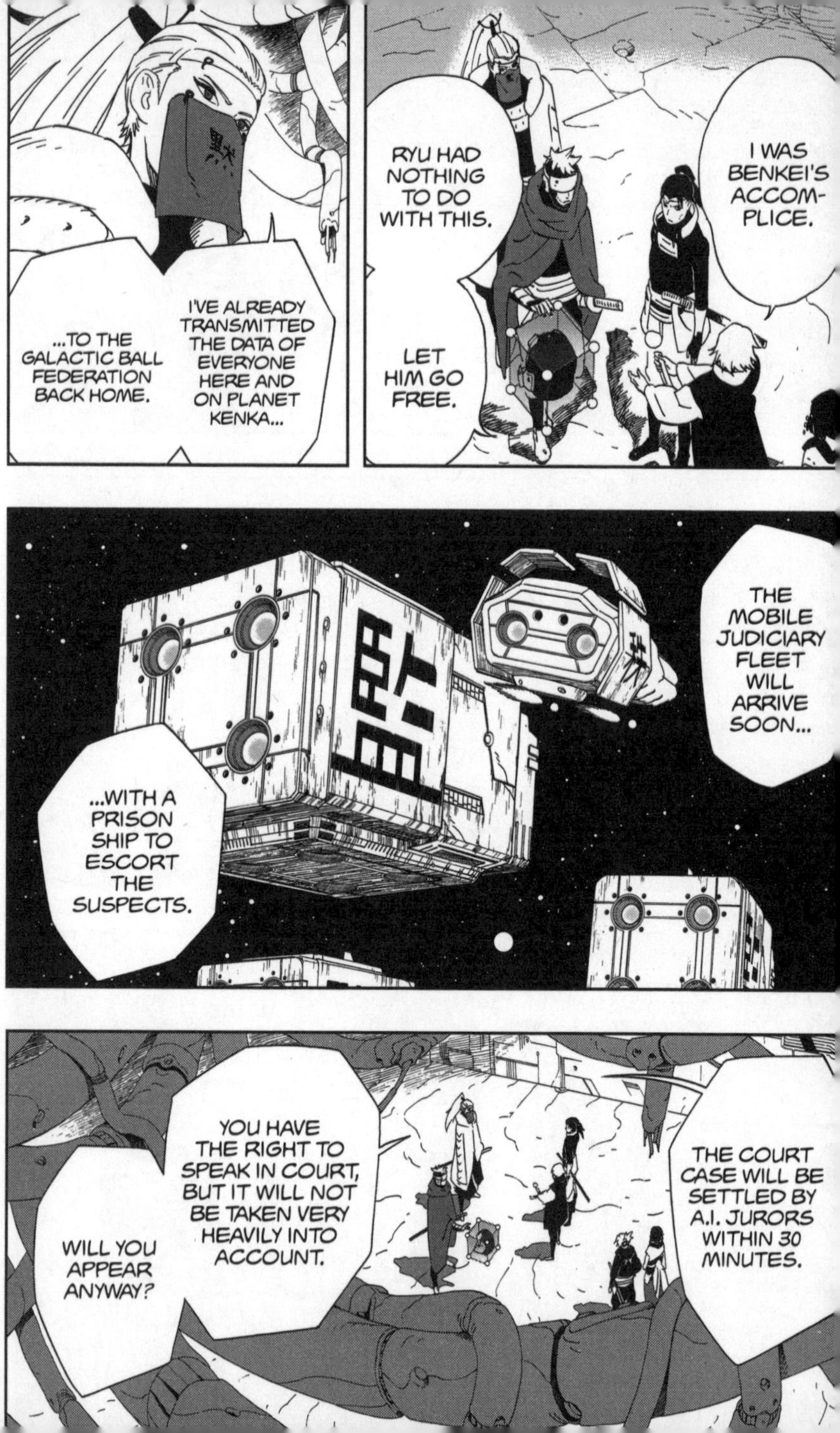
I WAS BENKEI'S ACCOMPLICE.
RYU HAD NOTHING TO DO WITH THIS.
LET HIM GO FREE.
I'VE ALREADY TRANSMITTED THE DATA OF EVERYONE HERE AND ON PLANET KENKA...
...TO THE GALACTIC BALL FEDERATION BACK HOME.
THE MOBILE JUDICIARY FLEET WILL ARRIVE SOON...
...WITH A PRISON SHIP TO ESCORT THE SUSPECTS.
THE COURT CASE WILL BE SETTLED BY A.I. JURORS WITHIN 30 MINUTES.
YOU HAVE THE RIGHT TO SPEAK IN COURT, BUT IT WILL NOT BE TAKEN VERY HEAVILY INTO ACCOUNT.
WILL YOU APPEAR ANYWAY?

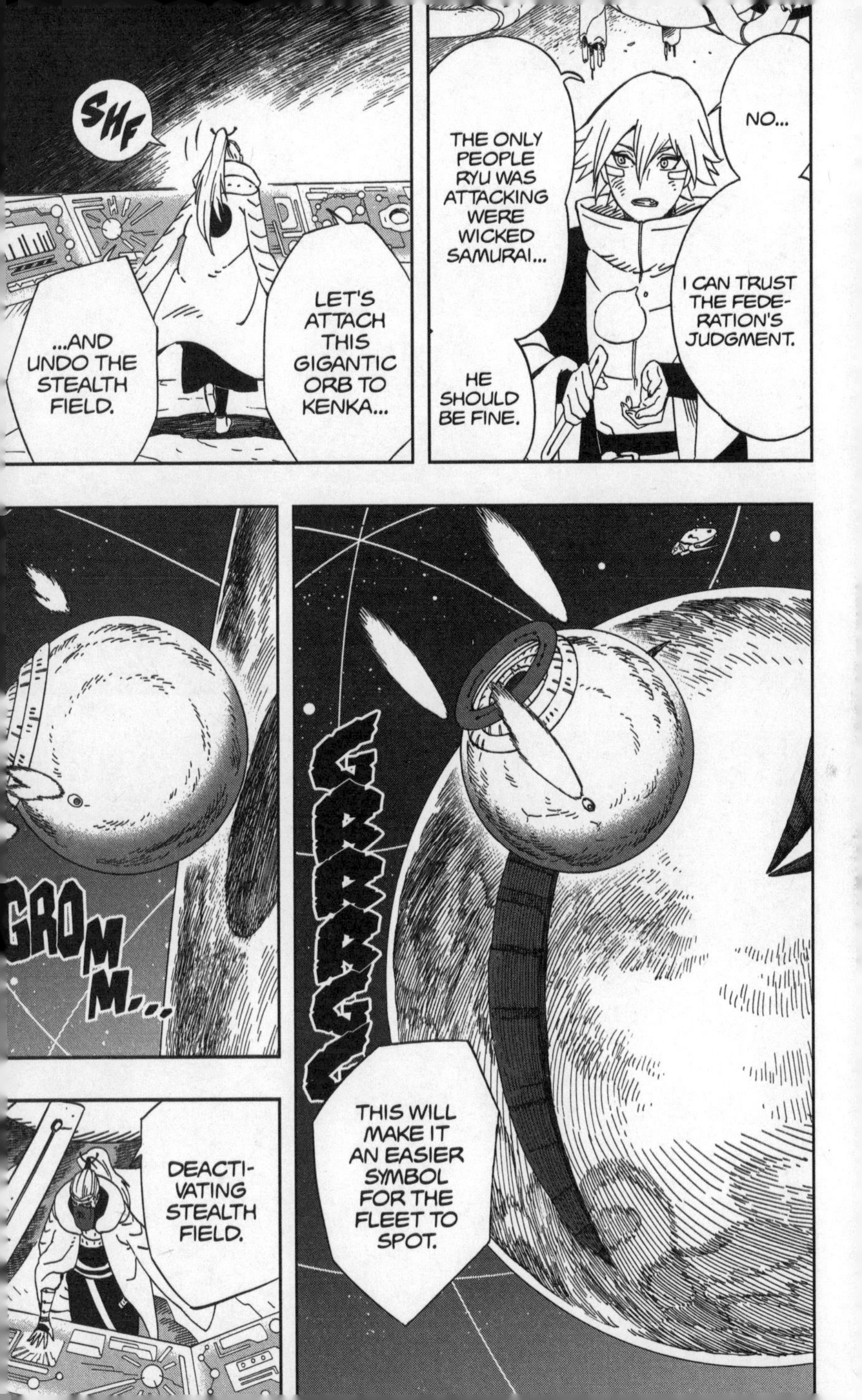
NO...
THE ONLY PEOPLE RYU WAS ATTACKING WERE WICKED SAMURAI...
I CAN TRUST THE FEDE-RATION'S JUDGMENT.
HE SHOULD BE FINE.
SHF
LET'S ATTACH THIS GIGANTIC ORB TO KENKA...
...AND UNDO THE STEALTH FIELD.
THIS WILL MAKE IT AN EASIER SYMBOL FOR THE FLEET TO SPOT.
GROMM...
DEACTI-VATING STEALTH FIELD.

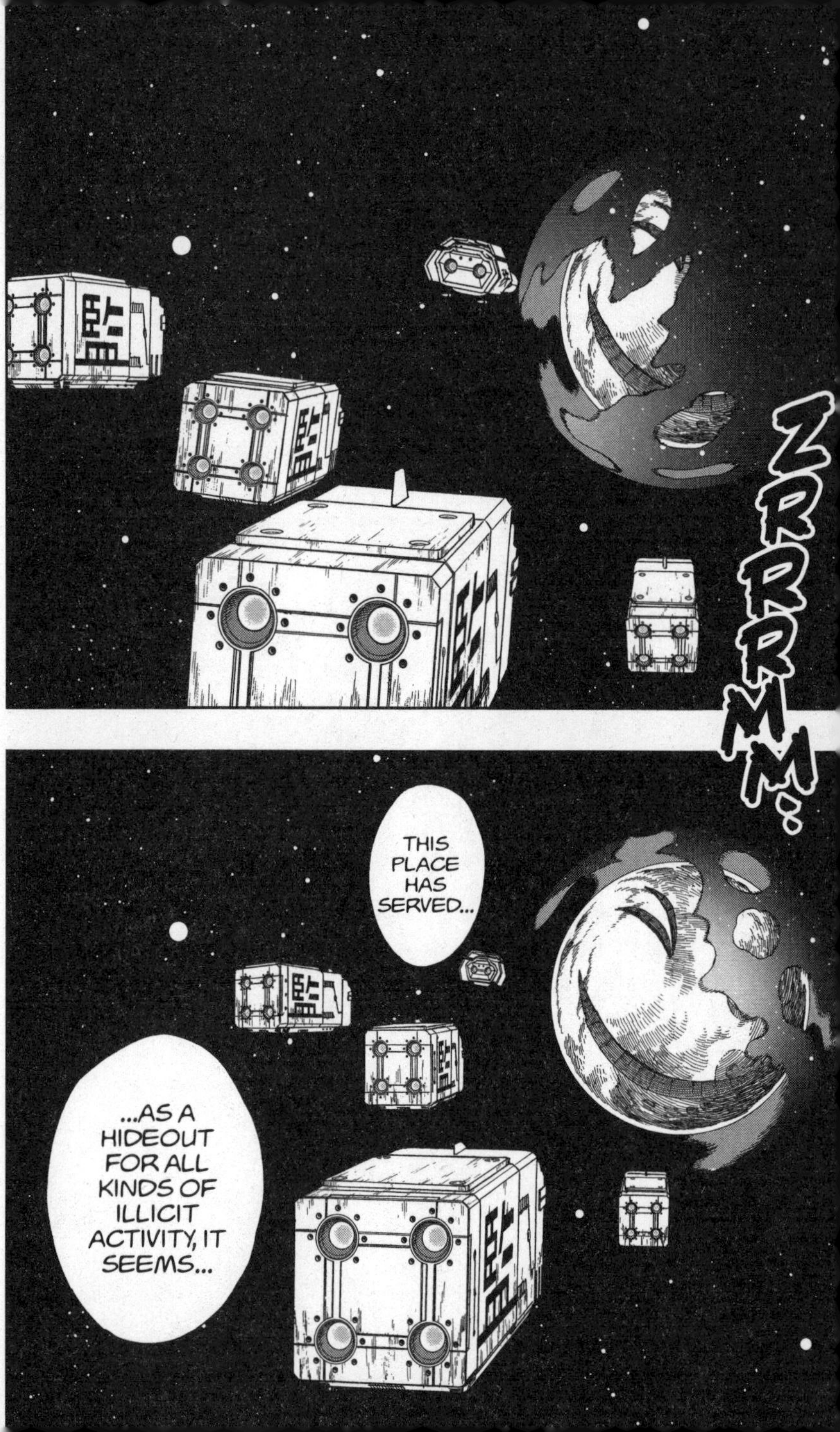
ZRRRMM!
THIS PLACE HAS SERVED...
...AS A HIDEOUT FOR ALL KINDS OF ILLICIT ACTIVITY, IT SEEMS...

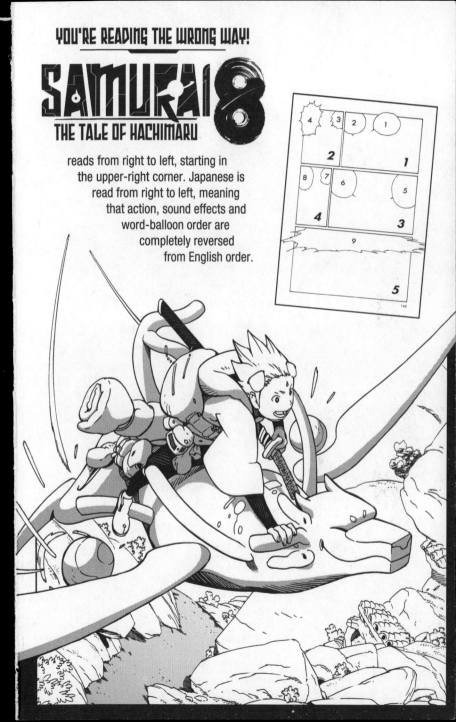

YOU'RE READING THE WRONG WAY!

SAMURAI 8
THE TALE OF HACHIMARU

reads from right to left, starting in the upper-right corner. Japanese is read from right to left, meaning that action, sound effects and word-balloon order are completely reversed from English order.

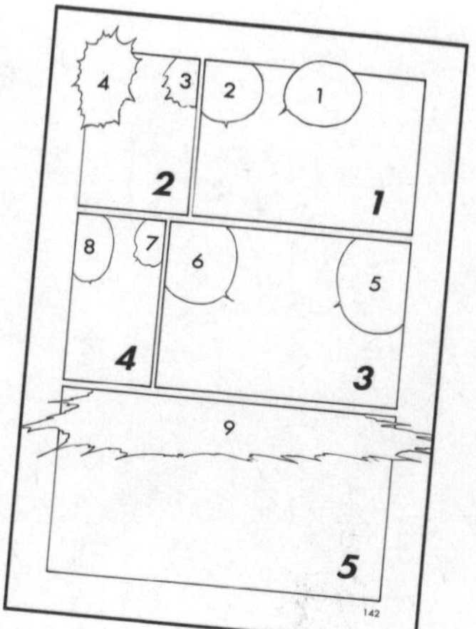

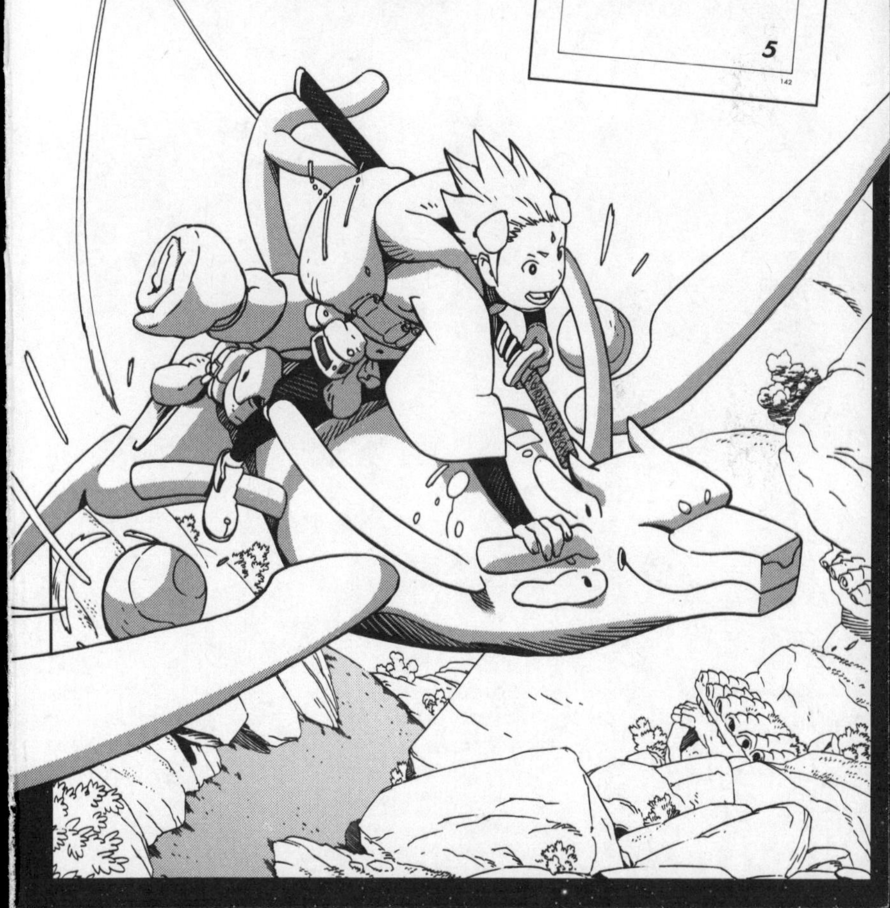

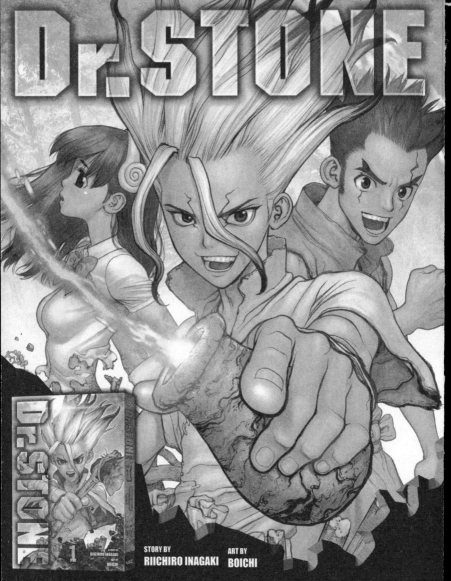

Dr. STONE

STORY BY
RIICHIRO INAGAKI

ART BY
BOICHI

One fateful day, all of humanity turned to stone. Many millennia later, Taiju frees himself from petrification and finds himself surrounded by statues. The situation looks grim—until he runs into his science-loving friend Senku! Together they plan to restart civilization with the power of science!

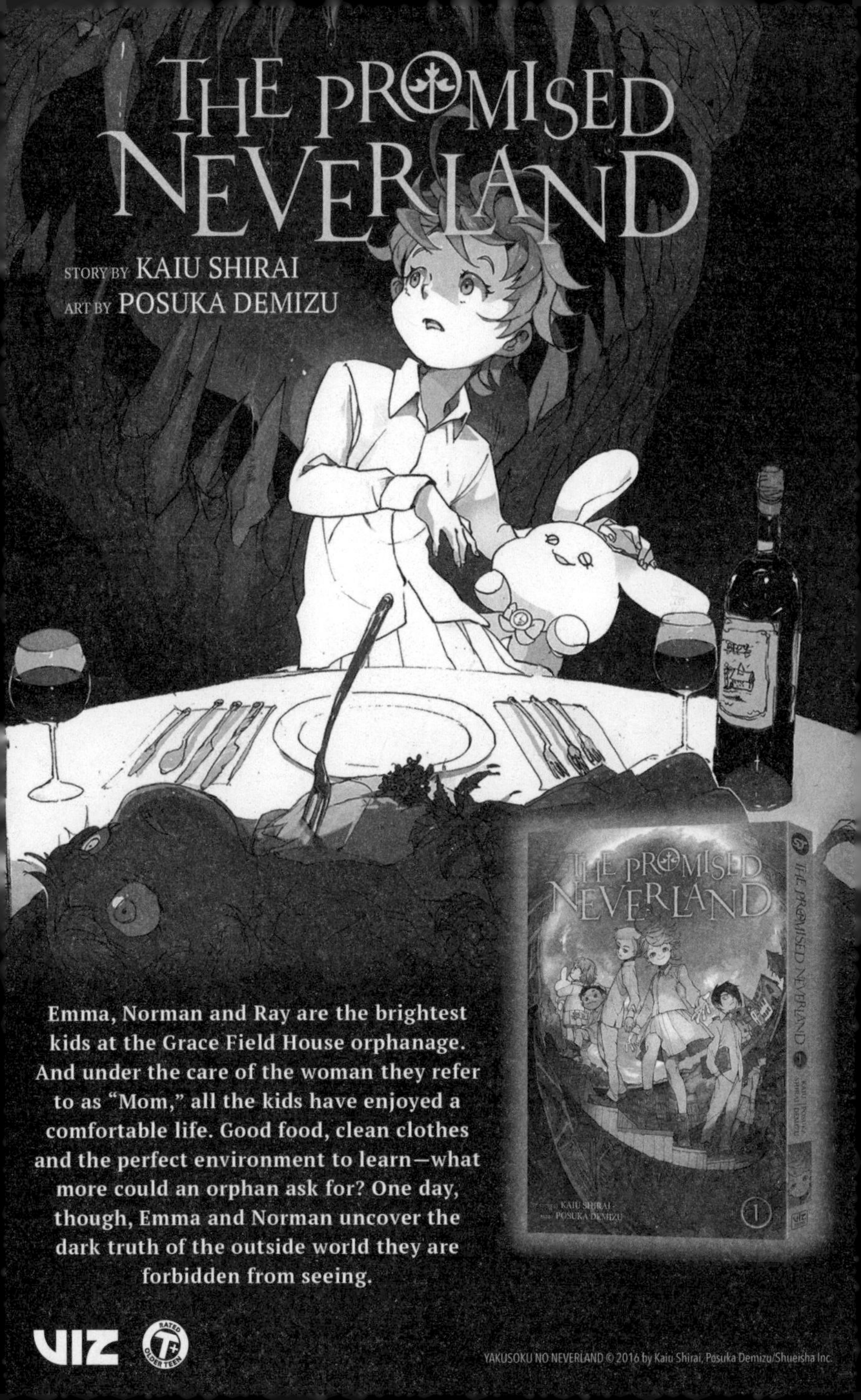
THE PROMISED NEVERLAND
STORY BY KAIU SHIRAI
ART BY POSUKA DEMIZU
Emma, Norman and Ray are the brightest kids at the Grace Field House orphanage. And under the care of the woman they refer to as "Mom," all the kids have enjoyed a comfortable life. Good food, clean clothes and the perfect environment to learn—what more could an orphan ask for? One day, though, Emma and Norman uncover the dark truth of the outside world they are forbidden from seeing.
VIZ
RATED T+ OLDER TEEN
YAKUSOKU NO NEVERLAND © 2016 by Kaiu Shirai, Posuka Demizu/Shueisha Inc.

Pre-Series Rough Designs (Okubo)

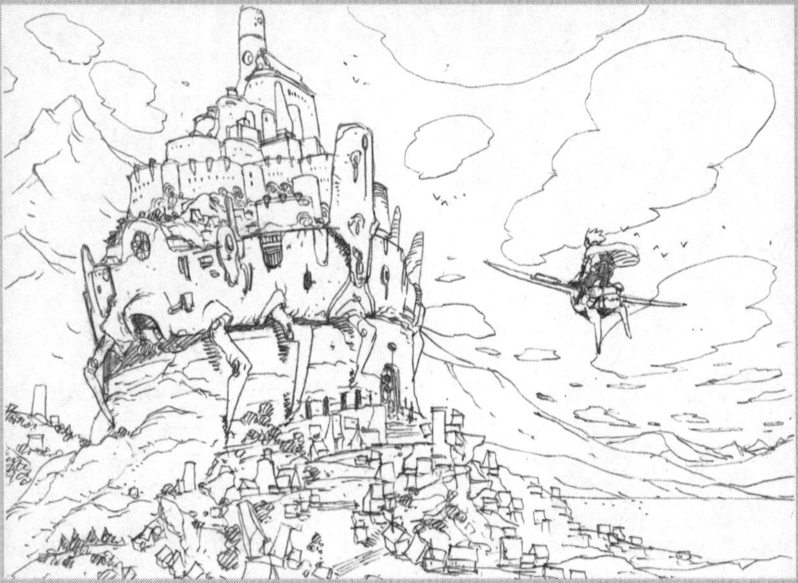

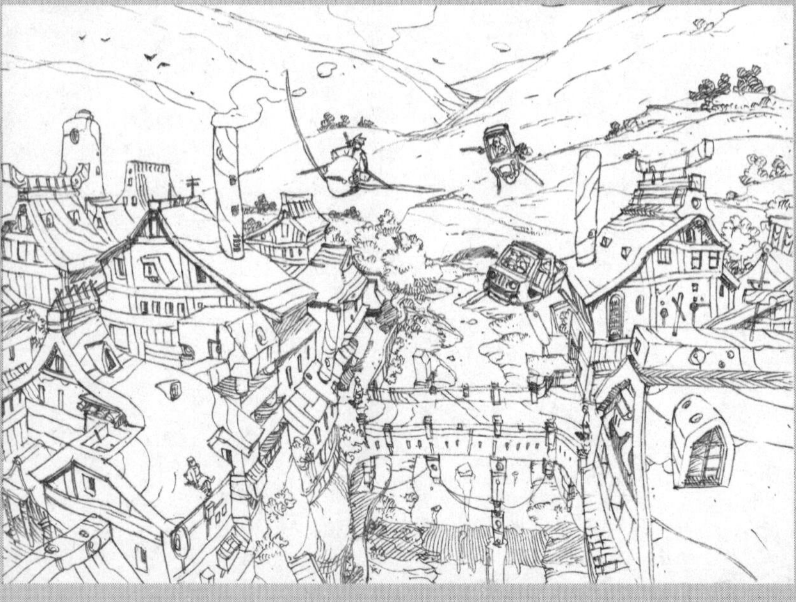

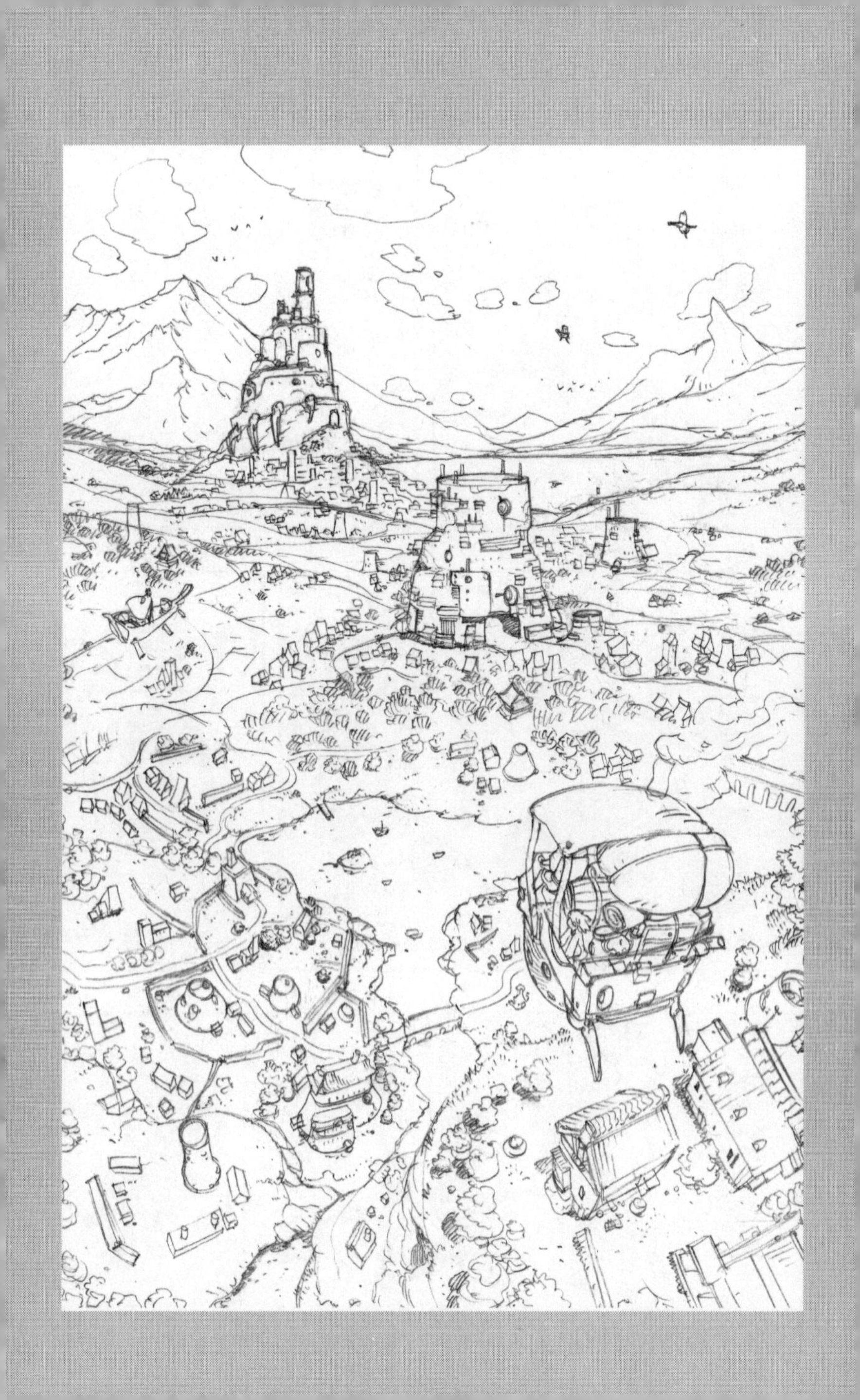

EXTRA STORY

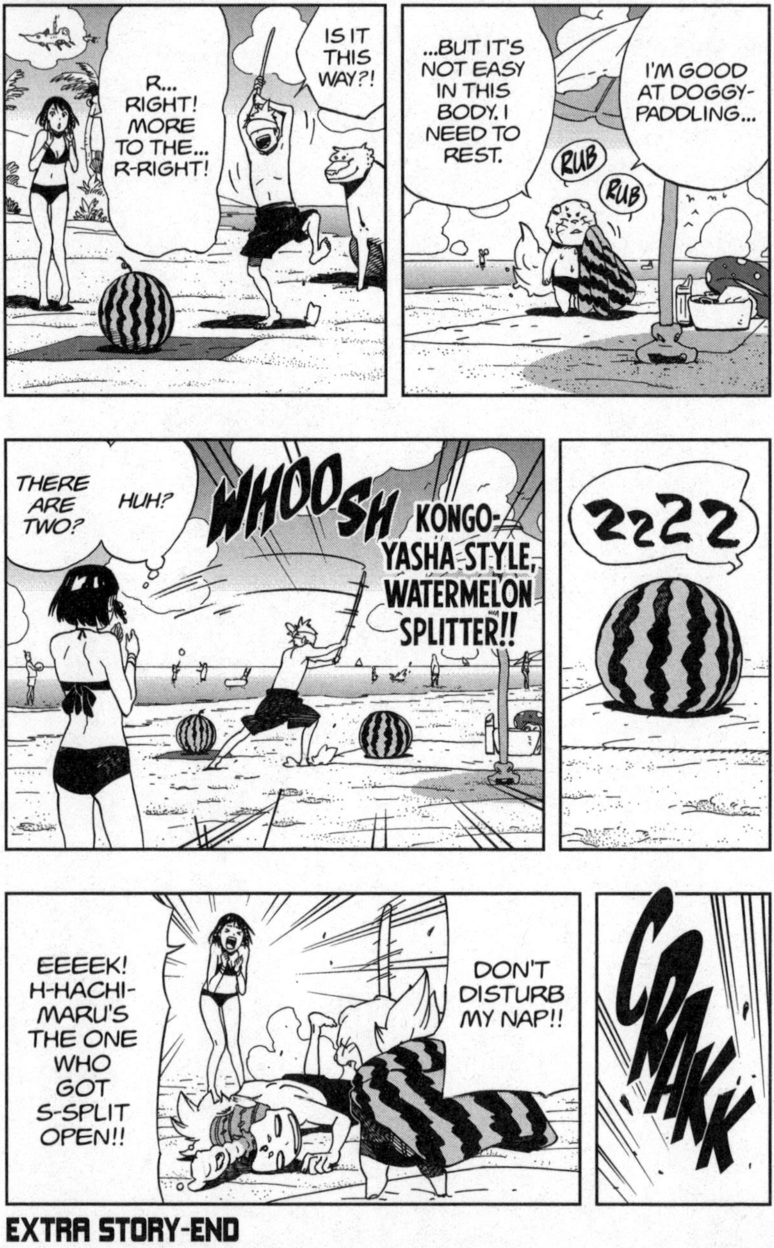
I'M GOOD AT DOGGY-PADDLING...
RUB
RUB
...BUT IT'S NOT EASY IN THIS BODY. I NEED TO REST.
IS IT THIS WAY?!
R... RIGHT! MORE TO THE... R-RIGHT!
ZZZZ
KONGO-YASHA STYLE, WATERMELON SPLITTER!!
WHOOSH
HUH?
THERE ARE TWO?
CRAKK
DON'T DISTURB MY NAP!!
EEEEK! H-HACHI-MARU'S THE ONE WHO GOT S-SPLIT OPEN!!

EXTRA STORY-END

SAMURAI 8
THE TALE OF HACHIMARU

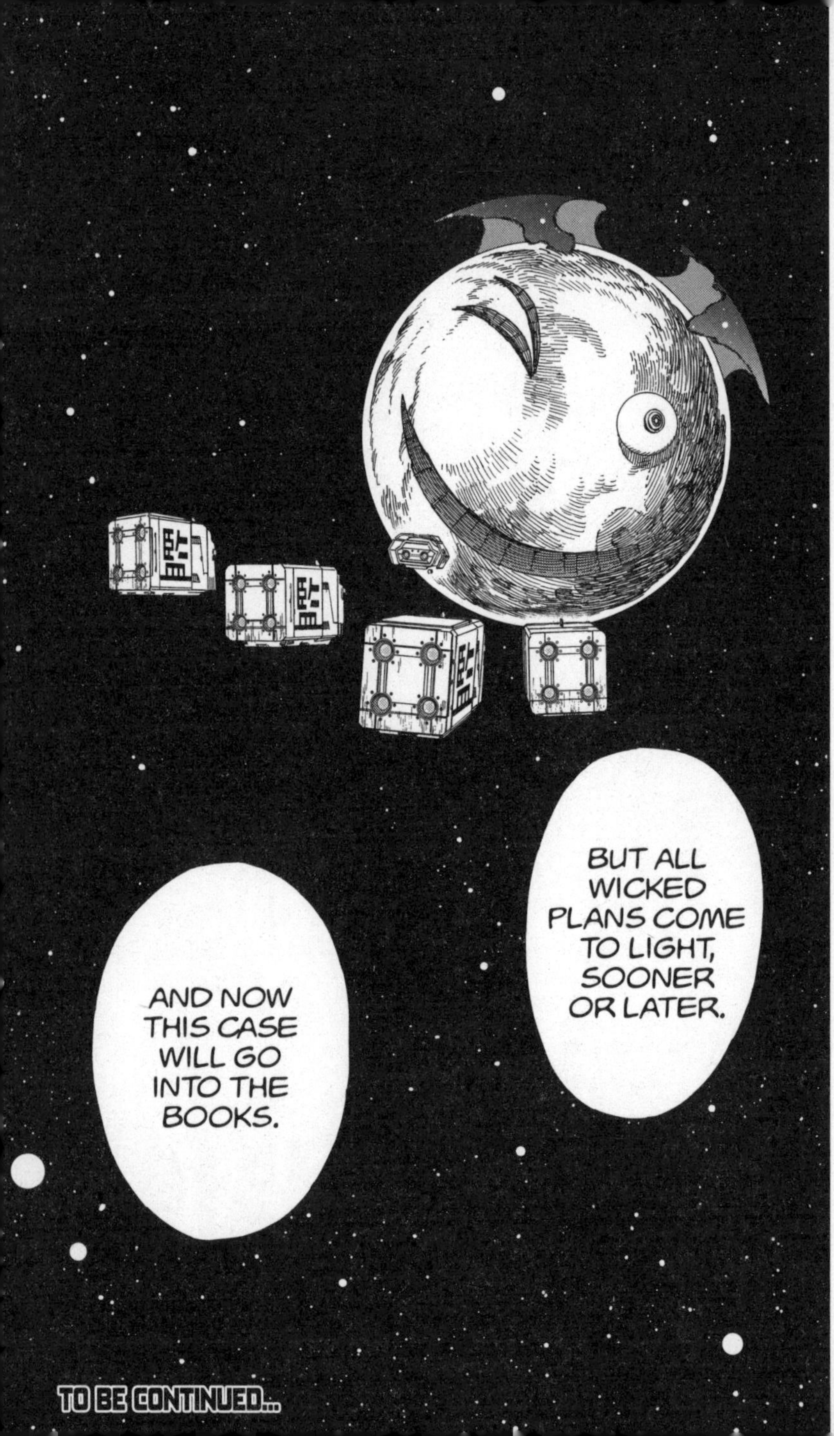
BUT ALL WICKED PLANS COME TO LIGHT, SOONER OR LATER.
AND NOW THIS CASE WILL GO INTO THE BOOKS.
TO BE CONTINUED...